Luis Muñoz Marín:

Puerto Rico's Democratic Revolution

Luis Muñoz Marín:
Puerto Rico's Democratic Revolution

A. W. Maldonado

LA EDITORIAL
UNIVERSIDAD DE PUERTO RICO

Luis Muñoz Marín:Puerto Rico´s Democratic Revolution
A.W.Maldonado

ISBN 0-8477-0158-1 (softcover)
ISBN 0-8477-0163-8 (hardcover)

Typesetting: EDUPR / Salvador Rosario
Cover design: Yolanda Pastrana
Editors: Javier Ávila
        Madeleine Colón-Terry

La Editorial
Universidad de Puerto Rico
Apartado 23322
San Juan, Puerto Rico 00931-3322
www.laeditorialupr.com

Table of Contents

Part Four: Serenity: 1953-1980

Acknowledgements

Miguel Vásquez Deynes, the former President of Triple S, and the late Frank Unanue, President of Goya Foods in Puerto Rico, made this book possible with their generous grants that allowed me to work on it full-time.

Back in 1995, Victor Pons, former Chief Justice of the Puerto Rico Supreme Court, and Antonio García Padilla, then chairman of the Luis Muñoz Marín Foundation, now President of the University of Puerto Rico, encouraged me to proceed with this book, offering me the facilities and support of the Foundation. I am grateful to Foundation Director José Roberto Martínez. Muñoz, like his father, Luis Muñoz Rivera, was an extraordinarily prolific writer. I am particularly grateful to the curator of the archives, Julio Quirós, for guiding me through the thick forest of the documentation and the enormous body of Muñoz's writings.

Victoria Muñoz, Luis Muñoz Marín's daughter, and Carmen Palacios, his step-daughter, were generous with their time and assistance, and provided important insights into his family life. Jaime Benítez and his wife Luz, "Doña Lulú," were especially helpful, as was José Trías Monge.

These are just some of the many people that contributed to this work. I am also indebted to the hundreds of men and women, many of them political and ideological opponents of Muñoz, many who served in his administrations and in La Fortaleza as his aides, that through the decades helped me to understand this powerful, unconventional and complex political leader.

I first covered Muñoz as a reporter for *The San Juan Star* in 1959. In the early 1970s, Muñoz made an unusual request. He had retired from the governorship in 1964 and nothing had gone as he had hoped and planned. The man he handpicked to replace him turned against him. The political party he had created in 1938 lost for the first time in 1968. Spending two years in Europe, he dedicated himself to writing his memoirs. Frustrated, he asked me, among others, to "help" him.

He handed me several hundred pages of manuscript, asked me to read them, then to "interview him." At the time, I was the Executive Editor of *El Mundo*, the island's leading daily newspaper. Muñoz had never seen me as anything but an independent journalist. Born and brought up in New York City, he knew I was not a member of his party, or of any party.

Muñoz always enjoyed seeing himself as a poet, and a "journalist", and was attempting to be as "objective" as he could in describing, not only his successes, but his failures – there were several big ones – and the many things he could have done but did not. So the "help" he wanted from me was to conduct as "objective" and "critical" an interview as I could.

The "interview", conducted two to three times a week, lasted over four months. Muñoz himself recorded it, but often turned off the big machine, wanting to talk "off the record" about critical and sensitive periods of his life. I thought I knew him well, but this experience helped me get through the crossroads of his long political and ideological journey.

The "interview" did not, in the end, achieve its purpose. Muñoz died in 1980 without completing his memoirs. But for me, it was the genesis of this book.

Prologue

Charisma, columnist and writer William Safire wrote in 1968, is the ancient Greek word for *gift*. He goes on to quote Thomas P.F. Hoving, then Director of the New York City Metropolitan Museum of Art:

> Power is the chief element, power and style. Style is choice—when to talk, when to shut up, when to move, when to be still, a kind of sex appeal (not good looks) that comes with conviction. Style must be accompanied by power to become charisma, but power without style is not charismatic.
>
> The man with the most charisma I ever saw is Muñoz Marín of Puerto Rico. The moment he walks into the room, you feel it whether you know who he is or not. The same is true of Picasso...and de Gaulle, Pope John has it... Khrushchev had it and Stalin didn't.[1]

Hoving was not alone in placing Luis Muñoz Marín in such company. Washington insider and Supreme Court Justice Abe Fortas wrote that Muñoz was "a spectacularly great figure . . . [who] in his restricted sphere has no less greatness than Roosevelt: and that, as a matter of fact, has some qualities of greatness which Roosevelt lacked."[2]

In 1940, Muñoz led a democratic revolution convincing the *jíbaro*, the typical poor mountain man, not to sell his vote. In the following years, he led an administrative revolution with the invaluable assistance of Rexford

---

1. Safire, *The New Language of Politics*, 71.
2. Kalman, *Abe Fortas: A Biography*, 166.

Tugwell, creating in Puerto Rico the first modern, efficient, and honest public administration in Latin America. Then Muñoz unlocked the maddening riddle that had baffled and defeated both Puerto Ricans and Americans for half a century: how to lift over two million Puerto Ricans, all American citizens, from extreme poverty. Operation Bootstrap (the industrialization of the island) driven by Teodoro Moscoso, was called an "economic miracle". It was.

When Muñoz died on April 30, 1980, at the age of 82, he left behind a volume of writings on his social philosophy, what he described as his intellectual and emotional "civil wars." In the 1940s he asked himself what was the deeper purpose of politics and parties. Into the 1950s and for the rest of his life, he questioned the purpose of economic development, urging his people to embrace what he called "Operation Serenity."

But that rare blend of power and style that makes extraordinary political leadership was not always evident.

When the last American Governor of Puerto Rico, Rexford Tugwell, arrived on the island in 1941, he saw in the Puerto Rican *político* a lot of style but a grossly unreal sense of power. Muñoz had become President of the insular Senate the year before and considered himself the island's supreme political leader. But many on the island as in Washington considered this a fluke. His party had gained control of the Senate with only 37 percent of the votes in the 1940 elections, less than the opposing party.

Tugwell, charter member of Roosevelt's "Brain Trust" and one of the innovative forces behind the early New Deal, was intrigued that Muñoz acted as if he had received a mandate to make sweeping and profound changes in this woebegone American territory. If nothing else, Muñoz certainly had a "gift" for words. For years, he had been a relentless advocate of Puerto Rican independence, a potent writer for newspapers and magazines, in English as well as in Spanish. And in 1940, he had indeed used his command of words to spellbind thousands of illiterate *jíbaros* to vote for him.

The perception of Muñoz among Americans, especially in Washington, Tugwell continued, was particularly negative:

Muñoz was [seen] as an inconsequential son of a notable father, lamentably lacking in any quality of application, persistence or ability: an incorrigible bohemian, living his life in cafés, talking largely with miscellaneous and impermanent crowds of acquaintances: he had literary leanings, fancied himself a poet – *El Vate* – his detractors called him, but he never worked hard enough to accomplish anything even at this amateur occupation...[3]

There were reasons to consider the 43-year-old Muñoz a failure. He had been a poor, undisciplined student who barely received a high school education, had never held a steady job, and was never able to support his wife and two children. As a young "Marxist radical" in the 1920s, he brazenly attempted to ignite a "class war". He failed and the pro-labor, non-revolutionary Socialist Party was pleased to see him leave. In the 1930's he was expelled from the Liberal Party—the party his father had founded—after failing in another brash scheme to boycott the elections. He was blamed for the collapse of a multimillion-dollar effort to bring Roosevelt's New Deal programs to the island, and then for the ignominious Liberal Party defeat in 1936.

His personal life was not much better: a heavy drinker and chain smoker, a womanizer, and overweight, he was already warned by doctors that unless he radically changed his lifestyle he would face an early death. Separated from his family, by 1941 he was living with a common law wife and their two small children.

What seemed most tragic was that he had failed to live up to the legacy of his illustrious father, Puerto Rico's dominant political leader at the turn of the century, Luis Muñoz Rivera. "I never knew anyone," Tugwell wrote in his 1946 memoirs, "even his detractors, who spoke of him at any length and did not in the course of their remarks deplore the waste of his abilities."[4]

Tugwell left the island in 1946 disillusioned, convinced that the reforms accomplished during his turbulent governorship would sink into the quicksand of the island's tribal partisan warfare. He titled the gloomy memoirs of his years on the island *The Stricken Land*.

---

3. *The Stricken Land*, p. 10
4. Ibid, p. 9

But a decade later he was amazed by the transformation that had taken place in Puerto Rico. He was even more astounded by what this lazy *político* "who had never worked hard enough to accomplish anything", had accomplished. In 1958 he compared Muñoz to two other great practitioners of "the art of politics," Roosevelt and New York Mayor Fiorello La Guardia. Tugwell wrote:

> Muñoz lead a movement and created a party, which consolidated the latent power of the stricken Puerto Rican mass and used it to force into being a disciplined program for rejuvenation. This effort had significance beyond itself. It soon became a wonder of a world looking for the means to lift backward peoples from the stew of poverty and demagoguism, which had become so characteristic of all the old colonial area. He was the creator, as much as one man could be, of a new status for a whole people and a new relationship among political entities. The Commonwealth of Puerto Rico was a brilliant invention and it's bringing into being a remarkable achievement.[5]

This is the story of the transformation that took place in Muñoz. For it is in the internal political, ideological, emotional "civil wars" within him—how they were fought, won and lost—that the drama unfolds of how Tugwell's "*Stricken Land*" became "a wonder of the world": the story of Puerto Rico's democratic revolution.

---

5. Tugwell, *The Art of Politics*, vi.

PART I

God's Agitator
1898-1933

"All this digression so that you will realize that I am no longer an ogre, without repenting for a moment my actions in island politics. I am sorry with all my heart for the ridiculous fanaticism and aggressions that accompanied my actions."

—Luis Muñoz Marín
1922

1 The Father: *El león*

Luis Muñoz Rivera was an imposing man: his huge handle bar mustache dominated his "Nordic-type" face, his intense blue eyes projected a commanding, authoritative, autocratic presence. Deeply rooted in 19th century Hispanic literary and political culture, his writings fused poetic imagery with potent advocacy. Style was as important as content. Leadership was exercised through the power of the pen. Insular partisan politics were driven not by policy or program, but by concepts: honor, dignity, and sovereignty. By the turn of the century, the life-long journalist, poet, and essayist had become Puerto Rico's principal political leader.

As the 19th Century came to a close, Puerto Ricans were the only Latin Americans not to have joined the movement for independence. While the Cubans fought a bloody war against the Spanish, Muñoz Rivera campaigned for an autonomous status within the *Madre Patria*—the Mother Country. In November, 1897, he achieved his goal. In a desperate last minute attempt to avert war with the Americans, the Spanish regime granted Cuba and Puerto Rico an autonomous government. The Cubans immediately rejected it. In San Juan, Muñoz Rivera proclaimed joyously in his newspaper *La Democracia*, "Puerto Ricans govern Puerto Ricans!" Three months later, on February 11, 1898, the Spanish Governor General appointed Muñoz Rivera to head the new Autonomous Government. In the eyes of the Puerto Ricans, *El León* was either a magician or a genius. This was what he had battled for all his life, and it seemed that he had single-handedly engineered this historic event.

Luis Muñoz Rivera was born on July 17, 1859 in the small mountain town of Barranquitas. His ancestors were part of Spanish colonial history in the Americas. His grandfather, Luis Muñoz Iglesias, who came from a well-to-do family dating back to 16th century Old Castille in the wind-swept plains of central Spain, abandoned medical school at the age of fourteen to battle Napoleon's invading army in 1810. He decided to make his career in the military, came to the New World as a Spanish officer, and fought in Venezuela in the wars of independence. He followed his commanding officer, Miguel de la Torre, to Puerto Rico after the failed Venezuelan campaign. Appointed the island's Governor General, De La Torre named Muñoz Iglesias to municipal posts. The young officer married a Puerto Rican woman and fathered twelve children. He settled for the rest of his life in a 400-acre farm in the scenic town of Cidra, where he was appointed its mayor. At the age of 54, having reached the rank of colonel, Muñoz Iglesias retired from the military.

One of Muñoz Iglesias's sons, Luis Muñoz Barrios, went to live in scenic Barranquitas, a remote town up in the highest mountain range near the center of the island, favored by the island's elite as a refuge from the stifling summer heat. It was also close to the town of Comerío, the home of the attractive young woman he was courting and would marry, Monserrate Rivera Vásquez. Muñoz Barrios, very much within his father's pro-Spanish mold, became the head of the Conservative Party in the region. Admired and respected as a solid, dependable man with deep religious convictions, described by his friends as "grave and distinguished," Muñoz Barrios was an officer in the Puerto Rican militia, had a long career in civil government, served as secretary of several towns throughout the island and as mayor of Barranquitas.

His son Luis Muñoz Rivera had an uneventful and relatively comfortable early life. He received a traditional Spanish education in European classical literature and was expected to carry on his family's businesses. He dreamed, instead, of being a poet, spending long hours with friends exchanging views and arguing over the latest trends in Latin American and European literature. It seemed that he had inherited his father's respect for authority. He was "quiet, respectful, timid and somewhat serious."[1] Up to the age of twenty-five, according to one of his

---

1. Negrón Sanjurjo, *Los primeros treinta años de Luis Muñoz Rivera*, 23.

closest friends, he showed little interest in island politics. Gradually, however, he began breaking away from his father's conservatism. In 1887, he was named President of the Barranquitas Autonomist Committee. Two years later, at the age of 30, he closed the dry goods store he and some relatives had established, and left for Ponce, the island's largest city on the Caribbean coast, and the hotbed of Puerto Rican nationalism.

THE AUTONOMIST

In 1890, Muñoz Rivera founded the newspaper, *La Democracia*, which was to become the "voice" of the autonomist movement and the island's most influential publication. His political mentor since 1883, the out-spoken autonomist advocate, educator, playwright and journalist, Ramón Marín y Solá, owned the printing press. Persecuted by the Spanish authorities, Marín had seen his elementary schools and several newspapers shut down by the authorities in San Juan. He was jailed in 1868 after the pro-independence uprising, *El grito de Lares*.

The September 23, 1868 uprising against Spanish rule, in the small mountain town of Lares, confirmed his forewarning. Organized by Ramón Emeterio Betances, the exiled French-educated abolitionist, the plot was easily uncovered by the Spanish. Twenty-four hours after the rebels had declared the "independence of Puerto Rico," the uprising was crushed. The several hundred rebels, mostly planters indebted to Spanish merchants, were, in fact, led by a Venezuelan and an American, both island residents.[2] The Puerto Rican *jíbaro* was indifferent. *El grito de Lares* became an emotional symbol, but as a political realist, Muñoz was convinced that Puerto Rico had to seek other means to achieve self-government. He was by nature a politician, not a revolutionary nor an ideologue.

Although in Cuba a truce declared in 1878 ended the Ten Year War, the jittery Spanish continued to persecute the Puerto Rican separatists and autonomists. In 1887, the island was subjected to still another wave of

---

2. Morales Carrión, *Puerto Rico: A Political and Cultural History*, 111.

political suppression called *"los compontes"*. Governor General Romualdo Palacio de González vigorously rounded up and in some cases tortured those suspected of belonging to an "illicit society" which included any political group not vociferously true to Spain. For a time, the word "autonomy" was banned.[3]

Young Muñoz considered the government inept and repressive. Ramón Marín, after all, would reopen the schools and newspapers shut down by the regime by merely changing their names or by replacing himself with family members. But General Palacio's *compontes* were dead serious. In 1887, the irrepressible Marín was again arrested, thrown into a dungeon in *El Morro* along with one of the founders of the Autonomist Party, Ramón Baldorioty de Castro. This time Marín believed that they would be executed. But once again a sudden political shift took place in Madrid. The despised Palacio was recalled, replaced by a moderate Governor General who promptly released the Puerto Rican leaders.

Three years later, Muñoz Rivera was himself detained and jailed briefly in Cayey. Questioned about his alleged membership in an "illicit society," the young man was treated with deference. His grandfather and father, after all, were respected government officials in this region, well known for their bed-rock allegiance to Spain. Muñoz, however, was shaken when he saw the large number of men that had been rounded up and packed into small cells, most of them illiterate *jíbaros* who, he was certain, had no idea why they were jailed. After his release, back in Ponce, he received news that four of the political prisoners had died.

On August 12, 1890, just weeks after founding his newspaper, he wrote a stinging denouncement of the tragedy. He was careful, however, not to get himself arrested again for sedition. He criticized the local authorities without questioning the legitimacy of the Spanish regime. Muñoz had begun to develop the art of walking the thin line between passionate advocacy and hard-headed pragmatism. He had no intention of becoming a martyr. One of Ramón Marín's sons, a captain in the Cuban Liberation Army, had been killed fighting the Spanish in Cuba.

---

3. Trías Monge, *Puerto Rico: The Trials of the Oldest Colony in the World*, 10.

While Muñoz wrote articles lamenting what he perceived as the appalling apathy of the Puerto Ricans to fight for their rights, he was convinced that to emulate the Cuban rebellion was doomed to failure. One-twelfth the size of Cuba, there was simply no place to hide on this island.

Throughout his life, Muñoz was often criticized and often confused his own supporters by his seeming inconsistencies. He was a prolific writer, mostly of newspaper columns written in the heat of the moment. To his opponents, he was a talented demagogue, a manipulator of words and always willing to sacrifice principles for political expediency. Muñoz Rivera, his opponents argued, possessed no fixed ideals.

His thinking was in fact driven by contradictory emotions. Puerto Ricans, a "people" with their own national, cultural identity, he believed, were honor-bound to favor independence just as all other Latin Americans. But he was also proud of his Spanish blood. Spain was the *Madre Patria*. There were in Puerto Rico, as in Cuba, a small number of people that favored the United States "annexing" the island. It seemed outlandish to him that two such distinct civilizations could be successfully blended. The idea, he wrote in 1895, was "absurd, depressing and inconceivable."

THE SAGASTA "PACT"

In 1893, Muñoz Rivera married the daughter of Ramón Marín, Amalia Marín Castillo, an outspoken young woman who performed theatrical works in Ponce. Soon after, Muñoz made his first trip to Spain where he remained for three years. The handsome and articulate young man was well received by Spanish political leaders in Madrid. He became a student of Spain's labyrinthine ever changing politics; its seemingly endless constitutional crisis. For sixty years, since 1833, Spain had had seventy-five governments and "a blizzard of constitutions."[4] There was one issue, however, where all Spaniards seemed to be of one mind. Writing for his newspaper from Madrid,

---

4. Trías Monge, *Puerto Rico: The Trials of the Oldest Colony in the World*, 8.

Muñoz Rivera reported that the Spanish people would never allow its leaders to give up Cuba.

When Muñoz Rivera returned to Puerto Rico, he saw his opportunity to make a move for autonomy. Spain was under growing pressure from the American Congress and journalists to end the bloodshed in Cuba. President William McKinley attempted to avoid war with Spain by getting Madrid to grant Cuba a high degree of self-government. This was precisely what Muñoz Rivera was demanding for Puerto Rico. On October of 1896 he returned to Madrid with a commission from Autonomist Party leaders. Five months later Muñoz was back in San Juan with a "pact" signed by the veteran opposition leader of the *Partido Liberal Fusionista*, Práxedes Mateo Sagasta. The former prime minister, as all Spanish politicians, had refused to even entertain the idea of "autonomy," a word "still hateful" to his ears.[5] But Sagasta saw that unless Spain yielded to American pressure, it would lose Cuba. In negotiations with Muñoz, he agreed that if he returned to power, he would grant Puerto Rico, as well as Cuba, an Autonomy Charter. Puerto Rico would have a total of nineteen delegates in the Spanish Parliament, all voting as members of Sagasta's party. While remaining under the ultimate sovereignty of the Spanish Governor General, the island would now exercise nearly complete authority over local government.

That summer, Sagasta was back in power. On August 8, 1897, Prime Minister Antonio Cánovas del Castillo was shot and killed near San Sebastián. Sitting at his old, familiar desk as Prime Minister, Sagasta was shocked to learn how much the situation in Cuba had deteriorated. Late reports described the Spanish land forces, now around 225,000, as "exhausted and bloodless, filling the hospitals, without the power to fight or hardly even to lift their arms."[6] General Valeriano Weyler's ruthlessness in attempting to "starve" the rebellion revolted world opinion. But there was brutality on both sides. Rebel leader Máximo Gómez was carrying out his own "scorched-earth" campaign. Behind the exaggerations of the American sensationalist and jingoistic press, the fact was that Spanish atrocities converted Cuba into a killing field. By Spain's own estimates, the plan to depopulate the Cuban countryside to concentration camps called

---

5. Ibid., 12.
6. O'Toole, *The Spanish War: An American Epic*, 88.

reconcentrados, resulted in "more than three hundred thousand...dying of hunger". This was one-fifth the total Cuban population.

Sagasta moved quickly. He called off the *reconcentrados* campaign and recalled Weyler, revered in Spain and among Cuban loyalists, but demonized as "the Butcher" by the international press. He accepted the American demand for an autonomous status for Cuba. Honoring his "pact" with Muñoz Rivera, the Puerto Rico Charter was, in fact, more liberal than Cuba's. In his race against time, Sagasta officially issued the Charter without submitting it to the *Cortes*, the Spanish parliament, as required by the constitution, knowing that it would have been rejected.

In San Juan there was an explosion of joy. Euphoric, Muñoz Rivera wrote in his newspaper that the Sagasta decree "destroys, without traces, the last vestiges of the old colonial regime...Puerto Rican, cry out with us: Long live Spain! Long lives the Liberal government! Long lives Puerto Rico, free and prosperous, in the heart of the Mother Country!"

THE CUBAN WAR

In Havana, however, there was a different cry. News of the Sagasta decree ignited riots by Spanish and Cuban loyalists: "Long live Weyler! Death to Autonomy!" On February 15, 1898, three days after Muñoz Rivera was designated to organize the new autonomous government, the USS Maine blew up in Havana's harbor, ending 286 American lives. President McKinley, a Methodist Episcopalian pacifist, still hoped to resist the country's war fever. He ordered a thorough and impartial inquiry of the explosion. The painstaking, month-long investigation revealed that the blast had occurred outside the ship: it was not an embarrassing on-board accident. But the commission was unable to determine the actual cause. Nearly a century later, another commission reported that it was almost certainly an accident.

Meanwhile, in Puerto Rico, Muñoz Rivera was in his own desperate race against time. If war between Spain and the United States was inevitable, certainly the island would be spared if it proceeded quickly to organize the autonomous government that the Puerto Rican leaders manifestly wanted for themselves. In the March elections for the new legislative body, Muñoz's party won overwhelmingly, as expected. Preparations began for the formal installation of the new government in May.

On the morning of May 12, Muñoz Rivera, his wife Amalia, and their three-month-old son, José Luis Muñoz Marín, were awakened by thunderous blasts. Huge American war ships, firing from 1,000 to 2,000 feet from San Juan harbor, bombarded the massive fortifications. Irrationally, senselessly, it seemed to Muñoz, the war to liberate Cuba, a thousand miles away, and the war on the other side of the globe, in the Philippines, had come to this peaceful island that had begun to organize its own government. The bombardment caused panic in San Juan. It was so intense that Admiral William T. Sampson's command battleship, the USS Iowa, "was enveloped in smoke and vivid with jets of fire."[7] The *El Morro* lighthouse took a direct hit.

For years the Muñoz family recalled the reaction of their Chinese servant to the bombardment. The family cow was out to pasture in the fort's open field. The servant, one of the hundreds that the Spaniards had brought to build streets and roads and had stayed, was ordered to go out to get the cow. He refused. "You should be ashamed of yourself," he was admonished. "By not daring to go, you are denying this baby his milk!" "If it is such a big honor," the man quietly replied, "why don't you go get the cow and bestow the honor on yourself." Instead, Amalia "Maló" Muñoz packed her baby and family members and fled for Río Piedras, a few miles from San Juan.

Muñoz Rivera remained behind. As Puerto Rico's civil head of government, he and party leader José de Diego urged the Governor General to arm the population in order to resist the expected invasion. But three hours after the bombardment began, suddenly the American cannons went silent. The war ships slipped away into the distance.

The day before, when a reporter asked Admiral Sampson if he intended to take San Juan, he quipped: "Well, if they want to give us the city, I guess we can't refuse it."[8] But his mission was to locate and destroy the Spanish fleet. Sampson believed that he had trapped Admiral Cervera y Topete and his warships in the San Juan bay. But the Spanish Admiral had no desire to engage, the American navy and had sailed instead to the island of Martinique. Sampson gave the order to move on to Cuba.

---

7. Friedel, *The Splendid Little War*, 42.
8. Ibid., 42.

In San Juan, the disappearance of the American ships was as baffling as the horrendously loud bombardment. The smoke that had enveloped the American war ships also enveloped Muñoz Rivera and the shaken Puerto Ricans in uncertainty. What did the Americans want? Would they return? And if they did, then what?

They did return. On July 25, 1898, the head of the U.S. Army, General Nelson Appelton Miles, along with 3,415 American foot soldiers, came ashore without resistance from the Spanish troops or Puerto Rican militia at the sleepy, south coast town of Guánica. There were only several skirmishes as four columns of American troops made their way up the island. Nineteen days later, word was received that an armistice had been signed. The Puerto Rican campaign was over and four centuries of Spanish rule had come to an end.

"THEN WHAT?"

No one was more confused by the new American rulers than Muñoz Rivera, who turned 39 on July 17, 1898. Days before the American invasion, he had again sworn his allegiance to Spain: "We are Spaniards and wrapped in the Spanish flag we will die."[9] But the Puerto Ricans had received the Americans, not as invaders, but as liberators. The last Spanish Governor General, Manuel Macías y Casado, cabled Madrid: "The majority of this country [does not] wish to call itself Spanish, preferring American domination. This the enemy knows and it is proven to him today by greetings and adhesions in towns that are going to be occupied."[10] Muñoz Rivera, interviewed by an American reporter, replied with caution. He recognized that "the island accepted the invading army with great rejoicing," but advised islanders to wait "until the thinking and actions...of Washington were manifest."[11]

What indeed were the Americans' intentions in Puerto Rico? Days after landing in Guánica, General Miles issued a proclamation in the city of Ponce:

---

9. Musicant, *Empire by Default*, 521.

10. Ibid., 536.

11. Morales Carrión, *Puerto Rico: A Political and Cultural History*, 142.

"We have not come to make war upon the people of a country that for centuries had been oppressed, but, on the contrary, to bring you the protection, not only to yourselves but to your property, and to bestow upon you the immunities and blessings of the liberal institutions of our government...the advantages and blessings of enlightened civilization."[12]

Island leaders took this literally. Quoted endlessly, it was interpreted as a solemn commitment coming directly from the President to incorporate the island into the United States. Muñoz Rivera's political rival, the black physician educated at University of Michigan, José Celso Barbosa, who spoke English, made his views known immediately: "We aspire to be another State within the Union in order to affirm the personality of the Puerto Rican people."

At first, Muñoz went along with Barbosa, reversing his earlier rejection of annexation. He and his newly formed Federal Party came out in favor of "incorporation." But his opponents did not trust him. This was, they insisted, another example of his political expediency. Muñoz Rivera, after all, could not change his convictions: he was still "Spanish to the core," still enamored with the *Madre Patria*. The Americans did not trust him. "A political agitator," the military Governor General Guy W. Henry informed Washington, "that is bound to make trouble in the future."[13]

If Muñoz Rivera was confused as to why the Americans had taken Puerto Rico, he, Barbosa, and all other island leaders were even more perplexed about American intentions towards the island. Historian Ivan Musicant points out: "The subject of Puerto Rico hardly rose in American political and expansionist circles during the diplomatic activity that led to the war."[14] It was always assumed in Washington that if the Americans went to war to liberate Cuba, it would have to also "take Puerto Rico" to cut the Spanish military supply line. And, of course, as a moral crusade against the "evil" Spanish, it made little sense not to expel them totally from the Western Hemisphere.

---

12. Ibid., 132.
13. Ibid., 146.
14. Musicant, *Empire by Default*, 517.

The little thought that was given to Puerto Rico was mostly given by the expansionists, Assistant Secretary of the Navy, Theodore Roosevelt, Senator Henry Cabot Lodge, and their mentor, the influential naval historian, Captain Alfred Thayer Mahan. Looking forward to the "isthmus canal," the expansionists saw Puerto Rico as the "Malta of the Indies." Their concern was that this small, poor island would be overlooked. "Puerto Rico is not forgotten and we mean to have it," Lodge assured Roosevelt.[15] But while the American civilian and military policy makers discussed whether to "take Puerto Rico" before or after the Cuban campaign, no one asked, much less answered the question: "Then what?"

It was not a trivial question. For on this dot on the map, there were a million people almost all living a depth of deprivation that shocked the young American soldiers and officers, but at the same time a proud cultural nation with four hundred years of history, a developed literary and artistic elite, and with an amazingly intense political life. Americans, intoxicated with the stunning display of naval power in crushing the Spanish, looked forward to their new naval bases in Puerto Rico. But the last thing the Americans had in mind was that they would spend the entire 20th century wrestling with the island's intractable economic realities and its equally intractable status dilemma.

---

15. Ibid., 520.

2 The Son of Muñoz Rivera

Luis Muñoz Marín was born into a world of political and military warfare. He was born near the *El Morro* fortress, on February 18, 1898, three days before the "Maine" blew up in Havana, five months before General Miles finally got the order to proceed to "take Puerto Rico." His first memory was of partisan conflict. He heard a commotion outside the house on La Fortaleza Street. Someone cried that it was another *turba republicana*, another "Republican mob," harassing his father. The three-year-old boy ran out to the balcony and shouted: "*¡Muerte a Barbosa!*" Death to Barbosa! These were words he had heard before, but not knowing, Muñoz wrote decades later, "who he was, nor what death was."[1] Barbosa was his father's political opponent. But the boy's shout angered Muñoz Rivera, who pulled his son inside and reprimanded him. The boy obeyed his father's command and returned to the balcony to whisper, weakly: "*Viva Barbosa.*" Long live Barbosa.

Politics had turned uglier since the arrival of the Americans. The Puerto Rican parties, the Americans found, were essentially driven by personalities and ideology. This was in part the result of centuries where Puerto Ricans had virtually no power in local government, but it was also cultural. Island leaders had little interest in administrative policies and programs.

When a civilian government was finally established by Congress in 1900, after two and a half years of military rule, island leaders were bitterly

---

1. Muñoz Marín, *Memorias*, 1898-1940, 26.

disappointed. The Foraker Act was economically generous. It exempted the island from all U.S. taxes and established free trade. But no one was more crushed than Muñoz Rivera: "the Foraker Act does not fulfill the aspirations [of Puerto Rico]...it satisfies nobody..." Puerto Rico now had less autonomy than under the final months of Spanish rule. Since the mid-19th Century, island politicians seemed obsessed with the status issue. The Foraker Act left the island's ultimate status in limbo. The political passions that Muñoz observed as a child flared up like never before.

Muñoz Marín's early memories were also of the smell of ink, the clatter of the printing press putting out his father's newspaper. And he recalled the night of another *turba republicana*, this time breaking into his home, the men damaging the press, the galleys, and the classified advertisements, scattering them all over the floor. He recalled his alarm, thinking that those galleys never again could be put back together.

To escape the violence, Muñoz took the family to Caguas, 15 miles south of San Juan. Then he decided to move again, this time to the United States. He would learn English, publish a newspaper in English, and continue his life-long battle for autonomy. In April, 1901, Muñoz Rivera, his wife, Maló, their three-year-old son, and several other family members disembarked from the USS Philadelphia. They moved into an apartment at 156 Fifth Avenue. Soon, the first issue of *The Puerto Rico Herald* came out, again attacking the Foraker Act as "indecent...there is not the slightest shade of democratic thinking..." The article was written as a "Letter to President McKinley." But on September 6, McKinley was shot and killed in Buffalo, New York. "The sudden advent of Theodore Roosevelt in the White House," historian David McCullough writes, "was to mark the most dramatic shift in Presidential style and attitude since the inauguration of Andrew Jackson...it can be said that the twentieth century truly began when he took the oath of office."[2] For Muñoz Rivera, once again everything seemed to change.

---

2. McCullough, *Truman*, 247.

For the son, however, the move to New York was to prove decisive in his intellectual and emotional formation, as well as in his political career. The passions, shouting, and violence of Puerto Rican politics were now accompanied by a new world—the streets of the big city. Yet he had no identity problem. "I lived two childhoods," he wrote years later, "the one in New York and the one in Puerto Rico... I do not recall during those four years being an American child, or not being one." He felt living in New York was "as natural" as living in San Juan. "I recall no moment in which I did not speak in English and I do not recall any moment in which I did not speak in Spanish."[3]

Muñoz missed his father who went back to the island for the 1904 elections, returned to New York in December and went back to Puerto Rico in February. This was not a happy marriage. His father, always distant in his own world of politics; his mother, a tough-minded, opinionated, demanding woman, dedicated to her son, accepting her lot in life as the wife of a "great political leader," and accepting the fact that her husband, and as it seemed every other island leader, had "another family," wife and daughter.

In this new century the American blueprint for extending the "blessings" of American democracy and prosperity to millions of immigrants was cultural assimilation. To ensure that the islanders were Americanized, all students in the public schools were to be taught in English. For seven-year-old Muñoz, now back on the island, this was a boon. After a brief stay in a Catholic school, Muñoz was placed in the first grade of a public school named William Penn. However, the fact that he was the only student who spoke English became a source of grief. The other students laughed at his unusual Spanish tinged with a New York accent. At the same time, it was embarrassing when the teacher would turn to him to correct his own English, instructing the students to "say it as José Luis does."

Muñoz was unhappy about something else. He was skipped to the third grade. One reason, of course, was his English. But it smacked of favoritism. He was "the son of Muñoz Rivera." As much as he revered his father, he

---

3. Muñoz Marín, *La historia del Partido Popular Democrático,* 74.

resented having to live up to his father's reputation. He flunked his third grade tests.

Muñoz Rivera was concerned about his son. He was definitely not a good student. Getting him a basic education had become a chore. He took the family temporarily back up to his mountain hometown, Barranquitas, in the summer of 1908, and hired a private tutor. But that also did not work. The tutor took the advanced payment and disappeared. The boy appeared to have natural intelligence, but was undisciplined, too much a free spirit. He much preferred to wonder off to gaze and appreciate the beauty of the Barranquitas countryside; to climb to the top of surrounding hills with friends and to repeat old tales of magical and miraculous events in the dark rivers and valleys.

Back in San Juan, Muñoz Rivera attempted still another approach with his ten-year-old son. He placed him in an experimental private school where the instruction was in Spanish. The boy adopted well to the freedom—there were no grades—and to the creative teaching methods of the school's owner and teacher, Pedro Mozcó. For his father's political cronies, *republicanos* were "bad." But it was evident to the boy that his teacher was a "good" *republicano.* "It was a contradiction," Muñoz Marín wrote years later, "typical of Puerto Rican life that made the emotional violence of our politics more bearable."[4]

Young Muñoz's new success at school pleased his father, but he was still worried. In a 1909 letter thanking Mozcó, he wrote: "I think that the boy's intelligence is pretty clear, but it is also my view that his negligence is difficult to correct."[5]

Young Muñoz preferred to live in his world of daydreams of adventure and romance. He was Alexander Dumas' D'Artagnan, or a brave pirate in a Robert Louis Stevenson novel, or a composer of romantic ballads. The boy fell in love and became "the lover, albeit platonic and respectful" of a Mexican actress performing in *The Merry Widow* in San Juan. Decades later Muñoz still recalled detesting her husband, the show's producer, and still recalled his name, Gutiérrez.[6]

---

4. Muñoz Marín, *Memorias*, Vol. I, 10.
5. Rosario Natal, *La juventud de Luis Muñoz Marín*, 17.
6. Muñoz Marín, *Memorias*, Vol. I, 12.

His favorite daydream was of being a war correspondent for his father's newspaper, *La Democracia*. In his fantasy, Japan, as he heard from adults, a new world power after demolishing the Russian army and navy in 1905, attacked Puerto Rico and captured San Juan. But there appeared Colonel Theodore Roosevelt, leading his Rough Riders to the rescue, capturing the town of Cataño on the other side of the San Juan Bay, then crossing the bay and liberating the capital city. War correspondent Muñoz Marín, behind Roosevelt's lines, wrote his dispatches at an inn on the road from Cataño to Bayamón. But how did he get his sensational reports back to *La Democracia* across the island to Ponce? First the reports were taken by horse to Bayamón, and from there to Ponce by telegraph. "The son of Muñoz Rivera" was now celebrated as the island's best reporter.

As Muñoz entered his teens, his daydreaming gave way to real-life historical events that he discussed with his father: the French Revolution and then the socialist revolutions between 1848 and 1870. He now dreamed of being a "revolutionary." But the one role he did not see for himself was following in his father's footsteps. Yes, he shared in the satisfaction of family and followers at his father's ability to "win" elections, but he disliked being forced into political rituals, such as wearing red and white ribbons on election day (the colors of his father's party) while the sons and daughters of the Republicans expressed their pro-Americanism with red, white and blue ribbons. "I never dreamed of being a politician," Muñoz wrote, "and later dreamed often of no longer being one."[7]

In 1910, his father was elected Puerto Rico's resident commissioner in Washington, the island's lone, non-voting member of Congress. His parents' marriage had deteriorated further and now they lived separately. Muñoz Rivera took a small apartment in Washington and installed his wife and son in New York. The boy's erratic education included a short time in a New York public school, and again classes with a private tutor.

The following year, his father brought him to Washington to enroll him at the University of Georgetown High School, the oldest Jesuit school in the nation. Muñoz Rivera was drawn by the school's reputation for "creating character," demanding "precision," and above all, instilling "discipline" in

---

7. Ibid., 12.

the small student body of 150. This was precisely what this "difficult" thirteen-year-old needed.

Muñoz Marín was enrolled under the name "José Luis Muñoz Rivera." For his fellow students he was "Joe Rivera." Again the young man was bored by the regular classes—Latin, Greek, religion, geography, and modern languages. He briefly took up piano lessons and engaged in several sports programs, but the courses he found interesting were literature and history. Unfortunately, he proved to be a poor student again. His school record indicates that he had to repeat his second year (1912-13). "In those three years," Muñoz confessed, "I didn't learn much."

In 1914, when his father returned to the island to campaign for reelection, he dropped out of school. Spending the summer with his mother in New York, he read in the newspapers the increasingly alarming reports of the furious arms race taking place in Europe. Britain and Germany's political and military leaders were as much disciples of the American military visionary Alfred Thayer Mahan as Theodore Roosevelt was. Muñoz was aware that these events affected Puerto Rico and his father's crusade for self-government. That summer of 1914, for the first time a ship traversed Roosevelt's Panama Canal. Puerto Rico became, as Mahan had predicted, strategically important. But young Muñoz's mind and emotions were elsewhere: "I was more interested in the dance hall in upper Broadway and spending Sundays at the beach in Coney Island than in the Kaiser's armies or President Wilson's proclamation."[8]

One of Muñoz Rivera's most famous poems is based on the Greek myth of Sisyphus, the legendary king of Corinth sentenced to an eternity of futility: condemned to push a giant rock up a steep hill, only to have it come tumbling down again after reaching the summit. Now, in Congress, Muñoz Rivera again demonstrated his tenacity. First, he had to master English. In 1911 he wrote to his close friend, José de Diego, "In June, I will go to a mountain or a beach, with my books, practice English without speaking another language. When I master it, I will feel better prepared for the decisive campaign. I have progressed a lot. I need much more. I will never be an orator...but neither was I in my own language."

---

8. Ibid., 13.

Muñoz Rivera was also tenaciously determined not to give up on his son. He decided he should study law. The seventeen-year-old protested: this was the last thing in the world he wanted to do with his life. *But what is it that you want?* his father demanded. The son had no answer, except for a vague calling for "journalism". He had written a few stories and published several newspaper articles in his father's newspaper back in Puerto Rico, under the initials "JLM." Even as a poet he was not very promising. Years later, asked about that first poem, now lost, Muñoz commented: "It was very bad, which is the only thing I remember about it."[9]

Muñoz Rivera persisted, forced him to take the high school equivalency exams, and enrolled him in a Georgetown Law School night program. This was made tolerable by working with his father in the daytime as his "personal secretary." He loved the excitement and the power of the Congress of the United States. But his university studies were disastrous. He passed only one course, Criminal Justice, with a high mark, and failed to complete all the others. Years later he commented that from this period of his life two books remained in his memory: "A biography of Goya that my father asked me to translate from French to Spanish, and a law school text on real estate that I sold the first chance I got."[10] That was the end of Muñoz Marín's legal career.

Young Muñoz was in fact now getting an education crucial to his life. His classroom was his father's office. He found himself in the maelstrom of a major political drama: for his father, the biggest battle since the arrival of the Americans. Finally Congress was responding to his 16-year campaign to repeal the Foraker Act. The new bill would significantly increase self-government, creating a fully-elected Legislature with power over the still presidentially appointed Governor. Dealing with Puerto Rico's status had always been frustrating for Congress, an issue its members found difficult to understand and much preferred to leave alone. But with world events again highlighting the island's strategic importance, Congress decided to act.

---

9. Rosario Natal, *La juventud de Luis Muñoz Marín*, 26.
10. Ibid., 26.

Economically, Americans felt good about what had been done on the island. Taking advantage of free trade between Puerto Rico and the mainland, American corporations made significant investments in sugar. From 1901 to 1909, the value of sugar exports to the mainland more than tripled from $4.7 to $18.4 million. The American government, meanwhile, made a major effort to improve the people's health, sanitation, communications, and education. In 1902, there were 874 schools on the island. Seven years later there were 1,912.

Nothing had a bigger impact than Dr. Bailey K. Ashford's breakthrough. The handsome Virginian came to the island with the American troops in 1898. He remained and discovered the parasite that caused the anemic disease that afflicted the *jíbaros*, one of the reasons why Americans found them so listless. Ashford founded the Institute of Tropical Medicine, which eventually became the University of Puerto Rico's School of Medicine. Along with the big American investment in sanitation, Ashford's pioneer work lowered Puerto Rico's death rate from 30 to 22 per thousand. The birth rate, however continued high, further speeding up the island's rapid population growth.

The prevailing attitude was expressed by President Roosevelt in 1906. Returning from a visit to Panama, Roosevelt—the first American president to travel abroad—stopped over on the island where he was enthusiastically received. He praised the American administration: "We are giving them good government...and the island is prospering."[11]

A few years later, however, Secretary of War Henry L. Stimson, after a prolonged visit through the West Indies in 1911, warned President William Howard Taft of the growing anti-American sentiment among Latin Americans. With American security concerns in the Caribbean heightened by the Panama Canal, Stimson took a strong interest in promoting political reform in Puerto Rico. He established a close relationship with Muñoz Rivera to work for changes, including American citizenship for Puerto Ricans. The following year Taft asked Congress to repeal the Foraker Act and to replace

---

11. Morales Carrión, *Puerto Rico: A Political and Cultural History*, 163.

it with an autonomous government modeled after British self-governing colonies. Taft agreed with Stimson that statehood "would not be of benefit to either Puerto Rico or the United States." The "link" between the island and the U.S. would be American citizenship.[12]

Woodrow Wilson, elected president in 1912, had demonstrated special interest in the political fate of the Philippines, Cuba, and Puerto Rico since his days as President of Princeton University. He warned Congress that America's position as leader of the free world demanded action towards the colonies: "Our treatment of them and their attitude towards us are manifestly of the first consequence in the development of our duties in the world..."[13] Wilson, the champion of self-determination, had another reason to attend to the American possessions. In 1915, a German submarine sunk the British passenger liner *Lusitania*, killing 1,200 people, 139 of them Americans. Still insisting in American neutrality in the devastating European conflict, Wilson began preparing the United States for war.

Americans believed citizenship was the greatest "gift" they could give to the islanders. There was little question in Congress that the vast majority of Puerto Ricans also welcomed it. José Celso Barbosa's pro statehood party was, of course, delighted. But what was Muñoz Rivera's position on citizenship? The master trapeze artist in Puerto Rico's ideological wars was in danger of losing his balance. Citizenship forced him to take a definitive stand on the island's political future. Beyond politics, it epitomized his personal ambiguity. Emotionally he dreamed of eventual independence. His deep Hispanic cultural roots made it difficult for him to suddenly embrace American citizenship.

Muñoz's inner turmoil became dramatically manifest on March 5, 1916. He gave a speech on the House floor that was meant to finally define his and his party's position. But he seemed to argue both in favor and against American citizenship. He declared that if the earth were to swallow the island, Puerto Ricans would prefer American to any other citizenship in the world. But as long as the island existed, the islanders preferred Puerto Rican citizenship. What did this mean? To members of Congress, attempting to follow his convoluted reasoning and fantastic analogy, he was clearly

---

12. Ibid., 171.
13. Ibid., 193.

attempting to appease his critics back home. But to his congressional colleagues, he seemed to be accepting citizenship. It was indeed a high-wire act.

In May the House passed the citizenship-reform bill introduced by Congressman William F. Jones of Virginia. But in the Senate, in spite of a personal campaign by the President, a last minute effort to attach a prohibition amendment that would have made rum illegal on the island stalled the bill. Anticipating that it would be approved early in the next session, Congress suspended the general elections in Puerto Rico scheduled for November of that year, 1916.

Young Muñoz witnessed his father's anguish. "The question of American citizenship," he wrote a half century later, "was for Muñoz Rivera the most difficult issue."[14] Yes, he wanted his father to win this battle just as he always wanted his father to win. But he did not feel part of the emotional conflict. For him, citizenship did not define his identity. Whether in New York or San Juan, in Washington or up in the Barranquitas mountains, there was no question in his mind as to what he was:

> I did not feel "American" nor did I feel that I was not "American," nor did I have a sensation of being in a limbo. I was from Puerto Rico, with all the naturalness of what is not questioned. I did not feel different after the approval of the Jones Act with its citizenship and all...If anyone asks me what country I am from, I would answer Puerto Rico. If I'm asked what my citizenship is, I would answer of Puerto Rico and of the United States. If I'm asked if I'm willing to fulfill my duties to both Puerto Rican and American citizenships, I would say yes to both alternatives—Puerto Rican because I am from here and that is what I am, and American because I have accepted it in good faith."[15]

There was something else young Muñoz noticed. In the battle between his father and de Diego that took place in the assemblies of the party leadership and in Congress, Muñoz asked himself, what do the people of Puerto Rico

---

14. Muñoz Marín, *Memorias*, Vol. I, 15.
15. Ibid., 18.

themselves want? Nobody is asking—not the members of Congress nor the Puerto Rican politicians.

Muñoz Rivera returned to Puerto Rico in what should have been the crowning moment of his political life. As his son wrote years later, he had won "his second great battle for autonomy." The first had been the 1897 Autonomy Charter. This one, Muñoz Marín wrote, was "more restrictive... but perhaps with more potentiality." Puerto Rico was finally freed from the Foraker Act that the political leaders despised.

Several days after his return, writing in his newspaper, *La Democracia*, Muñoz Rivera called on all Puerto Ricans to accept American citizenship. Although no one had asked the Puerto Ricans, there was little doubt regarding what they wanted. The law provided the opportunity for any islander to reject it and remain only a citizen of Puerto Rico. Muñoz Rivera knew that very few would.

The Lion's Death

Thousands of Puerto Ricans gave Muñoz Rivera a wildly enthusiastic reception when he arrived on the island, but Sisyphus' rock had clearly taken its toll. He looked older than his 56 years. He was physically and emotionally exhausted. A month later, he was ill from an infection caused by a ruptured gall bladder. On November 15, 1916, Puerto Rico was stunned by the news that Muñoz Rivera had died.

The entire town of Barranquitas waited patiently for the body of Muñoz Rivera to return home. Puerto Rico had never seen such an outpouring of grief as during the funeral procession across the island and up into his birthplace in the mountains. Some recalled his triumphant visits to these small towns during his many political campaigns. Hundreds of Unionists, all bearing flags, singing the party's battle song, came riding on horseback in what was the most spectacular event since the previous election campaign. Behind, finally, that imposing, majestic figure that projected such power and self-confidence would appear.

But on this day, on both sides of the main street stood young girls dressed in white, each with black ribbons around her waist, each holding flower bouquets. When the funeral procession appeared, a chorus of Catholic priests began a solemn chant, pierced by the anguished cries of women and children. An endless caravan of cars followed: some reports said there were five hundred, others a thousand. The girls in white threw the bouquets in front of the cortège slowly passing by while in the background a group of violinists from Mayagüez played a mournful funeral march. Then a band from Comerío played, slowly, *La Borinqueña*, the island's anthem, as the casket was carried up the church steps. "You have a very noble heart," the parish priest declared, "and that is why you earned the love of the Puerto Rican people."

Muñoz Rivera's niece, the poet Mercedes Negrón Muñoz, who published under the pen name, Clara Lair, wrote that the secret of the extraordinary affection that Puerto Ricans displayed for this man was his virility: "His campaigns, more than political, ideological or cultural, were virile political campaigns...with the avalanche of his virility, more than deeds or ideas, he annihilated the adversary." It was not, she wrote, what Muñoz Rivera offered the people in his hand, it was that "the people adored the hand."

President Wilson signed the Jones Act on March 2, 1917. For Puerto Rico's political leadership, the ordeal of the unworkable administrative and political hodgepodge created by Congress in 1900 was finally over. Few Americans, however, noticed. Ten days later, on March 12, an American ship was sunk by a German submarine. Three more were sunk four days later. On April 2, 1917, the United States entered the World War.

FATHER AND SON

The death of his father evoked in Muñoz Marín pain and resentment. Contemplating the imposing face, now silent and frozen in death, he felt anger. He was silently resentful of the parade of men and women attempting to console him, assuring him that "Muñoz Rivera is not dead...Muñoz Rivera lives..." But he *was* dead. Like his father, young Muñoz was not a religious man. There was no escape in faith or dogma to find comfort, justification or explanation to something so pointless, so irrational, as his father's death in the prime of his life.

Days later he broke down and cried as he opened his father's briefcase and saw the things that back in Washington his father had meticulously packed inside—shaving razors, combs, black ties, a used collar, false cuffs, cuff links and bottoms, and a check book with a balance of $600, what remained from his last payment as resident commissioner. These ordinary objects of his life, more than words, more than all the eulogies he had heard, seemed to encase his father's spirit, his presence, his voice, and made the pain of his loss worse.

Muñoz was confused. Almost to his last breath, Muñoz Rivera had manifested his concerns about his son, whispering to a friend at his bedside that he was an "intelligent young man," but after a pause, he asked himself if, after all, that was just "paternal blindness."

Muñoz Marín's mother was worried. "The death of his Papá," she wrote to a relative, "has made such a deep impression on his spirit that he has totally changed his behavior. It seemed that he was going to cause us trouble, being so given to attending parties, but today he is too quiet for his age."[16]

What, Muñoz Marín asked himself, had his father expected of him? Certainly he would not be his political heir. He disliked politics and politicians. He disliked what they had done to him, what they had forced him to say and do: all the twisting and turning, the compromising, the contradictions.

During the days and nights of his father's agony, the large house of his friend and benefactor, the sugar-baron Eduardo Georgetti, was filled with followers and adversaries, irresistibly grouping themselves to engage in endless *tertulias*—in conversation and comradery—where the burning topic was, as always, politics. Muñoz was not interested. Instead he gravitated toward the clusters of his father's literary friends, the poets and writers Nemesio Canales, Luis Lloréns Torres, Antonio Pérez Pierret, Epifanio Fernández Vanga, and Miguel Guerra Mondragón.

He savored the animated talk about the great Nicaraguan poet Rubén Darío and English writers George Bernard Shaw and Oscar Wilde, breaking out of the stifling insularity. Muñoz was especially interested in listening to Canales talk about the irreverent and witty Fabian Socialists of Great

---

16. Rosario Natal, *La juventud de Luis Muñoz Marín*, 54.

Britain. He relished the irony of hearing these Puerto Rican socialists denouncing the evils of capitalism at the Georgetti mansion.

In attempting to answer the question of what his father expected of him, he had to face his pride and annoyance at being "the son of Muñoz Rivera." The title took on a sinister weight: the weight of obligation, of duty, to his family, his followers. His father's death, paradoxically, threatened his free spirit. His emotions were confused, contradictory. How could he not dedicate himself to live up to this man who, in death, was being deified? But he also had the right to be himself, and in his own way, with his own ideas and goals, somehow make up for the great injustice that death had dealt Puerto Rico—and him. Writing in his father's newspaper, *El Diario de Puerto Rico*, directing his words to *Borinquen*, Puerto Rico's indigenous name, the eighteen-year-old melodramatically pledged: "...if someday you need my blood, it is yours. It is red blood, the same that ran in his veins. I was his son and my gratitude will be eternal."

The two biggest influences in his life, Muñoz wrote decades later, were his upbringing in two worlds—Puerto Rican and American—and his father. He wanted to emulate his personality, at once imposing without being overbearing. Always being himself, acting the same with the famous and powerful political leaders in Washington as he did with a *jíbaro* from tiny Barranquitas. Muñoz Rivera had profound self-confidence. He had commented after returning from his first trip to the United States in 1899 that "at no time did I feel envy." The son believed he had inherited this from his father. "Growing up," Muñoz Marín wrote, "I saw myself as a person among other persons—Americans, Puerto Ricans, shoe polishers, industrialists, businessmen, *jíbaros*." He wanted to believe that, like his father, he had no need for recognition, for important titles, for the seemingly never-ending *reconocimientos*, the testimonial banquets and speeches beloved by the *políticos*.

And the son, like the father, instinctively rejected violence, verbal as well as physical. Muñoz never forgot his father's first lesson and admonition: never "*Muerte a Barbosa.*" Always "*Viva Barbosa.*"

But what, Muñoz now asked himself, was his father's legacy in Puerto Rican history? As hard as he fought for self-government, Muñoz Rivera was never "anti-Spanish" nor "anti-American." But was there a core, a consistency in his life? He found an article his father had written back on July 12, 1910, responding precisely to his opponent's accusation of "ideological inconsistencies." Published in *La Democracia* under the title "What I Was, What I Am, What I Will Always Be," Muñoz Rivera wrote:

> Listen to me well, those that want to argue with me: if any nation of this planet, not only Spain, the discoverer and civilizing nation... or be it Italy, England, Russia, Turkey, monarchies with their kings, emperors, Caesars, and sultans, would have guaranteed to me, for my poor tropical rock, Self-Government, I would have become Italian, Russian, English, Turkish, all: because by doing so I would not become a Turk, an Englishman, a Russian, an Italian, but instead I would be the only thing that I am, what best fulfills my native thinking and desires. Because that is what I am: Puerto Rican!

Muñoz was aware that his father, like almost all other island political leaders, was much more interested in the island's political status conflict than in the abysmal economic and social conditions. But Muñoz recalled a June 28, 1915 letter his father sent to Antonio R. Barceló, a leader of the Union Party, in which he complained that their party was not doing enough in behalf of "the abused" island workers. "We are accomplices," he wrote, "by our inexcusable silence." And Muñoz recalled that it was his father who first introduced him to "socialism," spending evenings alone with him at his small Washington apartment, listening to him describe the progress of "international socialism" in France, England, Germany, and most recently, Russia. Late in life, Muñoz Marín wrote of those evenings: "That was a deposit of ideas, like a bank savings account in my mind. Later I was to draw from that account."[17]

Culturally, however, Muñoz Rivera and Muñoz Marín were different. Both never doubted their Puerto Rican identity, but the imprint of American culture was as strong on the son as the Spanish was on the father. The son lived ten of his first eighteen years on the mainland. Up to the age of thirty-three, he had moved so often between the mainland and

---

17. Ibid., 20.

the island that he could call both, or neither, home. Muñoz Marín never had to learn English as a second-language: it coexisted with Spanish as his "first language." There was no need to translate one into the other. From his earliest memory, there were always two words for everything, one in Spanish, and the other in English. "By a fortunate coincidence of my early years," he wrote in 1942, "I think that English, in its American expression, and Spanish, in its Puerto Rican expression, understood each other pretty well within me."[18]

That Spanish and English "understood each other pretty well" made him different, not only from his father, but from all other Puerto Rican political leaders. At the root of his father's battles since the arrival of the Americans—the distrust of American generals, the Foraker Act, the agony over American citizenship—was the cultural gap that made island politics incomprehensible to Americans, and American culture and politics incomprehensible to Puerto Ricans. Muñoz was still years away from deciding what to do with his life, but the stamp of this essential bridge that transcended the gap of cultural misunderstanding between Americans and Puerto Ricans was already imprinted on him.

---

18. Muñoz Marín, *La historia del Partido Popular Democrático*, 86.

3 "I want to be a giant..."

In the December 2, 1916 issue of satirist Nemesio Canales's literary magazine, *Juan Bobo*, young Muñoz appeared in a photo, dark and handsome like a Latin movie star. The large black Spanish eyes he had inherited from his mother stared at the camera. He had one hand in his pocket, the other on the wooden cross over his father's grave. "I want to be a giant to embrace the mountains that he contemplated as a young man...and that today bury his body. I want to be a giant to press against my chest the entire people of Puerto Rico.... I want to be a giant to finish the work of Luis Muñoz Rivera."

In spite of his words, the 18-year-old Muñoz, in his actions, continued to resist and resent the pressure to fill his father's shoes. In Ponce one day, while attempting to promote a new magazine he and friends had put together, a potential advertiser responded favorably, pointing out that it was the least he could do for "the son of Muñoz Rivera." The young man snapped back that he was Luis Muñoz Marín, and had no intention of living off his father's reputation.[1]

Economically, however, he did. Muñoz Rivera died poor, leaving his family in debt. His capital consisted of a small residential lot in the Miramar sector of San Juan, where he planned to build for his "retirement," a $5,000 life insurance policy, and the debt-ridden newspaper, *La Democracia*. But he also left behind a network of wealthy and loyal patrons,

---

1. Ibid., 60.

land-owners and businessmen who had supported him and his Unionist Party. The sugar baron Eduardo Georgetti and a small group of friends took over the finances of *La Democracia*, insuring its survival and guaranteeing the widow and the son a small but steady income. Free from financial obligations, Muñoz could dedicate himself to his education and writings. As long as *La Democracia* existed, Muñoz also knew that his writings would be published. His articles had been appearing in the newspaper since 1915. He discussed topics such as the war in Europe, "the submarine of the future," and occasionally the need for Puerto Rico to become independent.

Back in New York in December of 1916, living in an apartment on 141st Street and Broadway, Muñoz enrolled at Columbia University. While assuring his mother that he intended to finally get a degree in journalism, instead he took courses in play-writing and dedicated himself mostly to writing a collection of short stories and a play, completed in one month. In July, *La Democracia* compiled them into a book, *Borrones*— "Blemishes." The title, wrote Epifanio Fernández Vanga, the famous writer and politician, "is, in part, modesty; in part, it is true." Muñoz himself agreed.

"This was not," Muñoz wrote years later, "a good book." It consisted of amateurish imitations of popular Spanish and Latin American writers. The stories took place in Atlantis, the North Pole, in imaginary lands; one story included gruesome scenes of cannibalism, another was the tale of the rejected son of a prostitute who murders his own son, who is also the son of a prostitute. The characters philosophize over the superiority of the "noble savage," pure, pristine over modern man, contaminated, brutalized by civilization. Readers looking for the seeds of his father's literary talent didn't know what to make of this strange book. Indeed, one thing was clear. The young man deliberately made no effort to imitate his father. Puerto Rico and Puerto Ricans did not appear in this book.

"THIS IS FINAL!"

Muñoz could not avoid finding himself embroiled in the island's partisan politics. When he returned to Puerto Rico in the summer of 1917, he found the island preparing for its first general elections under the new Jones Act.

To his surprise, he was met with sneering comments by the opposition. The Ponce newspaper, *El Día*, reported that "the prodigal son" had been corralled and imported by the Unionists to campaign for his father's party. Nothing to be concerned about, the newspaper commented, since it was already evident that the son could not begin to fill his father's shoes. But this was not what Muñoz had in mind. He had come to supervise the printing of his book. In an angry reply, he declared: "I have an illustrious name that honors me, but does not glorify me. He achieved his glory and it belongs to him only." Muñoz went on to defend "his party's" support of "freedom"— independence—"always in harmony with the generous spirit and sense of justice of the American people." Muñoz ended again in his pontifical style: "This is short. This is clear. This is final!"

It wasn't. Muñoz could not resist jumping into one of the most volatile issues in the political campaign, and his brashness and arrogance provoked another stinging attack. He was vehemently opposed to Prohi-bition and criticized the women activists that supported it. Consumption of liquor, he argued, is not the cause of the inferior status of women in society. Women don't drink. The cause is their ignorance, spending their time at home cooking and sewing instead of reading books at a library. The response of one activist, Dr. Dolores Pérez Marchand, was quick and devastating. It was he who was "ignorant" of the great progress made by women in professions around the world as doctors, lawyers, war nurses, even train conductors in London. How dare someone with such poor formal education smear all Puerto Rican women!

This time Muñoz was hurt. "I, a vile person who insults women?" He always thought he had defended, not insulted women: "But, how bad it is to play the role of Redeemer! One always ends up crucified."[2]

Demonstrating that the reference to his poor education had hit a nerve, Muñoz then released the emotions churning within him, this time not in parables and sophomoric imagery as in *Borrones*:

My education *has* been very poor. After all, I attended a Jesuit school. But now my ideas are iconoclastic. Today's monstrous organization

2. Ibid., 51.

frightens me. I simply can't understand why it is that way, how is it that human beings can accept such an imbecile, idiotic, more anachronistic regime. There are times when I believe that my poor brain is going to explode. Many, many unbelievable things are occurring today in the world in general, and in Puerto Rico in particular.

Beneath the bravado of his posed photographs and extravagant words, Muñoz's skin was still too soft and thin for island politics. He ended this article, published in *La Democracia* on July, 9, 1917, in a tantrum. Mimicking the repetitious prayer in a Catholic mass, he recited: "Blessed be Puerto Rico...blessed be its tall and gentle palm trees...blessed be the hills that house the *jíbaros*...blessed be the sky, blue as a child's dream...blessed be the sun that warms our veins, our Latin blood, blessed be all of this, but damn, a thousand times damn, the crushing, ridiculous, anachronistic environment of the provincialism in which we are born, live and die!"

Muñoz, the iconoclast, was absolutely certain of what was wrong in Puerto Rico and the world. Everything. The banality, superficiality, and poison of Puerto Rican politics—the poison that had finally worn down the monumental figure of his father—was only a manifestation of the mindless destruction overtaking the entire world. If the absurd death of his father had left him emotionally reeling with confusion and resentment, how could he not be affected by the "murderous insanity" of the war raging in Europe? The great outburst of nationalism and idealism that had sent British, French, and German youths to the battlefront, now joined by the Americans, signing patriotic hymns, had bogged down into the idiotic slaughter of trench warfare "a gangrenous wound across France and Belgian territory...the brutal, mud-filled, murderous insanity known as the Western Front..."[3]

But for all his disdain for modern civilization, Muñoz needed something positive in his life. In 1917, a "great deed" seemed to have taken place in far-off Russia. His father had once spoken to him of a different concept of civilization—*socialism*. There was at least the promise that the Russian

---

3. Tuchman, *The Guns of August*, 487.

Revolution, a true socialist and democratic revolution, he believed, would bring about the world he wanted to live in.

EL GRAN GALEOTO

That summer, with his mother Maló back in New York, Muñoz began to exercise his new freedom in Puerto Rico. His father's friend and patron, Georgetti, had urged him to stay at his magnificent residence, but Muñoz preferred his aunt's much more modest home, which was nearby in Santurce and had "a piano and a poetess"—his cousin, the poet Clara Lair, a beautiful woman two years older—"who played Chopin and Beethoven" on the piano. Muñoz was also attracted to the Latin American, Dominican, and Puerto Rican writers that frequented the house. In the long *tertulias* that continued into the early morning hours at the Old San Juan restaurant *La Mallorquina*, there was endless and passionate talk on poetry, art, and philosophy.

The increasingly troubling reports that his mother received about his late night lifestyle, his drinking and womanizing, Muñoz admitted years later, were mostly true. Finally, he received a "hysterical" letter from her. How could he tarnish her reputation, and that of his legendary father? Muñoz answered in a sharp cable: "Damn the *Gran Galeoto!*" He thought this was a clever smokescreen: the *Gran Galeoto* was "the great galley slave" in a theatrical farce on the Spanish propensity for spreading vicious rumors.

The cable, however, ended up on the desk of a postal censor in New York. It was 1917 and America was at war. Two stern American agents appeared at the door of his mother's apartment in New York. Who, they asked, is the *Gran Galeoto?* Shown her son's cryptic cable, terrible ideas ran through her mind. What was her son involved in? She had no idea, she shot back, who the *Gran Galeoto* was. But did they know who *she* was. The widow of Luis Muñoz Rivera! Did they understand that she was a "lady" that possessed a "historic position" in her land? The two agents, unable to understand, decided to turn and leave.

When her son returned to New York, her first question was, "Who is the *Gran Galeoto?*" "How could you forget?" he asked incredulously. She herself, an amateur actress back in Ponce, had seen the Spanish farce several times. "Oh yes," her face brightened, "that's who he is!"[4]

In part to allay his mother's fears, Muñoz went to work for the new resident commissioner in Washington, Félix Córdova Dávila. She agreed to join him in Washington. Córdova, as many other island politicians, was also a poet. He and Muñoz often recited poetry, Córdova's classical and Muñoz's vanguard poetry. But soon it became difficult for Muñoz to concentrate on his clerical work. His mind would easily wonder off in absurd directions. He found his work extremely monotonous. In December 1917, he had enough and found an excuse to quit and return to Puerto Rico.

THE PRODIGAL SON

The excuse was to sell subscriptions and advertisements for still another "literary magazine." As he traveled from town to town, 20-year-old Muñoz saw his idealized Puerto Rico as an island of great scenic beauty and extraordinary poets. The small town of Guayama, nestled between a range of richly green hills and the pale blue Caribbean Sea, seemed to him "an Athens donated to Puerto Rico," in his eyes, a caldron of poetic creativity. He quickly gravitated to its nucleus, the *Café París* in the town plaza, where every evening a surprisingly large number of writers, poets, musicians, painters, and teachers came together.

Among them was a young poet his own age, a school teacher who every weekend came down from the *Carite* mountains. The thin, pale Luis Palés Matos was already something of a town celebrity. Unlike the confused reaction to Muñoz's *Borrones*, Palés's first book of verse had been received with high praise. Barely subsisting on his rural teacher's income, in this small town "dying of nothing," Palés became Muñoz's close friend and poetic soulmate. They spent hours composing verses, each attempting to get as close as possible to the style of an admired Latin American poet.

---

4. Muñoz Marín, *Unedited Draft Memorias*, 17.

Muñoz could not prevent, however, the other Puerto Rico of poverty and exploitation from intruding his dream-like world. The Guayama area was dominated by the big American sugar mill, *Central Aguirre*. One of the regulars at *Café París* was José Buitrago, the head of the local Puerto Rico Socialist Party and the town's only doctor. One afternoon, Muñoz noticed Buitrago walk out to attend to a man being carried on a stretcher from the countryside. Another labor stoppage at the *Central* had turned violent. Cane workers were beaten by police and company guards.

But young Muñoz would not allow these ugly intrusions of reality to spoil the enchantment of this land of poetic and scenic splendor. He convinced Palés to accompany him on to Barranquitas, still supposedly to promote his new magazine, and then to Ponce for a few days, the city that called itself "The Pearl of the South" and had for Muñoz an "aura of romanticism." It was there, twenty-six years earlier, that his father began his political crusade, publishing his combative newspaper *La Democracia*. Soon after their arrival, *El Día*, the small paper that had published the nasty stories about him several years earlier, ran a letter from an obscure Colombian poet expressing his "solidarity" with Ponce's poets and writers as an example of how free men extend their hands overseas and "over the broken backs of slaves." It was not clear to anyone just what the Colombian meant, but the Ponce poets considered this an "event" of extraordinary importance. Young Bolívar Pagán was especially proud: the letter was addressed to him.

Pagán went on to become one of the island's political leaders: historian, president of the *Ateneo Puertorriqueño*, an organization that promotes Puerto Rican artists, writers, and scientists. He married the daughter of the founder and president of the Socialist Party, labor organizer Santiago Iglesias, eventually becoming the party's president, the island's resident commissioner in Congress, and by the 1930's and early 40's, one of Muñoz's principal political opponents. But earlier in their lives, Pagán and Muñoz became good friends, collaborating in literary works.

Muñoz and Palés Matos, meanwhile, saw themselves as the literary incarnations of the controversial and influential vanguard Uruguayan poet, Julio Herrera y Reissig, a role model and a martyr. Herrera had died eight years earlier, at the age of 34, in abject poverty. He had turned his back on his well-to-do family to lead a life of defiance and insolence in

Montevideo, writing highly original and provocative verse meant to shock the bourgeois society he rejected. Muñoz and Palés attempted to capture his idiosyncratic style that at times, Muñoz wrote later, seemed to border on lunacy, but that often possessed "beautiful simplicities."

After Palés Matos was forced to return to his job and income in Guayama, Muñoz decided to write a play on Herrera's tragic death. Quoting "many of his most extravagant verses," Muñoz wrote it in four days sitting at a borrowed desk in the newspaper *El Día*. Bolívar Pagán wrote the introduction. Muñoz got the play performed by an Italian drama company that happened to find itself idle in Ponce. He thoroughly enjoyed the rehearsals, but its title, *In Silence*, proved to be prophetic. On its one and only performance, it played to a silent and empty theater. In Muñoz's own words years later, "the play was not a success, critically or at the box office."[5]

Muñoz's doomed play and his fascination with Herrera were to resurface a few years later. Part of Herrera's mystique of rebellion was his supposed use of drugs. The magazine *Revista de las Antillas* had published a photo of Herrera where he was apparently taking morphine. Years later, after Muñoz entered partisan politics, his opponents accused him of taking drugs. The origin of the attack, Muñoz was convinced, was his association with the striking and incriminating Herrera photograph. Yes, Muñoz answered his opponents, he was indeed guilty of "various sins" in that period of his life. But taking drugs was never one of them.

NEMESIO CANALES

Young Muñoz's mentor at this stage of his life was Nemesio Canales. Born in a small town, Jayuya, in the central coffee-growing mountain area, Canales's well-to-do family sent him to Spain to study medicine. After the Spanish American War, Canales convinced his father to allow him to transfer to the University of Baltimore to study law. He quickly mastered English and graduated with honors. Back in San Juan, he seemed well on his way

---

5. Ibid., 74.

to a successful and lucrative legal career. But law interested him little more than medicine had. His true vocation was satire, trenchant wit, often biting social criticism. He joined Muñoz Rivera's party, serving in the Legislature, started a newspaper in Ponce in 1912, and several years later the literary magazine, *Juan Bobo*, John the Fool. Finally abandoning his legal profession, Canales left Puerto Rico in 1918 for Panama, where he founded and published what became a showcase for progressive Latin American writers, the magazine *Quasimodo*.

Twenty years older than Muñoz, Canales introduced the young man to the ideas and writings of the prominent Fabian Socialist writers, George Bernard Shaw, Sidney and Beatrice Webb, and the works of H.G. Wells, Joseph Conrad, and Henrik Ibsen. In the spirit of their namesake (Roman general Fabius Cunctator, famous for outlasting superior forces by avoiding direct battle) the London Fabians advocated that socialism would eventually defeat capitalism through criticism, satire, education, and perseverance. This was, Muñoz recalled, pretty much what his father believed: socialism, morally superior to capitalism, would eventually triumph, not through the force of arms, but through the force of ideas. But as much as he listened to and admired Canales, Muñoz was still enamored of the Russian Revolution. He read Marx and Engels. The class struggle so simply and powerfully described in *The Communist Manifesto* seemed irrefutable. However, as he tried to "get into" Marx's *Capital*, as he put it years later, he was able to go only "several pages deep" before having to come up for air and surrendering.

MUNA LEE

Back in New York in the spring of 1918, Muñoz and a group of Latin Americans rented a small apartment on Broadway and 39th street where they met, talked, drank, and set out to publish another literary magazine, this one bilingual, called *Revista de Indias*. It had the same fate as Muñoz's other literary enterprises: it failed after only three issues. One of the Latin Americans was the Nicaraguan poet, Salomón de la Selva, active in New York's literary circles. Fully bilingual, De la Selva introduced Muñoz to a wide circle of progressive and socialist writers and intellectuals, including Edwin Markham, who was to become another major influence in his life and thinking, and to an Irish poet and author of anthologies on Latin American literature, Thomas Walsh. In February, 1919, Walsh, in turn, introduced him to an attractive young friend and poet, Muna Lee.

Lee and Muñoz had a lot to talk about during their long strolls through Central Park in early 1919. She was an interesting woman. Born in Mississippi in 1895, she took off on her own to Oklahoma to teach school. Soon she was bored and decided she wanted to live in New York. She applied for a job in the U.S. Post Office in New York as a Spanish linguist and was able to crash course enough knowledge of Spanish to get the job. She soon dedicated herself to her vocation. She wrote commentary and criticism of Latin American literature, became active in the women's rights movement, and achieved some fame as a poet, having won, in 1915, an award from *Poetry* magazine.

Muñoz and Lee shared the views of other socialists that "the war had given the old belief in the sacredness of private property a blow from which it could never recover..."[6] Capitalism, they were convinced, was reeling. But still she warned Muñoz to be cautious about expressing in writing his increasingly radical views and provoking the postal censor. After all, she worked at the postal censor's office. Muñoz readily agreed with her, recalling his mother's frightening experience with his *Gran Galeoto* cable.

Muñoz and Lee were married on July 1, 1919. A woman whose life and habits reflected the economy and precision of her verse, she soon learned that her handsome husband was uncaring, even irresponsible with money. They decided to make their way down to Washington, at times hitchhiking, occasionally taking a local trolley or ferry. In Philadelphia they ran out of money. It occurred to her that she might get a magazine that published her verse to cable her a small advance. It worked. However, that night, as they waited for the money, Lee and Muñoz slept on a Philadelphia park bench.

They stayed in Washington for several weeks, seeking the company of whatever young Puerto Rican or Latin American writers were to be found that summer in the city. Muñoz was pleased to locate and spend time with

---

6. Schlesinger, *The Crisis of the Old Order*, 39.

Tomás Blanco, another medical student who had a successful literary career. He would eventually write several books that would influence the debate on Puerto Rican culture and national identity in the following decades.

Muñoz decided to take his wife to the office of the resident commissioner in Congress, Félix Córdova Dávila. Coincidentally, they came across a commission of insular politicians, including the island's top leader, Antonio Barceló. The 50-year-old President of the Senate let out a howl of surprise and joy when he saw the young man. Barceló had been his father's close and trusted colleague, now the heir as head of the Unionist Party. He had always treated Muñoz as his own son, and greeted him with a warm, fatherly hug. But Muñoz felt awkward. He knew that he in his weather-beaten clothes and his "Bohemian" American wife were a rare sight for these well-dressed, formal, self-important Puerto Rican leaders. He suspected that behind their smiles, they were asking themselves, once more, "What in God's name has become of the son of Muñoz Rivera?"

4 God's Agitator

There were reasons for Luis Muñoz Rivera's disciples to wonder if the "prodigal son" would ever amount to anything. On February 18, 1920, Luis Muñoz Marín celebrated his 22 birthday, but in fact he had little to celebrate. His ventures into literary magazines had all failed. Without a profession and without discipline, there were reasons to doubt that he would ever hold a steady job. Married to the Mississippi-born poetess, Muna Lee, under pressure to make money, he worked as reporter and translator for short periods of time in two commercial magazines, *The Spanish American Trade Journal* and *American Exporter*. Soon again unemployed, he depended almost entirely on the meager income his wife's writings produced, occasionally supplemented by whatever his mother could provide.

Unable to afford to live in Manhattan, Muñoz and Muna rented a small room in a Staten Island house for five dollars a month. The room had a stove and little else, but it had a great attraction. They were now neighbors of the world famous 68-year-old social protest poet with the big white beard, Edwin Markham. Nearby there was also a branch of the Carnegie Library of New York, where Muñoz read whatever books on socialism he could find.

The gatherings of academics, intellectuals, and poets at Markham's home, the books brought home from the library, the frequent correspondence with Nemesio Canales in Panama, the Spartan simplicity of his and Muna's living, and indeed, the poverty in which they struggled, all came together in Muñoz's emotions and thinking. In this semi-rural area, light years away from the island, he felt free from the pressures and demands of the patronizing bourgeois politicians that to a great extent had controlled his father's life.

He was now, at least, writing regularly: columns for *La Democracia* back home, articles and poetry for *Quasimodo*, and increasingly for liberal U.S. publications, including H.L. Mencken's *The Smart Set*, all infused with strong doses of what he called "proletarian protest". He was deeply moved by Markham's acclaimed 1899 poem, *"The Man With the Hoe."* Inspired by a painting by the French artist Jean-Francois Millet, Markham's brutally dehumanized farm worker, "bowed by the weight of centuries," was, for Muñoz, an exact, heart-wrenching portrayal of the Puerto Rican *jíbaro*, the sugar-cane cutter.

Who made him dead to rapture and despair,
a thing that grieves not and that never hopes,
Stolid and stunned, a brother to the ox?

Muñoz knew the answer: the American capitalist system: the absentee-owned sugar corporations in Puerto Rico, supported by the American colonial government. With Markham's permission, Muñoz translated the poem into Spanish and published it in Puerto Rico and in Latin America.[1] Even though he was a harsh critic of his own writings, Muñoz was pleased with the result.

In March 1920, Muñoz wrote and published a series of seven poems, strongly influenced by Markham and Carl Sandburg, whom he described as "not only a great poet but a good socialist."[2] In these self-portraits, Muñoz attempted to set a goal for his life. Among them was what was to become his most often quoted poem, *"Panfleto:"*

I have broken the rainbow
Against my heart
I am God's pamphleteer....
God's agitator

---

1. Rosario, *La juventud de Luis Muñoz Marín*, 102.

2. Muñoz Marín, *Unedited Draft Memorias*, 34.

And I go with the mob of stars and hungry men
Toward the great dawn...

The pamphleteer now had a message for his people—radical socialism—and he made a decision: the time had come to become also the "agitator."

THE SOCIALIST

From Panama, Canales invited Muñoz to join him in Buenos Aires to publish his magazine *Quasimodo*. But Muna, who was pregnant with their first child, made a quick review of their economic situation and convinced him that it made no sense. Muñoz, in fact, had other plans: to return to Puerto Rico where his mother and family would attend to Muna's childbirth. Twenty-two-year-old Muñoz had decided to join the island's principal political "agitator," Santiago Iglesias Pantín, founder and leader of the Puerto Rico Socialist Party.

Everyone, including Santiago Iglesias, was stunned. Iglesias had been one of his father's severest political critics. In turn, Unionist leaders saw the Spanish-born labor organizer as an "anarchist" and a "Bolshevik." As Muñoz stood before him, Santiago Iglesias cried in disbelief: "Boy! Do you know what you are saying?" Iglesias didn't know what to make of this. On the one hand, the conversion of "the son of Muñoz Rivera" to his party was a political coup. The November elections were six months away and certainly having this attractive, articulate young man by his side would add votes. But on the other hand, Iglesias did not want to be accused of having politically seduced this naïve "boy" who had lived most of his life outside the island.

Muñoz answered that he would join the typesetter's union, which qualified him for the Socialist Party. Let's do this, Iglesias relented. The following day he was going to visit the Fajardo area where cane cutters had declared a strike. "It has become violent," Iglesias warned. The laborers earned less than a dollar a day and were demanding two and a half dollars. The post-war demand has increased the price of sugar from six to twenty dollars a hundredweight. "The *Central* is answering our demands by cracking heads. Before you make your decision, you come with me and see for yourself if this is what you want. You are an adult and I will respect your decision."[3]

With Iglesias on the road from Carolina to Loíza, on to Río Grande and finally to Fajardo, for the first time in his life Muñoz witnessed Puerto Rico's "class war." The first line in Marx and Engel's *Communist Manifesto*— "The history of all hitherto existing society is the history of class struggle."— came to life before his eyes. Iglesias was right. There was violence as the companies, backed by the island police, attempted to break the strike.

Muñoz was deeply affected. "My indignation grew by the hour and by the minute during that trip," he recalled years later. "The *jíbaro* had been for me a figure within a landscape, poor, but as natural as the trees and the thickets and brooks; now he was transformed into a human tragedy..."[4]

Muñoz had another experience that shook him. He was surprised to come across Luis Palés Matos, his young poet friend from his dreamlike stay in the south-coast town of Guayama three years earlier. Palés, then a half-starved public school teacher, was now working for a municipal government newspaper, controlled by the Fajardo Sugar Company. He was also leading the publicity campaign against the cane-cutter's strike. "What are you doing here?" Palés asked Muñoz. Remembering the famous exchange between Emerson and Thoreau, Muñoz snapped back angrily: "What are *you* doing here?" Palés, who had lived in poverty back in Guayama on a school teacher's salary, was now making $50 a week with the government newspaper.

Years later Muñoz regretted the harsh and accusatory exchange. Palés Matos went on to become one of Latin America's most admired writers of Negroid poetry, capturing the rhythms, sounds, and euphony of black slave culture. Muñoz considered him Puerto Rico's greatest poet. "Only softer than his heart," Muñoz wrote, "was his willpower."

On the way back to San Juan, Muñoz and Iglesias stopped in Río Grande where one of the strike leaders pleaded for help. "Comrade Iglesias," Muñoz cried out. "I'll stay with him!" No, Iglesias shot back. He didn't want the responsibility of anything happening to this young warrior much too eager to battle capitalism. "I brought you here and I will bring you back home!"

---

3. Ibid., 39.
4. Ibid., 42.

At home Muñoz was met by a storm of disapproval. His mother, the custodian of his father's legacy, could only gasp that she would have a heart attack. ("She lived," Muñoz dryly commented decades later, "thirty-seven years longer.") "Why are you doing this?" a Unionist friend interrupted her to ask the grim Muñoz. "What have we done to you that you should join that destructive anarchist?" "It's not what you have done to me," Muñoz replied. "It's what you are doing to the proletariat." We are all "socialists," another family friend said. But "good socialists" like those good people he had seen in New York handing out jars of hot soup to the poor. That, Muñoz said angrily, is exactly the trap of the "bourgeois socialism" that Marx and Engels had exposed: to delude the proletariat with jars of "stale soup" into accepting their "chains."

The only explanation Unionists could give themselves for his incomprehensible behavior was that "he is crazy."[5] How could "the son of Muñoz Rivera" become an "agent for disorder" promoting the destruction of, more than his father's party, his father's world. Then it occurred to one of the Unionist leaders, Celestino Iriarte, head of the San Juan committee, to attempt to jolt the young man back to reality. He invited him to attend a Unionist meeting in San Juan, and see for himself that these simple people of modest income are the "proletariat" as much as the cane-cutters in Fajardo. Surely the young man would "admit his error."

Muñoz accepted eagerly. The meeting was held in the second floor of a wooden house on Calle de San José. Up the stairs, he could hardly get into the steamy room packed with sweating bodies that overflowed out into the balcony. At the other end Iriarte sat behind a table. He stood up, opened the way for Muñoz to come forward and sit beside him. Muñoz could sense the great curiosity in the room. These people were asking themselves, "Is this really the son of Muñoz Rivera?" Muñoz was perplexed. The Iriarte plan to jolt him seemed to be working. These common-place people wanted to be reassured that he was not "crazy." He merely went for a recreational outing with Iglesias. It had all been a misunderstanding. He looked around and saw the faces of men that had followed and loved his father. Of course, he felt absolutely no animosity toward them. Certainly they were not the "enemy." Like Palés Matos in Fajardo, they, too, were victims of the capitalist

---

5. Muñoz Marín, *Memorias* Vol. I, 45.

system. Muñoz grew impatient to speak to them while a Unionist *político* rambled on in an endless, meaningless, florid *pico de oro* speech. Muñoz finally got his chance. The "pamphleteer" knew exactly what he was going to say.

In contrast to the Unionist orator, Muñoz began to speak softly and slowly. What is happening in Puerto Rico today, he began, is much more than another political contest between parties. It is a class struggle. A political party cannot pretend to defend both classes at the same time, for to defend one is to attack the other. The Unionist Party, which controls the government, wants them to believe that it is on the worker's side, but it is in fact on the side of the ruling class. So is the Republican Party. He, Muñoz, was on the right side, the side of the proletariat, the side where those in this room all belonged.

As Muñoz spoke he sensed a growing restlessness in the room. The last thing these party militants expected was an abstract lecture. The only "war" they were interested in was the war against the Republican and Socialist Party "enemy." The only thing they wanted to hear from Muñoz was whether he was with or against the Unionist Party. Muñoz spoke faster, hoping he could get to the end of his lecture, but then someone shouted angrily: "Let him go!" Then another "We don't need him!" Iriarte jumped up and demanded that he be allowed to finish. "I have finished," Muñoz declared suddenly, getting up to leave. His cousin, Miguel Muñoz, "fortunately muscular," came to his side to make way for his departure and insisted on accompanying him to ensure that he returned unharmed to his mother's house.

Muñoz would not make that mistake again. He would preach his gospel, to him so self-evident, to the working class in the Socialist Party, men who would listen and understand. As part of his intense campaign in the following weeks he gave scores of political speeches at party rallies throughout the island. It occurred to him to attempt a novel way to lecture on the *Communist Manifesto*. He spoke at movie houses relating and interpreting movie plots, however varied, to illustrate his explanations of class warfare and economic determinism. Everything evil seen in the movie was the result of "capitalism," every worker a victim of "exploitation," every young soldier on the battlefield a victim of "militarism and imperialism."

Muñoz's vigorous campaigning had an impact. The Unionist Party again won the elections, but the Socialists doubled their votes. Before the elections, however, Muñoz had an experience that affected him as much as his initial visit to the Fajardo labor strike.

DISILLUSION

Several months before the elections, Iglesias called a meeting of the party leadership held at the Municipal Theater in San Juan. Muñoz, attending as delegate of the Alto del Cabro section of Santurce, where he lived, quickly noticed that there was something odd. Several delegates, led by Prudencio Rivera Martinez, head of the party's strongest union, the Tobacco Workers, reported that they had received a proposal from the island's Republican Party to form an "alliance" for the November elections. Pooling their votes, they hoped to defeat the Unionists, control the Legislature and thus the patronage. Muñoz was aghast. Had no one listened to him? The alliance would bring together the two social and economic classes that were at war with each other. This was not an "alliance." This was capitulation. Was the Socialist Party fundamentally no different from the Unionist and Republican parties? As he listened to the debate, Muñoz saw that Iglesias himself, not Rivera Martínez, was the author of the idea. Denouncing it as the betrayal of the working class, Muñoz, followed by four other delegates, walked out in protest.

Later that night, Muñoz received a message that Iglesias wanted to see him at his home. He found the party leaders gathered there, quietly waiting for Iglesias to speak. Yes, he began, he had seriously considered the alliance. It was a matter of political reality. Obviously the Socialist Party could better serve the island workers by sharing its power with the Republicans. But he made up his mind that he would not accept the Republican offer unless there was unanimity among the party leadership. Nothing would be gained by dividing the working class. In view of the Muñoz protest, he said, the offer was rejected.

Muñoz won this battle but he lost his leader. He had deluded himself from the beginning. Of course, Santiago Iglesias's goal was to win the elections in Puerto Rico, and yes, he was a true labor reformer, as well as a tough political boss. But he now shared the political conservatism of his mentor, American labor leader Samuel Gompers, and represented in Puerto Rico the American Federation of Labor. To attack him as "anarchist" and "Bolshevik" was absurd. Instead he had become decidedly "pro-American." In 1898 he had been jailed in *El Morro* by Muñoz Rivera for his labor agitation. He was released by the Americans, who guaranteed his right to organize unions. Although Iglesias insisted on keeping the political status issue separate from the Socialist Party's economic reform program, he was known to favor statehood, rejecting independence as economically disastrous. Now Muñoz wondered if the 48-year-old Iglesias was beginning to act like the other island *políticos*. Political status had to be a major reason why Iglesias had considered associating with the reactionary but pro-statehood Republican Party.

After the elections, Muñoz published a new magazine, *Spartacus*, the Marxist "organ of class struggle." The April, 1921 issue declared: "*Spartacus* favors, politically, any practical goal that will unleash the power of the proletarian revolution... the Puerto Rican proletariat needs complete freedom of action to carry out its mission of renovation." The magazine called on the island's youth to attend the Spartacus School of Social Science. It announced the creation of the "Proletarian Library" of "books written for workers and persons interested in the international proletarian movement, which interprets History and Social Science from the point of view of the Working Class." Thirty titles were offered, seven of them by Marx or Engels.

The magazine, as the others Muñoz had started, failed. Only two issues were published. His career as a radical "pamphleteer" came to an end. In 1921, Muñoz returned with his family to New York. This time he remained there for five years.

"DE-DOGMATIZATION"

Muñoz, Muna, now with two children, Luis and Munita, and his mother, Maló, moved into a house in West Englewood, New Jersey. Maló had finally sold Muñoz Rivera's residential lot in Miramar and used the money to buy the house.

Once again, Muñoz had in effect escaped. It was evident that as "agitator" he had done more to create fear than to promote an understanding of "true socialism." Responding to one of his critics, he wrote: "None of the hysterical alarmists can define the principles of the 'bolshevism' that they so feared."[6] There was little hope for a "proletarian revolution" on his island. During the campaign, visiting the huge tobacco factories, he observed the men hired to read out loud books and magazines, whatever would help the workers get through the monotony of their work. What an opportunity, Muñoz thought, to indoctrinate these loyal union members, the backbone of the Socialist Party, with the works of Victor Hugo, Marx, Kropotkin, Bakunin, and Proudhon. But it was all mixed in with popular novels, many romantic, some of them "pornographic," for Muñoz, a "grotesque combination" that could only confuse the workers.

Meahwhile in the U.S. the Wilson presidency had killed the illusion that Muñoz and Muna had shared with their generation of socialists, that the World War would fundamentally change America. "Disillusion began to be an epidemic in 1919, not only...in Washington, in New York [but] soon in every city in the country." On New Year's Day, 1920, Wilson's Attorney General, Alexander Mitchell Palmer, having escaped death from a terrorist bomb placed at his house, launched a massive persecution of socialists and radicals: 6,000 were rounded up and jailed. Among them was another of Muñoz's heroes, socialist leader Eugene Debs. From prison, running again for President of the Socialist Party of America, Debs got 915,000 votes that November. Muñoz had quoted in his magazine *Spartacus* Debs' indignant rejection of Wilson's last minute offer to grant him a pardon. "No man in public life in American history," Debs wrote, "ever retired so thoroughly discredited, so scathingly rebuked, so overwhel-mingly impeached and repudiated as Woodrow Wilson."

That year Americans elected Republican Warren Harding. In their small house on Teaneck Avenue behind a big apple tree, there was little for Muñoz and Muna to celebrate: the campaign slogan "Back to Normalcy" signaled the return to reactionary, isolationist government. From his detached tranquility, Muñoz had the time to think hard about his experiences in Puerto Rico, and about his life. "It's almost a year since I have been living

---

6. Rosario, *La juventud de Luis Muñoz Marín*, 113.

in this countryside in New Jersey," he wrote to a family friend on July 4, 1922, "almost completely isolated from the currents of life. No one visits me here nor do I go anywhere. I eat, sleep, and walk around the area, and I read."[7]

His friend and mentor Nemesio Canales broke his isolation one day, on his way back from Buenos Aires to the island. They agreed to meet in a small Italian restaurant in New York where they would drink "bad bootleg wine." Muñoz found Canales also "defeated and disillusioned," not only by the failure of his magazine in Buenos Aires, but also by the direction that the world socialist movement had taken since Lenin's attempt, through his 1920 Third International, to place it under Soviet control. Canales was repulsed by the goals and tactics of the Leninists. What, in fact, was happening in Russia? Had the Revolution become totally oppressive, or was Lenin's hand forced by the czarist and capitalist-inspired counterrevolution? When Canales left, Muñoz reflected on his experiences, his observations and his mood. Years later, he reported, "It was probably in that conversation in the Italian restaurant with Canales that I began a process of revision in my mind..."[8]

Muñoz returned to the books that Canales had brought to his attention years earlier, to the Fabian Socialists, the works of Shaw, Webbs. He read Bertrand Russell's *Proposed Roads to Freedom* and attended his conferences in New York. He also read works of "devastating criticism of the style of living in the United States apart from social theories": the Sinclair Lewis novels as well as H.L. Mencken's iconoclastic social criticism. He began to question whether he had "fallen too quickly into an ideological formula" that oversimplified Puerto Rico's realities. Muñoz, the free spirit, had allowed an ideology to imprison his thoughts and emotions. He had to get out.

Santiago Iglesias, Muñoz thought, had also gone through a process of "de-dogmatization"—from Spanish anarchist to "Americanized labor leader, Samuel Gompers style." His rethinking was taking a different route, "from Marxist dogmatism of the Second International, and at times the Third, to intellectual Fabian socialism."[9] Muñoz had begun his own "de-dogmatization."

---

7. Ibid., 141.
8. Muñoz Marín, *Unedited Draft Memorias*, 58.
9. Muñoz Marín, *Unedited Draft Memorias*, 66.

His father, known as "the Lion" for all the roar in his writings and speeches, and for all the passion in the island's partisan warfare, had never lost his humanity and his tolerance. Muñoz the son realized that his arrogance as the self-anointed "God's agitator" had led him to act cruelly to many good people in Puerto Rico. He had violated his father's "¡Viva Barbosa!" lesson. He had treated mistaken but good people as "enemies."

One of them was Eduardo Georgetti: the wealthiest insular "sugar baron", his father's close friend and benefactor. It was in Georgetti's San Juan house that Muñoz had died on November 15, 1916. Now, on July 4, 1922, the son wrote to Epifanio Fernández Vanga: "I have treated Georgetti and his family recently in a way that would be ridiculous if it were not also very painful, and abominable if it had not been totally fanatical."[10] Socialist doctrine, he wrote, presented itself to him as a perfectly symmetrical conflict between the "forces of Good and the forces of Evil." "My vision of class struggle was of a crude purity: all workers were angels, and if not it was the fault of capitalism, and all capitalists, by the mere fact of being so, were devils that fought to keep the angels in slavery..." Why, he asked, should he judge others on the basis of "the standards of my world if they don't even know my standards..." Muñoz confessed:

I have lost my inverted class prejudice. Moreover, I now feel more sympathy for individuals than for groups and their masses. It seems to me that it is more worthy to seek happiness within its many multiple and delicate individual forms than in its wholesale form of justice. I believe that each individual's aspiration to happiness is as deep, as strong and as venerable, [and] that it is almost a crime to put on those aspirations the obstacles needed for social existence... All this digression so that you will realize that I am no longer an ogre; that, without repenting for a moment my actions in the island's politics, I am sorry with all my heart for all the ridiculous fanaticism and aggressions that accompanied my actions.

Muñoz asked forgiveness of Georgetti and "all those that surround him." At twenty-four, he had done more than rediscover his father's tolerance. In

---

10. Rosario Natal, *La juventud de Luis Muñoz Marín*, 140.

feeling "more sympathy for individuals than for groups or their masses," he was placing the concrete reality of flesh-and-blood men and women—a phrase he was to use countless times in his career—over theory or ideology. Muñoz was still far from discovering what to do with his life, but he had discovered what was to become the essential approach, the foundation of his political thinking and political life.

In the Spring of 1923 Muñoz returned temporarily to Puerto Rico to put together and publish the journalistic writings of his father. The experience moved him further into his "de-dogmatization." For the first time, he confronted the contradictions, the twisting and turning of his father's ideas and conclusions. "Reading Muñoz Rivera's newspaper articles," he wrote a half century later, "produced in me a strange sensation."[11] How to make sense of his father's writing during 26 years of constant political and ideological battle? "My father's life, I knew, had been an honorable life, in service to Puerto Rico, without personal benefit for himself or his family, and for this I held for him great respect and admiration. I was confronting, without knowing or understanding it well, the torture of an intellectually honest man whose expressions at times reflected his sense of responsibility, and at times the truth, which do not always coincide..." This conflict that Muñoz saw in his father, between intellectual honesty and political responsibility, was also to become a source of "torture" in his own life.

The death of Nemesio Canales in September of 1923 devastated Muñoz. Years later, recalling how much Canales had influenced his thinking, he wrote: "In the years of service to my country I missed him—missed him often!" His death led to still another experience of "de-dogmatization." Santiago Iglesias asked him to replace Canales in a commission to represent the Puerto Rican Legislature at the American Federation of Labor convention in Portland, Oregon. The assignment came with a weekly stipend of $30 plus hotel and food expenses.[12] Muñoz buried his old disagreement with Iglesias and accompanied him and the commission across the country by train.

The United States of America, Muñoz wrote years later, "now passed physically before my eyes as the stage where the romance of the pioneers

---

11. Muñoz Marín, *Unedited Draft Memorias*, 63.

12. Rosario Natal, *La Juventud de Luis Muñoz Marín*, 163.

took place: immense in its plains, dramatic in its mountains—the scene of the great democratic accomplishment of an anonymous people creating a nation. The history of brutal 19th century capitalism after the Civil War, now merged in my mind with the epic poem of Walt Whitman's people. I asked myself: which of the two are the real American people?"[13]

Muñoz was surprised to see that the Palmer "Red Scare" of 1920 had not stamped out American socialism. He found pockets of progressives in power in several cities, including socialists in the Milwaukee municipal government and "representatives of the working class" in the Minneapolis government. At Portland he got the convention to approve a resolution, much publicized in Latin America, condemning the Juan Vicente Gómez dictatorship in Venezuela. Muñoz, Iglesias, and the others continued their trip down through California, stopping over in San Francisco. Here Muñoz was "really surprised" to find a large Puerto Rican community made up of laborers that had migrated in 1900. He was impressed by the progress they had made. These former sugar cane cutters had become professionals and businessmen living much better than the minute middle class back in Puerto Rico. Muñoz had been strongly opposed to the migration of Puerto Ricans to the mainland as a means of slowing the island's population growth. Now he rationalized the impressive gains of these migrants under American capitalism: "[Their progress] is due to the economic independence that they enjoy, the economic independence that Puerto Ricans in Puerto Rico are to enjoy once they organize themselves and fight for it."[14] A highlight of the trip was meeting one of his socialist heroes in Los Angeles, writer Upton Sinclair.

Muñoz's "de-dogmatization" journey brought him to a critical juncture in his life. "Men who carry through political revolutions," writes British historian Paul Johnson, "seem to be of two main types, the clerical and the romantic."[15] Lenin was a "clerical revolutionary...his humanitarianism was a very abstract passion. It embraced humanity in general but he seems to have had little love for, or even interest in, humanity in particular."

---

13. Muñoz Marín, *Memorias*, I, 57
14. Rosario Natal, *La juventud de Luis Muñoz Marín*, 168.
15. Johnson, *Modern Times*, 51.

Muñoz had entered the 1920 Socialist Party campaign a "clerical revolutionary" driven by a "very abstract" commitment to "groups and classes." Two years later he emerged from his isolation in Staten Island, his confessional letter to Fernández Vanga, and his trip across America, a "romantic revolutionary". His humanitarianism had come down to earth. As his father had never been, Muñoz would never again be an ideologue.

Muñoz emerged also with a different kind of passion, grounded in what he saw each time he returned to the island. To be motivated by "humanity in particular" meant facing the brutal economic realities of the Puerto Rican *jíbaro*. Muñoz had never questioned that Puerto Rico's natural status should be political independence. Culturally Puerto Rico was as much a "nation" as all other Latin American countries. It was also self-evident to him that Puerto Rico's enormous social and economic ills would never be tackled, much less resolved, until the island broke free from America's reactionary government. Muñoz's passion became independence for Puerto Rico.

THE REILY NIGHTMARE

Would Puerto Ricans follow Muñoz's dream of independence? Was his father's instinct right, that suppressed within every Puerto Rican was a nationalistic desire for "freedom?" President Harding's appointment of a new Governor, Emmet Montgomery Reily, a Kansas City mortgage broker, provoked the worst political crisis between the island's leadership and Washington since the arrival of the Americans in 1898. And in Muñoz's eyes, "The Reily Nightmare" answered the question of what lay in the hearts of all Puerto Ricans.

On November 20, 1921, a fire broke out in the passenger ship bringing the Governor to New York. Soon after entering the harbor and after the passengers disembarked, the ship sank. Reily was convinced that it was a Puerto Rican plot to kill him. It was sensational news in the American press. A *New York Times* editorial speculated that there was something terribly wrong going on in Puerto Rico, for just months after Reily's appointment, commissions of Puerto Rican political leaders were descending in Washington demanding his removal.[16]

---

16. Aitken, *Poet in the Fortress*, 71.

A fervent supporter of Harding and a "superpatriot," Reily was convinced that to favor independence was un-American. Egged on by local pro-statehood Republicans, he carried out his own "Red Scare"—a campaign directed at any Puerto Rican in government that expressed support for "freedom."

By now Muñoz had mastered Mencken's iconoclastic style. Reily's fears that Puerto Ricans were out to kill him, Muñoz wrote in a January 4, 1922 article published in *The New Republic*, were ridiculous. Through several centuries, Puerto Ricans had tried to harm not a single one of its many colonial rulers. But, he added sardonically, "rumors express desires when they do not express facts or fears. What, then, is the basis of this desire on the part of the majority of the natives to eliminate Mr. Reily, if not from the world, at least from their island?" It was his persecution of Unionists. But it was even more absurd, Muñoz went on, to believe that Unionists posed a threat to American rule, much less to an American governor. This was the party of the wealthy and "very few wealthy Puerto Ricans sincerely believe in independence." It was all talk and even the Unionists themselves were dumbfounded that the Governor took their pro-independence rhetoric seriously.

But in fact something new was taking place in Puerto Rico. For the first time, a colonial governor was subjected to brutal public ridicule. In songs and plays he was derided as *Moncho Reyes*, an absurd play on his name. Reily's radical pro-Americanism radicalized island politics. His persecution pushed the new generation of leaders and activists towards a more militant support of independence. Another effect of the "Reily nightmare" was the emergence of a new political movement. A small group of Unionist intellectuals bolted the party and organized the Nationalist Party of Puerto Rico.

Harding removed Reily in early 1923. That summer, traveling to the West Coast, the President fell ill. Several days later, on August 2, he died. The taciturn vice president, Calvin Coolidge, became the 30th President of the United States. He expressed his political and social philosophy in a few words: "The chief business of the American people is business." As historian Arthur Schlesinger put it: "For Coolidge, business was more than business: it was a religion."[17] It was all coming together in Muñoz's mind. Reily's

---

17. Schlesinger, *The Crisis of the Old Order*, 57.

bumbling entanglement in island politics awakened the "nationalist" within each Puerto Rican. There was no hope for reform under the U.S. flag. Muñoz had a new goal through his writings: to convince American public opinion that Puerto Rico represented a tragic and inexcusable American failure, and that it was in America's best interest to let go of the island and its people.

WHAT IS NORMAL?

"It is time," his mother wrote Muñoz in 1927, "for you to have a normal life." But what was "normal" in his life? Although he was pleased with his growing success in getting articles printed in Latin America and Europe as well as in the United States, nothing seemed to work out in Puerto Rico. In 1926, he returned to the island as editor of *La Democracia*. He and Unionist leader Barceló agreed that he would write the editorial, expressing his own views, while Barceló would write his own column with the official Unionist Party position. Inevitably, the columns clashed: Muñoz attacking the absentee sugar corporations, Barceló in the uncomfortable position of having formed an alliance with the conservative, pro-sugar Republican Party. A year later Muñoz was back in New York.

"Normal" for Muñoz was also never being able to make ends meet. "These were years," he wrote years later, "of Bohemian life and indigence."[18] His main source of income was the $25 Mencken paid him for his monthly articles in *The Baltimore Sun*. In 1927, his wife Muna, in Puerto Rico with his mother and two children, expressed her exasperation after receiving still another plea for money:

> Your cable yesterday afternoon inspired me (you will forgive me?) with a wild desire to shriek with laughter. You must learn to select, to control, to manage, Luis, if you are ever to have any comfort or pleasure in life—or any freedom. I know you have had a very difficult two months. So have I... I not only cannot help you in any

---

18. Muñoz Marín, *Unedited Draft Memorias*, 73.

financial way but I shall be utterly lost and undone if you cannot manage to help us immediately. Believe me, our need is desperate, or I should not beg for money—and continue to beg...[19]

Muñoz's "life of indigence," his irrepressible restlessness, back and forth between Puerto Rico and the mainland, and his frequent separations from his family allowing him to indulge in his "Bohemian life" seriously strained his marriage. In 1923, Muna published a book of verse, *Sea Change*, in which she expressed her love, frustration and resignation:

I make no question of your right to go—
Rain and swift lightning, thunder and the sea,
Sand and dust and ashes are less free!
Follow all paths that wings and spread sail know,
Unheralded you came, and even so,
If so you will, you may take leave of me.
Yours is your life, and what you will shall be.
I ask no questions: hasten or be slow."[20]

In 1927, Barceló once again came to Muñoz's rescue. He assigned Muñoz to carry out a Legislature-sponsored campaign on the mainland to attract industrial investment. This was an unlikely mission for this anti-capitalist, but it represented, for Muñoz, an economic windfall. Now with an income of $500 a month, he lived in the Vanderbilt Hotel on Park Avenue, supposedly his "promotional office," entertaining potential clients at expensive restaurants. He tackled the job with energy. Using his good relationship with American reporters, newspapers published positive stories about the island's attractions: abundance of low-cost labor, political stability and government incentives. But this economic bonanza ended quickly. The publicity generated hundreds of inquiries, more luncheons and meetings, but not a single new investment on the island.

Muñoz made other attempts to get a steady income: he worked for a short time for the Associated Press Latin American news desk. Later, also

19. Rosario Natal, *La juventud de Luis Muñoz Marín*, 197.
20. Ibid., 155.

"for a few days," he was a reporter for *The New York World*. Through a Puerto Rican friend employed by a New York public relations firm, Muñoz was hired as a Washington lobbyist to get Congress to lower the tariff on Argentinean grapes. His assignment was to convince members of Congress that the grapes would become raisins, not the prohibited wine.[21]

In 1928, he accompanied his wife to the Pan American Union Conference in Cuba, a meeting of the hemisphere's heads of state attended by President Calvin Coolidge. Muna Lee was director of Public Affairs for the Union's Inter-American Commission on Women. Known in Latin America as a pioneer leader in feminist rights, she was invited to address the conference in representation of the National Women's Party of the United States. She got Muñoz hired as a "technical advisor on languages," a translator, for which he was paid $100.

Muñoz's stinging 1925 article in *The Nation*, "Tyranny and Torture in Venezuela," had made him a celebrity in the Venezuelan exile community. He organized in New York a Venezuelan labor union and assisted in a plan to overthrow Venezuelan dictator Juan Vicente Gómez. With the help of the Mexican government and Mexican labor leaders, he coordinated a plot to infiltrate Venezuela through the Colombian border, bring arms and organize workers' cells throughout the country. He worked with a Venezuelan "adventurer general" and one of Mexico's top labor leaders, Luis Morones, "a big and heavy man who wore many diamonds whose labor followers justified saying that if capitalists can wear diamonds, why not their own leader."[22] The "invasion" lasted three days. In New York, Morones confessed to Muñoz that he never believed that the plot would work. Regarding the Venezuelan general, he said: "We have many like him in Mexico, and they are no good for revolutions."

Another exile venture involved going to Cuba with the brother of Nicaraguan rebel leader, Augusto César Sandino, as part of a plot to get Sandino into power following the withdrawal of the American military occupation. Muñoz got his good friend Roger Baldwin, head of the American Civil Liberties Union, to contribute $200 to the cause. The trip to Cuba

21. Muñoz Marín, *Memorias* Vol. I, 65.
22. Muñoz Marín, *Unedited Draft Memorias*, 68.

never took place and nothing came of the plot. Muñoz never again saw or heard from the brother, Socrates Sandino, who simply disappeared.

"In the jungle of the twenties," Thomas Aiken wrote in 1964, "it was perhaps miraculous that the tall and handsome son of Puerto Rico's greatest political figure, bereft of money and position, never lost sight of his island home and the tragedy that was stifling the lives of so many of her 'pale men of the mountains.'"[23]

But the reality was that approaching thirty, nothing seemed to work in his life. His determination to expose the "failure of American colonialism" on his island was faced with another failure: that of his own life.

---

23. Aitken, *Poet in the Fortress*, 76.

5 "America's Favorite Daughter"

To convince Americans that they had indeed failed in Puerto Rico, which was so evident to Muñoz, was no easy task. For several American Presidents and Governors, nothing was further from the truth. President William Howard Taft described the island as "The favorite daughter of the United States" in a special message to Congress back on May 10, 1909. If Americans could be blamed for anything, he said, it was for being overly generous.[1]

A decade later, Governor Arthur Yager titled his 1919 report to Congress "Twenty Years of Progress." The Kentucky-born Yager, a liberal Democrat, classmate and close friend of President Wilson and former university president, served as Governor for an unprecedented eight years, from 1913 to 1921. He was one of the few that had a good relationship with Unionists. Puerto Rico, he declared in 1919, was bustling with development and contentment. Americans could be proud of the achievements: the number of children in school had grown tenfold since the turn of the century; there were 52 new hospitals, 37 water and sewerage systems, 267 new kilometers of roads were built or improved. In addition to Dr. Bailey K. Ashford's pioneer work discovering the cause of endemic anemia, massive public health programs and universal inoculation against smallpox and tuberculosis had lowered the island's appalling 25.3 death rate. Just as dramatic was the improvement in the quality of government: an impartial and honest judicial

---

1. Morales Carrión, *Puerto Rico: A Political and Cultural History*, 166.

system now existed, along with honest municipal governments, a modern police force, and an equitable tax system.[2]

Yager was particularly proud of one statistic: of the 5,935 civil servants, all but 208 were Puerto Rican. Of these, 148 were young, idealistic American men and women who had come to teach at public schools throughout the island, many of them under the physical and emotional hardship of working in such an exotic, hot, and culturally foreign environment.

"In everything that enters into or indicates the life of the people," Yager wrote, "there is [a great deal] to be seen [in] this marvelous change and progress...in the architecture of their homes and hotels, in the traffic and character of the crowded shops and the traffic on the busy streets and the fine roads, in the voluntary organizations formed for pleasure and for social welfare and especially in the number and quality of the newspapers that make up the press, in fact, in everything one sees there is written the record and proof of 20 years of the most remarkable progress." That record, he wrote, "cannot be equaled by any people anywhere in the world for the same length of time." And the future was just as bright. Yager predicted that "the next two decades will see even more wonder and progress and development."

American private capital, meanwhile, had modernized the island's sugar production. The old, inefficient industry, fragmented into 446 small and primitive sugar mills, had been replaced by giant, multi-million-dollar American-owned *Centrales*. Americans introduced new varieties of cane, extensive irrigation, and heavy use of fertilizers. They built railroad and dock facilities in San Juan and Ponce. The four biggest sugar corporations, which controlled about half of the island's entire production, built attractive, well-groomed housing and recreational complexes for its managers and production workers. Productivity per acre doubled: total production increased more than tenfold, from 70,000 to 800,000 tons a year. The island's tobacco industry was also modernized by new American owners. The entire economy expanded greatly: the value of exports, which was $17 million in 1901, had grown to $200 million by 1928.

In 1928, President Calvin Coolidge, in what was for him an unusual display of emotion, echoed the words of President Taft two decades earlier.

---

2. Yaeger, *Twenty Years of Progress*, 10.

In a letter addressed to his appointed Governor, Horace M. Towner, Coolidge wrote: "It would not be difficult to demonstrate that the existing status of Puerto Rico is much more liberal than any other status in its history; that its people have more control of their own affairs, with less external intervention; that its people enjoy freedom and the protection of the law; and that its people and its government are receiving substantial assistance due to their association with the United States."[3]

Coolidge made an elaborate comparison of Puerto Rico under the Spanish and now under the Americans. "We found the people of Puerto Rico poor and defeated, without hope for the future, ignorant, victims of poverty and disease, without knowing what constituted a free and democratic government, and without the experience of ever having participated in self-government." He went on to painstakingly list all the benefits and privileges bestowed from the very moment the American soldiers stepped on the island: from zero public schools under Spain, there were now 991; from 29,182 children in school, there were now 213,321; American citizenship, free trade, total exemption of U.S. taxes, the U.S. excise tax "rebate." Coolidge repeatedly returned to his fundamental argument: the United States had given Puerto Rico more privileges and actual power to govern themselves than any other territory in American history.

"A LAND OF BEGGARS AND MILLIONAIRES"

Writing from New Jersey, using the same statistics as the presidents and governors, Muñoz got the support of liberal American journalists to debunk the rosy picture of Puerto Rico. The relationship between Muñoz and Mencken went back a decade. In the early 1920s, he had published Muñoz's and Lee's poetry in his important literary magazine, *The Smart Set*. Later, as editor of the *Baltimore Sun*, Mencken named Muñoz a freelance "special correspondent." By the end of the decade, Muñoz had become the first Puerto Rican, and one of very few Latin Americans to appear regularly in the mainland American press.

---

3. Bothwell González, *Puerto Rico: cien años de lucha política,* Vol.II, 382.

Another influential journalist who enthusiastically took up Muñoz' cause was Ernest Gruening, the editor of *The Nation*. Gruening possessed extraordinary energy and aggressiveness in pursuing his many liberal crusades, from racial justice at home to anti-imperialism in Latin America. The son of a Prussian immigrant who became a successful physician in New York City, Gruening graduated from the Harvard Medical School only to quit medicine for a successful career in newspapers and magazines in Boston and New York. Muñoz's exposure of American "colonialism" fit perfectly into Gruening's latest crusade, a campaign to get American marines out of Haiti and the Dominican Republic.

In 1925 Gruening published the first of several articles by Muñoz: "Puerto Rico: the American Colony." The essence of the problem in Puerto Rico, Muñoz wrote, could be stated in one word: sugar. "Profits have been known to surpass 100 percent per year, and a very large share of it leaves the island never to return. That is the secret glory of colonialists. And even this ghastly spectacle of wealth drained from a starving population into the richest country on earth is sanctimoniously entitled in the official reports 'A Favorable Trade Balance.'"[4]

The often cited examples of "American generosity," Muñoz insisted, were detrimental. The beneficiaries of free trade were the American sugar corporations that exported their product to the mainland. The *jíbaro*, paid starvation wages by the rich corporations, at the same time was condemned to "buy his staples in the same market where the American banker and bricklayer buy theirs. [That] evil cannot be corrected so long as we remain within the customs system of the United States."

In 1929 he wrote in Mencken's *The American Mercury*:

The development of large absentee-owned sugar estates, the rapid curtailment in the planting of coffee—the natural crop of the independent farmer—and the concentration of cigar manufacturing into the hands of American trusts, have combined to make Puerto Rico a land of beggars and millionaires, of flattering statistics but distressing realities. More and more it becomes a factory worked by peons, fought over by lawyers, bossed by absent industrialists, and

---

4. Muñoz Marín, *The Nation*, April 8, 1925, 379.

clerked by politicians. It is now Uncle Sam's second largest sweat-shop.[5]

For Muñoz, the solution to Puerto Rico's enormous ills was evident: massive land reform by taking land from the sugar corporation and giving it to the *jíbaros*. "Puerto Rico," he wrote in *The Nation* in 1929, "is small, not very complex, and the task was—and is—an easy one..." Using its borrowing capacity, the island government should begin to gradually "shave" land away from the *centrales*—as long as the island remained so dependent on sugar—until 100,000 families live and farm on their own land. At five acres per family, each would not only produce much of its food, but would be also required to plant a minimum acreage of sugar to meet the needs of the existing mills. Not an unreasonable proposal, Muñoz argued: "Surely if it has not been considered excessive heretofore for less than five entities to own one-third of the land, it cannot be considered excessive for half the people to own one-forth of the land."[6]

THEODORE ROOSEVELT, JR.

On September 13, 1928, a hurricane settled the issue of what was "the real Puerto Rico." "*San Felipe*," historian Morales Carrión recorded, "marked the end of the era of flattering statistics. The era of dismal statistics then began."[7] Even more ferocious than 1899's *San Ciriaco*, *San Felipe*'s 160-mile-an-hour winds devastated the island's economy. The following year Puerto Rico suffered another crushing blow—the full brunt of the world-wide Great Depression. "There was...hopelessness among the *jíbaros* of Puerto Rico," Morales wrote.

In 1929, Puerto Rico was hit by a storm of another kind. President Herbert Hoover named Theodore Roosevelt, Jr. the island's governor on October 7, 1929. He arrived on the island with his father's great enthu-siasm and energy: instead of acting like a "colonial viceroy...he tackled his

---

5. Muñoz Marín, *The American Mercury*, 1929, 139.
6. Muñoz Marín, *The Nation*, Nov. 20, 1929, 608.
7. Morales Carrión, *Puerto Rico: A Political and Cultural History*, 212.

job with great zeal and gusto".[8] But no optimism or enthusiasm could erase what he witnessed in a Puerto Rico still deeply affected by *San Felipe*.

Before his arrival, 42-year-old Roosevelt and 31-year-old Muñoz met in Roosevelt's New York apartment and took to each other. They were both sons of extraordinarily successful political leaders. Roosevelt had partially followed in his father's footsteps. After serving in World War I as colonel, and as assistant secretary of the Navy from 1921 to 24, he had also run for Governor of New York. Unlike his father, he was defeated. Already influenced by Muñoz, once on the island, according to Earl Parker Hanson, "Roosevelt was the first to look at people and not statistics and to say: 'This is awful!'"[9]

Roosevelt confirmed Muñoz's view of the island's dismal condition. He published in *The New York Herald Tribune* an article titled "Children of Famine." Visiting the center of the island, he witnessed "farm after farm where lean, underfed women and sickly men told and retold the same story— little food and no opportunity for work...poverty was widespread and hunger [had intensified] almost to the point of starvation...."[10]

Muñoz did something he had never done before: he praised an American governor. "Governor Roosevelt," he wrote in 1931, "has probably presented the case of Puerto Rico, both in its immediate and far-reaching aspects, more completely than any other American or Puerto Rican has done in the past thirty years."[11] He described Roosevelt's success in attracting large sums of money to the island—$8.15 million from the U.S. government for hurricane relief, $3 million more to help small farms, $7.3 million to combat disease and malnutrition. All this, Muñoz insisted, was "palliative, based on philanthropy." While applauding Roosevelt's attempts at "equitable land distribution" and rural education programs, he pointed out the magnitude of the island's excess population and its impact on all the social and economic ills.

This was another critical point of agreement between Muñoz and Roosevelt. Unlike other Puerto Rican politicians, Muñoz had been as "fanatical" a Neo-Malthusian as he had been a socialist ideologue. Several years earlier he had shocked the island's Catholic clergy and laymen with a

---

8. Morales Carrión, *Puerto Rico: A Political and Cultural History*, 213.

9. Hanson, *Transformation: The Story of Modern Puerto Rico*, 62.

10. Ibid., 63.

11. *World's Week*, July 1931, 21.

series of newspaper articles calling for voluntary, government-supported birth control to stem the island's population explosion. One anti-birth control doctor not only warned him about the harmful effects of contraceptives, such as cancer, but said that it was morally wrong to deny the "queen of the house of the little flowers that perfume her home." Muñoz replied sarcastically that far from "perfuming the homes," each new child became one more competitor for the scarce bread in the homes of half-starved Puerto Rican families. Puerto Ricans, he decried, were "breeding for the cemetery" since one out of every three children died before reaching the age of five.

When the Catholic Bishop entered the heated debate reprimanding Muñoz, the then-25-year-old replied with several long philosophical articles, quoting from Saint Paul and freely borrowing from Nietzsche and Mencken's anti-clericalism. He will not, Muñoz advised the Bishop, lose sleep over the threat of being excommunicated since he had "felt himself excommunicated" since the age of eight when his father gave him, and he read, *The Three Musketeers*.[12]

Muñoz agreed with Roosevelt on another point. "A country with a population such as the one Puerto Rico is called upon to support," he wrote, "cannot subsist decently without industrial development." Notwithstanding his personal, futile attempt to attract factories to the island in 1927, he agreed that the island possessed the ingredients to become "the workshop of the Caribbean, in some sense as England was the workshop of the world during the nineteenth century." Muñoz even allowed a note of optimism into his writing: "Not quite two years ago Theodore Roosevelt was appointed governor of Puerto Rico. He has governed it, but he has done more. He is on his way to solving the problems of Puerto Rico."

In February, 1932, President Hoover named Roosevelt Governor of the Philippines. Roosevelt left the island with strong opinions as to its future. He was convinced that the attempt to culturally "Americanize" the island was doomed to failure. Economically as well as culturally, Puerto Rico was simply too different from the United States. The aspiration of eventual statehood, he believed, was also futile. Instead, he wrote in his 1937 book *Colonial Policies of the United States*, "a dominion status is best, with the island realizing self-government within its borders."[13]

---

12. Rosario Natal, *La juventud de Luis Muñoz Marín*, 160.

13. Morales Carrión, *Puerto Rico: A Political and Cultural History*, 214.

Now that there was no issue over the "real Puerto Rico," the question was why? What went wrong? On Puerto Rico's political future, Muñoz disagreed with Roosevelt's eventual "dominion" status. "What went wrong," he was still convinced, was American colonialism. And the only solution was independence. This received a powerful boost from the 1931 book, *Porto Rico: A Broken Pledge*, by Bailey W. and Justine Diffie. American attempts to govern and lift the island from centuries of poverty, the Diffies wrote, were indeed a dismal failure. After the Americans arrived in 1898, unemployment increased from 17 to 30.2 percent in 1927, *before* the Depression. America had indeed made this pathetic island a "land of beggars and millionaires." While American companies made great profits, its sugar workers earned from 40 cents to two dollars a day: its tobacco workers ten dollars a week, women four dollars a week.

> Puerto Rico is at once the perfect example of what economic imperialism does for a country and of the attitude of the imperialists towards that country...Puerto Rico can hope for no relief under the existing system.[14]

Diffie's book, depending heavily on arguments and statistics provided by Muñoz and his followers, reached the inevitable conclusion that as long as Puerto Rico was under the American flag, it was doomed. Muñoz was right: the only "solution" was independence.

But was it? In 1930 the Brookings Institution published the results of the most exhaustive independent study ever done on the Puerto Rican economy. The two-year investigation attempted to get to the root of Puerto Rico's poverty. Unlike Diffie's book, it was free of any political or ideological influence. The study was conducted by a team of seven academics and professionals led by Dr. Victor S. Clark, who had served as the island's education commissioner. It was filled with statistics and charts along with long, graphic descriptions of the people's living conditions. Titled "Puerto Rico and Its Problems," the 700-page report was anything but a whitewash

---

14. Diffie, *Porto Rico: A Broken Pledge*, 220.

of American rule. After three decades, Brookings declared, "in spite...of the efforts [that] have been made to relieve the situation... the condition of the masses of the Island remains deplorable."

But in answering the question "why," Brookings arrived at a fundamental conclusion diametrically opposed to that of Muñoz and Diffie. Puerto Ricans and Americans were wasting their time looking at the island's political status. The cause was not "American imperialism," nor the excessive profits of American-owned sugar corporations. It was excessive misgovernment, inordinate partisan politics, and above all, too many people on too small an island.

If Puerto Rico was a "victim," it was of good intentions. Americans were able to greatly decrease the death rate through their health and sanitation programs, but not the birth rate. Already overpopulated with nearly a million people when the Americans arrived, the island had since experienced a population growth of 62 percent: one and half million people, 450 per square mile, packed on this mostly mountainous island. Brookings went further. It attacked another of Muñoz and Diffie's irrefutable "truths." Enforcing the federal law that limited corporation land ownership to 500 acres was exactly the policy that would make everything worse. On the contrary, Brookings suggested, the sugar industry should be made more efficient and significantly more competitive with other major sugar producers such as Cuba and Hawaii, allowing the corporations to control and cultivate *even more land.*

The Brookings Report created a serious intellectual problem for Muñoz. He could not dismiss it as more of the same reactionary bias. Brookings, after all, was seen as a liberal think tank and he could not refute its objectivity. In *The Baltimore Sun* of July 23, 1930, Muñoz wrote that the report "for painstaking thoroughness, for intelligent fact-finding, for a clear-cut dramatization, in diagrams and figures, of a collective tragedy... deserves all praise. No longer will it be possible to claim, on the basis of travestied trade [reports], that Puerto Rico is a happy child, tucked away [under] the American flag like a baby in its mother's [arms]." And yes, "the American regime must be credited with tremendous progress in road-building, education (quantitatively at least) and sanitation..."

Paradoxically, Muñoz argued, its tragic flaw was precisely its rigorous scientific approach. It dehumanized the Puerto Rican tragedy. "When it comes to solutions, the Brookings authors assume the character of scientific farmers dealing with a large farm and harboring good intentions toward the hired help..." This deeply offended Muñoz as a condescending, colonialistic, "reactionary" approach to the island's flesh-and-blood reality. The Brookings experts, he wrote, where right in describing at great lengths the "evils of politics" in Puerto Rico. But the cure was worse than the disease: it "recommends the abolition of all vestige of democratic government in Puerto Rico... Thus Puerto Ricans, on the basis of minor administrative difficulties—many of them true enough—would be tied hand and foot, hamstrung, knocked out, and in all ways incapacitated to develop their own policy for their own country, against their own hunger and economic servitude..." Crushing what exists of democracy on the island, in the name of scientific "efficiency", Muñoz indignantly declared, "is the theory of the Latin American dictatorships."

That Brookings so deeply disturbed Muñoz was made evident by his reaction to the report's fundamental argument: that the root of the island's "deplorable" condition was overpopulation. Of course, he wrote, this was a major factor. But he now rejected that it was the most important factor. While Puerto Rico's population had grown by over 50 percent, he argued that during the same period the value of exports had grown by over 1,000 percent. This, Muñoz insisted, proved that the cause of the island's misery was indeed American "colonialism" and "imperialism."

Muñoz ended *The Baltimore Sun* article with a warning. "Since the publication of the report there has been a trend towards nationalism, a feeling easy to lull but hard to kill even by policies far more intelligent than that which the United States seems able to adopt." Island political leaders were now denouncing the report for exposing an evil Washington "conspiracy" against the island. Muñoz did not believe that it represented official Washington thinking and intentions. "The United States does not wish to have a small Ireland on their hands by establishing a permanent satrapy in Puerto Rico."

It was an ominous and, it turned out, accurate forewarning.

6 The Nationalist Challenge

Muñoz's threat of a "small Ireland" was underscored by the emergence of a new voice in Puerto Rican politics, a young Harvard graduate who had become a fervent admirer of the Sinn Fein Irish nationalist movement: Pedro Albizu Campos. While Muñoz and Puerto Rico debated the Brookings Report, Albizu and his Peruvian wife, Radcliffe educated Laura Meneses, arrived in Puerto Rico after two years in Latin America advocating independence for the island, and quickly took over the Nationalist Party of Puerto Rico. They turned it into a force of radical nationalism and uncompromising anti-Americanism.

Born in Ponce in 1891, Albizu was the son of Alejandro Albizu Romero, a U.S. customs official from a well-to-do family of Spanish immigrants. Albizu was not raised by his father. In fact, his father hadn't officially acknowledged him until he was a 23-year-old student at Harvard. His mother, Juanita Campos, a domestic worker and the daughter of a slave, died when Albizu was a child. A promising student, Albizu graduated from Ponce High School, a public school predominantly for the city's white elite. With the encouragement and help of its American principal, Charles H. Terry, Albizu received a scholarship in 1912 to study at the University of Vermont.

In 1918, the attractive young man volunteered for the U.S. Army following America's entry into the First World War. Of the 236,000 Puerto Ricans that volunteered to serve, only 4,000 were accepted, almost all of them serving in Panama. Albizu, however, was assigned to a black American regiment.

He attended an officer's training school. After the war, the first lieutenant returned to Harvard, where he earned a law degree in 1923.

In Puerto Rico, Albizu was one of the new generation Unionists that demanded stronger, more aggressive militancy for independence. Like Muñoz, Albizu abhorred the posturing and rhetoric of traditional island politicians. The Unionist leadership ignored his proposal for a constitutional convention that would unilaterally declare the island a Republic. He was further dejected in 1924 when he was not selected as one of the Unionist candidates for the Legislature. Albizu broke from the party and joined the group of dissidents that back in 1922 had formed the Nationalist Party. But he was again disappointed to discover that far from a radical *independentista* movement the party was little more than an elitist "semi-private cultural club." Its leaders were intellectuals and writers who dedicated themselves to giving passionate speeches to other intellectuals and artists at the *Ateneo Puertorriqueño*. In its short history, its five presidents were all lawyers, white, and Catholic.[1] The founder, José Coll y Cuchí, educated in Spain, elected several times to the island Legislature, was a noted journalist and university professor. Although he had led the pro-independence rebellion in the Unionist Party, he displayed respect and admiration for the Americans. During President Hoover's visit to the island in 1931, he urged Puerto Ricans to give him a warm welcome. Albizu made no secret of his contempt for Coll y Cuchí's "attitude of fraternal solidarity with the enemy." It was obvious that these intellectuals displayed little interest in mobilizing the Puerto Rican masses. In the 1924 elections, the Nationalist Party got 399 out of the total 253,520 votes.

Albizu, however, was quickly made party vice president. He convinced the leaders to finance a trip to Latin America to raise awareness of the relationship between Puerto Rico and the United States. In mid-1927 Albizu and his wife began a two-year "pilgrimage" that took them to seven Latin American nations. They were well-received by governments, academics, students, and cultural groups. Puerto Rico was a mystery that baffled Latin American politicians and intellectuals. Albizu and Meneses answered their question as to why the island had not achieved its independence: ruthless American repression.

---

1. Ferrao, *Pedro Albizu Campos y el nacionalismo puertorriqueño*, 40.

Albizu was pleased with his success but deeply resented the lack of support and interest on the part of his party's leaders, and, at times, their failure to respond to his urgent request for money. When Albizu and his wife returned, they expected a triumphant reception, but not a single member of the Nationalist governing board was at the pier in San Juan to welcome them, only two minor party workers.

Albizu set out to take over the party by provoking confrontations with the leadership. He flatly refused to submit to the party president, Antonio Ayuso Valdivieso, the powerful publisher of the daily newspaper *El Imparcial*, any accounting or written report on his trip. Within weeks, he saw that his style, cutting directly to the jugular of American "colonialism," attracted militants to the party. On May 12, 1930, the party held its annual convention, packed with his fervent followers impatiently awaiting the formality of making him party president.

Albizu spoke for over two hours, bitterly criticizing the "old guard." Hurt by his harsh language and the reaction of his inflamed followers, party founder Coll y Cuchí walked out, declaring that he was resigning: "I cannot belong to a party that adopts the politics of hate and insult."[2] The following day, in a long statement published in *El Mundo*, Coll y Cuchí predicted that Albizu's intolerance and fanaticism was going to alienate the Puerto Rican people from the independence ideal.

Moments after his election as party president, Albizu declared: "I never believed in numbers, independence will be achieved instead by the intensity of those that devote themselves totally to the nationalist ideal." The "old guard" long gone, he commanded all those present to stand, raise their arms, and take an "Oath of Honor." "We hereby solemnly swear that we will defend the Nationalist ideal and that we will sacrifice our belongings and our lives if necessary for the independence of our fatherland."[3]

What occurred that day, according to Albizu biographer Luis Ángel Ferrao "was not merely a change in the party's leadership," but the beginning "of a totally different dynamic in the struggle" for independence.[4] It ended the era of "the gentlemanly...well-mannered" style of the traditional

---

2. Ibid., 46.

3. Bothwell González, *Puerto Rico: cien años de lucha política*, Vol.II, 395.

4. Ferrao, *Pedro Albizu Campos y el nacionalismo puertorriqueño*, 46.

independentistas. From the days of Muñoz Rivera, independence was a romantic ideal: a personal, intimate belief that was separated from the conduct of one's daily life and career. José de Diego, the island's most prominent *independentista* until his death in 1918, was a corporate lawyer for American sugar companies. From an intellectual, poetic, and partisan standpoint, Albizu was determined to transform the struggle for independence into a Sinn Fein-type war of "sacrifice" and, when necessary, death. But to conduct a war, one must have an "enemy." For Albizu, any contact with the American "colonial master" contaminated Puerto Ricans. Americans were evil and the battle to expel them from Puerto Rico a jihad, a Holy War that went beyond politics, economics or even ideology. To liberate Puerto Rico, to sacrifice one's life for the *patria* was a process of mystical "purification"—a word he used frequently.

Among those who went to embrace Albizu at the Nationalist assembly were several of the most promising young Unionist leaders, including Ernesto Ramos Antonini, Samuel Quiñones, and Vicente Géigel Polanco.[5] Several days later, on May 18, 1930, these and twelve other new generation Unionists issued a "Manifesto in Favor of Independence." Using much of the language of Albizu, the manifesto strongly attacked "the thirty-two years...of absolute *yanqui* imperialism." The new leaders, however, as moved as they had been by the mesmerizing effect of Albizu's acceptance speech, were not ready to give up on their traditional party. Instead they organized themselves into a formal youth movement with the sole mission of driving the party to fight in earnest for independence.

In the labyrinth of island politics, Albizu also received vital assistance from the conservative, pro-American Republican Party. The Republicans were anxious to have Albizu and the Nationalist Party on the 1932 ballot and thus split the Unionist vote. The Republican Coalition, in control of the Legislature, attempted to amend the electoral law to legalize the Nationalists without having to register as a new party, a cumbersome process that required thousands of signed and certified petitions. The Unionists were able to block the amendment. The Republicans then proceeded to lend their own party machine to gather the Nationalist petitions. Governor James Beverley, who had been appointed by President Harding in January, 1932,

---

5. Bothwell González, *Puerto Rico: cien años de lucha política,* Vol.II, 363.

reported to Washington that the Republicans provided 30,000 inscriptions to place Albizu and his party on the ballot.[6]

ELECTRIFYING EFFECT

Albizu's radicalism had an electrifying effect on island politics. He was treated with deference by the island's newspapers. He made news by attacking not only the Americans but many of the icons of Puerto Rican culture, such as Epifanio Fernández Vanga, Jose S. Alegría, himself a former president of the Nationalist Party, and even the venerated poet, Luis Lloréns Torres for having written a poem that praised Governor Theodore Roosevelt.

In spite of its conservative owners and editorial policy, *El Mundo*, the island's leading daily newspaper, gave Albizu and his activities prominence and invariably published his statements and press releases. Two of the paper's top reporters, Manuel Rivera Matos and Fernando Sierra Berdecía, became Albizu followers, active in the Nationalist 1932 campaign. Albizu, meanwhile, did not pander to the press. In one of his radio speeches in 1931, angered that the newspaper had "sided with the government" in a University of Puerto Rico student conflict, Albizu attacked the paper as the paid puppet of the colonial government.

His prominence in island politics became evident when the paper's owners, Ángel Ramos and Antonio Coll Vidal, responded with a long and emotional defense of their paper and themselves, extensively reminding the public of their favorable treatment of Albizu and his party. Albizu's outburst, however, paid a price: the reporter Rivera Matos—who along with Sierra Berdecía later played important roles in the Muñoz government—felt obligated to resign from his job.

On April 16, 1932, in a speech in San Juan, Albizu was interrupted and informed that the Legislature had approved a bill making "the Puerto Rican flag" official. Originally designed by Puerto Rican exiles in New York in December 17, 1895, the flag, three red strips with a star within a blue triangle, was identical to the Cuban except that the colors are inverted. The

---

6. Mathews, *Puerto Rican Politics and the New Deal*, 35.

Republican action was now seen as yet another political ploy meant to confuse the pro-independence voters. For Albizu it was more: having the flag represent the "shameful colony" was a desecration. He called on his people to follow him to the Capitol building. About 800 Nationalists, armed with planks of wood yanked from a miniature golf course along the way, entered the Capitol. Climbing the stairs to the legislative chambers, they were stopped by a small contingent of police. There was pushing, a scuffle, the rail of the stairs collapsed, and one young man, Rafael Suárez Díaz, plunged to his death.

Senate leader Santiago Iglesias, heckled and booed by Albizu's followers at Nationalist rallies, believed that he was the target of the mob. He blamed the police for being too lenient with these fanatical youths, all of whom, he said, were from the middle and upper classes. If they were from the working class, the Socialist Party leader said bitterly, "all their heads would have been cracked." Unionist party leader Antonio Barceló also attacked the police, but for being excessively aggressive. The Nationalists, he said, had been provoked by the cynical action of the pro-statehood legislators who had always "despised" the Puerto Rican flag. "It is only a sentiment of protest," Barceló declared, "aroused, if you will, but only protest and nothing more than protest."[7]

But it soon became more than protest. In the summer of 1932, Nationalist leader Luis F. Velásquez penetrated the office of the Chief Justice of the Supreme Court, Emilio del Toro Cuevas, struck him on the face, challenging him to a duel. The Nationalists were angered that the judge, who had been president of the *Ateneo Puertorriqueño*, agreed to serve as the chairman of a local committee to commemorate the bicentennial of George Washington's birthday. Again, Albizu turned the incident to his favor as he served as Velásquez's defense attorney in a highly publicized trial.

Albizu decided to humiliate his old party. He and his followers stormed into the Unionist Party convention with a great clamor and up to the stage forcing party president Antonio Barceló to interrupt his speech. Barceló's reaction was to appease the Nationalist leader. He effusively greeted Albizu and turned the meeting over to him. Albizu took full advantage and went on

---

7. Pagán, *Historia de los partidos políticos puertorriqueños*, Vol. II, 32.

to "harangue the gathering for over two hours on independence." When he finished, Barceló embraced him.

RHOADS' MODEST PROPOSAL

A bizarre event in early 1932 gained the Albizu campaign even greater notoriety. Luis Baldoni, a young Nationalist that worked in the Presbyterian Hospital in San Juan, delivered an astounding document to Albizu. An American doctor, Cornelius Rhoads, in Puerto Rico on a project of the Rockefeller Institute, wrote a letter expressing his disgust for Puerto Ricans and his hope for their extinction. Rhoads boasted that he was doing his part: "I have done my best to further the process of extermination by killing off eight and transplanting cancer into several more." [8]

A political earthquake erupted when the newspapers received copies of the letter from the Nationalists. The island's medical profession expressed shock at this atrocity. Even staid Governor Beverley, a seasoned observer of island political fireworks having served as the island's attorney general since 1928, moved to prosecute the doctor. Expressing that he was disgusted and sickened by the letter, he accused Rhoads not only of a vicious "libel on the Puerto Rican people" but of a "confession of murder." The story was picked up in major mainland newspapers and national magazines.

Rhoads had ended his assignment and returned to the mainland. He cabled the Governor that it was all meant to be a joke, that the letter was a "fantastic and playful composition...entirely for my own diversion" to make fun of Americans who do hate Puerto Ricans. Beverley's investigation found no evidence that Rhoads had in fact attempted to harm anyone.

But for Albizu and the Nationalists it could not have been a more auspicious beginning the 1932 campaign. He was running for Senator-at-large. If his denunciations that the Americans were a pestilence that threatened the very existence of Puerto Rico seemed to some excessive, even outlandish, in the eyes of his followers, the Rhoads letter was the proof.

---

8. Mathews, *Puerto Rican Politics and the New Deal*, 34.

Muñoz admired Albizu Campos, seeing in him more "patriotism than partisanship."[9] He first heard him speak at a political rally in Ponce back in 1926. Albizu recognized him and invited him to come up to the platform to address the crowd. Muñoz declined. Their styles were different but Muñoz felt that they had much in common. Albizu had repudiated the Nationalist Party veterans just as Muñoz had disowned the old guard of his father's party. They both rejected the florid style of political rhetoric. It was evident that Albizu had become a major political attraction in the 1932 campaign, his powerful, slashing speeches drawing ever larger crowds. In what Muñoz saw as the hypocrisy that permeated Puerto Rico's political culture, Albizu's cutting-edge authenticity was refreshing.

But there was something that concerned Muñoz. One evening, dining at the Palace Hotel in San Juan, Muñoz saw Albizu sitting alone at another table and invited him to join him. Since the Ponce rally, they had met several times, but now, for the first time, they had a long and intense discussion. They agreed on just about everything. But as Albizu talked, Muñoz sensed a divergence. Albizu's emotions, Muñoz wrote years later, were directed at "getting rid of the Americans...For me, it was getting rid of hunger."[10] Then Albizu made a statement that impressed Muñoz. The American governor, Albizu said, is really not important: he is "merely a puppet of the *Central Guánica*"—the biggest sugar corporation on the island. "Whom we have to kill is not the Governor, but the administrator of Guánica." Muñoz was momentarily taken aback by the casual remark. Certainly Albizu was engaging in hyperbole for dramatic effect. As passionate, as fanatical as his campaign was, certainly Albizu was not literally talking about "killing" anyone. Muñoz decided to ignore the statement. But he was to recall that conservation for the rest of his life as a forewarning of what was to take place in Puerto Rico and in his own life.

Muñoz believed he could bring Albizu around as he had many of the impatient young Unionist *independentistas*. Following that encounter, they

---

9. Muñoz Marín, *Memorias*, Vol. I, 63.
10. Ibid., 63.

met regularly, as often as two or three times a week, at the Palace Hotel. Muñoz argued that even with all its defects, the Unionist Party was the only realistic hope to take Puerto Rico to independence. It was evident that there was no possibility of the Nationalists winning the 1932 elections. And obviously it was essential to defeat the pro-statehood Republican-Socialist Coalition. As in the United States, Muñoz insisted, these were going to be watershed elections that would decide the future of the island. There was absolutely no possibility, however, of influencing Albizu's thinking. Albizu expected to get elected to the Senate, believing that he had great popular support. In Muñoz, in spite of his misgivings, Albizu had one vote. Questioned by a reporter, Muñoz revealed that although he was backing the Liberal Party, he would also cast his vote for the Nationalist leader.

It was evident to Muñoz that whatever hope there was of converting the Liberal Party into a true instrument for independence rested on its ability to hold on to its young, talented, motivated new generation of leaders that was so impressed by Albizu's intensity. In addition to the young lawyers Ernesto Ramos Antonini and Samuel Quiñones, there was the charismatic women's leader Felisa Rincón, as well as the brilliant University of Puerto Rico professor back from Georgetown University and the University of Chicago, Jaime Benítez. Talented and articulate young professionals such as university professor Antonio Colorado and writer José Buitrago had already joined Albizu and were actively campaigning for him.

Although Muñoz described himself as a "radical nationalist," and Albizu had his vote, they had in fact become competitors. Puerto Rican politics was entering a generational sea-change. Which of the two would step in and take command of the new generation of leaders, all these bright professionals, and thus take command of the battle for independence?

Muñoz Decides

On March 12, 1932, Muñoz answered the question. He attended a party meeting convened to officially change its name from Unionist to Liberal. In another ploy to confuse Unionist voters, the Republicans, through legal maneuvers, had the island courts rule that Unionists could no longer use their old name. Muñoz was outraged by this absurd "dirty trick." It was his father that had given the party its name. As in the days when his father struggled with the difficult issue over American citizenship, the party was again in danger of dividing into two ideological camps: the autonomists that sought a relationship with the U.S. somewhere between statehood and independence, and the *independentistas*.

Muñoz brought to the meeting his own draft of the party's program and an incentive to approve it. If both factions agreed to go to the elections militantly in favor of "independence now," Muñoz would finally jump off the fence and campaign in favor of the party and its program. Before the meeting, party leader Antonio Barceló agreed to support it. To Muñoz's great surprise and relief, the ideological clash between the two camps that seemed inevitable did not take place. His radical pro-independence program was overwhelmingly approved. There was no debate, no opposition.

This was a surprising victory for Muñoz. He had achieved his goal: the clear-cut status plank would make the elections a referendum on independence. And, of course, the party could now snatch the independence battle flag from Albizu Campos and the Nationalist Party.

But Muñoz was still not certain that he wanted to get into another political campaign. He asked himself if he had in fact achieved his goal. Never in his life had partisan politics interested him. He was driven by independence as the tool to bring about profound social and economic reform. He included in his draft program a list of the economic reform measures that he considered essential. But the delegates had no interest in the economic content of the program. It was not clear they were even interested in the status content. Their only concern was party unity. It was enough for them to witness Muñoz enter the theater alongside the leader of the autonomist wing, Guillermo Esteves—a clear sign that they were in agreement—for the convention delegates to break out in a roar of approval.

Meanwhile, the Liberals themselves wondered if Muñoz, for the first time, was serious. They had seen him test the waters of island politics before, only to go running off to New York at the first sign of battle. At the party convention, the test came quickly. Mistakenly believing that he wanted to go to Washington as resident commissioner, unidentified Liberals began a smear campaign that he was still "taking morphine." Everyone tensely awaited Muñoz's reaction. He deliberately heightened the anticipation by remaining silent. Finally, he took the floor to declare that he did not want and would reject the nomination for resident commissioner. Then he raised his powerful voice:

> Throughout the island someone has carried out a campaign of defamation against me... I don't know, gentlemen, who that person or those persons are... But I do know that the delegates that are meeting here know who those persons are ... It is on you that the poison has been spilled. Therefore, I accuse now, at this solemn moment, the person, or persons, of being ruffians, cowards, dogs: I accuse them because I do not know them, but I know that you know them...It is possible, even probable, that the defamers are here in this assembly. You look at him, or them, because I do not know them! I am going to stop now so that, if they dare, the ruffians will show their faces....[11]

There was silence. Several delegates looked around to see if anyone moved. More silence. No one moved.

Muñoz continued. If the purpose of the defamation was to have him running off again, this time it would not succeed. "I cannot disappear from Puerto Rico. It's necessary for me to stay here and it is here that I am going to live in a glass showcase so that everyone will see me."

The Liberal Party delegates were impressed. Aroused, the son of Muñoz Rivera had roared like his father. Even more, the poet, *El Vate,* had revealed his killer instinct. And it seemed that Muñoz would stay this time. At thirty-four, Muñoz had finally decided what to do with his life.

---

11. Ibid., 88.

PART II

The Deranged Saraband
1932-1940

"It was during. . . that process of familiarizing myself with the New Deal and its people, with the profound changes taking place in the United States, that there emerged before my eyes a new panorama for Puerto Rico."

Muñoz Marín

1933

"And so ends the most glorious, the most fair minded, the most generous, and the most dastardly four years of the American regime in Puerto Rico."

Muñoz Marín

1936

7 The Minority Senator

"What are those things that look like little cages?" asked one of the hundred thousand people gathered at the United States Capitol on March 4, 1933 to witness the swearing in of a new president. "Machine guns," someone answered.[1]

Fear gripped the country: fear that unless Franklin Delano Roosevelt, the thirty-second President of the United States, "did something...the farmers will rise up. So will labor. The Reds will run the country—or maybe the Fascists."

Fear also gripped Puerto Rico as one calamity seemed to follow the other. On September 26, 1932, six weeks before the elections, the island was ripped by another hurricane, *San Ciprián*, its 120 mile-an-hour winds killing 225 people, injuring 3,000, and leaving over 100,000 homeless. The island economy, still not recovered from the devastation of *San Felipe*'s 160 mile-an-hour winds back in 1928, suffered another $30 million in property damage. Island agriculture, especially the coffee industry, was again decimated.

Muñoz had not anticipated that fear would play such a big role in the elections. His campaign to make independence the principal issue for the Liberal Party backfired. For the first time in 28 years, the Unionist-Liberals were out of power. Muñoz himself was elected to the Senate, but the voters turned the Legislature over to the conservative and pro-statehood Republican-Socialist Coalition.

---

1. Schlesinger, *The Crisis of the Old Order*, 1.

Once again, as he had been in the 1920 Socialist Party campaign, Muñoz was shaken. Then he crashed against the impossibility of carrying out a Marxist revolution in Puerto Rico. Now he crashed against what he saw as an irrational, demeaning "fear of independence." Since returning to the island, he had ridiculed the belief that "freedom" would bring political instability, violence, and dictatorship. The surest way to bring violence to Puerto Rico, he argued in a 1931 newspaper interview, was to make the island a state.[2] Look at the violence on the U.S. mainland against the striking steel workers in Pennsylvania, against the coal miners in West Virginia, against the textile workers in Massachusetts and New Jersey. And as to violations of civil rights, Muñoz insisted, look at the state of California, throwing labor organizers into jail for six or ten years: look at the execution of Sacco and Vanzetti by the state of Massachusetts. Talk about "dictatorships," look at Huey Long in Louisiana. The states, Muñoz went on, were in fact "colonies of the Great Imperial Council called the Supreme Court," itself controlled by the great economic interests. "And at this very moment," he said, "in very few states of the North American union—if indeed in one—are there no constitutional violations in one way or another of the people's wishes."

Sounding much like Nationalist Party leader Albizu Campos, Muñoz appealed to patriotic emotions: "freedom is not sold...freedom among men is not debated." American economic assistance, "which we have the little integrity to accept, converts the American flag into a blanket that covers the warts of a beggar, under which a grateful slave rots away and dies of misery and hunger." No need to fear freedom, Muñoz declared confidently: it will work out for "those who have confidence in themselves and claim the widest horizons to create their own destiny."[3]

The November elections in the U.S. offered little comfort to Muñoz. He had no illusions that the patrician Governor of New York would change anything fundamental on the mainland, much less on the island. But on March 4, 1933, as millions of Americans listened on the radio, Muñoz was moved by Roosevelt's words: "Let me assert my firm belief that the only thing we have to fear is fear itself—nameless, unreasoning, unjustified terror which paralyzes needed effort to convert retreat into the advance."

---

2. El Mundo, "Hablando con Luis Muñoz Marín".

3. Ibid.

Yes, Muñoz thought, this described the real crisis in Puerto Rico: the only thing Puerto Ricans had to fear was "nameless, unreasoning, unjustified, terror" of its own freedom. He heard Roosevelt ask Congress for the equivalent of war powers: "broad Executive power to wage a war against [any] emergency, as great as the power that would be given to me if we were in fact invaded by a foreign foe." Was it true, Muñoz asked himself, as Roosevelt solemnly now declared, that "the money changers have fled from their high seats in the temple of civilization?" Was it possible that he was wrong about the new president? Would he make a difference?

RUBY BLACK

Muñoz had an eyewitness to the drama taking place in Washington that would answer this question. Before returning to the island in 1931, his wife Muna introduced him to a diminutive Southerner also active in liberal politics and women's rights, newspaper reporter Ruby Black. A correspondent for several out-of-town newspapers, she was described by her colleagues as "the first lady of the Washington press corps" because of her professional reputation, but also because she was a personal friend of Eleanor Roosevelt.

Black was more than an observant reporter: she provided access to the new President and his administration. Muñoz named her Washington correspondent for *La Democracia*. Soon she reported on a major development: it was virtually certain that Roosevelt would make history by naming, for the first time, a native Puerto Rican as Governor of the island. Martín Travieso, a respected former judge and corporate lawyer with good political and administrative experience, well-known by several members of Congress, and former interim Governor.

But to the surprise of the White House, this seemingly unassailable appointment was opposed by the newly-elected Resident Commissioner in Congress, Santiago Iglesias. The Coalition insisted that if a Puerto Rican were appointed, he should belong to the party that won the elections. Travieso identified with the minority Liberal Party. The objections from American residents on the island were even stronger. They argued that the island was not prepared for a Puerto Rican Governor, even one as conservative and "Pro-American" as Travieso. Puerto Ricans still needed an American that remained above the ravages of island partisan politics. Outgoing Governor James Beverley, who was credited with supervising the relatively honest and peaceful elections of 1932, agreed that this would be impossible for any Puerto Rican. In fact, Roosevelt had already made his decision, and it was not a Puerto Rican.

ROBERT HAYS GORE

Black was embarrassed and the Puerto Ricans dumbfounded. After an exceptionally long consultation process by the War Department's Bureau of Insular Affairs, and the White House itself, the President selected the candidate proposed by the head of the Democratic Party, Postmaster General James Farley, an insurance businessman and publisher of small newspapers in South Florida. Robert Hayes Gore expected a better reward for his political contributions, but he accepted the appointment. Two days later, on May 1, 1933, Black interviewed him. She reported to Muñoz that he was certainly lively, enthusiastic, and friendly; it was easy to see how this good salesman had become rich in the insurance business. "He chews gum," she wrote. "He is short, baldish, plump with a dimple." But don't be misled, she warned Muñoz, "The boys who know him tell me to warn you to nail down the furniture."[4]

Gore knew nothing about Puerto Rico, but before he arrived on the island he decided to go to Chicago to give a speech on its future. Comparing the island to southern Florida, he predicted a similar economic development. He went on to express optimistically that the island would enter the American union as a state. He assumed that this was what the islanders and his own Democratic Party wanted. Statehood for Puerto Rico, after all, was part of the party's platform.

Gore quickly discovered that he had made a mistake. The War Department sent him an angry telegram: "Puerto Rico is not believed even appro-

---

4. Mathews, Puerto Rican Politics and the New Deal, 56.

ximately prepared for statehood." Furthermore, offering statehood was a policy matter for the War Department, the President, and Congress. The whole point of naming an American, not a Puerto Rican, was precisely to avoid this kind of political pitfall. After arriving on the island, Gore acknowledged his error in a letter to the President, assuring him that he now understood that "it will take a long time before Puerto Rico can qualify" for statehood.

The Liberal Party, still stung by the November defeat, decided to ignore Gore's faux pas. Muñoz accompanied party leader Antonio Barceló to La Fortaleza. He had the party newspaper, *La Democracia*, welcome the new Governor, praising his inaugural message as a commitment to bringing Roosevelt's progressive policies to the island. Gore replied expressing his appreciation. His note was also published in the party newspaper.

Gore soon made another discovery. For island leaders, especially *independentistas* like Muñoz and Albizu, the Governor represented the power of American "colonial imperialism." But before long, Gore asked himself: what power? The fact was that the U.S.-Puerto Rico relationship had become a tangled maze of confused and contradictory lines of authority. One New Deal historian described it in 1990 as a "deranged saraband of responsibility."[5] To begin with, to whom did Gore respond? Politically, as Gore understood it, to Democratic Party Chairman James Farley. Officially, of course, to the President that nominated him and the Congress that confirmed him. Administratively he was under the War Department's Bureau of Insular Affairs. Another major abnormality was that he did not appoint key members of his own to the island's administration. The President nominated and Congress confirmed the island's attorney general, the auditor, the commissioner of education, and the members of the insular Supreme Court. How exactly, was he supposed to "govern" this island?

The judicial foundation of the very relationship between Puerto Rico to the U.S., the source of the obsession of island leaders, was shrouded in a thick haze of legal fog. Under the "territorial clause" of the Constitution, Congress had absolute authority over Puerto Rico as well as all other American possessions. But the U.S. Supreme Court had ruled in the 1901 "insular cases" that Puerto Rico was not an "incorporated" but an "unincor-

---

5. Watkins, *Righteous Pilgrim*, 527.

porated territory," a new status created to fit Puerto Rico's unique conditions. The Court declared that Puerto Rico "belonged to" but was not a part of the United States. What did this mean? Chief Justice Melville Fuller, in a dissenting opinion, decried that "Congress has the power to keep it, like a disembodied shade, in an intermediate state of ambiguous existence, for an indefinite period." Three decades later, Gore found that this had not changed.

The island leaders that vociferously decried "colonialism," Gore found, acted as anything but "colonial subjects". They were acutely aware that as American citizens, they were protected by the fundamental civil and political rights guaranteed by the American Constitution. To safeguard those rights, there was a U.S. federal court on the island. In defense of their rights, Puerto Ricans could go all the way up to the U.S. Supreme Court. And, like any other American citizens, they were free to circumvent the Governor taking their case directly to the White House and Congress. And Gore was surprised to see how often they did, and often members of Congress, and the President himself, became directly involved in island conflicts.

The "Expatriates"

Gore had another factor to deal with. There was on the island a small group of "expatriate" Americans, some of them in local committees of the national Republican and Democratic parties. Although island residents did not vote in presidential elections, and were represented in Congress by a non-voting Resident Commissioner, the national party committees sent voting delegations to the national conventions the same as the states. Gore's Democratic Party activism being the sole reason for his appointment, he felt that he could at least expect support and understanding from the local Democratic Party committee that had backed Roosevelt at the national convention. The insular Democrats, in turn, after two decades of Republican administrations, expected to be influential with this Governor as well as to have a say in federal patronage on the island.

Two recent arrivals to the island were of particular importance. James and Dorothy Bourne had been neighbors of the President and close friends of Eleanor at Hyde Park. Dorothy came to Puerto Rico to train social workers through the University of Puerto Rico. Communicating directly with Roosevelt and Eleanor, they were among the few that had recommended that a Puerto Rican be named governor. Both were fervent New Dealers and saw their mission as helping to bring the new liberal programs and attitudes to the island. Both shared the surprise and disappointment of some Puerto Ricans when their friend in the White House named Gore as Governor.

"MY PRESIDENT"

Still another factor confronting Gore was the entry of Muñoz into partisan politics. As editor and columnist of *La Democracia*, writing in both Spanish and English, and now as minority Senator, Muñoz introduced a new style into the island's political discourse: a style honed with the hard edge and the biting sarcasm of the American "muckrakers" and social critics of the 1920s that he so much admired and had emulated.

Muñoz called himself a "nationalist" and considered himself as determined an *independentista* as Albizu Campos. But he was not anti-American. The real "enemy," as he had told Albizu, was "hunger," and the cause was "capitalism." If Ruby Black's enthusiastic reports were accurate, there were profound changes taking place in Washington that required serious rethinking. He wondered if he could appeal to a new liberal conscience in Washington. Was Roosevelt sincere in his stirring inaugural message, and could Muñoz convince him and the American people that they had a moral obligation to work out a formula to give Puerto Rico its "freedom" without the people having to pay an impossibly inhuman price of even worse economic misery?

But how to work around the enigma of the 1932 elections? The Puerto Rican people had turned to the right electing the Republican-Socialist Coalition, while the United States had turned to the left. The enigma was compounded by Roosevelt's still baffling decision to appoint a Governor who was clearly incapable of bringing deep reforms to the island. Gore, in fact, had already begun to gravitate towards the most vocally "pro-American" leaders. But they were also the most conservative, many of whom had supported the Republican Party and were now dead-set against the New Deal.

For Muñoz, the enigma struck home. As had his father before him, he had dedicated his life to the goal of "Puerto Ricans governing Puerto Rico." But now, to bring the New Deal reforms to the island, he would have to circumvent not only Governor Gore, but the Coalition-controlled Legislature. To the degree that he succeeded in connecting with the new President and his liberal administrators, he would, in effect, be annulling the people's verdict in the 1932 elections. Wasn't this an absolute negation, contradiction, of his crusade for self-government? How could a fervent *independentista* justify going up to Washington to undermine the authority of the men and women democratically elected by the people of Puerto Rico?

Muñoz had an answer. He argued that the Liberal Party, because it got more votes than either one of the two Coalition parties, had "a moral victory" and thus a mandate to represent the island in Washington. Privately, the dejected old warrior, Antonio Barceló, commented that he much preferred real victories: "What you are saying has to be said, but the truth is that I'll be damned by moral victories!"[6] But Muñoz rationalized that it was common sense that the vast majority of the people, the half-starved *jíbaros*, would want him to do everything in his power to bring the programs that would lift them from extreme poverty. This was the deeper meaning of having obtained a moral victory.

Muñoz experienced the frivolity of island politics during his first Senate session in 1933. The Senators locked horns in an endless debate over a congratulatory message to be sent to President Roosevelt. The pro-statehood Coalition demanded that it be addressed to "our President." This offended the Liberals, who argued passionately that since the island was an American "colony," Roosevelt was not "ours." Muñoz participated, but he felt that this was just another example of how legislators wasted their time.

Decades later, however, Muñoz saw prophetic symbolism in the debate. Events were to reverse the traditional alignments of Puerto Rican status politics. "A few months later," Muñoz wrote, "it became evident that the President was really ours, apart from legal reasons, ours, of the Puerto Ricans that aspired to a great reform in our country."[7]

---

6. Muñoz Marín, *Memorias* Vol. I, 92.

7. Muñoz Marín, *Unedited Draft Memorias*, 94.

8 Eleanor Roosevelt's Good Ear

On October 23, 1933, Governor Gore wrote an anguished letter to President Roosevelt: "Mr. President, I have been here four months under the most distressing circumstances. I have been exposed to the most damnable political intrigue ever devised..."[1]

Island historians baptized his six-month stay in Puerto Rico as "Gore's Hell." Just three weeks after his arrival on July 23, 1933, Gore set off another political time bomb. Convinced by the Coalition that the Liberals were deliberately instilling "anti-American" separatist sentiments among public school children, he accused teachers of disloyalty. The island specialists in the War Department were again dismayed by Gore's bumbling. Why was he unnecessarily reviving this bitterly divisive issue? Back in 1921, the Bureau had instructed the beleaguered Governor Reily that "in the absence of any evidence to the contrary, Puerto Ricans must be presumed to be loyal citizens." Now Gore had fallen into the same trap: unless a Puerto Rican educator professed 100 percent Americanism, he or she was deemed to be treasonous.

Gore appeared to have become obsessed with removing Education Commissioner José Padín. Responding to his insistence, the War Department sent Wellesley College professor Dr. Leland Jenks down to the island in August to evaluate the educator's performance and report back on his "loyalty." Jenks wrote: "I must frankly say, that in my judgment a policy of furthering Americanization in Puerto Rico by political authority would be

---

1. Mathews, *Puerto Rican Politics and the New Deal*, 94.

almost the most unfortunate development which could take place for the two countries...it is hopeless folly now to talk of Americanizing the *jíbaro*."

As to Padín, it was evident that Gore had been duped by the Coalition *políticos*. "It is ridiculous," Jenks continued, "to refer to his policies as anti-American unless the New Deal, Teachers' College or John Dewey's educational philosophy are so termed...I do not believe that it is possible to make the islanders good Americans by education, except as they can be made good Puerto Ricans."[2]

Jenks's report was backed by the respected James Beverley, the former governor who had remained on the island. He wrote: "the charge of anti-Americanism against Dr. Padín would be laughable if it were not outrageous. It is a terrible charge to make—tantamount to treason. Dr. Padín is not pro-American: he is an American in the finest sense of the word."[3]

"YOU ARE A DAMN LIAR"

Muñoz was incensed. "Reily's nightmare" was being repeated. But it got worse. Misinterpreting instructions from the War Department, Gore made the off-hand remark that it was now the norm that all appointees to positions of trust would submit undated letters of resignation. Liberal Party president Barceló denounced this as a gratuitous degradation of all Puerto Ricans, and angrily withdrew the names of all Liberal candidates for public service. Gore was delighted to get the "disloyal Liberals" out of the way.

Muñoz, as editor of *La Democracia*, asked Ruby Black to query the White House. She cabled back quoting the President that it all sounded to him like a "fairy-tale." According to Gore the "fairy-tale" was the news story "fabricated" by the Liberals. For Muñoz, the President contradicted Gore. On September 6, 1933 Muñoz published an editorial in English under the title, "Governor Gore You Are a Damn Liar."

Reacting in part to Muñoz's tirade, a massive student protest broke out at the University of Puerto Rico, supposedly against Gore's appointment of

---

2. Ibid., 81.

3. Ibid., 96.

the Speaker of the House, Socialist Party leader Rafael Alonso Torres, to the University's board of directors. Gore saw the university crisis as part of the "anti-American" conspiracy engineer not only by the Nationalists, but by Muñoz and the Liberals. The Liberals were further outraged when they learned that Alonso intended to fire a number of University administrators identified with their party, including the communications director, Muñoz's wife, Muna Lee. "The University," Alonso disdainfully commented, "has no more need for a publicity director than I do for a poodle dog."[4]

Gore feared for his life. He reported to Washington that over two thousand students paralyzed the University and then marched to La Fortaleza carrying a casket, demanding his resignation. Several weeks later, a bomb went off at the Governor's summer home up in *Jájome*. Soon after, four sticks of dynamite were found within La Fortaleza. Led by Police Chief E. Francis Riggs, the dynamite was safely removed. Gore asked the War Department to send the FBI to investigate the "anti-American conspiracy" on the island, including the Education Department. The Department rejected the demand.

Muñoz and the Liberal Party stepped up their ruthless campaign. After the bombs and dynamite scares, *La Democracia* blasted him with still another diatribe: "Mr. Gore will disappear from Puerto Rico as a liar, for his ineptness, for his vindictiveness, for his fantasy, for being useless, for his incompetence, for his stupidity, for being uncivilized, for his unconscionable betrayal of the highest ideals of the American people that sent him here as their representative."[5]

James and Dorothy Bourne were alarmed. They wrote to the President and Eleanor: "There is tension quite noticeable among all classes of people from the lowest all the way through to the top that is most distressing. Anti-American feelings are growing rapidly among all classes." Informing the Governor that she was traveling to Washington to attend a Labor Department child health convention, Dorothy instead met with Secretary of War George Dern. Then, accompanied by Ruby Black, she went to the White House, met with Eleanor and stayed for dinner with the President. The island, she gravely warned, was drifting towards "anarchy." The Governor's bumbling was playing into the hands of Albizu Campos and the Nationalist Party.

---

4. Ibid., 93.

5. Bothwell, *Puerto Rico: cien años de lucha política* Vol. II, 426.

Muñoz also traveled to Washington determined to somehow convince the President to remove Gore. On November 7, 1933, through Ruby Black, he was invited to Eleanor's informal White House tea. It was a big day at the White House. Roosevelt had extended diplomatic recognition to the Soviet Union. Later in the afternoon, he was to receive the first Soviet ambassador, Maxim Litvinov. As Muñoz and Black were led up to a small room on the second floor, she whispered to him that Eleanor did not hear well from the left ear: "Remember, the right ear is the right ear." Almost half a century later, Muñoz wrote: "It was through that good ear that I talked for the first time to the most liberal part of the New Deal government."[6]

Eleanor was questioning a visiting journalist and his wife, who had recently returned from the Soviet Union, when she turned to Muñoz and Black and asked: "What *is* happening in Puerto Rico?" Muñoz was struck by the "beauty of her eyes—understanding, tender, serene" and made a conscious effort to respond with the same serenity. Governor Gore, he began, was not an evil man: he was personally honest, well-intentioned. But as Muñoz talked, his tone changed. Puerto Ricans, buried under terrible economic and social problems, now have to cope with "the block-headedness of a governor with a strange and complicated psychology, dealing stupidly" with these enormous problems.[7] Eleanor was listening intently when suddenly Roosevelt appeared. Lifting himself from the wheelchair with his strong arms, he sat between his wife and Muñoz. With his familiar, spirited voice "that seemed to emerge from his good humor," he asked the same question. Muñoz tried to match the good humor: "Mr. President, the weather has not changed..." Roosevelt got the message: "It's the psychological climate that seems to be overcast..." Roosevelt asked Muñoz to come back the next day to the White House to continue the discussion.

The following day, accompanied by War Secretary Dern, Roosevelt listened to Muñoz's detailed description of the Gore calamity. The real crisis, he repeated, was the waste of time and energy caused by Gore's blind, bumbling entanglements with Puerto Rico's vicious partisan politics. Muñoz repeated what he had written two weeks earlier in a much softer, conciliatory

---

6. Muñoz Marín, *Memorias* Vol. I, 99.
7. Ibid., 100.

article in *La Democracia*: "It is essential that the governor does not at any time depart in word or deed, publicly or privately, from the concept of his office as a non-partisan moderating power...it is essential, under the present status, that every last citizen of Puerto Rico consider the governor his high servant and not his petty enemy..."

The President asked about the University student protests. Having been informed that Muñoz had instigated the disruptions, he asked if he, Muñoz, approved of this conduct by "people too young to vote." Describing the meeting decades later, Muñoz commented: "Roosevelt, in his sea of liberalism, had small islands of conservatism, and one of them was his lack of confidence in young people." Muñoz dodged the question pointing out that the parents, all of voting age, were totally behind the students. Roosevelt laughed, and then became serious again: "These matters cannot be resolved from one day to the next, but they will be resolved soon. Do me the favor of telling your people in Puerto Rico to stop their attacks of Governor Gore because it makes it difficult for me to act while he is under fire."[8] Muñoz agreed, leaving the White House wondering if he had succeeded.

Keeping his side of the bargain, Muñoz sent a telegram to Barceló back in Puerto Rico to suspend all the attacks on Gore. Now it was a matter of waiting to see if Roosevelt would keep his word. Muñoz decided to remain in Washington until Roosevelt made his decision. The wait lasted two months.

The War Department, declining Gore's demand for an FBI investigation, decided to send another educator to report back on just what was happening with the island's educational system, the President of Dartmouth University, Dr. Ernest Hopkins. His conclusions were even more revealing than the earlier Dr. Leland Jenks' report and it sealed Gore's fate. "He is probably the worst blunderer that ever came along... He has the genius for doing things wrong and has a feeling of hostility or suspicion towards anybody not connected with the political group with which he is working."[9] Echoing Jenks's words, Hopkins expressed equal scorn for the Coalition *políticos* who had made a "political racket" out of Americanism: "...the irresponsible elements," he wrote to War Secretary Dern, "the ignorant and lawless

---

8. Muñoz Marín, *Memorias* Vol. I, 102.
9. Mathews, *Puerto Rican Politics and the New Deal*, 109.

factions, and the sordidly acquisitive groups are all too dominant in the Coalition Party for the United States Government to wish to subsidize it at all in influence and/or prestige... Washington ought not to allow itself to become too closely identified with them."[10]

On January 12, 1934, Gore's "resignation" was accepted. "Gore's Hell" had lasted six months. In Puerto Rico, it was a remarkable political triumph. The restless Bohemian, *El Vate*, a lone minority Senator, had gotten the President of the United States to remove a Governor. For Muñoz, this was a display of the President's trust in him. Believing that Roosevelt was indeed "his" President, Muñoz could now return to Puerto Rico.

In the wake of victory, Muñoz felt remorse. His anger became pity. From a colonial ogre, Gore now emerged in Muñoz's mind as a tragic victim. Not only was he ruthlessly criticized, but his dignity was assaulted. In Washington, Muñoz had observed Gore's humiliation. The press was aware that while Muñoz had access to the White House, Gore was unable to see the President to defend himself. When Roosevelt finally received him on December 27, it was to confront him with Dr. Hopkins's devastating report.

Gore left the island physically and emotionally broken. He had been terrified by the possibility of more bombs and threats that he and his entire family would be "poisoned" at La Fortaleza. Depressed, admitting his failure, he wrote to War Secretary Dern: "I have made the mistake there of being too outspoken in my conversations and too frank in my dealings. Someone who has lived there for twenty-five years might begin to assimilate the moods and mysteries of the people..." His appointment, Gore admitted, had been an error: "...the only governor who can be successful is one who knows them intimately and has had a long association with them."[11]

Muñoz, whose attacks had been brutal, sent Gore a personal letter declaring that in all the criticisms aimed at him, his integrity had never been in question. Muñoz agreed with Gore: the problem had been his total ignorance of the people and the country he had been unrealistically assigned to "govern."

Muñoz sent another letter to the President with a personal pledge: "I hope that mere politics can now be adjourned among Puerto Ricans, and I

---

10. Ibid., 109.
11. Ibid., 111.

shall certainly bend all my efforts to that end so that the economic implications of the New Deal shall have as full an opportunity for beneficial application to Puerto Rico as possible."

A NEW PANORAMA

During Muñoz's two-month wait in Washington another crucial change took place in his thinking and emotions. Were Ruby Black's glowing reports of a remarkable transition taking place in Washington true? As editor of *La Democracia*, Muñoz was a member of the Washington Press Club. He accompanied Black to a more lively "informal press club," the second floor of a brick house on 13th Street where White House correspondents and other reporters gathered daily to eat "good spaghetti and drink awful wine," still illegal as the states were in the process of repealing Prohibition. The contacts with the press became "an observatory" where Muñoz could anticipate developments within the White House and other agencies of great interest to him and Puerto Rico, such the administration's new policies on sugar tariffs and subsidies being worked out in the Agriculture Department.

Another key "observatory" was Black's home in Alexandria. She and her husband invited key government administrators, such as Donald Richberg, a close colleague of Interior Secretary Harold Ickes and assistant head of the National Recovery Administration, the director of the Agricultural Department's Sugar Bureau, A.J.S. Weaver. Muñoz met Harry Hopkins, the Federal Emergency Relief administrator and later Roosevelt's alter ego. He was also introduced to one of Roosevelt's original "brain trusters," the brilliant and controversial economics professor, Rexford Tugwell. Major labor leaders, including John L. Lewis, whom Muñoz had first met at the American Federation of Labor convention in Portland, would walk into Black's weekly open house. One of the journalists Muñoz befriended was Felix Belair of *The New York Times*. The following year, Belair tipped Muñoz on a developing story that was to have a big impact on Puerto Rico and on Muñoz's career.

It was another irony of island politics. While the Coalition leaders saw themselves as the "loyal Americans," they were in fact the outsiders in

Washington. Muñoz, the *independentista*, was the insider. Politics was a factor. Muñoz felt ideologically at home with the liberals that he met at the press clubs and at Black's home. But more important was the cultural affinity. Muñoz spoke and acted as "an American." His sense of humor was "American." The Coalition leaders felt and were treated as "foreigners;" they were seen as "Spanish," stiff, formal people who could hardly make themselves understood in English.

This political and cultural affinity proved crucial in Muñoz's life. A half century later, he wrote: "It was during those conversations in that process of familiarizing myself with the New Deal and its people, with the profound changes taking place in the United States, that there emerged before my eyes a new panorama for Puerto Rico."[12]

The new panorama made Muñoz question the foundation of all island politics and of his own thinking: that Puerto Rico was a victim of "colonialism." What, after all, he asked himself, are colonies for, if not to squeeze the subjected people for the benefit of the imperial power? Had he not spent his adult life describing and denouncing the absentee-owned American sugar corporations' exploitation of Puerto Rican workers? But what would have been an unthinkable possibility began to take shape in his mind. Days after Roosevelt had taken the oath of office, on March 10, 1933, Muñoz had written: "Independence is economically necessary. It's not just that it is possible. It's not just that it is convenient or desirable. It is necessary. Without independence we will march towards our ruin, a sudden, inevitable, irreparable ruin."[13] Now he asked himself if it was possible that they could be separated. Was it now possible that the catalyst for a social and economic revolution could come from Washington, from the new reformist, "anti-imperialist" philosophy that he was witnessing?

"The perception of this possibility," he wrote years later, "put on alert my power of reasoning. It did so against my power to rationalize."[14] But his "power to rationalize" was still dominant. He was not ready; indeed he was far from abandoning his ideal of independence. The ideological conflict within him, what Muñoz was to refer to as one of his internal "civil wars," had begun.

---

12. Muñoz Marín, *Memorias* Vol. I, 105.

13. Bothwell, *Puerto Rico: cien años de lucha política* Vol. II, 406.

14. Muñoz Marín, *Memorias* Vol. I, 106.

On December 8, 1933, he sent another note to Eleanor Roosevelt:

There is in Puerto Rico a generation that has risen to power in all the political parties—that has been educated in the United States. It is familiar with and feels the deepest sympathy for the best manifestations of American life...that wants to fight against hunger, not through welfare but with social justice, operating within an economy that should be autonomous and should plan as far ahead as it is possible. It wants to break the monopoly of land and return it to the people that will work it; it wants to diversify the crops, grow foodstuff, emancipate the people from the constant threat of congressional action regarding sugar: it wants to promote industrial development to help to sustain our relatively enormous population. It wants, finally, to impart dignity and purpose to political action.[15]

Muñoz felt that he had not only, finally, found "purpose" to his own political life, but exactly what to say to "the good ear... of the most liberal part of the New Deal Government."

"He has overthrown his first governor!" journalist Rafael Torres Mazzorana cried out to a tumultuous multitude of over 50,000 enthusiastic Puerto Ricans that received Muñoz as the "conquering hero" upon his arrival on January 21, 1934. It was an outburst of national pride that transcended party and ideological lines. The conservative newspaper *El Mundo* published on the front page a large photo of the tall, dark young man with his entire family.

As he and Liberal Party leader Antonio Barceló made their way out of San Juan, Muñoz was overwhelmed by the staggering celebration. But again his inner emotions were contradictory. Yes, he had helped to give the Puerto Rican people more power. But if Puerto Rico had had self-government, it would have removed a bad Governor through the power of its voters, and not through the pleading and maneuvering of a minority Senator in Washington.

But beyond that, he thought, this wild demonstration was happening for the wrong reason. What was really important, and what Puerto Ricans

---

15. Muñoz Marín, *Memorias* Vol. I, 108.

should have been celebrating, he believed, was not that he helped to overthrow an inept Governor, but his pledge to Eleanor and Franklin Roosevelt to end Puerto Rico's cannibalistic partisan politics. The real achievement, he insisted, was bringing back the hope of the New Deal: for the first time, the hope of bringing social and economic justice to Puerto Rico.

9 "A Distinct Sense of Betrayal"

Muñoz's new mission placed him and Albizu Campos on a collision course. The ultimate goal was still the same: independence. But for Albizu and the traditional *independentistas*, to link Puerto Rico's "freedom" to materialist economic considerations was sacrilege. For Albizu the road to independence was "war" against the Americans. Now Muñoz, the self-proclaimed "radical nationalist" of just a year earlier, promised the Puerto Ricans that Roosevelt's reforms would generate "an ascending spiral of prosperity and economic security". On January 24, 1934, he asked island political leaders to stop wasting their time and energy with "cheap tribal politics. I wish that the people would insist, within all the parties, that the political leaders accept the grave responsibility of this moment and that they give all their thinking and energy to the problems of life and death that Puerto Rico is confronting."[1] For Albizu there was only one problem of "life and death" in Puerto Rico: how to expel the Americans from the island.

Violence was rare in Puerto Rico's political culture. Puerto Rico was the only Latin American country that never rebelled against the Spanish. The short-lived *Grito de Lares* uprising in 1868 failed to move the people. The *turbas republicanas*, "the Republican mobs" of the early century, were outbreaks of tribal partisan politics. Bumbling governors, such as Reily and Gore, had provoked political hysteria, but nothing approximating a rebellion.

But there was now verbal violence in Albizu's speeches—what Nationalist Party founder José Coll y Cuchí had denounced in 1930 as "the politics of

---

1. Bothwell, *Puerto Rico: cien años de lucha política* Vol. II, 444.

hate and insult." Muñoz saw it still as the understandable reaction of one passionate man to the reality of Puerto Rico's "colonial" condition. Muñoz himself, in his long dinner conversations with Albizu at the Palace Hotel, had brushed off his casual remarks about political assassinations. When the sticks of dynamite were found at Gore's home, Muñoz's *La Democracia* suggested that they might have been placed there by Gore's own people in another absurd effort to gain public sympathy.

Albizu had suffered a humiliating defeat in the 1932 elections. The more radical he became, the more he seemed to drift from the real world. He saw his tiny party as the incarnation of *la patria*: "the fatherland organized to rescue its sovereignty."[2] By the early 1930s, he seemed to speak as if the island were already a "republic" with himself as "President." The 1898 Treaty of Paris was "null and void;" Spain had no right to "cede" Puerto Rico to the United States. He named Nationalist Party "emissaries" to other countries: he designated Mexican-born José Vasconcelos as the "Nationalist Party Plenipotentiary Delegate to Europe."

In 1931, the Nationalist Party attempted to sell "Republic of Puerto Rico Bonds" on the island and the mainland. Queried about the legality of the bond issue, then Governor Theodore Roosevelt, Jr. advised the War Department to simply ignore it. The Bureau of Insular Affairs sought a legal opinion that declared that the bonds were fraudulent since, of course, the Republic of Puerto Rico did not exist. But the War Department, following Roosevelt's advice, decided that this was another quirk of island politics and did not take legal action.

As with the Irish Sinn Fein, rejection at the polls drove Albizu and the Nationalists to emulate the fascist movements in Europe and Japan. Albizu would never again participate in any elections. In 1932, he trained a small group of University of Puerto Rico Nationalist militants into quasi-military "Cadets of the Republic." A Nationalist Party newspaper published Italian dictator Benito Mussolini's "Ten Commandments of Fascist Youths". "God and Fatherland" above all else; total surrender of "body and soul" to the Leader; total discipline all hours of the day; "learn to suffer without complaining," among others. In Albizu's meetings with the Cadets, he stressed physical health, personal valor, use of arms, rejection of "empty

---

2. Ferrao, *Pedro Albizu Campos y el nacionalismo puertorriqueño*, 135.

words" to be replaced by direct action. The Cadets used black shirts as their uniform, and a black flag with a cross as their symbol. In late 1931, the Nationalist newspaper published articles on Hitler and "applauded" Japanese incursion into the Caribbean.[3] By mid-1932, the Cadets, now organized throughout the island, with "officers," captains and lieutenants leading each "division", were holding "military drills" with wooden rifles. In May they held a "black shirt parade" before Albizu and other Nationalist leaders in the mountain town of Utuado.

All this "military" activity, the drills and parades, became a newsy novelty amply reported in the island's principal independent newspapers. Albizu and his followers were perceived as a curiosity, a picturesque sideshow to the furious partisan clashes between the Liberal and Coalition parties. One of the flaws of island politics, Muñoz lamented, was the propensity of Puerto Ricans to see politics as entertainment, more as "opera instead of foundry of democratic action".[4] The more outlandish Albizu's actions, the more entertaining he seemed to be to the island media and other *políticos.*

Albizu's "opera," however, was being played on a stage of all too real economic and political deterioration, and some business leaders began to take it seriously. One group organized a Citizen's Committee for the Preservation of Peace and Order and on December 29, 1933 sent a panicky cable to the President: ".... a state of actual anarchy exists. Towns in a state of siege. Citizens unable to leave home. Police impotent. Business paralyzed."[5]

What was evident to everyone in Washington, however, was that Gore's bumbling had excessively agitated the Puerto Ricans, and a new Governor was needed to cool off the island. In a message to the War Department, former Governor Beverley asked: "Is General Winship available for a position of this kind?" Blanton Winship, the War Department's Adjutant General, seemed to Beverley the ideal person to repair the damage of the Gore debacle: a highly-decorated veteran of the Spanish-American and First World Wars. He had served in Cuba, the Philippines and Mexico. He had carried out several delicate diplomatic missions in Europe, Africa and Latin America. He knew his way in Washington, having served as the President's military aide in the late 1920s. Roosevelt agreed that the retired General was precisely the man to restore the authority and dignity of the Governor's office.

---

3. Ibid., 321.

4. Muñoz Marín, *Memorias,* Vol. I, 91.

5. Mathews, *Puerto Rican Politics and the New Deal,* 112.

Muñoz was stunned. He believed that he had returned to Puerto Rico bearing the President's sincere commitment to extend the New Deal to the island. Wasn't this, after all, the deeper purpose of getting Gore out? Had he not convinced the President that it was the hope of economic and social reform that would "calm down" Puerto Rico? Instead, Roosevelt was sending the first military officer as Governor since 1900. When an American newsman shouted at Muñoz: "What do you think of that bird?", for a moment Muñoz thought of expressing his deep disappointment, but he decided to hide his feelings. "The feathers look good, but all I can see are the feathers."

Albizu Campos and the Nationalists did not hide their feelings. The appointment of a military officer and not a New Deal reformer was proof that what Muñoz had brought were empty promises and that the Americans were taking their "war" seriously. That Winship's primary mission was to crush the Nationalists, they believed, became evident when the new Governor promptly set out to "militarize" the island police and armed it with machine guns and the latest riot control equipment. Winship spent his weekends inspecting the new vigorous police training camps. For Albizu and his "army of patriots," the "enemy" had finally joined the battle.

The Nationalists were encouraged by signs that Puerto Ricans were finally shaking off their history of "docile" acceptance of colonial rule. Many no longer jumped to their feet when the American national anthem was played. Some had already begun to ridicule Blanton Winship as they had Gore: "And what do you think of Winship?" one would sing. And the others would answer in chorus: "*Blandón, Blandón!*" —softie, softie. Seeing in the conservative, stately career military man the personification of "*Yanqui* repression," the Nationalists set out to prove that the General was indeed a "softie" about to be overwhelmed by a tidal wave of militancy that would shatter Puerto Rico's centuries-old tradition of non-violence.

"General Blanton Winship," wrote Earl Parker Hanson, who worked under him in Puerto Rico, "a southern gentleman in the finest sense of the word—correct, hospitable, polite, decent and pleasant in his personal relations—was certainly not the man to rule Puerto Rico in those turbulent days. Like thousands in his class, he was utterly bewildered by the New Deal and all it stood for."[6]

---

6. Hanson, *Transformation: The Story of Modern Puerto Rico*, 164.

Roosevelt's confidant, Rexford Tugwell, commented after being named Governor of Puerto Rico in 1941 that he was still baffled: "What were the mental processes which led Mr. Roosevelt to the selection, I could not for the life of me imagine."[7] Decades later Muñoz wrote: "For different reasons in relation to Gore, it proved to be another bad appointment...he was the most disastrous Governor that Puerto Rico has had in this century."

The "Novelist's Fantasy"

At the same time, however, in Muñoz's view, some good decisions were being made at the White House. One was the reappointment of José Padín to a new term as commissioner of education, putting aside the disruptive and emotional issue of "Americanizing" the public school system. Padín was expected to continue to "completely divorce the Department of Education from local politics." Another was the naming of the liberal James Bourne to head the new Puerto Rico Emergency Relief Administration. Under Harry Hopkins's federal ERA program, the administration had an initial grant of $900,000 for work-relief projects, to distribute food, and to participate in road construction and disease control programs. In December, 1933, Bourne sent the President a "Constructive Plan for Puerto Rico" that included expanded building and significant tax and civil service reform. Roosevelt responded favorably, informing War Secretary Dern: "I think this memorandum from James Bourne has much of real merit."[8]

Muñoz agreed, but for him "economic reconstruction" must begin breaking up the large, absentee-owned American corporations and distribute the land to the *jíbaros*. Land reform would gradually push the island economy to its authentic, natural state based more on coffee, tobacco, fruits, and vegetables. This would return dignity and self-esteem to Puerto Ricans, freeing them from the "dependence mentality." His reforms would also liberate the economy from the insecurity, even paranoia, that at any moment the President and Congress would remove the "privilege" of tariff protection and other subsidies that propped the sugar industry.

---

7. Tugwell, *The Stricken Land*, 39.

8. Mathews, *Puerto Rican Politics and the New Deal*, 150.

But was Muñoz's apparent obsession with bringing the sugar industry to its knees really economic or political? The island's business class and opposition leaders had no doubt that Muñoz was still an unrealistic "poet" romantically longing to return to the past. With all its flaws, the fact was that Puerto Rico had a life-and-death dependence on sugar. If allowed to tamper with the industry, already suffering from non-competitive high costs of production, Muñoz was going to prove a calamity worse than Reily or Gore.

Muñoz found essential support from the New Dealers. Interior Secretary Harold Ickes was one. In a January 15, 1935 letter to Senator Duncan Fletcher, Ickes wrote that "Puerto Rico...has been the victim of the laissez faire economy which has developed the rapid growth of great absentee owned sugar corporations, which have absorbed much land formerly belonging to small independent growers and who in consequence have been reduced to virtual economic serfdom..."[9]

During his stay in Washington, Muñoz followed the heated debate over the Costigan-Jones Act to stabilize the price of sugar. The Cuban sugar industry had long resented and denounced what it considered favoritism for Puerto Rico's high cost sugar at its expense. Congress increased the Cuban sugar quota and decreased Puerto Rico's from 875,000 to 821,000 tons.

This was predictably seen by the island's industry and Coalition leaders as still another economic catastrophe. But for Muñoz, it was precisely the opening he needed, and there was a big surprise. The law imposed a special tax on sugar producers to be used to compensate the farmers affected by the reduced production. Muñoz was tipped off by his friend, *New York Times* reporter Felix Belair, to look into this since the law gave the President and his Agriculture Secretary latitude in spending the tax revenue. Muñoz asked Ruby Black to investigate, and she came up with the stunning news that Puerto Rico could receive from $23 to $40 million from this fund.

Muñoz envisioned an incredible scenario: the absentee-owned sugar corporations themselves, through the new processing tax, would finance his massive land distribution reforms. Black enthusiastically informed him that in Washington, "a completely planned economy for Puerto Rico is expected from the sugar stabilization plan."

---

9. Ibid., 215.

There was more good news. Muñoz was informed that one of the four big corporations, the United Puerto Rico Sugar Company, owner of five mills and large tracks of land, was up for sale. He recruited the island's two most prominent academic agriculture experts, University of Puerto Rico chancellor Carlos Chardón, and the head of the university's chemistry department, Rafael Fernández García, both sympathetic to the Liberal Party. They put together a plan to have the government purchase the company through a "public corporation" that would operate its mills and launch land reform by distributing the excess sugar lands to truck farmers.

On February 14, 1934, Muñoz decided to make the plan public in a Senate speech. The Coalition senators were quickly convinced that this was more of *El Vate*'s day-dreaming. Yes, of course, they responded sarcastically: this certainly sounded like a wonderful plan. But where was he, Muñoz, going to get the millions needed to carry it out? He had it, Muñoz answered: up to $23 million. "My response," Muñoz wrote years later, "exceeded all frames of reference. It seemed to be delusion of grandeur or a novelist's fantasy." This was twice the budget of the entire Government of Puerto Rico. *Where is it?* the Coalition leaders demanded. Muñoz was determined not to give the corporations and Coalition leaders the opportunity to sabotage his plan in Washington. Finally Muñoz answered: "I have it in my pocket." The Coalition senators were delighted. They had succeeded in getting Muñoz to expose himself as a charlatan. What he had in his pocket was a copy of the Costigan-Jones Act.

When the news of the economic windfall finally hit Puerto Rico, and Muñoz's "fantasy" began to emerge as a reality, even New Dealers Dorothy and James Bourne were worried. Muñoz was indeed tampering with something he did not understand. Echoing the 1930 Brookings Report, James wrote to Harry Hopkins: "To substitute a less efficient system of land utilization for a more efficient one in an island which badly needs its yield for the support of an excessive population is economic nonsense."[10]

Muñoz realized that if his initiative was to have any opportunity, it could not be seen as "politically motivated." Already known as the "Muñoz Marín Plan," he wanted it called the "Chardón Plan". Carlos Chardón, a Cornell University graduate, former commissioner of agriculture, like José

---

10. Ibid.,149.

Padín, was one of the few Puerto Ricans that were considered in Washington, as on the island, above island politics. He had earned his reputation as a scientific researcher, an expert on sugarcane diseases, and had proven to be a good administrator running the University of Puerto Rico with a firm and steady hand. His plan could not be so easily dismissed as "economic nonsense."

ELEONOR'S VISIT

Ruby Black informed Muñoz that Eleanor Roosevelt was coming to Puerto Rico. More good news. If he could reach her, he would overcome the escalating opposition. Working in a small room at the Normandie Hotel in San Juan, Muñoz followed closely the details of her visit. She brought along a team of experts from the Federal Emergency Relief Administration and other agencies, and a small group of journalists, Ruby Black among them. With her friend Dorothy Bourne as her guide, she spent three days seeing for herself the terrible conditions of the *jíbaros* throughout the island, the putrid slums in San Juan, movingly bringing to life the worse she had been told and read of this "broken American pledge."

Muñoz carefully prepared her exposure to his plan. She asked Governor Winship to convene a "round table" meeting at La Fortaleza on March 10, 1934, bringing together twenty-eight government, business, and religious leaders for a free discussion that would come up with concrete proposals she could take back to the President. Muñoz told Ruby Black that he did not want to be present, but Carlos Chardón would be there.

The meeting began with an extensive discussion of the Bournes' "Constructive Plan for Puerto Rico" that the President had initially endorsed. Throughout the meeting, Chardón remained silent. As the meeting was winding down, he put forward an outline of his plan, emphasizing that the public corporation that owned and operated the United Sugar Puerto Rico Company would be run as a private business. This was not "socialism" but the reaction was strongly negative. Chardón, after all, was an academic not directly involved in an industry in economic trouble. American policy, one sugar representative insisted, should be to support, not further damage the industry. Governor Winship expressed his view that the island's best hope was to develop tourism. The long meeting ended without the concrete proposals Eleanor wanted.

Before she returned to Washington, however, Muñoz was able to meet with her privately and finally get to her "good ear." He strongly urged her to take the Chardón Plan back to the President.

Muñoz didn't know it, but the plan, in fact, already had strong support. In another stroke of luck, Assistant Agriculture Secretary Rexford Tugwell, while not part of Eleanor's visit, had been on the same airplane with his own team of land use experts. Tugwell, like the others, was astounded by the magnitude of this island's economic ills. His initial reaction was skepticism that anything could be done to make a real difference. He immediately saw the root cause: overpopulation. "There are a dozen children behind every bush," he wrote to Agriculture Secretary Henry Wallace, "many of them indifferently nourished. But nature aided by our doctors has only added to the prevailing difficulty by such a growth of population that it outruns any possibility of furnishing opportunity in our terms."

Invited to attend Eleanor's "round table" at La Fortaleza, Tugwell returned to Washington, not only impressed with Chardón's presentation, but favoring an even more radical plan. He was precisely the advocate Muñoz needed in Washington. Incubator of several of the more innovative New Deal programs, Tugwell was in the key administrative position to push land reform. Tugwell also loved a good battle, especially against "reactionaries" that cringed at the idea of "socialism." After hearing the opposition and fears expressed in San Juan, he looked forward to taking on the sugar barons. "The facts are," Black reported back to Muñoz, "that Tugwell and some of the other boys want to use considerably more than $40 million of the sugar processing tax for Puerto Rico..."[11]

Through Tugwell, a Puerto Rican Commission was established. In addition to Muñoz's original planners, Carlos Chardón and Rafael Fernández García, it was decided to name a moderate member of the Coalition Party, agriculture commissioner Rafael Menéndez Ramos. Black informed Muñoz that there was the desire to name him but he declined, insisting on his strategy of not provoking more political opposition.

---

11. Ibid., 158.

Black, in fact, underestimated Tugwell's enthusiastic and radical approach. In April Tugwell wrote a memorandum describing "the possibility of socializing the sugar industry of Puerto Rico and running it both economically and for the benefit of Puerto Rico as a whole, on somewhat the same lines as a collective farm in the U.S.S.R. This might be legally accomplished through a public corporation."[12]

Tugwell was already the lightning rod for the anti-New Deal members of Congress. If word got out of what he had in mind, Muñoz feared, all would be lost. Tugwell decided to have the Commission and Muñoz, as its "consultant," come up to Washington to work secretly in an Agriculture Department office.

The President, meanwhile, took another step that pleased Muñoz. On May 23, jurisdiction over Puerto Rican matters was transferred from the "conservative" War Department, to Harold Ickes's "liberal" Interior Department. An early supporter of Theodore Roosevelt's Progressive Party, Ickes was an advocate of Indian rights and had aspired to join the new administration as head of the Commission of Indian Affairs. He was surprised by his appointment to head the Interior Department. According to Tugwell, "it does not appear that Mr. Ickes had any interests in the affairs of Territories and Possessions, or that he had any ideas about colonial policy, or even concern as to whether there should be a policy."[13] Ickes was a down-to-earth, tough administrator, sensitive and jealous of his prerogatives, who called himself "the Old Curmudgeon." He was also fiercely loyal to the President and determined not to let him down with this new assignment.

Everything seemed to be falling into place for Muñoz. The young minority Senator continued to demonstrate a remarkable ability to get things done in Washington. He seemed to be lining up a New Deal powerhouse—from Eleanor Roosevelt to Harold Ickes to Rexford Tugwell—behind his ambitious economic reforms.

But as the Roosevelt administration attempted to work out the details of the Chardón Plan, it found itself sinking deeper into its scope and complexity. It would reduce sugar production, diversify Puerto Rican agriculture, increase local food production, "eliminate land monopoly,"

---

12. Ibid., 162.
13. Tugwell, *The Stricken Land*, 2.

finance social improvements, create 10,000 subsistence homesteads, create 17,000 new jobs, and increase milk supply by 12 percent and pork by 30 percent. There were new and difficult questions of implementation. Still unresolved was the basic legal issue of whether the Secretary of Agriculture was in fact authorized to spend the sugar processing tax fund for such a wide and diversified economic reconstruction plan. Another serious legal complication was the old 500-acre law approved by Congress back in 1900 to limit corporate ownership in Puerto Rico. The U.S. Controller General and Agriculture Department questioned whether the U.S. government itself would be violating federal law through the Chardón Plan.

And regardless of the President's conceptual endorsement, the administrators could not ignore the opposition coming from Puerto Rico's private sector, backed by Governor Winship, that beyond politics and ideology, the plan would end up making the island's economic crisis even worse.

In June, 1934, it was announced that the President would visit Puerto Rico. Before the trip, Roosevelt took several actions to underscore his support. On the 16th, he convened a White House Conference on Puerto Rican Affairs where high-level administration experts analyzed the Chardón Plan in detail. Roosevelt then announced the creation of an Inter-Departmental Committee for the Economic Rehabilitation of Puerto Rico. Oscar Chapman, assistant Secretary of the Interior, Rexford Tugwell, representatives of the Treasury Department, and other key agencies were given the task of "coordinating" the plan.

For Muñoz, all this meant more studies, more bureaucracy, and more delay. With all the power he had mobilized behind the plan, beginning with the President himself, he sensed that it was in trouble. He decided to jolt the President with a dramatic, emotionally-charged appeal: "...the people of Puerto Rico are now living literally on faith—faith in you, faith in your sense of justice, in your reconstruction policy."[14] Without this faith, he warned, "the economy of the island could stop and break down... no unemployed worker would be able to buy a pound of rice on credit, no mortgage would not be foreclosed, there would be no credit, the economy of the island would stall and collapse." He expressed his own sense of frustration. Because of his confidence in Roosevelt, he considered it his job to "hammer into the

---

14. Bothwell, *Puerto Rico: cien años de lucha política* Vol. II, 481.

public conscience" not to lose its faith. He pleaded that Roosevelt, once in Puerto Rico, "announce his support of the reconstruction policy clearly and strongly."

The President arrived on July 1, 1934. He wrote to his wife that he was moved by the mass of islanders that cheered him "all the way" and by the enormous expectations he had aroused in them: "a really pathetic faith in what we are trying to do."[15] But while endorsing the plan in principle as consistent with fundamental New Deal goals and Agricultural Department policies, he acknowledged that there were still difficult, complex issues to iron out. He gave no timetable for its approval. This was different from of the "clear and strong" announcement Muñoz had expected.

"A Distinct Sense of Betrayal"

Soon after the President's return to Washington, Muñoz saw the plan sink deeper. Three agricultural experts selected by the Inter-Departmental Committee arrived on the island. One of them, Dr. Julius Matz, an Agriculture Department specialist, had lived and worked in Puerto Rico in 1919 and had already reached his conclusions. In a letter written two days after his arrival, he warned Secretary of Agriculture Wallace that the people that knew most about Puerto Rico's agriculture and sugar in particular "express their amazement at the fantastic and impractical so-called Chardón Plan."[16]

Matz was quickly admonished by the Department: his mission was not to pass judgment on a plan that had the President's blessing. But removing Matz did not solve the problem. The technical committee's final report, while avoiding Matz's blunt language, sustained his position that the plan was unrealistic and eventually destructive. Noting that the report would "embarrass" the Division of Territories and Insular Possessions, and thus the President himself, Roosevelt's Inter-Departmental Committee decided to suppress it. But a month later, Coalition Party leader Santiago Iglesias,

---

15. Pike, *FDR's Good Neighbor Policy*, 147.
16. Mathews, *Puerto Rican Politics and the New Deal*, 177.

the island's resident commissioner in Congress, inserted its damaging conclusions into the Congressional Record. The Coalition then had the entire report printed and distributed throughout Puerto Rico and Washington.

Muñoz had kept his part of the bargain with Roosevelt. He had worked hard "to adjourn politics in Puerto Rico." He had gone further, pledging that the Liberal Party "does not expect any appointments, nor patronage, nor any other rights."[17] But the President did not keep his side of the bargain. Ten months had passed since Muñoz's initial meetings with him at the White House: a month and a half since Roosevelt's visit to the island. Muñoz's promise of a New Deal "ascending spiral of prosperity and security for the Puerto Ricans" was turning into a cruel hoax. The Costigan-Jones Act went into effect, seriously hurting the island through its reduction of the sugar quota. But the $23 million Muñoz symbolically pulled out of his pocket, the windfall from the processing tax that would finance the Chardón Plan, were nowhere in sight.

Muñoz sent another cable to the President, this one written with the clipped urgency of an SOS message from a rapidly sinking ship:

> Costigan Act applied as to restrictions but unapplied as to compen-
> sations. Credit paralyzed. Cane dried up. Mills decapitating farm-
> ers; 98% cane workers unemployed, starving. Misadministration
> from Washington of policy intended to do opposite has accelerated
> tremendously process of last thirty years... I try hard to keep confi-
> dence while criticizing petty Washington official for criminal negli-
> gence. Situation growing rapidly unmanageable. People being as
> good as they can about it but there is a distinct sense of intolerable
> betrayal from Washington throughout population.[18]

The "distinct sense of betrayal" was, of course, his own. "Can anything be done?" Roosevelt asked as he handed the cable to Rexford Tugwell. Tugwell turned it over to his Agriculture Department colleague, John F. Carter, who had accompanied him on the trip to Puerto Rico. Carter replied: "I concur with Mr. Muñoz Marín in laying the blame for delay, confusion and

---

17. Bothwell, *Puerto Rico: cien años de lucha política* Vol. II, 437.
18. Mathews, *Puerto Rican Politics and the New Deal*, 158.

suffering with this government."[19] He then added his own warning, even more ominous than Muñoz's desperate message: "unless the Administration takes a vigorous lead in dealing with the Puerto Rican situation, we may find blood on our hands, and not only political blood either. Riots and similar social and economic disturbances are quite probable in the near future unless the Government acts."

19. Ibid., 186.

10 The Deranged Saraband

The President's response to Carter's warning was to get Interior Secretary Ickes to name Ernest Gruening to head the new Division of Territories and Islands. Gruening, the intrepid former crusading newspaper and magazine editor, had direct access to the President. He also possessed the self-confidence and aggressiveness to break through the bureaucratic logjam that had stalled the plan.

Muñoz, Muna, and Ruby Black all celebrated the appointment. Muñoz rushed up to New York to meet the friend who a decade earlier had published his articles in *The Nation*. They drove down together to Washington. Muñoz spoke non-stop during the 12-hour car trip. "I began with Christopher Columbus's discovery of Puerto Rico on November 19, 1493 all the way to Antonio Barceló and the new generation in the Liberal Party," Muñoz reported.

In Washington, Gruening and Muñoz came up with an idea to once more pressure the President. Muñoz wrote a draft of a letter to the President as well as a draft of the President's response expressing his determination to get the plan implemented. Gruening took the drafts to Roosevelt who approved them. Gruening then made the arrangements to have Muñoz himself transmit to the island Roosevelt's reply on December 22, 1934 from a short wave radio station in Schenectady, New York. Muñoz and Jesús Piñero, the leader of the association of small farmers and a former member of the island's Republican Party, drove through a snow storm to get to the station.

Muñoz read his letter to the President "in the name of Puerto Rico and as the representative of the forces of the New Deal in Puerto

Rico..."[1] He repeated the alarmed warning in his June cable to Roosevelt. "Puerto Ricans now going through more hell than it has ever been their fate to experience before." The island, he warned, was on the verge of "total economic and social collapse—public order today hangs by a thread." Then Muñoz read the President's response: he shared the frustrations of the Puerto Ricans, but the delays "have been totally inevitable." Roosevelt went on to "assure" the people of his endorsement of the Chardón Plan and his "firm determination" to initiate it "as soon as possible."

The Liberal Party had placed radios in all the town plazas. It was estimated that over half a million Puerto Ricans heard Muñoz's voice that evening, nearly a third of the island's total population. Puerto Rico had never seen or heard anything like this before. Its political impact was as great as his triumphant return to San Juan a year earlier after the removal of Governor Gore. Muñoz was now speaking for the President of the United States.

The opposition was furious. This was, they insisted, a cheap political trick to take credit for the millions in federal funds coming to the island. How had the President of the United States fallen into this partisan trap? In an angry protest, Coalition senator Alfonso Valdés, one of the island's most powerful businessmen, expressed outrage that Roosevelt had not only "circumvented" the insular government—the American Governor and the elected Legislature—but made a "political hero" of Muñoz Marín and his party. "I beg to remind you," Valdés wrote, "that said Party has stood and stands for the Independence of Puerto Rico."[2]

The transmission achieved its purpose. Puerto Ricans, surviving on "faith," had their "credit" extended. But Muñoz paid a price. His efforts to place the plan, and with it the New Deal, beyond Puerto Rico's cannibalistic partisan politics—what he had considered absolutely vital—collapsed.

Governor Winship, meanwhile, in a long meeting with the President on October 13, 1934, added his own voice of alarm. Puerto Rico's condition was indeed deteriorating. Unemployment, already sky high, had grown by another 20 percent after the sugar restrictions. He pleaded for a vast increase in relief funds from $2.3 to $32.2 million, restoration of the sugar quota, and

---

1. Muñoz Marín, *Memorias* Vol. I, 134.
2. Mathews, *Puerto Rican Politics and the New Deal*, 202.

$950,000 to carry out his favorite project, the rehabilitation of hotels and beautification programs aimed at attracting tourists to the island.

Muñoz made an attempt to induce Winship to leave. It was evident how much the veteran military officer resented being ordered around by political "loose cannon" Ernest Gruening. Muñoz urged Gruening to burden the Governor with an endless torrent of instructions, and even petty, silly orders. This, Muñoz was convinced, would certainly drive Winship out of La Fortaleza. Receiving almost daily letters from Muñoz criticizing Winship's every move, Gruening did shell Winship with messages and instructions. But the strategy failed. Gruening changed course and now resented being pushed by Muñoz.

Muñoz had seriously underestimated Winship's determination to stay on. Contrary to Muñoz's perception of him as a tired, spent man seeking to get through his "semi-retirement" with a minimum of irritation, the Governor was dead set on protecting, as he saw it, his country and his President from the reckless schemes of irresponsible dreamers such as Muñoz and Gruening.

The PRRA

On May 28, 1935, the President signed Executive Order 7057. The Puerto Rico Reconstruction Administration was born. The Chardón Plan was finally approved. But who was going to run it? The name of the head of the new agency was omitted when the final draft of the order emerged from the White House. When it was signed, the name Ernest Gruening had been inserted. Interior Secretary Ickes was convinced that Gruening had maneuvered behind his back to get himself appointed to run this $35 million program.

"Ickes was not pleased," Gruening wrote years later, "and questioned me sharply. Had I requested the President to appoint me? Had I asked an intermediary to do so? Had I discussed the appointment with the President? The answer was 'no' to all these questions."[3] Gruening insisted he first learned of his appointment in the press.

---

3. Gruening, *Many Battles: An Autobiography*, 189.

Ickes also learned from the Interior legal staff that the executive order gave Gruening virtual independence in administering the program and its funds. This, he was convinced, was still another mistake. He considered Gruening a notoriously bad administrator, excessively authoritarian, who provoked needless confrontations and conflicts in Washington as well as in Puerto Rico. Ickes, who had never come to trust or like Muñoz, trusted and liked Gruening even less. The self-styled "Old Curmudgeon" felt it in his bones that he and the President were headed toward deep trouble.

In Puerto Rico the creation of the Puerto Rican Reconstruction Administration was greeted as another triumph for Muñoz. The Coalition leaders, who had spent so much energy in preventing the Bournes, the "pawns of the Liberal Party," from controlling the program, now found that it was placed under a man they considered "the pawn of Muñoz Marín," Ernest Gruening. The political implications of this were enormous. In a political culture based on patronage, this was the ultimate bonanza. To defeat Muñoz and the Liberal Party in the following year's election, the Coalition had to either get its hands on the $35 million, or ensure the Chardón Plan's failure.

No one believed that Muñoz meant it when he said that the PRRA and its funds would not be turned into patronage. In Washington, John Franklin Carter, Tugwell's advisor, did not believe it: "I am really afraid of this program being used as a pie-counter for the Liberal Party..."[4] Muñoz's own party did not believe him. He wrote years later: "No sooner than I returned to Puerto Rico I was confronted by the voracious appetite for patronage of the Liberals... I had spoken with total sincerity. But within the prevalent political culture my attitude seemed incredible. Undoubtedly it was considered a hoax, that due to a grave Puerto Rican cultural defect, was admired."[5]

And no one believed Gruening when he insisted that he was not Muñoz's pawn. Gruening, who had made a successful career as a hard-hitting journalist, was stung by the attacks: "the press soon began a campaign of intemperate denunciation that far exceeded any mainland expressions in my experience."

4. Mathews, *Puerto Rican Politics and the New Deal*, 194.
5. Muñoz Marín, *Memorias* Vol. I, 143.

Even apolitical Dorothy and James Bourne joined the attack. In the political whirlpool, the New Deal liberals found themselves aligned with their recent tormentors, the Coalition leaders. In an April 21, 1936 memorandum to the President, Bourne accused Gruening of "being perfectly willing to have it (the reconstruction program)...be a Liberal Party program and it has so turned out."[6] Mrs. Bourne added her voice in a letter to Eleanor: "The question of political affiliation of PRRA with the Liberals is...debatable wisdom in a reconstruction program because of its inevitable exclusion of different political elements..."

Gruening vehemently denied it. But four decades later, in his memoirs, he admitted that he had indeed fallen into the trap, inadvertently naming Liberals to five of the top six jobs. "I have to take the blame for that," he confessed.

THE 500-ACRE LAW

Nothing exposed the "deranged saraband" that the Puerto Rico-United States relationship had become more than the surrealistic fact that the island's economy was based on a flagrant violation of federal law. For Muñoz, the irony was that to bring about a radical land reform, all that was required was the enforcement of the law approved by Congress in 1900 limiting corporate ownership of land to 500 acres. It was enacted, in part, to protect mainland sugar producers from potential Puerto Rican competition. But the stated reason was precisely to avoid what in fact occurred. Congressman William H. Jones argued: "If such concentration of holdings shall become the case, then the condition of the population will, I believe, be reduced to one of absolute servitude. The people of Puerto Rico will be driven to cultivate these lands for these corporations at whatever daily wage they choose to pay them."[7]

The law, however, did not provide for its enforcement. There were 41 corporations on the island illegally owning and operating 249,000 acres of

---

6. Ibid., 240.
7. Perloff, *Puerto Rico's Economic Future*, 34.

land. All four of the American sugar companies that produced half of the island's sugar were in violation of the law.

So while the President endorsed the Chardón Plan, his appointed Governor and appointed attorney general, Benjamin Horton, were determined not only to block the enforcement of the 500 acre law, but were driving to amend it. Muñoz accused Winship and Horton of acting as the "advocates" of the sugar corporations, pointing out that Horton's office had requested the assistance and advice of the sugar lawyers. Gruening agreed. In late August, Muñoz and Gruening finally convinced the President to name Georgetown University Law School graduate Benigno Fernández García to replace Horton and thus become the first Puerto Rican to hold the post of attorney general.

Flush with victory, Muñoz renewed his campaign to finally drive Winship out of the island. Initially Gruening agreed: "I...received almost daily letters and memoranda from Muñoz Marín," he wrote years later, "appraising me of the activities of the Coalition leaders, and of their efforts to get the Governor to appoint their men to various offices. He often wrote of his frustration at not having a 'New Dealer' operating from La Fortaleza...and his complaints were justified."[8]

But Roosevelt, who had allowed Muñoz to talk him into removing Governor Gore, was not going to admit that he had made another mistake. Even though he was surrounded by enemies in San Juan and Washington, Winship was confident that he still enjoyed the President's confidence. He was right. "Roosevelt," Gruening wrote, "was imbued with a strong naval tradition; the Caribbean was an American lake." In any case, from the President's point of view, how could Gruening and Muñoz carry out their reforms without the firm hand of a "military man" keeping "peace and order" on this island?

---

8. Gruening, *Many Battles: An Autobiography*, 191.

11 Muñoz Hits Bottom

In the early morning hours of July 4, 1935, dynamite bombs went off at the Puerto Rico Reconstruction Administration office in Old San Juan and at other U.S. Government buildings. Later that month, after a large quantity of dynamite was reported stolen from various lime quarries, another bomb went off at the U.S. Court Building in Puerta de Tierra. The explosions continued into August. One targeted the telephone building on Tanca Street in San Juan; another, the island police station in Barrio Obrero. There were no deaths, but it was evident that Albizu Campos and the Nationalist Party had begun their "war."

The first clash took place on October 24, 1935. University of Puerto Rico students, angry at one of Albizu's ferocious speeches, announced that they were holding a rally to defend their honor and to censure the Nationalist leader. Albizu had attacked the male students as "effeminate" and the female as "prostitutes" for opposing independence and "accepting American domination." The Nationalists declared that they would thwart the anti-Albizu manifestation.

Governor Winship's police force, tense since the bombings in July and August and anxious to retaliate after the explosion at the police station, was prepared to stop the Nationalists before they reached the student rally. Several police patrol cars intercepted an automobile with four Nationalists, ordering it to proceed slowly to a nearby police station. Policemen stood on the running boards on each side of the car when suddenly there were gunshots between one of them and the driver, Ramón S. Pagán. Several other policemen emerged from another patrol car and fired at the Nationalists inside the car. A Nationalist "cadet" came running towards the car and was gunned down. When the shooting ended, the cadet, three Nationalists in the car, and one policeman were dead. The fourth passenger was seriously injured.

At the cemetery, speaking to an estimated 8,000 mourners, Albizu swore revenge. It was an event of strong emotional impact. Overhead, wreaths of white lilies and a big Puerto Rican flag were dropped from an aircraft. Accusing Winship and police chief Colonel Riggs of "deliberately murdering the Nationalist representatives of Puerto Rico," Albizu vowed that for every Nationalist life lost, an American would be killed. He did not exclude certain Puerto Ricans that were working for the Americans: Carlos Chardón, who was now heading the local PRRA office, the new attorney general, Benigno Fernández García, and other Liberal Party leaders.

Two months later, in early December, there was extraordinary anticipation and excitement at the Nationalist's annual assembly in Caguas. Albizu announced that the party was now a "Liberation Army." All Nationalists were expected to enlist in "compulsory military service". The party, of course, would not participate in the 1936 elections.

Albizu had crossed the line from politics as "opera" to openly calling for the violent overthrowing of the American government in Puerto Rico. Fearing for his life, Carlos Chardón obtained a gun permit and had guards posted at his PRRA office. Governor Winship got Washington to send a team of FBI investigators to the island. The agents found revolutionary literature at Nationalist "recruitment stations," signs on the walls calling for "funds to buy weapons," but, except for individually-owned guns, no cache of weapons to carry out the "war."

What, in fact, was Albizu's aim? Did he have a strategy? Was he deliberately provoking Winship and the United States to prosecute the Nationalist leadership for sedition? Was he seeking to have himself and his followers thrown into jail as martyrs? Or had he simply lost his senses?

To Muñoz, Albizu was still a paradox. His theatrics were clearly preposterous. There was absolutely no reality in Albizu provoking an uprising against the Americans. Like his father, Muñoz viscerally rejected violence. But he continued to see Albizu's extremism as a symptom of the desperation overtaking the Puerto Rican people. It gave credibility and urgency to his warnings to Roosevelt, Ickes, and Gruening that the "criminal" delay in beginning to fulfill the promises of the New Deal, which drove him to the very limits of his faith in the President, had public order "hanging on a thread."

SUNDAY MORNING MURDER

On the quiet Sunday morning of February 23, 1936, police chief Elisha Francis Riggs, after attending mass, walked down the steps in front of the Santa Ana Church in Old San Juan. He was approached by two young men. Elias Beauchamp shot and killed Riggs instantly. The police quickly apprehended Beauchamp and his companion, Hiram Rosado. Both were killed in the police station.

For the Nationalists, Riggs was the embodiment of the despised "Winship repression." For stunned Puerto Ricans, Albizu had carried out his threat at the gravesite speech where he had vowed revenge. Muñoz was in Washington. He knew Riggs well and liked him: a "humanitarian and liberal person...he was my personal friend, generous, of cordial good humor."[1] Riggs had gone out of his way to make friends with Puerto Rican leaders, including Albizu Campos. The news of his murder, Muñoz wrote decades later, "shook my spirit." And it intensified his ambiguity regarding Albizu.

Muñoz had to make a decision: whose side was he on? He deplored the murder of his "friend" Riggs but also the "police lynching" of the two Nationalists. The assassination made the front pages of major U.S. newspapers, provoking angry editorial comments. Why was there, Muñoz asked himself, no similar outrage at the "murder" of the two young Puerto Rican patriots?

There was no ambiguity in Gruening's reaction. "Riggs was not a typical police chief," he wrote. "A retired army colonel, he had served as a military attaché in various diplomatic posts abroad. He was a kind, cultured man, fluent in Spanish and sincerely interested in Puerto Rico's needs and aspirations."[2]

---

1. Muñoz Marín, *Memorias*, Vol. I, 147.
2. Gruening, *Many Battles: An Autobiography*, 197.

But unlike Muñoz, he was revolted by the description of Albizu and the Nationalists as misguided "patriots." Gruening was convinced that the source of Albizu's virulent anti-Americanism was his personal racial experiences in the U.S. after leaving Harvard. Among his many crusades, Gruening had fought against racial discrimination. Back in the 1920's, as editor of *The Nation*, he campaigned against the exclusion of "Negroes" from Harvard's freshman dormitories. He mobilized the alumni, initiated a letter-writing campaign, and finally succeeded in getting the reluctant university to change its policy. While at Harvard, Gruening wrote, Albizu "was not considered a Negro but a 'Latin American'" and did not "encounter the prejudice that he would have otherwise experienced...known as 'Pete', he was a popular student and was elected president of the Cosmopolitan Club whose membership consisted of students from foreign countries. When the United States entered the war, he was filled with patriotic fervor and wanted to be among the first to go and fight the Kaiser. He returned to Puerto Rico and was assigned to a Negro regiment. It was a new experience for Albizu Campos; his regiment trained in the South and for the first time he learned what it was to be a Negro, not only in the army, but in America. All his love for America turned to hate."[3]

Gruening asked Muñoz to condemn the Riggs killing. Muñoz refused, offended that Gruening seemed to be blaming all Puerto Ricans for the crime and showed no outrage over the "police lynching." Decades later, Gruening recorded his recollection of a bitter and fateful encounter with Muñoz. He quotes Muñoz as saying: "I have taken on the Coalition, I'm not going to take on the Nationalists, too." Gruening, "puzzled and indignant," answered: "You *should* take them on and denounce their campaign of terrorism." Muñoz again refused. Feeling his "indignation rise," Gruening said, "I'm afraid you are just another politician, I thought you were something different." But there was something else in Muñoz that made Gruening even angrier: megalomania. "He laid his hand on my shoulder. 'Ernest, you're excited. Many lives may have to be lost in the liberation of Puerto Rico. I take the long-range view in contemplating the destiny of my country.'" Gruening replied, "I'm afraid you are just contemplating the destiny of Muñoz

---

3. Ibid., 196.

Marín." Muñoz clarified: "The destiny of Muñoz Marín and the destiny of Puerto Rico are inseparable."

Gruening was crushed by what he saw as Muñoz's betrayal:

> I confess I was greatly disillusioned. I had had implicit faith in Muñoz Marín, in his integrity, his vision, and his statesmanship. Now by his silence he was condoning murder, and indeed the whole Nationalist campaign of violence... I was deeply troubled and after a sleepless night, I went to him and again pleaded that a simple statement of sorrow at Riggs' death was the minimum of decency. I could not budge him.[4]

If Albizu, the Nationlists, and now Muñoz, wanted "war," Gruening was prepared to draw the battle line. It was no longer between those for and those against the New Deal and the Chardón Plan. It was a battle between Puerto Ricans loyal and disloyal to the Americans, the same mindset of the American governors Montgomery Reily and Robert Gore. But for Gruening this was different. Muñoz, in siding with Albizu, had "betrayed" the Americans that had trusted and supported him, President and Eleanor Roosevelt, and above all, himself.

Several days after the nasty encounter, Muñoz sent a letter published in *The Washington Post* that did condemn "the three murders." But it was too late. Gruening, as in all the battles in his life, was relentless in his campaign against the man that he believed had stabbed him in the back. His "war" began in April of 1936, when in Gruening's own words, "a political bomb exploded" in the now shell-shocked Puerto Rico.

THE TYDINGS BILL

Senator Millard Tydings of Maryland, Chairman of the Senate Committee on Insular Affairs, favored independence for Puerto Rico. In a visit in December, 1933, he assured Puerto Ricans: "If you really want it

---

4. Ibid., 197.

[independence], I am willing to help you get it." A long-time opponent of American overseas colonies, author of the law-granting independence to the Philippines following a ten-year adjustment period, Tydings, convinced of the futility of "Americanizing" foreign cultures, believed that it was in the best interest of the Americans to somehow convince Puerto Ricans to follow the Philippines example.

But what he observed on the island was discouraging. Contrary to what Muñoz had been insisting for years, Puerto Ricans were not demanding their "freedom." Tydings informed Roosevelt: "I am sorry to report that there is no real independence sentiment here...it would certainly be better for us if we were out of this place, and, conversely, much worse for Puerto Rico."[5]

Even more than Gruening, the Riggs murder affected Tydings. He had recommended Riggs, a close friend, for the post in Puerto Rico and had convinced him to accept it. Now he called Gruening to his Senate office. "I've always been opposed to the United States taking over countries with cultures and traditions alien to ours," Tydings began. He asked the Interior Department to prepare a bill, modeled after the Tydings-McDuffie Act for Philippine independence, authorizing a plebiscite in Puerto Rico to be held in November, 1937. If Puerto Ricans chose independence, they would get it. This, Tydings pointed out, had always been American policy. Gruening asked if the President and Secretary Ickes were aware of this request. Yes, Tydings answered, and both are "all in favor of it." On April 23, 1936, the Senator introduced the bill. Breaking his commitment with Roosevelt not to present it as an administration bill, Tydings made it known that it had the President's blessing.

News of the "Roosevelt bill for independence" hit Muñoz like a thunderbolt. He had been excluded from its preparation. Gruening was temperamental and had clearly lost his bearings, but how to explain that Roosevelt himself was behind Gruening's "revenge...blaming the entire Puerto Rican community for the fanaticism of the Nationalists?"

As editor of *La Democracia* Muñoz had access to the Senate press gallery. He was typing a statement describing the bill as "*la ley de fuga*," the act of allowing a prisoner to escape in order to shoot him in the back, what Muñoz

---

5. Mathews, *Puerto Rican Politics and the New Deal*, 107.

believed had happened to the two Nationalists. Muñoz suddenly felt that there was someone behind him. It was Gruening reading over his shoulders. "I thought you were in favor of independence," he said. "That's right," Muñoz answered. "I'm also in favor of matrimony. But this bill is a whore."[6]

A "DIABOLICAL" SCHEME

Only Gruening's "twisted mind," Muñoz believed, could devise such a "diabolical scheme" to shoot and to kill independence in the back. It was "revenge disguised as political freedom...The bill says to the Puerto Ricans that independence can be of their own choosing and it paints a picture of hunger and terror as necessarily connected with independence."[7] It's economic provisions were harsher than Tydings's Philippine independence bill. Whereas the Philippines were given 20 years to phase in U.S. tariffs, Puerto Rico would have only four.

After his encounter with Gruening at the Senate press gallery, Muñoz made a personal attempt to persuade Secretary Ickes, Assistant Interior Secretary Oscar Chapman, and Ruth Hampton, a friend of Ickes in the Division of Territories, that the bill's real motive was to doom the Liberal Party in the elections. But with it, it would also doom the New Deal in Puerto Rico. Muñoz described it to Ruby Black:

> It happens that those who favor independence are, with slight over-lapping, those who believe in the New Deal and in economic justice, and those who are against independence, also with small overlap-ping, are those who are against the New Deal and against economic justice through the ownership and exploitation of selfish economic interests. Therefore, at one stroke, Gruening (but, officially, the administration) has placed control of the elective part of the Puerto Rican Government for many years to come in the hands of the anti-liberal, anti-economic justice, and anti-New Deal element and has

---

6. Muñoz Marín, *Memorias* Vol. I, 151.
7. Ibid., 149.

considerably weakened the liberalism of the Liberal Party which was the remaining engine for the protection of those helpless masses down there.[8]

Muñoz failed. Ickes, as much as he disliked and distrusted Gruening, was solidly on his side. Like Gruening, he resented that Puerto Ricans showed such little gratitude now that the American government was making a gigantic and costly effort to lift them from poverty. It seemed that the more the Americans did for them, the greater the complaining and protests. Perhaps Gruening was right. Referring to the Tydings bill, Ickes wrote: "I strongly urged its immediate introduction...because of the quieting effect that I anticipated it might have on Puerto Rican public opinion."[9]

Unable to budge Ickes and the New Dealers, Muñoz returned to the island on June 22, 1936 determined to convince the Liberal Party that the only way to avoid Gruening's "diabolical" ambush, and thus save the independence ideal as well as itself from a crushing defeat, was to boycott the November elections. In dramatic contrast to his previous triumphant returns, this time Muñoz slipped back into the island secretly under a false name. When he resurfaced several days later, he announced to the surprised reporters that he was resigning his Senate seat and would not run for any office in the coming elections.

Gruening's "revenge" apparently was working. As did Ickes and Gruening, Muñoz knew that there was no possibility of Congress approving the bill in this session. But the bill plunged the island into a political status frenzy. For the first time, independence emerged in the minds of Puerto Ricans, not as an abstract ideal, not as poetic political rhetoric, but as a reality. Many of Muñoz's young Liberal Party followers, joined by pro-independence university professors, lawyers, other professionals, and several Nationalists, took the bill seriously and organized a "United Front for the Constitution of the Republic of Puerto Rico."[10]

The Liberal Party leadership came under great strain. The aging Liberal leader, Antonio Barceló, ill and losing his sight, seemed disoriented. Pulled

---

8. Mathews, *Puerto Rican Politics and the New Deal,* 289.

9. Watkins, *Rightheous Pilgrim: The Life and Times of Harold L. Ickes,* 521.

10. Pagán, *Historia de los partidos políticos puertorriqueños* Vol. II, 78.

by Muñoz and the "independence wing," he approached the Republican and Socialist leaders to form a "united front" to boycott the elections. But then he was pulled in the opposite direction by the "autonomy wing." Convinced that the party was about to be returned to power, it was appalled by Muñoz' "anti-democratic" extremism. At one point Barceló favored Albizu's call for a "constitutional assembly" to unilaterally declare the island independent. But again he reversed himself and opposed it. Finally, Muñoz's demand for a boycott came to a vote among party leaders. There was a tie. Barceló himself cast the decisive vote. He finally made his decision. It was against Muñoz and in favor of the Liberal Party going to the elections.

The Republican Party leadership was just as confused. Rafael Martínez Nadal, the party's president and the island's principal statehood advocate, declared that the Tydings bill was so offensive to Puerto Rican dignity that if the plebiscite were held, he and his party would campaign for independence. Other party leaders, including Speaker of the House Miguel Ángel García Méndez, strongly disagreed. The Socialist Party, meanwhile, issued its own proclamation favoring the "decolonization" of the island, a plebiscite with also the options of statehood and autonomy, but prohibiting any party member from participating in any pro-independence activity.

Puerto Rico was witnessing a dizzying barrage of party conventions, assemblies, meetings –and a seemingly endless procession of *pronunciamientos* from all political leaders. As the idea that "independence is around the corner" took form, groups of students began to lower the American flag from the public schools, raising the Puerto Rican flag instead. At the Central High School in San Juan, the police arrested four students "standing guard" over the island's flag. University of Puerto Rico students carried out a demonstration: Albizu Campos was the principal speaker.

FEAR OF INDEPENDENCE

Ruby Black was worried about Muñoz. She feared that, like Gruening, he may have gone over the edge. On July 8, 1936 she sent him a long letter imploring him to change his mind. His campaign to "stop the elections", she pleaded, was a terrible mistake. It was not understood or accepted by anyone in Washington. Committing political suicide, she pointed out, was not the way to save the independence ideal. She even suspected that Muñoz was now thinking like a Nationalist. It was absurd, she wrote, to think that Puerto Rico could become independent through violence: "Our military and economic force is greater than yours."

Muñoz would not cross the line to join Albizu and the Nationalist "liberation army." Instead he was engaged that summer in a furious attempt to take over the Liberal Party. He organized what Barceló denounced as a "party within a party," the *Acción Social Independentista*.

The now open conflict between Muñoz and Barceló injected a wave of optimism into the Coalition. Martínez Nadal and Santiago Iglesias predicted a sweeping victory. The Union Republican Party leadership had finally come together, its program reiterating the party's historic demand for statehood, but turning to independence if Congress rejected the demand.

Gruening set out to purge the Puerto Rico Reconstruction Administration of Liberals. A "witch hunt," Muñoz called it. Gruening decreed that to favor independence was necessarily "anti-American" and thus unacceptable for employment in a U.S. agency. He queried American residents on the island for evidence of "anti-American activities" among government employees, including university professors and administrators. He sent Interior Department investigators to uncover political infiltration in the PRRA. They indeed found that employees connected to the Liberal Party had installed the old system of a ten to fifteen percent salary kickback among sympathetic PRRA employees.[11] Again Gruening reacted angrily to what he considered another form of betrayal by Muñoz, who had repeatedly assured him and everyone in Washington that he would not allow this to happen.

Earl Parker Hanson witnessed the effect of the purging. He wrote: "a stench of fear arose within the PRRA and smothered all enthusiasm and creative effort. Many employees, whose bread and butter depended on Gruening, were afraid to be seen with Muñoz. If for one reason or another they felt impelled to discuss something with him, they parked their cars blocks from his house and sneaked in the back way... All who stayed...went underground..."[12]

---

11. Hanson, *Transformation: The Story of Modern Puerto Rico*, 162.
12. Ibid., 160.

Hanson worked in the PRRA Planning Division under Chardón and defended the program with "almost religious fervor as one of the greatest rays of light in Puerto Rico's anguished history." He and a team of planners labored for four days preparing a rigorous study to document how a Tydings bill-induced independence would result in "starvation" and "chaos." Gruening, in fact, was well aware of the devastating economic effect of the bill. Privately he had admitted as much to Ickes: "I am convinced that independence for Puerto Rico would be folly and that the Island could not sustain itself either politically or economically. Our withdrawal would spell alternating periods of chaos and dictatorship. I venture this prediction without qualifications..."[13] But Gruening's reaction to the Hanson initiative was to reprimand him for "having dared to meddle in the matter and ordering me in no uncertain terms to collect and burn all copies of the report which might still be in San Juan."[14]

Gruening, in turn, believed that he had forced Muñoz to reveal his true colors: that he was working hard in Washington to convince Ickes and others that his, Gruening's, "persecution" of independentistas was responsible for provoking the violence. Muñoz, he believed, was also actively drumming up support for Albizu and the Nationalists in Latin America. He told Ickes that Muñoz had sent a Liberal Party militant to "attack United States imperialism" at the Pan American Peace Conference: "I pointed out that he was behind the anti-American attacks in Buenos Aires and as part of his policy to achieve Puerto Rican independence and become the first president of Puerto Rico, he was attempting to stir up as much antagonism as possible towards the United States, both in Puerto Rico and other Latin American countries."[15]

The trial in the U.S. District Court of Albizu Campos and seven Nationalist leaders for the Riggs murder, in the summer of 1936, indeed stirred up interest in Latin America as well as in the United States. The lawyers defending Albizu, including Liberal Party followers of Muñoz, argued that it was incongruous for the United States to prosecute Albizu for "sedition" when the American government itself was offering, if not actually pushing,

---

13. Watkins, *Righteous Pilgrim: The Life and Times of Harold L. Ickes*, 521.

14. Gruening, *Many Battles: An Autobiography*, 203.

15. Hanson, *Transformation: The Story of Modern Puerto Rico*, 168.

Puerto Rico towards independence through the Tydings Bill. From the insular House floor, one of Muñoz's closest followers, Representative Ramos Antonini, praised Albizu as a "patriot" and denounced the arrests of the Nationalists.

In Washington, ACLU head Roger Baldwin urged his friend and fellow civil libertarian, Secretary Ickes, not to try the Nationalists for conspiracy to overthrow the U.S. government because it would become a "political trial." Ickes confessed that Baldwin was correct, but his priority was stopping the Nationalist threat: "The life, not merely of government officials, but of peaceable citizens... are at stake," he wrote to Baldwin. "If assassinations cannot be stopped by ordinary legal processes, there will be no alternative but the highly undesirable one of declaring martial law." Distrusting the local courts, Ickes supported Gruening, who insisted that the Nationalists be tried in the federal court.

"The trials," Hanson reported years later, "created a certain amount of public sympathy for the Nationalists, as martyrs and patriotic Puerto Ricans, which they would not have enjoyed as murderers."[16] A mostly Puerto Rican jury refused to convict the Nationalists. A second trial, with ten of the twelve jurors Americans, ended in conviction. In June, 1937, Albizu and Luis Velázquez were sentenced to seven years in the Atlanta Penitentiary.

Muñoz, while not running for office, did campaign for other Liberal candidates. Puerto Rico, he insisted, could still work out with Congress a rational independence bill with an economic transition that guaranteed development and justice. But his campaign was undermined by the old warrior Antonio Barceló, who in typical island political *machismo*, proclaimed Puerto Rico's right to "independence even if we starve to death." Barceló, Muñoz complained, was communicating precisely the message from Gruening's "twisted mind" that "terrorized" island voters.

The Muñoz campaign to keep the independence "ideal" alive was also undermined by renewed Nationalist violence. Whatever popular support Albizu had generated during the "sedition" trial dissipated on October 25, 1936, one week before the elections. At a Coalition Party meeting in Mayagüez, a Nationalist fired five rounds at Santiago Iglesias, founder of the Socialist Party and the island's labor movement. Two bullets ricocheted

---

16. Ibid., 171.

off the microphone, slightly injuring Iglesias in the arm. The other three bullets somehow missed the party leaders surrounding Iglesias on the platform. "Victory [for the Liberal Party] was impossible," Muñoz wrote years later, "and it was made more impossible [by that attack], if there are degrees of impossibility..."

As Muñoz anticipated, the Tydings bill achieved its purpose of sending a tidal wave of fear over Puerto Rico. And as Gruening had anticipated, thousands of Puerto Ricans were terrorized into voting against Muñoz and the Liberal Party. Two weeks before the elections, on September 25, 1936, Muñoz wrote to Ruby Black: "The moment the Tydings bill is presented the Liberal Party has the elections as good as lost...Thus Ernest Gruening, with years of liberalism as his background, is solely responsible through a lunatic quirk in his mind, for having released the greatest reaction that Puerto Rico has even known."[17]

Muñoz Hits Bottom

The Liberal Party lost the elections. It got 252,467 votes, increasing its share from 46 percent in 1932 to 48 percent. The Union Republican-Socialist Coalition got a total of 296,988 votes. The veteran Liberal leadership blamed Muñoz for the defeat. There was now no question in the leaders' minds that if Muñoz had not gone on his "boycott tantrum," if he had not divided and demoralized the liberal vote by creating his own "party within a party," if he and his followers had appeared on the ballot, the Liberal Party would have won. Barceló was more than bitter. Like Gruening, he was wounded by what he considered the "betrayal" of this young man he had helped and supported, and now regretted having pampered and spoiled through the years. If the purpose of "Gruening's revenge," as Muñoz insisted, was to destroy him politically, he seemed to achieve it beyond his hopes. At the age of forty, Muñoz's political career "hit rock bottom." Historian Morales Carrión wrote: "Muñoz, who for a moment has been the great promise, disappears from the urban scene. His star is in deep eclipse, and he is now seen only as

---

17. Mathews, *Puerto Rican Politics and the New Deal,* 289.

a leader of a routed faction, a political Bohemian who had pilfered the treasure of a name and an illustrious tradition."[18]

With Muñoz's political demise, the Puerto Rico Reconstruction Administration virtually collapsed. "Whether among the *jíbaros*, or the sugar laborers, or the politicians, or the businessmen, or the professionals, or the sugar barons," Hanson wrote, "there could be no doubt that ...Muñoz *was* the PRRA."[19] Carlos Chardón and Rafael Fernández García, two of the three authors of the Chardón Plan, resigned. The third, the moderate Republican Labor Commissioner, Rafael Menéndez Ramos, left government. The Education Commissioner that Roosevelt had retained over Governor Gore's objections, José Padín, and who, as interim Governor, had dealt firmly and effectively with the student unrest after the introduction of the Tydings bill, also resigned. There were no winners. Ickes sent one of his assistants, Leona Graham, to the island to evaluate Gruening's performance. She reported that she had never seen "such amazing incompetence."

In her emotional letter to Muñoz back in July, 1936, Ruby Black lamented: "all our plans for Puerto Rico [were] smashed." The promise and exhilaration of bringing the New Deal to Puerto Rico had become a nightmare. Muñoz replied to Black: "And so ends the most glorious, the most fair minded, the most generous, and the most dastardly four years of the American regime in Puerto Rico."

GRUENING'S ASSESSMENT

But Ernest Gruening, who went on to conduct other battles in his long life, including statehood for Alaska as the territory's governor, and early opposition to the Vietnam War as U.S. Senator, never accepted that it was a failure. In his 1973 autobiography, he insisted that the Puerto Rico Reconstruction Administration accomplished a great deal on the island. Hydroelectric plants were constructed as well as dams and reservoirs, forty-five medical dispensaries and two hospitals were built, the University of Puerto Rico

---

18. Ibid., 139.
19. Gruening, *Many Battles: An Autobiography*, 193.

was expanded with eight new buildings, including a new School of Medicine. He cited the special emphasis placed on soil erosion programs; 30,490,000 trees were planted, nurseries were producing twenty million seedlings a year. He described the restoration of coffee and fruit producing lands. Family resettlement programs were established with schools and clinics. A major effort was made to push forward the core land reform program: one sugar mill, Central Lafayette, was acquired, its land divided into 500-acre tracts for the *colonos*. By the end of 1936, PRRA had spent $13 million, it had 3,635 administrative employees, and provided at least temporary work for 52,221 workers. By the end of 1938, the U.S. government had spent $56 million in PRRA programs.[20]

But as with other American efforts in the past, the massive spending in social programs, relief, and fundamental infrastructure hardly made a dent in Puerto Rico's extreme poverty. Puerto Rico's historical dependence on welfare worsened. Before PRRA, in mid-1934, 126,917 families (643,327 people) were receiving U.S. relief funds; by the end of 1938, this was up to 222,606 families, (1,121,938 people). As economists, local and American, had been pointing out for years, the population explosion made the island a "bottomless well" for federal spending.

THE PONCE MASSACRE

In mid-1936 Harold Ickes predicted that "there might be a first class blow-out one of these days in Puerto Rico for which [the President] and I would be held responsible."[21] On March 21, 1937, Palm Sunday, the "blow-out" occurred. The Nationalist Party was denied permission by the Ponce Municipal government to hold one of its "parades" in the town plaza. Governor Winship sent the head of police to Ponce to warn them that if the black-shirt Nationalists were allowed to march, it would provoke another violent confrontation with the police. There were reports that a band of heavily-armed Nationalists had left Mayagüez for Ponce.

---

20. Mathews, *Puerto Rican Politics and the New Deal*, 266.
21. Ibid., 314.

Coalition Party Mayor José Tormos Diego, however, revoked the decision and approved the "civic parade." Rushing back to Ponce, the police chief convinced the Mayor to change his mind. All morning and into the afternoon, Tormos and the colonel attempted to get the Nationalists to suspend the march. They failed.

About 80 Nationalist "cadets" and "Daughters of the Republic," followed by a small contingent of "Nationalist Nurses" dressed in white, lined up for the march. A police captain, backed by about 150 heavily-armed policemen, held up his hand ordering them to stop. But at that moment the Nationalist band began to play the island's then unofficial anthem, *La Borinqueña*. The marchers moved forward. A gun was fired. Instantly there was a barrage of gunfire from the police to the Nationalists and the crowd. When the firing stopped, more than one hundred Nationalist followers, spectators and policemen were wounded, and twenty people were dead, two of them policemen.

The Ponce Massacre was the bloodiest event in Puerto Rican history. The Nationalists marchers themselves were unarmed. The police, backed by the Governor and later Gruening himself, insisted that the initial shot came from the Nationalist Party headquarters behind the marchers.

The American Civil Liberties Union carried out an extensive investigation headed by Arthur Garfield Hays. The famous New York lawyer expressed little sympathy for the "fanaticism and intolerance...the seeds of fascism" among the Nationalists. He felt even less sympathy for its leader, Albizu Campos. In a private letter to Roosevelt he wrote: "Nobody but people with the martyr complex of a lunatic would lead a crowd to face machine guns."

But Hays and the ACLU placed the blame for the tragedy squarely on Winship, condemning him for his "gross violation of civil rights and incredible police brutality." This was a "police riot" where the heavily armed officers panicked at the first gun shot and fired indiscriminately, not only at the Nationalists, but at the men, women, and children in the crowd of spectators. Winship refused to budge. Eleven Nationalists were accused, tried, and all were acquitted.

Albizu and another Nationalist were taken from Puerto Rico on June 6 to the federal penitentiary in Atlanta to serve a seven year sentence for the Riggs murder back in February, 1936. The following day an assassination attempt was made against Cecil Cooper, the federal judge that had sentenced the Nationalist leader. When the news reached Washington, Ickes's investigation of the Ponce Massacre was cancelled. On July 25th, about to speak at the fortieth anniversary of the landing of American troops in Guánica, Winship himself was the target of another Nationalist assassination attempt. The Governor escaped without injury. All possibility of convincing the President to remove Winship had now vanished. Roosevelt was not going to yield to violence. He wrote to Ickes: "I am definitely convinced that the maintenance of Federal authority is the first consideration and that nothing be done until the Island thoroughly understands that Federal authority will be unhesitatingly maintained."[22]

Ickes, however, had finally decided to get Gruening out. But, like Winship, Gruening continued to stonewall his authority. Five months later, he had still not submitted his resignation. In May, after having summoned Winship and Gruening to a stormy meeting at his home, Ickes was rushed to the hospital with a heart attack. From his hospital bed, he angrily barked at one of his assistants: "If Gruening does not send me his resignation as Administrator I shall remove him at once."[23] A month later, on June 16, 1937, Gruening resigned.

A Barrel of Snakes

All of Puerto Rico seemed to go into an emotional tailspin. "The island now suffers days of intense political reaction," Morales Carrión wrote. "Albizu's extremism not only prejudices the evolution of the independence thesis, but also confuses and disperses the groups devoted to economic and social reforms. Without the energetic popular support which Muñoz had aroused in the beginning, federal aid degenerated into bureaucratic activity with sparse results. Psychological fatigue, disillusionment, and disorientation spread in the urban areas."[24]

---

22. Watkins, *Righteous Pilgrim: The Life and Times of Harold L. Ickes*, 526.

23. Ibid., 526.

24. Hanson, *Transformation: The Story of Modern Puerto Rico*, 171.

The fatigue and disillusionment gripped also those in Washington that most wanted to help Puerto Rico. Ruby Black, in a 1940 biography of Eleanor Roosevelt, wrote: "Increasingly frustrated, her ambitious plans snarled by petty politics in Puerto Rico, incompetent administrators and congressional opposition, the First Lady began to withdraw. It became less and less possible for Mrs. Roosevelt, 1,800 miles away, to untangle the truth from the lies, the just from the unjust, the right from the wrong."[25]

Secretary Ickes's attitude went beyond frustration. Seeing his worst premonitions come true in the relentless Puerto Rican crisis undoubtedly had contributed to his physical breakdown. When Rexford Tugwell approached him on a Puerto Rican matter, he found Ickes "as near to numbness as his nature would permit. It was not that he did not care what happened to Puerto Rico: he knew that, uneducated and exploited as the masses were, they could hardly be held responsible. But he had just about given up the struggle to do something for them... he regarded the island as a barrel of snakes for which no one could do much, and from which no one could get nothing in return for honest effort but recrimination, political bluster and personal attack."[26]

"In Puerto Rico," wrote Ickes biographer T. H. Watkins, "the Roosevelt years began badly and continued badly...an amalgam whose misery, complexity, and passion...would snarl the New Dealers in a tangle of frustration...nearly seven years of incomparably inept and strife-riddled attempts at reconstruction...invested with the character of a kind of grisly joke."[27]

ANTONIO BARCELÓ

Had Muñoz, who 26 years earlier proclaimed at his father's grave site, "I want to be a giant to finish the work of Muñoz Rivera," also betrayed the legacy of his father? Nothing dramatized Muñoz's personal drama as acutely

25. Black, *Eleanor Roosevelt: A Biography*, 297.

26. Tugwell, *The Stricken Land*, 8.

27. Watkins, *Righteous Pilgrim: The Life and Times of Harold L. Ickes*, 515, 528.

as his now embittered confrontation with the man who, since 1916, embodied his father's legacy. Antonio Barceló had joined Muñoz Rivera in 1899 to create the Federal Party and the origin of the Union and then Liberal parties that were to dominate insular politics into the 1930s. A member of the Legislature since 1906, Barceló was selected by Muñoz Rivera in 1913 to serve as party president. Four years later, after Muñoz Rivera's death, Barceló became the first president of the new insular Senate, for the next 23 years holding this paramount position of Puerto Rican political leadership.

The 68-year-old Barceló was now convinced that he had allowed his emotions, his loyalty to Muñoz Rivera, to overwhelm his judgment. He felt that he had permitted the son to take the party into political blind alleys with his recklessness, immaturity and arrogance. Muñoz, he believed, had a "destructive streak" in him that finally took him over the edge, dragging down the party with him. He blamed Muñoz for wrecking the party's relationship to the President, Secretary Ickes, and Congress. All Puerto Ricans, Barceló decried, must now pay the price for Muñoz's "personal punitive war" against Ernest Gruening. It was his thirst for "vengeance against Dr. Gruening" that drove him to demand that the Liberal Party commit political suicide by boycotting the election. Muñoz had only himself to blame for having crushed Puerto Rico's great hope for economic reconstruction.

Muñoz set out to prove that Barceló was wrong and that he was right. Days after the elections, he drafted a bill that would give Puerto Rico independence with generous economic conditions. He returned to Washington and got Representative Wilbur Cartwright to introduce it. Muñoz knew that, like the Tydings bill, it would not be approved, but he insisted that it had "educational value."

The bill, in Muñoz's eyes, unmasked Barceló's hypocrisy. Muñoz escalated his attack against the Liberal leader in the pages of La Democracia. The man who had cried out "independence even if we starve to death" was now opposed to a bill drafted precisely to guarantee that an independent Puerto Rico would continue to eat. Muñoz even saw in the old leader a tendency to cozy up to the despised Governor Winship—the "culprit" of the Ponce Massacre. Who was "betraying" whom?

Barceló had had enough of the "prodigal son." In a long "manifesto" directed at all the Liberal leaders, published on May 3, 1937, he openly accused Muñoz of having become a disciple of the Nationalist Party leader. His extremist campaign, Barceló said, was "imbued with the spirit of Puerto Rican nationalism...learned from the radical lips of Pedro Albizu Campos."[28] It was Muñoz himself, not Gruening that had planted fear in the hearts of Liberal voters and economic supporters with his ideas of "radical and demagogic socialism."

Reading Barceló's "manifesto," Muñoz felt that at the heart of Barceló's bitterness was something deeper than politics or status ideology. He replied that he "seemed to be hearing the voice of hatred, spiteful of the blood that Muñoz Rivera bequest to Puerto Rico in his son."[29] Muñoz went on: "I, Luis Muñoz Marín, do not hate Antonio Barceló. I am, whatever his attitude towards me, willing, to the best of my ability, to give Antonio Barceló all that he wants—honors, respect, positions, glory—all that he wants, but not the surrendering of the ideal and the division of our party."

Muñoz then made his most definitive statement as to his attitude, his relation to Albizu, and the Nationalist Party:

> Without offending the memory of George Washington, I should affirm once more that I reject violence as a political instrument in Puerto Rico. I reject it because I know that the American people would be incapable of denying Puerto Rico its independence if they knew that the majority of Puerto Ricans peacefully and in friendship desire it. I reject it because I know that once American public opinion acts over Puerto Rico, there is no liberal American government that will have interest in denying Puerto Rico its independence. And I reject it finally—and I have repeated these words on numerous occasions—because the use of political violence is the gravest harm that can be done to the success of independence...[30]

Three weeks later, at a meeting of carefully selected party leaders, Muñoz and his followers were expelled from the Liberal Party. Before walking out of the assembly, Muñoz brazenly declared: "You believe that you have expelled

28. Bothwell, *Puerto Rico: cien años de lucha política* Vol. III, 109.

29. Ibid., 122.

30. Ibid., 128.

us. But what you have done is expel the Liberal Party from the governing board. You have expelled the Liberal people from the Liberal Party." To reporters, he commented: "What has occurred here is the Massacre of the Liberal Party..."[31]

On July 27th, Muñoz met with delegates from 50 local party committees. A new entity that Muñoz called the "Authentic Liberal Party" was formed. At the same time, Muñoz and his family "rescued" his father's newspaper, *La Democracia*, taking it away from Barceló's control.

Ill and depressed, Barceló wrote again to Muñoz, who had just made one last highly publicized attempt to take over the party. Muñoz sent Barceló a letter demanding that he turn over "to the legitimate owners, the name, insignia, [and] all the rights of the Liberal Party." It was an unnecessary gesture since Muñoz had already effectively constituted his own party.

Barceló's reply, this time not in anger or "hatred" but with the pain of a heartbroken father: "You tried to destroy what you did not create... Give your own party the seed of your vagabond imagination, your unshakable loyalty, your steadfast devotion, your total sacrifice... Don't destroy it some day to see what is inside... Don't destroy the faith and morale of its soldiers in the decisive moment of the battle. Don't deliver it lifeless to the adversary, tied-up, at the last moment, in the net of an absurd and unexpected 'electoral boycott'... On the contrary, build it on the example of your father, Luis Muñoz Rivera, whom you never understood..."[32]

Barceló's indictment could not have been more devastating: that Luis Muñoz Marín had indeed betrayed the legacy of his father.

Three months later, on October 15, 1938, Barceló died. He had been in many ways an extension of Muñoz Rivera. He possessed the gift of eloquence, the ability to move crowds with words. He was undoubtedly the core of the Liberal Party's political dominance for two and half decades. Like Muñoz Rivera, he was scrupulously honest. But for Muñoz and his followers, he had been the master of the "old politics" of patronage and pronouncements without content, conviction, or consistency. During the crucial battles against Gruening in Washington, Muñoz wrote, Barceló "was in Puerto Rico, declaring himself frequently in favor, against, in favor, against, in favor,

---

31. Ibid., 132
32. Muñoz Marín, Memorias I, 170.

against, in favor of the revolution, of the boycott, of whatever there is in the Lord's Garden."[33]

No wonder the *jíbaro* sold his vote for two dollars every four years, convinced that it was worthless. Antonio Barceló had always played the game of island politics with good intentions and personal integrity, but to Muñoz, it was a game divorced from the horrible economic and social reality of the *jíbaro*'s day-to-day existence.

On July 22, 1938, Muñoz and a handful of followers began the inscription process of a new political party. This would, of course, doom his father's party in the eyes of many. For the unforgiving followers of Barceló, Muñoz had finally achieved his selfish ambition, "the title of party president." For Muñoz, he had finally liberated his father's legacy from the clutches of those that used it for the sterile politics of superficiality. On July 17, 1938, speaking before his father's tomb in Barranquitas at the anniversary of his birth, Muñoz vowed: "We are going to throw out the merchants of your name from the temple of your tomb!"[34]

Winship continued to baffle Muñoz. Defying everyone's expectations, he survived the wrath of Muñoz, Gruening, and Ickes, remaining as Governor until August 31, 1939. The following day, Hitler invaded Poland, plunging the world into another World War. Roosevelt replaced Winship with another military officer, the Naval Chief of Operations, Admiral William Leahy. Puerto Rico was again the "Caribbean Malta"—the strategically vital gateway to the Caribbean, the Gulf of Mexico and the Panama Canal. As Muñoz organized his new party in Puerto Rico, in Washington the spirit of Captain Alfred Thayer Mahan replaced the spirit of the New Deal.

---

33. Bothwell, Puerto Rico: cien años de lucha política, Vol. III, 126.
34. Muñoz Marín, Memorias I, 171.

12 The Beautiful Young Teacher

A beautiful young teacher entered Muñoz's life in 1938. Muñoz's cousin, Clara Lair, the poet, had a premonition. "There is a dangerous woman to see you," she warned Muñoz at his office in *La Democracia*. Lair was referring to Inés Mendoza's image as a fiery, 29-year-old "Nationalist school teacher" who had created a storm of controversy over the emotional issue of using English as the language of instruction in public schools. But she was dangerous for Muñoz in another way: her pitch black hair, ivory skin, large black eyes, slim body, combined with her notoriety, made her an exceptionally attractive woman. She walked into Muñoz's office and changed his life forever.

Dismissed from teaching for her campaign in favor of Spanish, Mendoza had appealed directly to Eleanor Roosevelt, who passed a note to the President. But the mood in the White House was unsympathetic. "The letter my mother received from Eleanor Roosevelt," her daughter Victoria recalled years later, "was a disappointment to her and all the Puerto Ricans who saw her as their liberal saint. In effect she answered that if Puerto Ricans want schools in Spanish, they might just as well ask for independence."[1]

The political violence in Puerto Rico had produced another backlash in Washington: a return to the idea that Puerto Rican children should be "Americanized." Roosevelt appointed Education Commissioner José Gallardo, who back in the early 1930s had been Governor Gore's candidate for the job, with specific instructions to intensify the teaching of English. On April 17,

---

1. Victoria Muñoz interview, 3-4-97.

1937, three weeks after the Ponce Massacre, Roosevelt sent a letter to Gallardo, drafted by Gruening, decrying that after 38 years under the U.S. flag and 20 years after being made American citizens, "hundreds of thousands" of Puerto Ricans could not read or write English. Roosevelt gave Gallardo specific instructions that it was "an indispensable part of American policy that the coming generation of American citizens of Puerto Rico grow up with complete facility in the English language. It is the language of our nation."[2]

The pro-American Coalition Party, flush from their 1936 election victory, spurred Gallardo to remove from the schoolrooms *independentistas* that opposed the English policy. Inés Mendoza, a popular Spanish teacher in Central High School in San Juan, had campaigned for Albizu Campos and the Nationalist Party in the 1932 elections. Accepting an invitation to testify before the Arthur Garfield Hays Commission investigating the Ponce Massacre, Mendoza denounced the revival of the old policy. Soon after, her teaching contract was rescinded "for the good of the service." American Civil Liberties Union head Roger Baldwin and Hays bombarded Interior Secretary Ickes, decrying this "gross violation" of Mendoza's civil rights. Ickes, like the President and Eleanor, sided against her. Joining the battle in Mendoza's behalf was Muñoz's wife Muna Lee, who commented to her: "You must meet my husband Luis."[3]

When she walked into Muñoz's office, Mendoza had broken with Albizu Campos and the Nationalist Party. Like many other *independentistas*, she found his call for violence repellent. While studying in New York in 1931 she married the artist, and later successful cartographer, Rafael Palacios. They had two children, Carmen and Rafael. Himself an ardent *independentista*, Palacios was particularly adamant in breaking her away from Albizu's influence. The break occurred when she heard Albizu comment to his wife, Laura, that it was necessary "to kill Americans." "My mother's reaction," her daughter Victoria said, "was more than opposition or even disgust. She was revolted by the idea of killing—of killing children."[4]

She was jobless and blacklisted from teaching. Her husband, Palacios, had left for New York to find employment. Other disenchanted Nationalists

2. Bothwell, *Puerto Rico: cien años de lucha política*, III, 40.
3. Luz Benítez interview, 3-21-97.
4. Victoria Muñoz interview, 3-4-97.

were gravitating to Muñoz's new *independentista* party. She turned to the publisher of *La Democracia* not only looking for a job, but to join this crusade for the island's "freedom."

Clara Lair's premonition proved right. Not long after her visit, Mendoza's friends began to sense that there would be "trouble" between these two, both married, both with children, both very much in the spotlight. "Have you noticed that man," her friend, Luz "Lulú" Benítez, asked provokingly. "That's not a question," Mendoza answered, "that's a statement." Muñoz was a striking presence: his large, dark eyes clearly feasting on beautiful women that seemed always to be within his visual range. *El Vate* had the reputation of being a Don Juan: his *machismo* essential to his image as a political leader. "She was a woman who took herself seriously," her daughter Carmen Palacios commented, "and men respected her. She was a devout Catholic and proper in every sense. But like our grandmother always told us, she was always flirtatious. She knew that she was, for men, a magnet."

To avoid the "trouble" that her friends feared, they urged her to join her husband and children in New York. But it was too late. Muñoz had fallen deeply in love with her. He was taken in by the intensity of her ideas and convictions, her intelligence and fine poetic sense. "For many years," Benítez said years later, "Inés was accused of breaking up Muñoz's marriage. It was already broken. It was Muñoz that broke Inés's marriage. She and Rafael Palacios had a good marriage. They got along very well. But Muñoz was simply crazy about her."[5]

Inés María Mendoza Rivera was born on January 10, 1908 in Yabucoa, a small town on the east coast. Unlike Muñoz, she had been a good student with a purpose in life: she never doubted that she had been born with the vocation to teach. Her father was illiterate but had worked himself into economic security. He owned a large house at the town's plaza and a large tract of land that produced sugar cane for the giant Fajardo Sugar Company. Inés was a spirited girl with strong opinions. One day she and one of her brothers hoisted a Puerto Rican flag over their house when this was considered by conservatives a gesture of Nationalist sympathy. Her mother, a staunch Liberal, quickly brought the flag down.

---

5. Luz Benítez interview, 3-21-97.

At the age of eight, her father died. To help support her mother, Jesusa Rivera, and brothers, Inés earned money sewing designs on tablecloth and bed sheets as she went to public schools in Yabucoa, Naguabo, and Humacao. By the age of seventeen she had earned her certificate and was teaching in rural schools. In 1927, the 21-year-old Inés graduated from the University of Puerto Rico, Magna Cum Laude, winning the first Carlota Matienzo Award for academic excellence. She was a student leader, president of her class and member of the Girl Scouts board of directors. She then returned to a rural classroom where she taught for the next three years. She recalled years later that the first day was spent cleaning out the nests of bats from the classroom and washing the heads of student girls with skin infections.

Still the rebel, she dismayed her family when, without informing them, she married Palacios in New York, where she was earning a degree at Columbia University's Teachers College. Back at the University of Puerto Rico, she became a disciple of the Nobel laureate Chilean poet, Gabriela Mistral. During her graduate studies, Mistral urged her to dedicate herself to Spanish literature and develop her sensitive, poetic writing style. But Mendoza was convinced that she was indeed "born to teach" and again returned to the classroom, this time at the Catholic Academy in Old San Juan. Soon afterwards, she was named public school principal. She then worked at the Model School of the University of Puerto Rico, and finally at the Central High School in San Juan.

By late 1938, Inés Mendoza was Muñoz's constant companion in the campaign to organize his new party. Rafael Palacios, still in New York with their two children, granted her a divorce. But she was determined not to be "Luis Muñoz Marín's woman." As long as it was kept discreetly quiet, it was accepted for island political leaders, and whoever else that could afford it, to have lovers. His father, Muñoz Rivera, had two daughters out of wedlock. Muna Lee had attempted to hold their marriage together by not infringing on Muñoz's freedom to come and go as he pleased. One often-told story had it that Muñoz said to her one evening, "I'm going out to buy cigarettes; be back in a few minutes," and did not return for three months. But for Muna what mattered was that he returned. Muna was certain that Muñoz would again return, that the beautiful "Nationalist school teacher" was another temporary infatuation.

Inés, a proud woman with deep religious convictions, pressured Muñoz to somehow convince his wife to grant him a divorce. She resented what seemed to be his reluctance. Muñoz acted as if he felt remorse for his treatment of Muna, a woman who had surrendered her life totally to his during his long years "in the desert" without a job, an income, a vocation, even, it seemed, a purpose in life. The marriage, of course, was long broken but Muñoz knew that asking her for a divorce would shatter her. When Muñoz finally did bring it up, he was not surprised by her refusal, but by the harshness of her reaction. She would grant it only on the grounds of adultery. Muñoz attempted to convince Inés to accept what seemed all too obvious: a hostile break-up would break the code of silence that had so far protected them in their relationship. Everyone, of course, knew that they were living together, and by 1939, Inés was pregnant with their first daughter. But not a word of this had appeared in print. For Muñoz's enemies, and as Muñoz would learn, for the hierarchy of the Catholic Church, this was another manifestation of a man without values, political, ideological, or moral. Muñoz pleaded with Inés to give Muna time to come around, not to risk the political damage of forcing the issue.

But Inés was insistent, at times thinking that perhaps Muna was right, that Muñoz had no intention of getting the divorce. Muñoz's fear was that she would carry out her frequent threats to leave him. After one of their many arguments, she did break up with him, joining Palacios and their children in New York. Through a torrent of letters, Muñoz convinced her to return. But she was as adamant as ever. They were both also under great pressure from their families. Muñoz's mother, Doña Maló, just as head-strong a woman as Inés, campaigned for her son to return to Muna. Inés's mother, Doña Jesusa, a devout Catholic, applied her own pressure. On one occasion when Muñoz accompanied Inés to her mother's home, she asked him to lower his head in the car so that she would not see him. Muñoz never forgot. A decade later, when Muñoz was Governor of Puerto Rico, he and Inés were rushing back to La Fortaleza during a Nationalist uprising. As their car entered the narrow streets of Old San Juan, fearing an assassination attempt, she again ordered him to lower his head. He shot back: "I did [that] once for Doña Jesusa, but not for Albizu Campos!"[6]

---

6. Muñoz Marín, *Memorias*, Vol. II, 237.

At this time, it seemed to many of Muñoz and Inés's friends that as ardent as the passion between them, there was simply too much going against them. It would take a miracle, they believed, for the relationship to survive.

"A big part of the bond that kept them together through this very difficult period and throughout their lives," their daughter Victoria said, "was that they complemented each other in different ways. They not only shared fundamental political and ideological convictions, but they had much in common beyond politics. They loved having poets and good writers around."[7] In other ways they were opposites, but their differences, she added, also helped to cement the bond. He had been the undisciplined son of a great political leader, a bad student, a heavy drinker, bilingual, bicultural, the product of New York and Washington as much as San Juan. She was the product of a small town, the daughter of a successful but illiterate farmer and of a traditional Catholic upbringing: she was disciplined, well-organized, had been a dedicated, successful student: she was a teetotaler.

And, Victoria said, she was never cowed by him. "My mother," Victoria said, "never feared my father, in the sense of being afraid to tell him exactly what was in her mind and heart. She gave her life to him, but never surrendered herself. She was always her own person. Her relation to him was one of collaboration. She joined him, but at the same time, she was very demanding. I know that my sister and I, as we grew up, feared her more than our father. And I think he too feared her."[8]

If the survival of their relationship surprised their friends, even more so was how Inés Mendoza, in the language of the *jíbaros*, "*enderezó*"— straightened out—Muñoz's life. As Muñoz immersed himself physically and emotionally into the *jíbaro* culture, now he was accompanied by a woman who clearly has *la mancha de plátano*—"the stain of the plantain" in her looks, her speech, the way she moved. She was undeniably Puerto Rican. Just having her by his side illustrated that Muñoz had indeed returned to his cultural roots. His personal life for the first time had a core that gave it stability. Inés was not going to make the same mistake as Muna: she was as strong as Muna had been pliant. She would keep Muñoz on a short leash. "My mother knew that she could not give my father an inch, because he would take a mile," said Victoria.

---

7. Victoria Muñoz interview, 3-4-97.
8. Ibid.

The discipline she imposed on his lifestyle and personal habits was vital for him to accomplish his mission. He was acutely aware that the grueling one-on-one campaign depended on his keeping his health. She saw to it that he did. She took along additional clothing, making certain that he changed his shirts, wet with rain or perspiration. She fed him a steady diet of "proteins" believing that it "protected his liver" from his drinking. To everyone's amazement, Muñoz reduced his drinking. Her harping against his chain smoking, however, was not to succeed for another decade, when his doctor, Roberto Busó, flatly assured her that Muñoz would not survive another five years unless he stopped. Muñoz never again touched a cigarette.

Their temporary home up in the Ellsworth farm in Cidra became a madhouse of visiting political leaders, *jíbaro* followers, reporters, and the always present procession of writers and poet friends. She imposed a degree of structure and order without restricting Muñoz's demand that the home serve as his movement's *batey*—the open, rural "town hall" where his "democratic revolution" was gestating. Even though they were always short of money, she managed to provide food and drinks for the guests. She helped control and organize the haphazard logistics of the campaign, attending to Muñoz's constant need for messengers and drivers.

She was his gatekeeper when Muñoz wanted to be alone to concentrate on writing a speech, statement or newspaper article. As gregarious as he was, a person who needed and thrived on human contact, Muñoz also valued periods of silence and solitude. He was a painstakingly slow reader and writer. He drove the typists crazy with his layers and layers of corrections, at times confusing them as they turned the pages around, sideways, upside down trying to follow his scribbled lines. Muñoz was obsessive in seeking always the exact word.

"Gandul"—the pigeon pea, a stable in the Puerto Rican diet—was a word she used often with him. One afternoon, pointing at a *jíbaro* walking down the road, Muñoz commented to her: "He doesn't know it yet, but he expects something out of me." Muñoz, she said, you know a lot about Washington and how to get things done in Congress. But never forget: you must "return to the *gandul*": You must return to your roots. Muñoz felt strongly that he had and didn't need anyone to remind him. "My father was more open to ideas and arguments than she was," Victoria said. "He loved to listen to everyone, to different ideas, and he loved to absorb. So I think that was why she was so persistent in keeping him focused on that *gandul*—on that *jíbaro* that had placed his hopes on him. In that sense, she was a critical influence on him."[9]

The tensions and frustrations of the 1940 campaign, to everyone's surprise, brought Muñoz and Inés even closer. The verbal conflicts between them continued, but Inés found herself increasingly drawn into what both saw as an essentially "educational crusade." Inés turned an old barn at the Ellsworth farm into a classroom and the word went out to the *jíbaros* in the area that she would give lessons every night. "First we talked about Cidra," she recalled years later, "about its land, its history, then about the rest of our country and then about the rest of the world. Some of them took notes and some read as they learned." She recalled that Muñoz, when he returned early from campaigning, as exhausted as he was, would join her in the classroom: "How beautiful and pure all that was! How simple, how easy!" One night, she turned to Muñoz: "If we lose, we must continue to teach. I know something, and you can help me."

"Aside from their personal relationship, my mother was one of the hundreds, then thousands, of young, talented men and women that joined my father in that period," said Victoria Muñoz, "because they felt intuitively that this was a unique, a once-in-a-lifetime opportunity to make history. My mother felt that very strongly and wanted to be part of it, and she found herself right in the very center of it."

Six years later, in 1946, Mendoza sent a letter to her friend Luz Benítez, wife of the Chancellor of the University of Puerto Rico, Jaime Benítez, with important news: *"el peninsular se casó"*—the "Peninsular finally got married." This was a joke between them as girls growing in the small town of Yabucoa, when a young woman in old Puerto Rico grew desperate waiting for her handsome Spanish fiancé, *el peninsular*, to finally make up his mind to marry. The "American Peninsular," Muñoz, got his divorce from Muna, decreed following a ten-year separation. The following day they were quietly married by Judge Emilio Belaval.

Inés's friend, Benítez, had learned of a small, concrete house with several acres of lush vegetation on the road to Trujillo Alto, a small town several miles southeast of San Juan, available for rental at $46 a month. Muñoz

---

9. Ibid.

and Inés and their two daughters, Viviana and Victoria, moved to what was to remain their home for the rest of their lives. Muñoz had become a "family man." The "dangerous" woman had transformed him as much as he was determined to transform Puerto Rico.

Muñoz wrote toward the end of his life: "In a sense that goes beyond the juridical, but deep and good in the human and spiritual sense, my marriage with Inés began in 1938... I imposed myself upon her spirit to change the course of her life."[10] "The truth is," she confessed, "that the heart takes one where one never thought of going."

---

10. Muñoz Marín, *Memorias* Vol. I, 184.

PART III

The Road to Reality
1941-1952

"An important part of what we Puerto Ricans believe is that freedom has to be understood more through the observations of reality than by the mere reading of political and legal documents."

Muñoz Marín
1949

13   The *Jíbaro* Campaign

O n July 22, 1938, the Popular Democratic Party was born in
Barranquitas, where Muñoz Rivera was born and buried, and in
Luquillo, the coastal municipality east of San Juan known for its beaches
and a rain forest located on one of the highest peaks in Puerto Rico, *El
Yunque.* Absolute secrecy in registering the name and emblem was essential
since island parties sometimes stole the names and symbols of new parties
by rushing to register them beforehand.

Muñoz wrote to Ruby Black on August 11, 1939 that his was the first
party in island history to organize committees in all 786 rural *barrios*
throughout the island. And it was carrying out a radically different campaign.
The reason he had to stop drinking was that he had set for himself the goal
of talking "face-to-face" to all 700,000 Puerto Ricans expected to vote in the
November 5, 1940 elections. There would be only a few mass assemblies
and rallies. Instead he would talk to small clusters of people, on a road
under a tree, in a home or *colmado*, anywhere he could get them together
for an hour or so to listen to him.

He was already talking to an average of 30,000 to 40,000 men and
women a month, he informed Black, and it all depended obviously "on my
health holding up...No other leader has done, or can do this." His message
was simple and direct: "We will not pay a cent for your vote and we will not
accept a single cent from the economic interests."[1] Muñoz expressed his
confidence that this new message would lead his Popular Democratic Party
to power.

---

1. Bothwell, *Puerto Rico: cien años de lucha política*, Vol. III, 207.

Muñoz's strategy and optimism seemed outrageously unreal. To convince the *jíbaro* not to sell his vote Muñoz had to break the tradition of strong and deep party loyalty. For the *jíbaros*, Muñoz wrote years later, "their party was like their nation, more than Puerto Rico. They belonged to it. To abandon the party made them feel like deserters. And that was something that a man did not do—without profound motive."[2] The only "profound motive" Muñoz could offer was his plea to "trust me." Trust that a vote for him would make a difference in their lives.

Absorbing the attitudes and emotions of the *jíbaro*, he realized that he had to convince them that these elections were not about the island's status. That was the "old politics" that made the elections futile: the leaders engaged in "patriotic" status rhetoric while the people continued to suffer all too real economic and social deprivation. The island's status, Muñoz insisted, would be decided in a future plebiscite totally removed from these elections. "Our principal concern is democracy," he wrote to Black. "And that means that the People of Puerto Rico itself, not the Popular Democratic Party, will have to decide with their own votes what they want as their final political status... these elections will be fought on the basis of democracy and exploitation."[3]

A Few Clear Words

Muñoz never forgot an experience from his first political campaign in 1920. He was scheduled to give a campaign speech in the central mountain town of Utuado. The people there had never heard him speak before and he decided to mimic a typical political orator, a *pico de oro*—a golden throat. It was, as he described it years later, a "crescendo of nonsense" describing the "dantesque illumination of twilight," comparing the hills of Utuado to the "peaks of the Himalayas," and paying homage to "the beauty of Puerto Rican women." He ended by raising his voice even more to describe his vision of "colorful flags descending from the clouds in the dawn between the sun and the moon..."

---

2. Muñoz Marín, *Memorias* Vol. II, 174.

3. Bothwell, *Puerto Rico: cien años de lucha política* Vol. III, 208.

The *jíbaros* in front of him broke out in wild applause. "When it died down," Muñoz wrote, "I began to speak again, this time in my normal voice, asking them: 'Why did you applaud?' Absolute silence. 'Why did you applaud if what I just said to you was nonsense?' What you need is not nonsense that sounds good. I see many feet without shoes: I suspect many stomachs with not much food other than bread and dark coffee: I see children with pieces of cloth scarcely covering their bodies; in all these hills I see shacks made of straw with the earth as the floor; I know of the miserable salaries when there is work and of the many days when there isn't. I have talked to you about none of this: but it is in relieving these ills that you should have your thoughts and your will..."[4]

There was another outburst of applause. "The wisdom of the *jíbaro* was stirred... I began to become aware [that]a few clear words, spoken with transparent good faith, moved them from unthinking to feeling, from not knowing to understanding... People with more, although insufficient, education tend to put up defenses for their prejudices: the *jíbaro* does not have a vested interest of an ideological nature, and does not reject learning more as automatically as do other cultural groups."

In spite of Muñoz's enormous personal effort, the inscription of the new party was not going well. By February of 1939, eight months after he had begun in Barranquitas and Luquillo, the party was registered in only twenty-three of the seventy-six municipalities. It was a laborious, tedious task that required having a local judge certify, one by one, each petition, a task easy to stall by unsympathetic judges.

Muñoz decided to hold a leadership meeting every Monday, the day of the week he was not campaigning, up in the beautiful, rustic hotel, Treasure Island, owned by his friend and fellow *independentista*, Elmer Ellsworth. Muñoz asked Jesús Piñero, the head of the Sugar Cane Farmers Association, to take charge and accelerate the inscription.

Those weekly meetings, to Muñoz's amusement, contributed to the impression that his new party was going nowhere. Visitors to Treasure Island spotted Muñoz there, sitting under a tree, smoking a cigarette, "doing nothing." The word got around that *El Vate* had again lost interest in his latest venture. One afternoon at the hotel, overhearing someone comment:

---

4. Muñoz Marín, *Memorias* Vol. I, 52.

"There is Muñoz Marín, doing nothing," an idea came to him. Why not put out a *jíbaro* newspaper, written in simple language so that no *jíbaro* on the island could fail to understand his message. He would call it *El Batey*, a rural meeting place.

There was a problem: "There was not a single cent for the publication of this newspaper".[5] Yet he decided to print 100,000 copies in the old printing press of *La Democracia*. He got a friend to donate $100 for the first issue to come out in March, 1939. He would publish it every two weeks, he hoped, by selling advertisement. Personally, "door to door," for fifteen, ten or five dollars.

El Batey

El Batey became Muñoz' vehicle for "clear words." In an April, 1939 issue, he asked:

> What is the vote? The vote is the only weapon that you have to defend yourself from exploitation. The vote is the only weapon you have to make a government that is yours and of men like yourself that need bread, land, justice and freedom. It is the only weapon that you have to make a government that is not of the big corporations that take millions from the misery of your family and the hunger of your children.
>
> If you were being watched by a bandit that wants to take your house and plow. And if you were given a weapon to defend yourself. Would you sell that weapon to the bandit for a few coins? Or would you use it to stop the bandit from taking your house and plow? If you are a man you will use that weapon to defend your home and your plow.[6]

On the road to Ponce, accompanied by local leader Andrés Grillasca, Muñoz saw a *jíbaro* walking alone. They slowed down the car, and Grillasca shouted:

---

5. Muñoz Marín, *La historia del Partido Popular Democrático*, 93.
6. Muñoz Marín, *Memorias* Vol. I, 261.

"Do you get Muñoz Marín's *El Batey?*" "El what?" he shouted back. "Never heard of it." "That's the newspaper of Muñoz Marín," Grillasca said, "this man here seated next to me." "Oh," shouted the *jíbaro*, with a quizzical look on his face, reaching into his sweat-stained shirt to pull out a carefully folded copy of *El Batey*. Then, with a smile, he asked: "Who knows if it's this newspaper I have here?"[7]

As a tool of "democratic training," Muñoz wrote to Black, *El Batey* proved more effective than "forty years" of university training: it was the "first bridge" that linked the "two cultures in Puerto Rico." By election day he would have distributed six million copies. It became Muñoz's principal campaign weapon, one that the opposition party could not match despite its huge advantage in funds and patronage. "I feel a very special pride regarding *El Batey*," Muñoz wrote towards the end of his life.[8]

By late 1939, the inscription was going so well that Muñoz predicted 345,000 for his Popular Democratic Party. Fate seemed to be turning in his favor.

The sudden death of Socialist Party founder Santiago Iglesias on December 5, 1939, set off another intense round of political negotiations between the traditional parties. The 69-year old leader had contracted malaria attending a labor meeting in Mexico City and died in Washington where he had served as Puerto Rico's resident commissioner since 1933. With both Iglesias and Antonio Barceló gone, their parties set out to form new coalitions to secure victory in 1940. This played directly into Muñoz's hands. His Popular Democratic Party, he vowed, would never join a coalition. He also benefited from the turn of the new Liberal leadership towards statehood, driving more local party leaders, many of them experienced vote-getters, into the Muñoz camp.

In the jockeying for new "winning combinations," a new party emerged from three splintered groups. José Ramírez Santibáñez, a 43-year-old lawyer who replaced Barceló as Liberal Party President, united with the Speaker of the House, Miguel A. García Méndez, who had split from the Republican Party, and Prudencio Rivera Martinez, a veteran labor leader who broke off from the Socialist Party. They formed "The Puerto Rican Triparty

---

7. Ibid., 177.
8. Muñoz Marín, *La historia del Partido Popular Democrático*, 93.

Unification"—"*El Tripartismo.*" Muñoz attacked this new group as the quintessential "*mogolla*"—the "stew" of the old politics where program and ideology are ignored. But in fact, this new group with the awkward name, the "Triparty," was to play a decisive role in the 1940 elections and in the following years.

Muñoz's growing optimism was further buoyed by an unexpected development. He had reacted skeptically to President Roosevelt's decision to replace Governor Winship with another veteran military officer. But to his relief, Admiral William D. Leahy quickly established his impartiality. On January 8, 1940, Muñoz wrote to Ruby Black: "Let me tell you something about Governor Leahy. I believe that this has been by far the best Governor sent to Puerto Rico since the beginning of the American regime here."[9] Leahy's fairness, he wrote, and his "evident skills are having a clear effect on public morale and are restoring confidence in the government."

Leahy's trust in Muñoz proved crucial. Several weeks before the elections, Muñoz went to see him with an important request. He wanted all Puerto Rican voters to know that the Governor and his administration were determined to prevent not only the buying of votes, but the old practice of inducing *jíbaros* known to favor the opposition, to drink rum and have a feast at special "parties" during the voting hours. For Muñoz, nothing better dramatized the "dehumanization" of the *jíbaro*, reducing him to the level of "beast." In many rural areas, these "parties" were held in corrals that were closed to guarantee that none of the *jíbaros* would leave to vote.

Muñoz suggested that the Governor issue an executive order with specific instructions to the police to act rapidly after receiving reports of vote-buying or the "corralling" of voters. Leahy asked Muñoz to draft the order. To implement it, the Governor established direct telephone communication between police headquarters and the central offices of all the parties, including the Popular Democratic Party. Muñoz got twenty telephones installed at his office at *La Democracia.* Now the problem was finding party workers that could be spared to answer the phones. He recruited a group of Spanish "Republican" exiles that had fled from the Spanish Civil War, most of them teaching at the University and strongly supporting Muñoz and his new party.

---

9. Bothwell, *Puerto Rico: cien años de lucha política*, Vol. III, 220.

Muñoz's "party of the poor," the party of the *jíbaro*, was in fact attracting a growing number of Puerto Rico's young, well-to-do, well-educated professionals, such as the thirty-two-year-old Jaime Benítez, a graduate of the University of Chicago, from a distinguished family of poets and political leaders. Benítez was an ardent *independentista* and an equally ardent foe of the Generalísimo Franco's *Falangista* regime in Spain. During the Tydings Bill "explosion" he attempted to organize a constitutional assembly to declare Puerto Rico "a Republic." Benítez became Chancellor of the University of Puerto Rico after the elections, a post he held for three decades.

Albizu's radicalism and violence continued to drive Nationalist sympathizers into the Muñoz party. Outstanding attorneys Ernest Ramos Antonini and Víctor Gutiérrez Franqui, who had personally witnessed the Ponce Massacre and successfully defended the Nationalists in the subsequent trial, and Samuel Quiñones, who went on to become Speaker of the House and then President of the Senate, joined Muñoz in the mid 1930s. They were followed by other young men who had been close to Albizu Campos, such as Manuel Rivera Matos, who later became Muñoz' press aide, Fernando Sierra Berdecía, future Secretary of Labor, writer José Buitrago, one of Muñoz's intimate friends.

Another Muñoz supporter was Felisa Rincón, a tireless, charismatic young woman who grew up in the thick of Liberal politics and was active in the drive for women's suffrage in 1932. While Muñoz much preferred to do his campaigning in the countryside, Felisa put together in San Juan what became within a few years the island's most powerful political machine. She dominated city politics for the next three decades, and was active in national Democratic politics, propelling her as the world-famous, colorful "Doña Felisa," Mayor of San Juan.

Also joining the new political movement was medical doctor Antonio Fernós Isern, the party's candidate for resident commissioner. Fernós was to author and manage through Congress the island's fundamental political reforms in the late 1940s and early 1950s, and served as President of Puerto Rico's Constitutional Convention. There were labor leaders and powerful local political leaders such as, like Andrés Grillasca in Ponce, Ildefonso Solá Morales in Caguas, and Cruz Ortiz Stella in Humacao.

One afternoon, campaigning in the mountainous Adjuntas area, north of Ponce, Muñoz made one of his most unlikely converts—the son of a conservative Republican and successful entrepreneur. Thirty-year-old Teodoro Moscoso was educated in the U.S. and slated by his father to run the family drug retail and wholesale business. Named after his father's idol, Theodore Roosevelt, young Moscoso was in almost constant disagreement with his father, appalled by his support of Generalísimo Franco and the Spanish "fascists," although he understood that it was because of his deep Catholicism as much as his anti-communism. A voracious reader, Moscoso escaped his humdrum existence in Ponce by reading all he could about the liberals now in Washington, longing to be part of the excitement.

Moscoso got the opportunity when Muñoz took ill and had to suspend his campaigning in nearby Adjuntas. With a fever and feeling awful, Muñoz sent for Dr. José Gándara, one of his followers in Ponce. Gándara invited his brother-in-law Moscoso to accompany him. When Gándara walked out of the coffee farm house where Muñoz was resting in a hammock, he signaled Moscoso to go inside to briefly greet him.

Over an hour later, Gándara looked in to see what was keeping Moscoso and finally pulled him out. On the drive back to Ponce, Moscoso was strangely silent. The meeting with Muñoz, Moscoso said years later, "left me in a state of shock for three or four days...I was aware that I had met a superior person...and everything from then on I was to assess in my mind had to be weighed against the standards that this extraordinary man had set for me in that conversation that lasted a couple of hours."[10]

The bond formed between them was to play a critical role in Muñoz's career. To his father's outrage, Moscoso became an active member of the Popular Party. The following year, he finally "escaped" from Ponce and spent the next two decades as Muñoz's "human dynamo," running Puerto Rico's economic development program, the transition from an agricultural to an industrial economy, called Operation Bootstrap.

In 1940, however, Muñoz had no idea of the consequences of his chance meeting with the young Ponce pharmacist. Nothing was further from his

---

10. Maldonado, *Teodoro Moscoso and Puerto Rico's Operation Bootstrap*, 5.

mind than a Puerto Rican "industrial revolution." His promise of a better life for the *jíbaro* depended on land reform, and the sensational news from Washington seemed to confirm that this was a promise he could keep. The 500-acre law had been challenged in the courts. On March 25, 1940 the U.S. Supreme Court upheld the law.

Within days, Muñoz bought radio time to talk to the entire island. The Supreme Court, he said, has finally put in the hands of the *jíbaro* the "weapon" to bring about his own social and economic justice. A vote for the traditional political parties would have the effect of annulling the court decision: of throwing that weapon away. The word "democracy" now had substance: for the first time in island history, voting will count: "your votes will decide if the corporations will continue to extract millions from the land of Puerto Rico, or if the millions produced by that land will benefit the workers, the farmers, and all the people of Puerto Rico. It now depends on you!"[11]

Muñoz got another opportunity to establish his credibility after Congress approved the Fair Labor Standard Act in 1938. He received a letter from workers of the sugar cane mill in Santa Isabela. The Aguirre Corporation, they said, refused to apply the 30 cent-an-hour minimum wage to them. Muñoz quickly dispatched his top lawyers, Ramos Antonini and Gutiérrez Franqui, to sue the company. The corporation lawyers quickly decided that they wanted no part of what would have been a highly-publicized political trial. The workers got the raise and the Muñoz campaign another boost.

Muñoz dreamed up an even more dramatic way to convince the *jíbaro* that this time his vote would count. He took time out from the campaign to sit down with a number of advisors and lawyers to draft the twelve most important economic reform laws that the Popular Party would enact if it won control of the Legislature. Muñoz himself wrote the bill he considered the most important, creating the Land Authority to carry out land distribution by implementing the 500-acre law.

On September 15, 1940, in San Juan, Muñoz did something unprecedented. Mass political rallies were traditionally "high opera." Festive events filled with bombastic speeches meant to fire up partisan emotions. Instead Muñoz read slowly each of the twelve reform bills. Then he called

---

11. Bothwell, *Puerto Rico: cien años de lucha política*, Vol. III, 230.

all Popular Party candidates for the Legislature to come forward, raise their hands and take an oath that if elected, they would vote for all the bills. Muñoz asked each *jíbaro* in every barrio in Puerto Rico, listening on the radio, to become part of the oath. Keep a record on a blackboard, he said, of the votes cast by each one of these candidates that gets elected. If you can't write, he said, get someone to do it for you. At the end of four years, if anyone voted against one of these bills, you take back the vote that you lent him: you vote against him.

"THE GREAT DECISION"

By early 1940 Muñoz was convinced that with so many things in his favor, it was essential to resolve the one issue that stood in the way of victory in November: the issue of independence. Years later he described his dilemma: "Since the Tydings bill took independence out of the realm of political discourse and of assembly debates, transforming it into the specter of an imminent reality, fear of independence was palpable: one could almost touch it in the air. For the immense majority of the *campesinos* and a great majority of the so-called middle class, independence became a fearful threat. The popular saying was that it was one thing to call the Devil, another to see him come."[12]

But he gradually began to convince himself that what he was seeing in the face of the *jíbaro* was not an irrational, mindless "fear of independence" instigated by political demagogues, as he had believed after his depressing experience in the 1936 electoral defeat. It was not even, as he had often lamented, a demeaning cultural defect of Puerto Ricans ashamed of their nationality. Muñoz was about to make the biggest and emotionally the most difficult decision of his political life. Eleven years later, speaking at his father's gravesite on July 17, 1951, Muñoz described this critical crossroad in his political evolution. During this campaign, he said:

> I learned that there is a wisdom among the people in the town and the countryside which education may lead, but cannot improve, in

---

12. Muñoz Marín, *Memorias* Vol. I, 186.

its magnificent human essence. I taught many of them something, but they taught me more. I learned that these people are wise— wiser than we think. I learned that to them freedom is something deep in the heart, in the conscience, in everyday life, in personal dignity, in the furrow, the plow, and the tool. I learned that among the simple people the nationalistic concept does not exist, because in its place there is a deeper understanding of freedom... And I learned even better something I already knew: that it is unworthy of the conscience, that it is the denial of all ideals, to risk, for abstract concepts, the hope for a better life, the deep belief in the integral freedom of the good and simple people... I learned all this and I also learned that the great majority of Puerto Ricans prefer close association with their fellow citizens of the American Union and with all men on earth, to the bitter narrowness of separation.[13]

It was precisely the Tydings bill in 1936, he continued, that had forced him to begin to rethink his fundamental assumptions about independence. "We have to be grateful to that bill that, with the force of a sledgehammer, forced many of us to think with much more care." He had taken for granted that it was a matter of will power—the will that the old Liberals never possessed—to work out an independence with Congress without the specter of starvation: the will to carry through sweeping economic and social reforms. If what he was "learning" from the *jíbaro* was right, then he had been wrong.

Aside from the "spiritually painful" conflict within him there was the political reality staring him in the face. Did the *jíbaros*, within themselves, without saying a word, see "the Devil coming" when he and his party leaders approached? And if they did, would they nod their heads as if they understood and agreed when he spoke of the desperate need for social and economic reforms, but then, in the secrecy of the voting booth, vote against him out of fear? Muñoz was convinced that he had to meet this head on.

"I realized," he wrote, "that with a program calling for separate independence we would never obtain the support of the people for economic development—equitable distribution and production—which the people

---

13. Hanson and Wells, *Annals of the American Academy of Political and Social Science 285*, 2.

needed so much... The Popular Party [had] a platform which was its own worst enemy—a platform in which the political plank (independence) could destroy the economic planks with the devastating fury of a tropical hurricane."[14]

To earn the trust of the *jíbaro* and carry out his democratic revolution, Muñoz had to resolve this dilemma. It was not enough to convince the *jíbaro* not to sell his vote. He had to communicate another message: *even though I and my party do believe in independence, if you give us your vote, trust me that we will not betray you and use it to take Puerto Rico to independence. Trust me that you, only you, not the Popular Party, not Luis Muñoz Marín, will decide the status of Puerto Rico.*

NICANOR GUERRA

The key to escape from the trap came to Muñoz in one of his small meetings with a group of twenty-five or thirty sugar cane cutters on the road between Río Grande and Palmer, several miles east of San Juan. Once again, Muñoz wrote in his memoirs, he made his case against vote-buying: "The argument was persuasive and I communicated it to them in the simplest terms possible. I could sense in the expressions and movements of their heads their agreement."[15] But he noticed the dark face of a tall, muscular man who was clearly having difficulty following him. He saw in the face "fear, doubt, anguish." Finally, the man, looking Muñoz in the eye, started to say: "Yes... but..." He made his statement with a gesture: he ran one finger across his neck. Muñoz wrote: "I understood immediately what he wanted to say. The heads of the others nodded in agreement, sharing the same profound fear. He agreed with all I had said about the vote and social justice. But he knew that the Popular leadership was *independentista*. In spite of our renovation program, he feared that his head would be cut off by independence."[16]

The Nationalist Party rhetoric and violence had clearly affected this physically strong *jíbaro* with visions of "violence, abuse, hostility, and

---

14. Ibid., 3.
15. Muñoz Marín, *Memorias* Vol. I, 187.
16. Ibid., 187.

carnage" under independence. Muñoz never forgot the man's name: Nicanor Guerra. "So deep was the impression made on me by that dramatic expression of what already intellectually troubled me, that I decided to deal with it at the first opportunity."

The opportunity came at a meeting in San Juan. A Party militant shouted at him the point-blank question: "What will the Popular Party do to reclaim independence if it wins the elections?" His instant answer was: "Political status is not the issue in these elections. The votes for the Popular Party will not be counted in favor or against any political status." Muñoz saw the man, obviously an ardent *independentista*, turn away dejectedly. He shared the feeling: "And I, still an *independentista*, understood the desolation in his spirit."

Muñoz had found the slogan that became the heart of his campaign. He would repeat it, "*el status no está en issue*" thousands of times. Muñoz had discovered the "few clear words" that would be understood by the *jíbaros* across all of Puerto Rico. For the rest of his life, Muñoz pinpointed the precise moment he uttered the words as the turning point in his party's campaign, as "the great decision" in his political career, and in Puerto Rican history.

It was at that very moment that the Popular Party assured its victory in 1940 and assured what it could do in the next thirty years for that man, for the future of his children, for more than two million souls, for the creation and development of a new middle class, for the transformation, from one generation to another, of the sons of sugar cane workers into medical doctors, technicians, professors, business administrators, skilled workers, that received more respect for their person, more security for their salaries and horizons of maximum opening for their children.

Any other answer would have caused the immediate defeat and probably the long delay, or the profound transformation, of the historic achievements of the next thirty years."[17]

Muñoz, however, had to convince not only Nicanor Guerra and hundreds of thousands of other *jíbaros*, but his own party leadership, almost totally

---

17. Ibid., 188.

independentista. The war now raging in Europe and Asia gave him an additional argument: This was not the time to bring the issue to President Roosevelt and the U.S. "Puerto Rico's position not only in the geography of the world, but in the geography of justice and hope, could not be an obstacle to the United States or to democracy."[18] No sooner the world crisis ends, he assured his party leaders, Puerto Rico will hold a plebiscite and then take the battle to Washington.

Most of the leaders, he believed, understood and accepted the message of Nicanor Guerra. Some were in fact pleased that Muñoz had finally removed this huge obstacle. But many were asking themselves if this was a clever Muñoz partisan tactic or a fundamental ideological change within their new party and, above all, within Muñoz himself. Several of his closest followers were convinced that he remained a die-hard *independentista*, and that once he achieved power, he would find the way to fulfill his status ideal.

Muñoz failed with an important party leader, the 36-year-old attorney Vicente Géigel Polanco. Géigel had been a youth leader in the old Unionist Party, a member of the governing board of the Liberal Party, and he was currently president of the *Ateneo Puertorriqueño*. He followed Muñoz out of the Liberal Party to found the PPD. Reading Muñoz's statement in the newspaper *El Mundo* that reiterated and emphasized that a vote for the Popular Party would not be interpreted as a vote for independence, Géigel was heartbroken and outraged.

As he was doing with other party leaders, Muñoz made a personal attempt to bring Géigel around. He invited him to lunch along with Manuel Rivera Matos and Fernando Sierra Berdecía, two of the more prominent *independentistas* that had bolted the Nationalist party to join the PPD. Two hours later, Muñoz had failed to convince Géigel.

Immediately after the meeting, Géigel sent a letter to four top party leaders denouncing Muñoz's action as "absurd, monstrous and immoral."[19] Is this the kind of "democracy" Muñoz is preaching—on his own, violating the agreements reached at the party's assemblies? Muñoz had unilaterally,

---

18. Muñoz Marín, *La historia del Partido Popular Democrático*, 68.

19. Bothwell, *Puerto Rico: cien años de lucha política* Vol. III, 222.

in effect, amended the essential plank in its platform. Wasn't this the old, "rotten" politics that had prompted all of them to organize the Popular Party?

"Muñoz Marín," Géigel wrote, "has our affection, our respect and our esteem, but he has no authority to discard, as he pretends to do, the political aspirations of this party that was created fundamentally to demand the recognition of our sovereignty." Géigel believed this was no mere political strategy for a moneyless party desperately trying to lure voters from the other parties. He sensed and he feared that the flame of the *independentista* ideal was indeed dying in his leader.

The letter did not succeed in igniting a rebellion against Muñoz. Géigel's indignation subsided and he himself came around and rejoined Muñoz in the 1940 campaign, and was elected to the Senate. Muñoz also decided to bury the protest as a natural, inevitable outburst of frustration and disappointment. In the next decade, he named Géigel as the island's attorney general. His intimate friend and collaborator, however, was to play an important role in a rebellion of another kind that took place in Puerto Rico in 1950.

14 The Democratic Revolution

Muñoz's campaign style, the free give and take with the *jíbaros*, made it impossible to keep a schedule. He was always running late. One evening, he arrived at an isolated rural area so late—already early morning—that the *jíbaros* had given up and returned to their homes. Muñoz, however, found a lone Popular Party worker who had not lost hope that he would arrive. The worker had managed to get a loud speaker, an amplifier, and a small generator. It was pitch black, the dots of fireflies crazily darting here and there. The excited young man handed Muñoz the microphone and told him to proceed to talk. "Talk to whom?" Muñoz asked. "Go ahead," the man insisted, "talk. Talk loud". Muñoz, exhausted, hoarse, wanted to talk to *jíbaros*, not to the black night. "Talk," the man demanded. "Talk!" All right. Muñoz stood on the running board of his broken-down Ford, and began to talk. "Just watch, don Luis, just watch," the young man said. Suddenly, in the distance, Muñoz saw a faint, flickering light: then another and another. "They are listening, Don Luis," the young man said. "They are lighting their candles to let you know they hear you. Go on. Talk to them." As he talked, it now seemed to Muñoz that there were as many candles lit in the dark as there were fireflies.[1]

In the town of Cidra, there was something about a small, thin, barefoot old woman that caught Muñoz's attention. Holding in his hand a friend's camera, Muñoz approached her, asking if he could take her photo. She snapped "no!"—suspicious that this *político* was up to something. Muñoz

---

1. Aitken, *Poet in the Fortress*, 135.

lowered the camera and, smiling, tried to talk to her about the Popular Party. "I have to go," she insisted, then added: "I have to put on my shoes." Muñoz suspected that there were no shoes. He tried again, relating his gospel to her fictitious shoes. She would not listen. As she disappeared into her wooden shack, Muñoz heard her saying to herself: "*No pico...no pico...*" I will not peck; I will not fall into your net. It was two weeks before the elections and Muñoz turned to his companions: "If we can get that little old woman to listen and understand from now to the elections, the Popular Party will win."[2]

One of Muñoz's followers, Manuel Seoane, later to become mayor of Caguas, after hearing of Muñoz's late night speech in the darkness, mounted a record-player, amplifiers, and battery on a mule, which he took to remote rural areas where Muñoz's car could not reach. There he held what he called "the meetings of solitude." After eight in the evening when the *jíbaros* retired to sleep, he arrived with his mule and his equipment, and began to announce that Muñoz was about to speak to them. He played a short recording of Muñoz's voice. Again, the *jíbaros* would begin to light candles in their homes. Scrapping some money together, Muñoz had scores of the recording duplicated to be played in every *barrio.* By election day, he calculated it had been played 30,000 times.

If Muñoz was counting on his pen—*El Batey*—to overcome the opposition's seemingly unlimited funds, party militants like Seoane were counting on his voice. Muñoz attempted to emulate his political idol, Roosevelt, in making as much use of radio as the limited funds allowed. His voice projected self-confidence, power, masculinity, but at the same time it was accessible and intimate.

In San Juan, meanwhile, as Muñoz described it, the political pundits converted the "restaurant table cloths into premature electoral tally sheets," at the beginning, jotting down only 5,000 votes for the "Popular Party." By now, several were jotting 50,000 votes. One noted newspaper pundit went out on a limb, venturing a guess that the most a party that did not buy votes could conceivable get was as many as 80,000 votes.[3]

Finally it was election day, November 5, 1940. In the early dawn, Muñoz returned to his temporary home in Cidra. The "restaurant tally

2. Muñoz Marín, *Memorias* Vol. I, 203.

3. Muñoz Marín, *La historia del Partido Popular Democrático*, 14.

sheets" were all wrong. He was certain of his victory. He could now break his promise of abstinence of hard liquor to Ruby Black. He took with him "a small bottle of brandy...to celebrate." Waiting for him were Inés, now expecting their second child any moment, and their one-year-old baby girl, Viviana. He had spent the entire day at party headquarters, the old *La Democracia* offices, attending to the special telephones installed by Governor Leahy. That morning, sitting on an old wooden table, he wrote his last radio message to the voters. The grueling 837 days of campaigning were over.

Now, as he staggered into the *ranchón*, owned by his "half ruined, half radical friend," Elmer Ellsworth, Popular Party candidate for the legislature, Muñoz found hundreds of *jíbaros*, many with their families, some of them sleeping wherever they could lie down, among boxes and crates. Those that were awake were singing and reciting *jíbaro* verses. Inés told him that the men, women, and children had begun to arrive the previous morning. The polls would not open until 1 p.m. and then locked at 3 p.m. with guards posted outside. Only those inside and registered could vote. This was the air-tight system approved by the Coalition to prevent multiple voting. With all the vote-buying and dirty tricks Muñoz denounced as "corrupting" island elections, he recognized that the "closed precinct" system was a guarantee against fraud.

The hundreds of *jíbaros* greeted him warmly, some had already begun to "celebrate." They were there, they said, because they did not want to risk a downpour raising the level of the rivers, or anything else that would make them "break the promise they had made to themselves silently, and to me."[4] One of his father's verses, lamenting the "anemia...the fever" that made the *jíbaro* passive and defeated, came to his mind. These *jíbaros* staying up all night, determined to vote, were breaking through the wall of hopelessness.

After a few hours of sleep Muñoz returned to party headquarters in San Juan. The phones were ringing constantly: Jaime Benítez and the Spanish "Republican" volunteers, with their thick accents, were taking the urgent calls. The reports of vote buying and corralling of voters were coming in furiously, but Muñoz's system of getting the police to act was working. At noon, an hour before the polls opened, he took a break. With his friend,

---

4. Muñoz Marín, *Memorias* Vol. I, 200.

journalist and writer Jorge Font Saldaña, he went to the González Padín department store to buy a crib for Viviana. In four days she would celebrate her first birthday.

There were close to one hundred people waiting silently inside the classroom which served as a voting precinct. When Muñoz arrived he saw that no one at the voter's identification table represented the Popular Party. He asked for a volunteer among the *Populares* present. There must be one present, Muñoz said to himself, but no one moved. He asked again. Again, there was no response. Then Muñoz turned to a well-known lawyer and member of the Coalition. Would he represent the Popular Party during the voting and the tally? The man agreed. The integrity of the voting in that precinct—the culmination of Muñoz's enormous, personal campaign—was now in the hands of a militant of the party that he had so ruthlessly attacked. Muñoz could not escape the irony. Decades later he recalled the man's name, Carlos J. Torres, who put "his democratic conscience above his partisan conscience." Eighteen of the hundred or so voters in that precinct were counted for the Popular Party. At the end of the day, Muñoz and his "democratic revolution" would need each one of them.

An hour after the polls closed, "unofficial" first returns began to be reported on radio. This was part of the island's election ritual. Each party released "unofficial" returns that indicated a great victory. The glowing numbers, breathlessly transmitted by the radio announcers, created great excitement at each of the party headquarters, celebrations that continued into the early evening as the reality of the official tallies slowly arrived.

The early scant reports seemed to indicate that the *jíbaro* had responded. One local leader told Muñoz that driving towards the town, he came across five or six men on the road from Comerío to Bayamón, all barefoot and soaking wet from the morning rains, probably with only a piece of bread and a cup of coffee for the day. The leader invited the *jíbaros* to jump into his car. They thanked him but declined: "Muñoz Marín told us to be sure to vote, and we only trust our feet." The driver identified himself as a *Popular*. Still, the *jíbaros* refused and continued walking.

By 8:00 p.m. Muñoz heard on the radio the first town won by his party: Coamo, near the south coast. He telephoned Francisco Anselmi, the local leader who was to become the region's political leader for the next two decades. Perhaps, he thought, it was time to begin to "celebrate." He reached for the jar that constituted the "Popular Party Treasury." That morning he had counted $56. Now there were only about five dollars, enough to buy a bottle of whiskey and coffee for the party workers. Muñoz recalled the little old woman who had refused to allow him to photograph her, running away saying to herself: "No pico...no pico..." He now said to himself: the barefoot *jíbaros* walking on the Comerío road did make it to the polls, and the little old woman "picó": she did understand.

The Death of the Old Politics

November 5, 1940, Muñoz exultantly declared, was now as historic a date as July 25, 1898 when the American troops landed on Guánica. The old politics were dead. Never again will the *jíbaros* sell their votes. Never again will the "corporations" control the government. As he predicted on July 17, 1938 at his father's gravesite, a "new personage," a new source of power had made its entrance to the Puerto Rican political stage: "the people of Puerto Rico." For Muñoz, this was not post-election bluster: this was not more empty rhetoric. He believed it literally and he saw Puerto Rico itself reacting as if it believed it. He wrote years later: "We ourselves felt, and the people felt that as a party we had defeated, not only the rival parties, but an epoch ...The faith in democracy of those *jíbaros* had moved the mountains of Puerto Rico."[5]

The Popular Party won control of the Senate. It just squeezed in getting ten seats to the Coalition's nine. For Muñoz, this meant that the Popular Party "won." He would be elevated to Senate President, the position of highest political leadership on the island.

But, in fact, the Popular Party got only 39 percent of the total vote, 214,857 votes, 7,566 less than the Coalition. This was far below the 345,000 Muñoz had confidently predicted in his August, 1939 letter to Ruby Black. But it exceeded by much the predictions of the pundits, the journalists, and his political opponents. Muñoz buried within himself his disappointment that hundreds of thousands of *jíbaros* he had spoken to, looked at in the eye,

---

5. Muñoz Marín, *Memorias* Vol. I, 210.

had *not understood.* Instead, he exercised his ability to use words not only to affect the perception of events, but the event itself. That night, Muñoz claimed a great victory.

The day after, however, the Coalition claimed victory. It elected Socialist Party president Bolívar Pagán to return to Congress as resident commissioner. It captured 37 municipal governments to the Popular Party's 29. In the Legislature, the Coalition and *Populares* were tied in the House, with 18 seats each. The Triparty got three seats in the House. The splinter group Muñoz had denounced as a "*mogolla*" now held the balance of power.

Hundreds of well-wishers invaded the ranch in Cidra, in spite of a fence that Inés, against Muñoz's will, had ordered put up to somehow control the growing flow of people. But the celebration was marred by incidents that troubled Muñoz. There was the man asking to be appointed justice of peace in a small town. Then there were two lawyers from Coamo, describing how they had helped to win that town, and asking for municipal contracts for legal work. Muñoz contrasted this with the *jíbaros* that had used their free vote for "justice that had to be taken from no one else," while these other men now wanted government jobs taken from the political adversaries.

But was he, who considered himself a political "realist," reacting as a naive idealist, a dreamer? How could he govern, carry out the "people's mandate" without a strong, disciplined, efficient political organization? And how to maintain a strong, motivated political machine without giving out favors, beginning with those who helped to get him elected? Requests like those of the lawyers from Coamo would now follow by the hundreds. During the campaign he had courted and won the vital support of the thousands of *público* owners and drivers who used their passenger cars to shuttle *jíbaros* to and from the voting precincts. How could he not reward these *público* drivers that made his victory possible?

Muñoz felt deeply that Antonio Barceló's pained denunciation of him as a person driven by a selfish passion to become the "president" of a political party, any political party, could not have been further from the truth. Like his father, he had no interest in titles. But now he had, not one, but two: He was "President" of the Popular Democratic Party. He was about to become "President" of the Senate. He would sit in the chair Barceló had occupied in the first 23 years of the Senate's existence. And he had still another title, the biggest of all. He was now Puerto Rico's *líder máximo.*

But was this really what he wanted out of life? Yes, of course, he had run a political and personal marathon to get the power that the *jíbaros* had put into his hands. And he was determined to use that power to the maximum to fulfill his promises. But this was a struggle, a conflict that Muñoz was never to resolve within himself. All his life he had been a critic, a faultfinder in the style and spirit of the American muckrakers he so much admired. Now as Puerto Rico's *líder máximo* all this changed. He had to pay a price. Almost to his very death he privately lamented to family and friends that he enjoyed less "freedom of speech" than any other Puerto Rican. He found himself in the same dilemma as his father: caught between what is "true" and what is "responsible." He was no longer free to say or write what he believed regardless of political or ideological consequences. He was now a prisoner of his political success and the power and responsibility that came with it.

The Terrible Question

Muñoz's health finally gave in, and he was confined to bed in early 1941. He began to put down his thoughts in what he hoped would be a book (never completed, its fragments published by his heirs in 1984, four years after his death), describing the nature, the uniqueness, the "soul" of his new political party. The party, he wrote, had undergone a fundamental metamorphosis during the campaign. Anyone who had observed its origins in 1938, left the island and returned in 1940, would not have believed that this was the same party. "It was not the result of a technique, mine or of a group of leaders. I myself was growing. The leadership of the movement was growing. We were all part of a spiritual organism in rapid development."[6] Muñoz described this "spiritual growth" in almost mystical terms:

As I went through the countryside, as I talked to the people and the people talked to me, as the people's instinct sensed the potential of what I brought, as the old hope in the people was becoming a famil-

6. Muñoz Marín, *La historia del Partido Popular Democrático*, 113

iar part of my spirit, the transformation was taking place. The doctrine of the Popular Democratic Party, the tonality of its soul, was the work of the *jíbaros* of Puerto Rico, of the workers and middle class of Puerto Rico. When I went through the countryside, people thought that I was campaigning among them. The deeper reality was that they were campaigning within me.[7]

As Muñoz lay sick in bed early in 1941, he felt that the most important thing that happened to him during the campaign was precisely his "communication" with the *jíbaro*. He was the first Puerto Rican leader ever to do so. He had formed a bond with the *jíbaro* that went beyond politics or ideology. "They developed in me," he wrote in his memoirs, "a solidarity, no longer intellectual nor of social doctrine, but of human affection."[8] The bond meant that he would never betray the *jíbaro*: that he would never put himself, his ideas, his goal, above the *jíbaro*.

But he was not ready, at his point in his life, to ask himself the terrible question: was independence possible without precisely betraying the *jíbaro*. Had he locked himself into having to "betray" one or the other—his beloved ideal, or his beloved *jíbaro*?

No, he would not confront that terrible question now. But, as he confessed a decade later, he was inexorably moving towards the ultimate frontier of his de-dogmatization.

"THE NEW DEAL PARTY"

The traditional parties in Puerto Rico, even the pro-statehood Republican Party, were "Spanish" in temperament, in their fixation with status ideology. Muñoz wanted the Popular Party to be the first "government party" in the island's history, an essentially American-style party. "The Popular Democratic Party," he wrote in late 1941, "is the first party to achieve power in Puerto Rico with its leadership fundamentally from the generation

---

7. Ibid., 113.
8. Muñoz Marín, *Memoirs*, I, 178.

most subject to American democratic influences." While Muñoz did not want it officially affiliated to the national Democratic Party, he described it as "The New Deal Party." Now, he said, liberalism in Washington under President Roosevelt, and in the insular Legislature under his new party, would "converge solidly" behind a social and economic reform program.

But what about the Governor? In his enthusiastic January, 1940 letter to Black, Muñoz sarcastically noted: "But Puerto Rico is so unlucky that it is said that Governor Leahy will not remain with us for long since he is too good a person for the position that he holds here."[9] He added that "it would be bad luck for us [if] some national emergency compelled the President to remove Leahy from the island before he could do more good." Muñoz's premonition proved unfounded. Roosevelt did not recall Leahy until December 5, 1940 to appoint him U.S. ambassador to the Vichy government following the Nazi occupation of France. By then Leahy had accomplished his primary mission on the island. He had overseen what threatened to be one of the most tumultuous, potentially violent elections ever on the island and became, instead, one of the most peaceful.

Roosevelt named Guy J. Swope, the island's auditor, to replace Leahy. Muñoz and almost everyone else assumed it was an interim appointment. Swope did not want the job. A former congressman from Pennsylvania, his experience on the island had convinced him that he wanted no part of the quicksand of island politics, and he made no secret that he was eyeing a position in Washington as head of the Interior Department's Division on Insular Affairs.

AN EXTRAORDINARY PRONOUNCEMENT

If Muñoz, after his victory, indulged himself with bouts of introspection and philosophy, something he would do periodically throughout his life, he had absolutely no doubts about what to do with the "power" now in his hands: he would take it as far as he could. On February 11, 1941, he made an extraordinary pronouncement. Moments after being elected President of

---

9. Bothwell, *Puerto Rico: cien años de lucha política*, Vol. III, 222.

the Insular Senate, he declared that not only the Legislature but also the Governor of Puerto Rico were bound by the people's "mandate" to enact each one of his party's reform bills. "The will of the people within the principles of democracy applies and should apply, in the conscience of the Governor's executive branch as much as in the conscience of the Government's legislative branch."[10] There were only three reasons, he said, that would permit the Governor to veto any one of these bills: if the Governor believed that there was a better way to fulfill the reform; if he believed that the bill violated the "people's mandate;" or if the bill obstructed American national defense.

Muñoz went further. The "mandate" extended all the way up to the White House:

> The same considerations are valid, and the same democratic prin-
> ciples govern, in regards to the President of the United States. The
> Governor of Puerto Rico is his representative. He had his backing.
> He executes his policies. Within the principles of democracy, in the
> person of the Governor reside the democratic policies of the Presi-
> dent and the democratic policies of the people of Puerto Rico.

Through all the celebrating, declarations and speeches, Muñoz did not mention the status question. But his intrepid pronouncement had changed the relationship between Puerto Rico and the United States. Legally the island was still a U.S. territory. For Puerto Ricans it was still "a colony." Neither the Governor nor the President were under any legal obligation to follow the Puerto Rican "mandate." On the contrary, the U.S. Constitution gave Congress absolute power over territories. But Muñoz was not talking about legal concepts. When he stated that the Governor and the President himself were now constrained by the "principles of democracy," that what in fact occurred on November 5, 1940, was a fundamental shift in power in Puerto Rico, Muñoz meant it.

---

10. Ibid., 329.

"What mandate?" asked the opposition Coalition leaders. "The Coalition won the elections," insisted Union Republican Party leader, Rafael Martínez Nadal. Muñoz's ascension to Senate President, he said, was the result of an electoral quirk: the defection of 60,000 Socialists and 35,000 Republicans to the Unification Triparty splintered group. In fact, Martínez pointed out, the Popular Party got 38,000 votes less than the old Liberal Party back in 1936 when it was able to elect only one Senator. Did Muñoz think he could bully his way into politics, in effect, annulling the real election results?

The elections, in fact, had created what seemed to be a recipe for gridlock. Muñoz and his "minority" party, by controlling the Senate, controlled most of the government administrative and judicial appointments. But without the House, he could not control the budget, nor carry out a single one of the promised social and economic reforms. Just as important, Puerto Rico's official spokesman in Washington, elected with an 8,000 majority to represent the island in Congress and before all federal offices, was Coalition leader Bolívar Pagán.

To break out of the opposition's vicious circle, Muñoz had to pull off an unlikely scheme. He had promised during the campaign that his party would never enter a "coalition." But there was no alternative. Either at least two of the three conservative Triparty representatives joined him to give the Popular Party control of the House, or his pronouncements after the elections would go up in smoke.

The Triparty leaders were precisely veteran practitioners of the "old politics" that Muñoz had proclaimed died on election day. Miguel Ángel García Méndez, former Socialist Party leader Prudencio Rivera Martínez, and former Liberal Party leader, José Ramírez Santibáñez, had no love for Muñoz and his Popular Party. But they "hated" the Coalition more. Muñoz knew that they could be motivated, not by a desire to turn the Legislature over to the Popular Party, much less to carry out Muñoz's sweeping reforms, but by the vengeance of denying the House to the Coalition.

This was a paradox Muñoz used in his favor. Since they were all in favor of statehood, he appealed to their "American patriotism," to their shared loyalty to the United States in the war crisis. This, Muñoz declared, was the bond between them: "I am talking about all those [elected to the

Legislature] that because of their ideas and purposes, because of their spirit of responsibility with the future, feel in their hearts that they are now part of the reality of democratic power that now extends over the seas from Puerto Rico to Washington and from Washington to Puerto Rico."[11]

Winning over the Triparty representatives became one of the most difficult periods in Muñoz's life. Having convinced the *jíbaro* not to sell his vote, he now had to "pay a price" for the Triparty votes in the House. From the November elections to his designation as Senate President in February, Muñoz played the old game of patronage. He knew that Prudencio Rivero Martínez's goal in life was to be named Commissioner of Labor. Years later Muñoz wrote: "The truth is that the price paid seems small compared to what we would achieve in renovating action. But in a more subtle way, it was not trivial: it etched into these new times certain hateful characteristics of the old politics."[12] Putting his emotions aside, Muñoz played to win and proved that he too could be a master of the "old politics." The Triparty leadership ordered its three representatives to vote with the Popular Democratic Party in the organization of the House and in favor of the PDP reform bills. Muñoz consolidated his power and was now in control of the Legislature.

But he was still not home free. A terrible battle erupted within his party. A bitter contest between the Ponce attorney who had been at Muñoz's side since the 1932 Liberal Party campaign, Ernesto Ramos Antonini and Samuel Quinoñes, the lawyer and writer who had taken on the critical assignment as the party's "electoral commissioner," the thankless job of supervising the registration process and making sure that the electoral laws were strictly enforced during the campaign and voting. Both were vital to the new party, but both emotionally wanted to be Speaker of the House. Muñoz favored Ramos Antonini. He kept this to himself, however, and Quiñones was elected. Ramos was not only hurt by his defeat, but bitter, convinced that he had been rejected because he was black. He announced that he would attend the inaugural session, vote for Quiñones, and then resign from the Legislature.

---

11. Muñoz Marín, *Memorias* Vol. II, 6.
12. Ibid.,10.

Muñoz was not only faced with the prospect of losing control of the Legislature, but he too was hurt by the accusation of racism in his party. The fact was that aside from the founder and leader of the Republican Party, José Celso Barbosa, few blacks were in leadership positions in any of the parties. To complicate this ugly conflict, there were rumors that although no one doubted Ramos's extraordinary political abilities, he would not be "accepted" in the United States, certainly not in the "Southern town" of Washington nor by the Southerners that controlled much of Congress. A "poison," Muñoz angrily declared, had penetrated the party.

He had to find a way to convince Ramos to stay. He must repair his injured self-esteem, his *dignidad* not only as a major political leader, but as a black man. Then it came to him. He sent him a letter declaring that a sudden, painful attack of neuritis made it impossible for him to take command of the Senate, prepare all the reform legislation, and remain as Popular Party president. Since Ramos was party vice-president, Muñoz was appointing him president during his illness. Ramos agreed to take over the presidency during "the emergency," and withdrew his resignation. Eight years later, Ramos became Speaker when Quiñones replaced Muñoz as Senate President, holding the post until his sudden death on January 9, 1963.

15 The Best and the Worst of Times

Two months after the elections, on December 24, 1940, Interior Secretary Ickes asked Rexford Tugwell to return to Puerto Rico on a delicate mission: to assess the consequences of Muñoz's victory, and specifically the effect of implementing the 500-acre law.

While in Puerto Rico Muñoz celebrated that finally there was a link between the Roosevelt administration and the insular government, in Washington Ickes was again worried about events on the island. Since the elections, Ickes was bombarded by Muñoz's political opponents and the insular business class. "The 'better element' was close to panic," Tugwell wrote several years later. "Its individuals were appealing pathetically to Mr. Ickes for protection... coiling serpentwise through the lobbies and bureaucracies of Washington, their demand for protection against 'communists' reached even the ears of the incorrigible progressive who was the Secretary of the Interior."[1]

Ickes had little sympathy for Puerto Rico's conservative politicians and the sugar industry. But he had never trusted nor liked Muñoz. His perception of the Puerto Rican leader had not changed since the bruising battles with Ernest Gruening back in 1936. For Ickes, as Tugwell found, Muñoz was still the "inconsequential son of a notable father."

Tugwell, then the head of the New York City Planning Commission, was anxious to return to Washington for some kind of "war work." He was certain that the war would reach the Caribbean and that keeping the lid on Puerto Rico was important to the nation.

---

1. Tugwell, *Stricken Land*, 7.

Back in 1939, Governor Winship reminded Washington of the "paramount importance of Puerto Rico as a strategic point of defense of the Panama Canal, the South Atlantic and the Gulf states, and the trade routes of the Caribbean."[2] The President and his military leaders were well aware of this. Plans were made to build major air force and naval bases in Puerto Rico. In September, 1940, Roosevelt and British Prime Minister Winston Churchill established a 4,500-mile "American defense line" for the Western Hemisphere should the British and French Caribbean colonies come under Nazi pressure. The U.S. gave Great Britain 50 "old destroyers" in exchange for U.S. use of naval bases from Newfoundland to Bermuda and the Caribbean islands of Bahamas, Jamaica, Trinidad, and Antigua.

Tugwell had carried out several missions for Roosevelt in the Caribbean in recent years and considered himself an expert on the region. He warned that it was vital for the Allies to attend to the serious political and economic problems in many of the islands. "How could we build a chain of fortresses on thickly settled islands that were hostile?"[3]

After another visit to the Caribbean in 1940, Tugwell came up with one of his grandiose schemes. He recommended that the United States, in effect, take over the entire region "as a Protectorate," and organize it under "a general Caribbean government of some sort." "We must work out a system of representation with full territorial status which will permit the free functioning of all our Federal welfare agencies within a plan authorized by Congress for rehabilitation."[4]

The President and State Department quickly rejected Tugwell's Caribbean Protectorate. But now that France had fallen and England was tottering under the German siege, his warning took on an added sense of urgency. Again he brought up the importance of getting the support of local populations. "It was not unthinkable," he wrote, "that we might be involved in serious local trouble exactly when we had, with our bases half ready, to brace ourselves against attack; and if it came it would be well planned, almost overwhelming, as Nazi attacks had been elsewhere."[5]

---

2. Morales Carrión, *Puerto Rico: A Political and Cultural History*, 248.

3. Tugwell, *Stricken Land*, 69.

4. Ibid., 97.

5. Ibid., 99.

The question Ickes wanted Tugwell to answer was whether the United States was again headed towards "serious local trouble" in that tropical "barrel of snakes" called Puerto Rico. Was Muñoz up to his old troublemaking, stirring up the desperately poor Puerto Ricans with promises neither he nor anyone else could keep?

What irked Ickes the most was Muñoz's attitude since the elections. He was talking and acting as if he did indeed run Puerto Rico. Who was going to pay for Muñoz's promises of massive social and economic reforms? As far as Ickes knew, no one had relieved him of his responsibility over Puerto Rico and passed it on to Muñoz. Ickes himself had no problem with expropriating thousands of acres owned by American corporations. He still had vivid images of the inhuman, "putrid slums" he had witnessed during his trip to the island. But Muñoz's radical plans would certainly end up on his desk and the Puerto Rican leader had committed the cardinal sin of not having discussed them with him, much less sought his endorsement.

Tugwell understood Ickes's anxiety. Somehow he had to bring Muñoz down to reality: "Muñoz, well as he should have known the United States, has fallen into the error of all insular politicians—he forgot that political victory in Puerto Rico was a matter of no interest to Continentals... Obviously my first task was going to be a diplomatic one: to persuade Muñoz that he had made a mistake which had better be rectified at once, and to win from the Secretary a pretty large tolerance for what he obviously regarded as a serious slight."[6]

As Tugwell and a team of agriculture experts made their way to San Juan at the beginning of March, 1942, again he felt overwhelmed by the magnitude and complexity of any renewed program to lift the island from its abysmal poverty. He recalled his great efforts to push the Chardón Plan forward, the millions spent on the island, hardly making a dent in the people's misery.

During his years in the Roosevelt administration, Tugwell initiated programs to combat rural poverty by resettling poor families from eroded to productive soil. But this approach was not possible in Puerto Rico: "The soil

6. Ibid., 13.

and the climate would not bear the burden of feeding two million people. The people themselves had outrun their food supply, if not their other resources."[7]

There was no more ambiguity over the implementation of the 500-acre-law. Ickes assured Tugwell that it was now Washington's "established policy." It was, after all, federal law upheld by the Supreme Court. But as Tugwell thought about this, he looked out the window of his aircraft flying over Haiti—a century earlier a rich exporter of sugar, molasses, coffee, and rum. After its revolution, the rulers carried out a land distribution reform similar to the one advocated by Muñoz. As the population grew, the land was divided into smaller and smaller farms, cutting production and its exports to about a tenth of what they had been, throwing the Haitians backwards into even greater poverty. Is this, Tugwell asked himself, where Muñoz is taking his island?

> The *Populares* in Puerto Rico appeared to be following the easy path down which so many other reform movements had gone. They were holding out to their followers "a piece of land," at once the most attractive and most betraying of promises a leader can make to an underprivileged people. It has always sufficed to get a group into power. But when put into practice it has always made the economy weaker by lowering total income. So that, although the incubus of exploiting landlords was thrown off, what had been taken in profits was seen to be a good deal less than what had been gained by superior management under their regime.[8]

Tugwell's foreboding only grew after he arrived in Puerto Rico and toured the island, revisiting some of the same horrid slums he had witnessed with Eleanor Roosevelt seven years earlier. He was again struck by the cruel contrast between the island's spectacular scenic beauty, along the coast and up in the mountainous central area, and the inhuman squalor of the people. If Muñoz's land distribution plan was not the solution, certainly the assault on the "absentee-owned sugar corporations" was justified. These

---

7. Ibid., 19.

8. Moscoso, *Annals of the American Academy of Political and Social Science*, 20.

companies, he was convinced, were "milking" the American consumer for $20 million a year in higher sugar prices. "Was it justified with higher wages and better living conditions in Puerto Rico?" he asked himself. "I thought not as I looked around...wages were miserable, living cost high, housing as bad, surely as any in the world, people half starved on a diet inherited by ration from the days of slavery, and sick with all the diseases to which malnutrition and ill-housed people are subject in the tropics."[9] Tugwell agreed with Muñoz "that some drastic change in the economy was needed, and certainly that it meant less emphasis on sugar."

KINDRED SPIRITS

Tugwell painted a vivid picture of Muñoz in 1941:

> I myself had not seen Muñoz for years and only recall him vaguely as a sad-eyed, companionable, heavy-mustached man. I liked him in the way one does like a casual acquaintance with whose views about the world are exchanged in a like-minded way. He was obviously a Spaniard by blood; dark and heavily built; and it was an added attraction that he spoke a full, flexible, meaty English without indication or origin, except, perhaps, a trace of New Yorkese in expression, though his tongue was altogether without accent. I remember saying a word of appreciation for that once and having him tell me humorously that his English was better than his Spanish. What was true, as he admitted, was that he was one of the few people who *felt* in two languages.

But while Tugwell was so taken by Muñoz' personality and intelligence, he shared the feeling of others that he "wasted his abilities...abilities even if inflated with the intoxications of discourse without responsibility."[10]

If Tugwell approached Muñoz with trepidation, Muñoz could not have been more pleased by his return to the island. Unaware of Ickes's fears and

---

9. Tugwell, *Stricken Land*, 34.

10. Ibid., 10.

resentment of his "serious slight," Muñoz saw the Tugwell commission as confirmation of the "convergence of the Roosevelt Administration and the Popular Democratic Party government." After the disaster of Governor Gore, and after two military officers, here was a man Muñoz considered a kindred spirit. Both had immersed themselves in Marxism, emerging with strong sentiments against all forms of totalitarianism and equally strong convictions that capitalist competition, fueled by greed, was at the root of the destructive impulses in humankind—including, Tugwell argued, the horror of modern war.

Both professed disdain for partisan politics: Muñoz rationalizing it, Tugwell maintaining his distance in undisguised contempt. But beyond their intellectual compatibility, there were important practical reasons for Muñoz to be pleased. Tugwell retained access to the President who continued to value his friendship and advice. As he had demonstrated in the Chardón Plan, he was a creative, innovative thinker who relished taking risks. His scholarly works, his years as a university professor, his experience in the federal government and later as the organizer and head of New York City planning had earned him an international reputation as an expert in public administration, especially in economic and physical planning. In the hard work of government, as distinguished from politics, Tugwell was everything Muñoz wasn't. For one who believed he was going to "run" Puerto Rico, Tugwell was a god-send.

There was still one more connection between the 43-year-old Muñoz and the 50-year-old Tugwell. They were both prolific writers, aspiring poets in their early years. Similar to Muñoz, Tugwell had grandiloquent aspirations for himself as a young men. He proclaimed in one of his early poems: "I shall roll up my sleeve—make America over!"

TUGWELL'S OTHER SIDE

There was, however, another side to Tugwell: what appeared to be a propensity for creating controversy by generating hostility. His advocacy of powerful central planning—what he called the "fourth power" of government, equal to the other three—was berated by conservatives as a euphemism for

Soviet-style economic state control. His contempt for "politicians," especially members of Congress, reinforced the perception of contempt for representative democracy. Tugwell attributed the extraordinary hostility not only of the anti-New Deal forces in Washington, but of newspapers and the advertising industry, to his campaign to give the old Food and Drug Administration the teeth to regulate the labeling and advertising of foods and drugs.

But it was also his personality. "Tugwell's own cockiness or condescension of manner only compounded his difficulties," wrote one of his admirers, historian Arthur M. Schlesinger, Jr. "His impatience with fools and bores and members of Congress (categories he sometimes found indistinguishable), his chilly refusal to accept businessmen at their own evaluation, his addiction to academic language and to soaring social speculation—all this complicated his position in Washington."[11] It would also "complicate his position" in Puerto Rico.

One afternoon, while Muñoz was relaxing with Tugwell and Jaime Benítez at the *Punta de Cangrejos* recreational area, watching the strong Atlantic tide crashing against the rocks, Muñoz, out of the blue, invited Tugwell to become Chancellor of the University of Puerto Rico. The idea took Tugwell and Benítez by surprise. Decades later Muñoz recalled Benítez, then the leader of the University reform movement, jerking his head up, his thick mane of hair blowing in the wind, his eyes fixed for a moment towards the sky, as if to ask: Good Lord, where did this come from? But he seconded Muñoz's offer. Tugwell expressed interest and promised to think about it.

Tugwell had another idea. Ickes originally asked him if he was interested in heading the Interior Department's Division of Territories. This was not what Tugwell was after. It would have been a demotion from his early New Deal days as Agriculture Secretary. Once on the island, Governor Guy J. Swope confessed that he was interested in that same Interior Department post. Tugwell asked himself: why not have Ickes go ahead and name Swope, and then have the President name him, Tugwell, Governor of Puerto Rico?

He was now convinced more than ever that this would be indeed vital "war work." Tugwell agreed with Winston Churchill and others that envisioned a gigantic Axis movement, the then allied German and Russian

---

11. Schlesinger, *The Coming of the New Deal*, 360.

forces meeting in the Middle East, moving on to India and meeting the Japanese. Then "it would be straight on to the Caribbean with South and North American flank movements branching out of that central Sea. San Juan might indeed soon be the center of the world at war!"[12]

Tugwell expressed his interest directly to Roosevelt, who quickly approved it. Returning to the island, he stunned Muñoz with the question: "Would Puerto Ricans rather have me as Governor or as Chancellor?" Muñoz answered exuberantly: "Both!" Tugwell agreed. Muñoz assured him that he would get a ten-year contract and that the Legislature would approve the university reform law for which Benítez and others were clamoring. They agreed that he would be named permanent Chancellor and temporary Governor. Although the University's board balked at the ten-year contract, on July 24, 1941, it proceeded to name Tugwell the Chancellor.

"Whatever he touched," Schlesinger wrote in describing Tugwell, "ran into trouble."[13] When the news broke early the next month that President Roosevelt had appointed him Governor and that he would occupy both posts, although with the salary of one, it ignited a political explosion. The island's principal newspaper, El Mundo, consistently critical of Muñoz, now declared war on Tugwell. The Coalition, led by resident commissioner Bolívar Pagán in Washington, immediately joined the battle. It was evident to Muñoz that he had made a mistake. Tugwell quickly agreed that he should step down from the university. As much as Muñoz's election, however, Tugwell's appointment as Governor sent tremors of fear throughout the Puerto Rican business world. The President had sent a "radical liberal"–Red Rex!—to La Fortaleza to join the "radical reformer" Muñoz and the Legislature controlled by his independentista party. Muñoz's seemingly preposterous rhetoric of an "economic and social revolution" loomed as a pending and terrifying reality. The war against Tugwell carried on by the Coalition and El Mundo was to continue unabated for the five years he remained as Governor.

A seemingly insignificant incident in Washington in August, 1941 took on still another menacing aspect in the eyes of the opposition. Eleanor Roosevelt invited Muñoz to a party at Hyde Park, and Muñoz, as had occurred eight years earlier at the White House, found himself seated close to the

12. Tugwell, The Stricken Land, 112.
13. Schlesinger, The Coming of the New Deal, 361.

President. When Roosevelt turned to introduce him to other guests, he referred to him as "what we can call the Prime Minister of Puerto Rico." Years later, Muñoz himself speculated whether this was Roosevelt's whimsical humor, perhaps he was momentarily confused as to Muñoz's real title. In any case, this was reported in Puerto Rico as further proof that Muñoz and Tugwell were engaging in secret, sinister plots to tamper with Puerto Rico's status.[14]

In Washington, the Coalition's Bolívar Pagán found the conservative members of Congress, Democrats as well as Republicans, eager to join the battle against their old adversary. Tugwell's Senate confirmation process, as expected, revived the intense hostility. Republican Senator Robert Taft described him as "the worst administrator who ever lived...a failure at everything he ever tried."[15] Tugwell was forewarned to prepare himself to be interrogated about rumors that, paradoxically, painted him not as a dangerous communist, but as a greedy carpetbagger. Conservatives were preparing to unearth evidence that he and his friend Charles Taussig "conspired" to introduce hairbrained "socialist" schemes that would greatly devalue Puerto Rico's sugar land. Taussig would then move in to snatch these lands at ridiculously deflated prices.[16] The "evidence" never surfaced and he was confirmed.

That the new Governor and Muñoz would work in tandem was confirmed in Tugwell's September 21, 1941 speech after taking the oath for office. Echoing Muñoz's campaign rhetoric, Tugwell proclaimed that the era of economic and political domination by "absentee capitalists" had ended. He criticized those Puerto Rican intellectuals and *políticos* obsessed with political status and "culture" while the island sunk in economic and social misery. He assured Puerto Ricans that their status would be determined by them: that their decision would be "totally respected." This meant, as Tugwell forcefully assured Muñoz, that the moment Puerto Rico asked for independence, it would get it.

Tugwell's vision of Puerto Rico's economic future also mirrored that of Muñoz and the Popular Party. He saw it almost exclusively in terms of

14. Muñoz Marín, *Memorias*, Vol. II, 57.
15. Tugwell, *Stricken Land*, 142.
16. Ibid., 136.

agricultural development and of agriculture-based industries, such as rum production. What were needed to make the island's land more productive were good "leaders, administrators, technicians."

The centerpiece of Muñoz's land reform was the Land Authority, a public corporation that would acquire land either though purchase or expropriation with compensation, and would then subdivide it into small farms. Muñoz himself had come up with a new scheme to overcome Tugwell's fear that Puerto Rico would repeat Haiti's costly error of unproductive farm fragmentation. "The proportional-benefit farm," economist Harvey Perloff wrote in 1950, "was Puerto Rico's original and ingenious answer to the dual need for land reform and the retention of the efficiency of large-scale operations in the highly competitive sugar industry." Was Muñoz, Tugwell asked himself, finally coming down to earth? His scheme would turn the big sugar plantations into profit-distribution cooperatives. Tugwell was now enthusiastically behind the reform. There was no holding back for implementing the 500-acre law. He wrote: "A more flagrant and irresponsible disregard of law—and a Federal law at that—would be hard to find in all of history."[17]

But as Muñoz and Tugwell pushed forward, the "war" against them escalated. By the Spring of 1942 a full-scale drive to oust Tugwell from Puerto Rico had begun. Now major labor unions joined the ranks of the Chamber of Commerce, the industrial and agricultural associations, and the opposition parties and newspapers. Bolívar Pagán's incessant attacks in Congress, meanwhile, were having an effect. The resurgence of "anti-democratic Red Rex" as a target for conservatives in Washington was timely. Was there anything more "anti-democratic" than Roosevelt's decision to run for a fourth term in 1944?

At times the unrelenting attacks got to Tugwell. "My years of public life ought to have taught me what to expect," he wrote several years later. "But I admit to having been surprised not only in Washington, but also a little later in San Juan, at the massiveness and determination of the opposition that I encountered."[18] The newspaper *El Mundo*, as historian Charles Goodsell described it in 1965, engaged in "an extraordinarily uninhibited

---

17. Ibid., 8.
18. Tugwell, *Stricken Land*, 137.

campaign against Tugwell, carrying almost every day one or more prominently placed articles on the latest demagoguery, rumors and allegations."[19]

The Empty Shell

And there was the old paradox of the office Tugwell held. While he listened to the Puerto Ricans riling endlessly against American "colonialism" as personified in the governorship, and while up in Washington the conservatives seemed to be losing sleep over his "socialist dictatorship," Tugwell felt more and more that he was, in fact, powerless, that decades of American neglect and ineptness had made the Office of the Governor an "empty shell."

> What I saw was the twilight of confused colonialism: the occupiers were defeated by their own bumbling and by the everlasting self-interest and intimate knowledge of the occupied. The shell of authority was empty. The generous subsidies were managed by subterranean machines. Governors seemed powerless to counteract, though as politicians they might understand it well enough. There was a delicious irony in the situation, quite to the taste of the islanders, and they smiled while [the Governor] would labor in futility, they had lost their colony but they had ruined its Government.[20]

For Muñoz, what was taking place in Puerto Rico was even stranger. It was, he wrote decades later, "a curious class war that took place during the next four years." On one side the Coalition and business leaders, backed by part of the Washington bureaucracy and a large part of Congress. On the other side was a populist political movement, seeking to represent the poorest of the poor: "a party, to the amazement of the 'good people' that had the support of Governor Tugwell, Interior Secretary Ickes, and the President of

---

19. Goodsell, *Administration of a Revolution: Executive Reform in Puerto Rico under Governor Tugwell 1941-1946*, 25.
20. Ibid., 81.

the United States: that is, those always personified as 'the imperialists' were now the reformers and revolutionaries."[21]

REVOLTING A HOTTENTOT

Nothing dramatized American failure as the gut-wrenching sights and revolting smells of *El Fanguito*. How was it possible that America had overcome the enormous plight of the Great Depression, was now taking on the greatest military and totalitarian threat to human civilization in history, but could not clear out this inhuman, putrid slum in San Juan?

Tugwell recalled his sharing with Eleanor Roosevelt a sense of shame during that visit back in 1934 and the resolution that this intolerable "disgrace to the American flag" had to be erased as soon as possible. Two years later, in January, 1936, not only was it still there, but worse. This time it was Ickes who was revolted by *El Fanguito* and other foul ghettos: "the worst slums I have ever seen... Open sewerage runs through the streets and around the buildings and there are no sanitary facilities at all. The children play in this sewerage, which in many cases is covered with thick, green scum..."[22]

Now, five years later, Tugwell told himself, if nothing else he would do something about it, and it would begin with Roosevelt himself. He had photographs taken, went up to Washington and placed them before the President. These were photos, he wrote, "that would have revolted a Hottentot—and on such questions, Mr. Roosevelt was never a Hottentot. He said that, damn it, he had told every Governor since he had been President that it was his business to clear up that disgrace to the flag—and now, eight years after he had begun to talk about it, I was showing him that it was many times worse than at the beginning."[23] Roosevelt called his secretary and issued an order: "The slums in Puerto Rico are a menace to public health. This should be attended by the Surgeon General of the Navy and

---

21. Muñoz Marín, *Memorias* Vol. II, 48.
22. Watkins, *Righteous Pilgrim: The Life and Times of Harold L. Ickes*, 512.
23. Tugwell, *Stricken Land*, 126.

the Medical Director of the Army. Then you should find a source of funds and get this project done."[24] Tugwell left the White House convinced that he had accomplished his mission: he had indeed "revolted the Hottentot."

THE BEST AND WORST OF TIMES

"Nineteen hundred and forty-two," Tugwell recorded, "will, in local history, be regarded as, at once, one of the most disastrous and one of the most fruitful of years." A day after declaring war on the United States on December 11, 1941, Hitler ordered Admiral Karl Doenitz's U-boats to cross the Atlantic to the American east coast, the Caribbean and the ports of the Gulf of Mexico, in a massive preemptive attack to cripple the American merchant marine and navy and cut Britain's vital supply line. By March of 1942, the German submarines had sunk 788,000 tons of American shipping, 375,000 tons in oil tankers alone.[25]

Tugwell's prediction proved right. The Caribbean was in the thick of the war. By the end of 1942, the shipment of food and energy to Puerto Rico was reduced to a trickle: from an average of 120,000 tons a month, down to only 7,000 tons. While the island's economy could have benefited from the great demand in the U.S. for Puerto Rican rum, due to the ban on alcohol production in the U.S., there was no way to get the rum to the mainland. The prices of staples leaped 53 percent from November 1941 to November 1942. Aside from military construction, Puerto Rico had no war-related industries. Unemployment jumped from 99,100 in July 1941 to 237,000 in September, 1942.

It was indeed the "worst of times." Squeezed by inflation and unemployment, the unions that had backed Muñoz and his pro-labor party were now bitterly protesting and calling crippling strikes. "Economic life is practically paralyzed," Tugwell cabled Washington.[26]

---

24. Ibid., 127.

25. MacGregor Burns, *Roosevelt: the Soldier of Freedom*, 243.

26. Goodsell, *Administration of a Revolution: Executive Reform in Puerto Rico under Governor Tugwell 1941-1946*, 21.

But 1942 was also the "most fruitful of years." Charles Goodsell compared the spring of 1942 to "the First Hundred Days in Washington in 1933: "Puerto Rican Legislature enacted a statutory program of monumental proportions...The ninety-odd days between February 9 and May 14, 1942 witnessed the passage and approval of a great share of the statutory underpinning of the Puerto Rican revolution. In a single week of this historic period no less than seven major public institutions were signed into legal existence, all of which were still functioning in the middle nineteen-sixties."[27]

Among the new agencies created were an independent Planning Board—although not as powerful nor as free from the executive and legislative branches, and from partisan politics as Tugwell wanted—that would control urban construction and establish economic and physical development priorities: the Budget Bureau, for the first time providing the insular government with orderly, coordinating program spending authorization that went beyond government patronage; a Transportation and Communications Authority to substitute the bankrupt and chaotic public transportation system in San Juan and to establish a telegraph network throughout the island. The Authority was authorized to acquire the private telephone company.

Also approved was a law to transfer to the new Aqueduct and Sewer Authority the small and inefficient systems in the growing metropolitan areas and in rural zones; a law authorizing the new Electric Power Authority (*Autoridad de Fuentes Fluviales*) to acquire or expropriate the several private power companies; a law declaring that the private sugar corporations constituted a "public service industry" under government regulation; a law to reform and depoliticize the University of Puerto Rico, removing from its board of directors the political appointees, the President of the Senate and Speaker of the House. Directly related to the war, the Legislature approved and Tugwell signed bills creating a Civil Defense Office and a State Guard to replace the National Guard that had been nationalized by the President. The young pharmacist from Ponce, Moscoso, now an assistant to Tugwell, convinced Muñoz and the Governor to create still two more entities: the Economic Development Company, which Moscoso himself organized and headed, and the Government Development Bank.

---

27. Ibid., 22.

Tugwell relived his exhilarating role back in 1933 in the "first hundred days" of the New Deal. "The second genuinely creative period of my public life was written on the lawbook and in the institutions of Puerto Rico before the end of the year." All this was, of course, "Muñoz's revolution." But Tugwell, resisting the relentless attacks on the island and from Washington, had reasons to feel that this was also his revolution. And most remarkable for Muñoz and Tugwell was that all this was accomplished while the island was being brutally strangled by the devastating economic effects of the Nazi submarine warfare in the Atlantic and the Caribbean.

16 Surviving Nazi Submarines and the U.S. Congress

Muñoz and Tugwell found themselves also with an "enemy within." The insular Attorney General George Malcolm decided that all the new agencies were "illegal." The Organic Act that regulated the Puerto Rican government specifically prohibited the creation of new departments. The Auditor, Patrick J. Fitzsimmons, joined Malcolm in pointing out that none of the new entities could spend over dollars without his approval, which he was denying.

The Auditor and the Attorney General were supposedly part of Tugwell's administration. But again, the organizational structure contradicted the function. Both were named by the President and confirmed by the U.S. Senate: both extended their loyalties and accountability, not to the Governor, but to Washington. As had Governor Winship, they were convinced that it was their duty to save the island and their nation from Muñoz and Tugwell's "radical schemes."

They found other means. The Organic Act required a balanced budget. A bookkeeping gimmick traditionally used by auditors to allow programs to proceed was to keep legislative appropriations "off the books" until the funds appeared. Fitzsimmons suddenly placed all the new agencies "on the books," grossly unbalancing the budget: another insular violation of federal law. A chart was published in *The World Journal*, the English-language newspaper published by *El Mundo*, depicting how Tugwell's "Mussolini-like regime... totalitarian monster" centered around the Governor's pride and joy, the new Planning Board.

The new agencies, Muñoz and Tugwell pointed out, were not government "departments" but "public corporations" meant to be self-sustaining through their own incomes and thus should not be included in the operational budget. Muñoz tried to appease the Auditor and got the Legislature to repeal many of the minor, non-essential spending allocations. Fitzsimmons persisted. Tugwell lambasted Fitzsimmons and Malcolm as "traitors" that had become the tools of the "reactionaries" in San Juan and Washington.

In their nights of socializing, Tugwell often thought that Muñoz was idealistic and even naive about what was happening in Washington. Muñoz talked as if the New Deal spirit of 1933 and 34 was still alive. It was not, Tugwell lamented. The war and the promise to make America the "arsenal of democracy," he argued, had forced Roosevelt to allow the selfish, greedy capitalists back into the temple. And Roosevelt himself, Tugwell continued, was "betrayed" by the many old New Dealers in Congress that now were part of the conservative wave that had taken over Washington. In the 1942 congressional elections, the Republicans gained 44 House seats and eight in the Senate. The Democrats barely retained control of Congress. All this, Tugwell warned Muñoz, meant that they had better prepare themselves for the political hurricanes sure to come from the opposition's forces converging in Washington—the "apolitical" assaults of Fitzsimmons and Malcolm, the endless diatribe of Bolívar Pagán, and now the powerful coalition of anti-New Deal Southern Democrats and Republicans that controlled Congress.

"I have a feeling," Tugwell noted in his diary, "that there is a whole crowd now determined to 'get' me, on manufactured evidence, if necessary. It is a feeling much like being very empty but not having hunger. It must be the same feeling that Jews have in Germany, or Negroes in the south."[1]

"WE WILL NOT PERMIT THIS!"

Tugwell's warning to Muñoz and his foreboding proved right. On January 6, 1943, Michigan Republican Senator Arthur H. Vandenburg introduced a bill to remove Tugwell. It declared the governorship vacant 60 days after

---

1. Tugwell, *The Stricken Land*, 399.

approval, then set a two-year term for future governors. That the Insular Attorney General Malcolm was also a Republican from Michigan seemed to Tugwell to be no coincidence. Resident Commissioner Bolívar Pagán followed quickly with an identical bill in the House.

Five days later, on January 11, Puerto Rico was again rocked by what Muñoz, decades later, described "as one of the most shameful actions of Puerto Rico's colonial system." Another Michigan Republican, Representative Fred Crawford, introduced a resolution to nullify, by congressional fiat, the new Muñoz-Tugwell government agencies. Bolívar Pagán pointed out that under the Organic Act, Congress had the power to annul any law approved by the island Legislature—a power Congress had never exercised.

Muñoz counterattacked. He sent a letter to Secretary Ickes decrying that "approval of the Crawford's resolution, I need hardly tell you, would create a condition of moral chaos in Puerto Rico."[2] At stake was much more than the new agencies. It told the *jíbaros* "that came down from the mountains on election day without breakfast, who were offered five and ten dollars for their votes and who did not take it, that the democracy they thought they were exercising is a damn lie."

In a scorching radio speech on January 18, after comparing the conspiracy of Bolívar and the "reactionary forces" behind the Crawford's resolution to the "satanic forces unleashed by Hitler on the people's freedom," Muñoz attempted to ignite a public protest against the measure: "Wherever there is a Puerto Rican with shame that is listening to me, he is repeating with me these words: We will not permit it! We will not permit it! We will not permit it!"

The Crawford's resolution was not approved or even considered. But on January 19, the Senate Committee on Territories approved Michigan Senator Vandenburg's "get rid of Tugwell" measure by a vote of nine to three. Secretary Ickes sent a memo stating that it was "unconstitutional... a bill of attainder... a legislative act which inflicts punishment without a judicial trial." The committee ignored Ickes.

Tugwell would, however, get his "trial." New Mexico Senator Dennis Chávez, who spoke Spanish and whose daughter, married to a Puerto Rican, lived on the island, headed a commission to conduct an on-the-spot

---

2. Muñoz Marín, *Memorias*, Vol II., 92.

investigation of the mounting charges against the Governor. Tugwell had every reason to fear this "investigation." Soon after arriving on the island, one of the Chávez committee members, Senator Owen Brewster, forewarned him: "You are up against it. Congress has a lynching party all prepared for you and I don't think it can be stopped."[3]

Tugwell had put up with the attacks from Pagán and *El Mundo*, and even the "traitors" within his own administration, but a congressional "lynching party" convinced him that he had had enough. He indicated to the Interior Department in Washington that he was willing to resign. This leaked to the press and the island media published headlines reporting his imminent departure. Coalition leaders "confirmed" that this was true. Fearful that it might be true, Muñoz insisted that Tugwell "stick it out." He assured him that during a recent visit to Washington, Secretary Ickes, his deputy, Abe Fortas, and the President himself had expressed their solid support.[4]

Tugwell and Muñoz were surprised by Chávez. Tugwell had been alerted by the Interior Department that Chávez was "anti-administration" and "was dancing cheek to cheek with Mr. Felipe de Hostos," the president of the insular Chamber of Commerce and one of Tugwell's most vociferous opponents. But the Senator from New Mexico decided to go beyond the formal testimony, mostly damning to Tugwell, to get the "view from the people." The committee made extensive visits to the island, up into the mountains and into remote rural areas. The Senators walked into *colmados*, across cane fields and into coffee farms, talking to as many *jíbaros* as they could. Gradually a picture emerged radically different from what they had been getting from Bolívar Pagán, de Hostos, and the other critics. "The Chávez group," Tugwell noted, "after a look for themselves, made up their minds that they had been hoaxed by their Washington informants."[5]

ROBERT TAFT

Even more unexpected was the apparent conversion of Senator Robert Taft, long one of Tugwell's harshest critics, expected to be at the front of the

---

3. Tugwell, *The Stricken Land*, 471.
4. Ibid., 433.
5. Ibid., 467.

"lynching party." Tugwell wrote years later: "the greatest surprise that the Committee had for us, after all the newspaper accounts, would be to discover how honest and sagacious Mr. Taft could be and how genuine an interest in Puerto Rico he would have." Tugwell had deliberately assigned Teodoro Moscoso, the head of one of the new agencies under attack, the Industrial Development Company, to accompany Taft during his entire visit. Moscoso, with his aggressive, no-nonsense demeanor, looked and talked much more like a young entrepreneur than a "socialist radical." He also testified before the committee. When Taft expressed his doubts that the island could attract significant private investments, Moscoso assured the Senator that if necessary he would "sell his soul to the Devil" to create jobs through private industrial investment. Muñoz and Tugwell cringed, but several years later Taft remembered the exchange and the young Puerto Rican's exuberance. Taft gave Moscoso critical support in launching Puerto Rico's industrialization.[6]

At one social gathering in an exclusive club in Ponce, a prominent and "expensive" sugar corporation lawyer criticized the new electric power authority as "unconstitutional." Tugwell, who was present, saw "Taft turn red," cutting the lawyer short. The fact that he was Republican and conservative, Taft shot back, did not mean that he did not understand the difference between "what is political and what is legal." Another Senator then broke in to remind the lawyer, "with some amusement," that it had been precisely Taft's father who, as U.S. Supreme Court Chief Justice, had established the constitutionality of the government operating power systems.[7]

After most of the Senators left the island, Taft stayed behind for a few days. Muñoz took him up to the beautiful *El Yunque* rain forest. "Taft," Muñoz wrote, "was really surprised by the irresponsibility of the attacks made against the Government of Puerto Rico. Personally he was against the government running business enterprises, but he certainly did not feel that it was a crime to do so, or that it was unconstitutional. Furthermore, he was now aware that the situation in Puerto Rico was so different to that in the United States, that public policies he attacked there could be justified for their urgent need here."[8]

---

6. Maldonado, *Teodoro Moscoso and Puerto Rico's Operation Bootstrap*, 39.

7. Tugwell, *The Stricken Land*, 469.

8. Muñoz Marín, *Memorias*, Vol. II. 108.

The opposition was amazed. By the time the Chávez committee had left the island on February 20, 1943, Tugwell and Muñoz had somehow transformed the "lynching party" into what the opponents nicknamed a "whitewash committee."

THE FIRING SQUAD

But Tugwell found himself again under congressional attack. The gun was being fired this time by a House of Representatives committee. Headed by representative Charles Jasper Bell, a lawyer and former judge from Missouri, the committee arrived on the island on May 31, 1943. Tugwell overheard one of Bell's staff members comment that this time there would be no disgraceful "whitewash." He was right. Having saved his neck, he now found himself facing what Muñoz called a "firing squad." Years later Muñoz wrote: "With the exception of one or two of its members, it became the shock troops of the Puerto Rican counter-revolution... The committee's public hearings were an orgy of reaction: a defense, with or without reason, of all that constituted minority private interests."[9]

Back in Washington, the committee had received extensive testimony from Fitzsimmons and Malcolm, including the "incriminating" chart depicting Tugwell's "totalitarian monster." Answering a question from the committee, Fitzsimmons assured the committee that Tugwell was repudiated by the vast majority of Puerto Ricans and that Muñoz "will be swept from power in the next elections."

So convinced were the representatives that Tugwell and Muñoz had imposed a regime of fear, that the committee announced that any person that was afraid "of reprisals" could testify in a closed session. One of the federal officials who did so was a former Interior Department supply officer, who described Tugwell and Muñoz as: "dye in the wool communists." Muñoz, he said, was a "Bohemian" dreamer while Tugwell was a "perfect surrealist" who himself did not believe in his unreal projects.

---

9. Ibid., 95.

The hearings lasted into July, by far the longest ever held by a congressional committee on the island. This time there were no conversions. The antagonism against Tugwell was inexorable. He noted in his memoirs: "Long as I had been used to hostility from those who dislike the cut of my political clothes and perhaps my ideological manners, I should hardly have believed it could run to such venom..."[10]

Muñoz retaliated in a harsh *j'accuse* letter to the committee, cosigned by House Speaker Rubén Arrillaga: "With what moral authority do you attempt to control what the people of Puerto Rico decide to do with the limited democracy that they are permitted to exercise...? The truth is that... we have much more reason to investigate your motives and intentions with respect to our democracy than what you may have to investigate our efforts to alleviate our own suffering."[11]

The Committee produced what it had intended, a stinging indictment of Tugwell's regime, including the testimonies of Fitzsimmons, Malcolm, and numerous other critics. But the 1200-page report, accompanied by a thick volume of the transcripts and exhibits, was not released until two years later, 1945, and by then it was ignored.

Puerto Rico had survived the congressional onslaught, but Tugwell was concerned about the emotional backlash on the young, talented Puerto Ricans he and Muñoz had recruited for government service:

> I had been trying to represent to my young men, the promising managers of a Puerto Rican irredenta, the new United States. I had never told them so, but I hoped they—and all Puerto Ricans— would infer from my position on all the public questions, by my loyalties and my conduct, that the United States was worthy of their patriotic regard. I hoped thus to destroy the last vestiges of colonialism in their minds and to give them a sense of oneness with those of us on the continent who were also liberals and to convince them that they might tie to us with gratitude and trust.[12]

---

10. Tugwell, *The Stricken Land*, 515.

11. Muñoz Marín, *Memorias*, Vol. II, 100.

12. Ibid., 536.

Tugwell was grateful that throughout Muñoz had remained steadfast: "And Muñoz had consistently contributed to the establishment of this concept. None of the thrusts at me and my policies in Puerto Rico had affected that—indeed they had strengthened the faith now growing in many minds. Not even the attacks of a partisan minority in Congress or the cruel lies and insinuations of the continental press affected it."

Muñoz, Tugwell had seen first hand, was tough. Working together, their "democratic revolution" had come through, but it has been a close call. The siege, Tugwell wrote, "nearly destroyed all Muñoz and I had built."

By the summer of 1943, Puerto Rico had also survived the Nazi submarine onslaught. "Rice and beans were plentiful again," Tugwell reported.[13]

---

13. Tugwell, *The Stricken Land*, 574.

17 A Great Victory and a Hard Question

On January 14, 1944, Muñoz gave an unusual radio speech. He attempted a "conversation" with the thousands of *jíbaros* listening to him. The Popular Party local committees had mobilized its followers and as many others as they could induce to form groups at homes with radios, at *colmados*, at the town plazas. Muñoz began by declaring that he was going to ask a series of questions. Each listener, in turn, should ask himself if he was hearing empty words, like the words of the old politicians, or if his words corresponded to what they knew, in their own experiences, to be true. Muñoz went on to ask about the improvements in their lives since 1940. Answer out loud, Muñoz said, and if you are not in a group, if you are alone, answer out loud to yourself.

This is not a battle, Muñoz insisted, against the opposition leaders or even reactionary forces. "The true battle in Puerto Rico, the only real battle in Puerto Rico, is the battle against hunger and extreme poverty and the misery and pain suffered by our people—it is a battle to reduce that hunger, that extreme poverty, that misery, that pain... Neither you nor I are fighting against the Republicans, the Socialists, the Coalition, because we get pleasure out of this fight. Damn be the pleasure it could give me, or anyone else, to engage in such a juvenile squabble!"

Muñoz concluded: "I say to those leaders: either join us in this battle, or get out of the way of the people, or the people, with their will, exercised through their vote, will get you out of the road!"

As Tugwell observed Muñoz in the 1944 campaign, there was no question that he had become an effective political leader. The power of the Popular

Democratic Party throughout the island was evident. A year earlier, 1943, Muñoz asked Ernesto Ramos Antonini to collect signatures in support of Tugwell to counteract the attacks from Washington. Ramos turned over boxes filled with notebooks with 314,000 signatures: nearly one hundred thousand more than the Popular Party votes in 1940.

But since arriving on the island, Tugwell had assigned himself another mission; not only to reform this tragically poor and mismanaged American "colony," but to reform this *político* that had so intrigued him. Could he transform this charismatic young man, this underachiever who had wasted so much of his talent, into a statesman?

At times, the teacher was pleased with his student. Muñoz clearly had an enormous appetite for votes, and the test was whether he could contain that appetite when it contradicted good government. A good "test" arose when the public school teachers threatened to go on strike in 1943, demanding immediate salary increases. Muñoz and the Popular Party had taken for granted the support of the underpaid teachers. One of his first reform bills increased their income by 20 percent. Now the conflict posed a serious political threat. Coalition leaders immediately announced their total support of the teachers' demand. What would it be, Tugwell asked himself? Would he be confident enough in his own political leadership to resist this demand?

Speaking at his party's daily radio program, Muñoz said that there were really two, not one, demands being made here: both totally justified, both needing solutions. One was the vocal demand of the underpaid teachers. The other was the demand of 200,000 children unable to go to school due to lack of funds for public education. The response of the "old politics," he went on, was to react only to the loud demand. The difference is that now there is a party that listens and responds to "the forgotten people of Puerto Rico." The party, he declared, would attend to both demands, but first the limited funds would be used to open new schools.

Yet, as the elections neared, Tugwell detected in Muñoz a "strange mixture of confidence and uncertainty which could torment him throughout the year."[1] The endless lecturing, preaching, cajoling, Tugwell felt, was not working. On November 28, 1943, dejected, Tugwell returned from another long and unsettling exchange with Muñoz. That night, he recorded his frustration in his diary:

---

1. Tugwell, *The Stricken Land*, 624.

A weekend at Jájome [the Governor's summer residence up in the mountains] ended friendly enough but had some bitter moments. I warned him frankly, as I felt it my duty to do, of the perils of some of his present policies. I tried to convey to him, what has been growing in my mind, that he had to discover new procedures and better organization or he will find that the movement is too large to be controlled. There is the further danger of the movement turning to other ends than those it began with. It has to keep close to the people and only his leadership, democratically managed, can ensure that. I urged strongly that he work now at renewing his hold on the people. This will be easy for him if his ideas are clear, and if he is persistent. He resented this analysis... His mind is full of fugitive, rather unorganized, but apparently unwise expedients. I urged a consistent course, above intrigue, above patronage, above recriminations. His hold on the people is such that it is not only possible for him but obviously indicated. He must strengthen his direct contacts with them and subordinate the local leadership to them and, as a result, to him. But he is afraid to try it, talks of my being an amateur, says that elections are won by contented party workers, etc., etc., all of which I have heard again and again. But my position is getting stronger because his policy is so obviously failing him. We went over and over these matters for many hours... It all came to no decision, of course... I did not even succeed in getting an admission that my analysis was correct...it was not a happy occasion and we were left in what appeared to be as complete disagreement as in the beginning.[2]

Muñoz's insecurity, Tugwell noted with amazement and amusement, extended even to national politics. Muñoz had convinced himself that Roosevelt would lose the 1944 elections, something Tugwell considered inconceivable. Tugwell noted in his diary: "Muñoz, these days, is in a strange state, a pitiable one... He cannot make up his mind even what the facts are—which I suppose is because he is unable to predict with the certainty which, for instance, I feel about certain matters in the future. He is still apprehensive

---

2. Ibid., 612.

about the [national] election and impressed with the likelihood that he may have to deal with a Republican administration."[3]

BLUNDERS

Muñoz, in fact, had committed what originally appeared to be a serious political blunder. In 1943, to everyone's surprise, Muñoz dramatically denounced his own Popular Party for approving a bill that he believed wrongly benefited the international gasoline companies that operated on the island. Since the 1900 Foraker Act, U.S. excise taxes on goods imported into the island, as well as on Puerto Rican goods imported into the U.S., principally rum and tobacco, were turned over to the insular Treasury. Now, during the war, the large amount of petroleum transshipped through Puerto Rico generated $4 million in tax revenue.

Muñoz angrily condemned as a "monstrous conspiracy" a law that turned these funds over to the petroleum companies. The blame fell on one of his closest, most loyal political lieutenants, the Speaker of the House, Samuel Quiñones, who was also a lawyer for the Shell Oil Company. A painstaking legislative investigation uncovered no evidence of "fraud" or conspiracy. Quiñones was exonerated but it was too late. Muñoz lost the crucial Triparty swing votes. Using his attack as an excuse, they joined the Coalition to remove Quiñones from the House leadership. Muñoz had not only committed a grave injustice against a person that had been by his side since the Liberal Party battles of a decade earlier, but he had also lost control of the Legislature. Quiñones was replaced as Speaker of the House by Rafael Arrillaga Torrens, of the Triparty. When he declared that he would be "neutral," he too was removed and replaced by Triparty representative Rafael Rodríguez Pacheco, who voted with the Coalition. Five months before the elections, the House was deadlocked. Major legislation was paralyzed, including a bill Tugwell considered essential, creating an apolitical civil service based on the merit system.

---

3. Ibid., 652.

This was an astounding victory for the Coalition. It had the potential of stopping the Muñoz-Popular Party juggernaut. The new fiscal 1944-45 budget was not approved. The impact on the elections was enormous. The existing $10 million unemployment insurance program had to be suspended. Thousands of Puerto Ricans, almost all of voting age, were faced with losing their unemployment payments on June 30, 1944.

Muñoz convinced Tugwell to proceed with the payments. A favorable legal opinion from the Attorney General, Manuel Rodríguez Ramos, declared that the $10 million allocation did not expire, but was to be considered part of the hold-over 1944 budget. The Coalition went to court and won. San Juan District Court judge Marcelino Romany issued an injunction. In defiance, Tugwell continued the payments. The judge ordered the arrest of the entire cabinet for "contempt of court." A panicky aide broke into Muñoz's Senate office: "The court marshals are now looking for the cabinet members with arrest orders!" Muñoz thought for a moment, then said: "Get in contact immediately with each one and tell them that my advice is to place themselves where the marshall will most easily find them." Muñoz paused. "Something else. And you, you get a photographer to go immediately to the prison gates."

The following day the photo appeared in the newspapers: the Tugwell cabinet staring out from behind the jail bars at the Princesa Prison in Old San Juan. Muñoz had the photo reproduced in his party newspaper, *El Batey*, with a simple explanation of why the Coalition had put the cabinet in jail.

"Never, in all my political experience," Tugwell wrote, "have I seen a campaign document so effective as the picture of those commissioners looking out determinedly from behind the bars in La Princesa. To the *jíbaro* and the *obrero* it was plain that the members of his government, all *Populares* but one, had suffered the humiliations of prison in order to protect their right to an income during unemployment. It seemed not unlikely, after this incident, that the *Populares'* victory might be so great as to be embarrassing..."[4] The magnitude of the blunder, Muñoz wrote years later, gave it a place of honor "in the rich world history of political error."

---

4. Ibid., 626.

Years later, the picturesque Judge Romany was again news. This time he captured a moment of American political history when, on national TV, as a member of the insular Republican delegation to the 1952 Republican Party Convention, he stopped the roll call on the verge of nominating Dwight Eisenhower for President when he asked for a polling of the tiny Puerto Rican delegation.

There were other blunders by the opposition. In May, Tugwell received at La Fortaleza a copy of an Associated Press story: "Resident Commissioner Bolívar Pagán in a statement and interview yesterday again demanded the resignation of Governor Tugwell. 'The island is almost on the verge of revolution,' Pagán said. If the American flag were not waving over Puerto Rico the people would already have gone into open revolt by arms... Tugwell's dictatorial attitude can be matched only by Hitler's and Mussolini's tactics... Sensible persons wonder how the United States can hold the banner as the champion of democracy throughout the world while two million American citizens continue to live under the most incapable, corrupt and undemocratic government."[5]

The Resident Commissioner asked Congress to cancel the 1944 elections. For Tugwell, this was ridiculous and he assumed it was also for Muñoz. But Muñoz, again demonstrating his jumpiness, overreacted and suggested to Tugwell that he step down temporarily. Perhaps, he added, Admiral Leahy, the Governor during the 1940 elections, could be brought back. "I was a little indignant," Tugwell wrote, "and, naturally, refused to entertain the suggestion that I should be publicly put in the position of admitting the reality of the fantasy creation by the *Coalición*."[6]

Tugwell knew that Pagán's bizarre request would backfire. In Washington, Interior Secretary Ickes declared: "This political attack in [a] time of crisis upon the representative of the United States Government in Puerto Rico is in reality an attack upon the people of Puerto Rico and upon the peace and security of the United States."[7] The President himself reacted. That summer he commented to Tugwell that, incredibly, Pagán had brought to him his demand to cancel the elections that he and his party were sure of

---

5. Ibid., 647.
6. Ibid., 627.
7. Ibid., 427.

losing. Tugwell wrote: "The President told him it was 'one of the most un-American suggestions' which have ever come to the White House and showed how little, after all, the gentleman understood our institutions."[8]

THE 1944 ELECTONS

The inscription of new voters early in an election year was considered an accurate indication of each party's strength. As the new voters exited the registration precinct, representatives of each of the parties requested their copy of the registration form. The forms were then used to update the party's voter's lists. Muñoz spent the day going from one precinct to another, counting the forms given to his people. At the end of the day, they totaled more than all the other parties combined. The Coalition leaders, however, announced that they would go to court to challenge the legality of the 85,019 Popular Party inscriptions. The district court ruled in Muñoz's favor, but the insular Supreme Court reversed the decision.

There was fear that the ruling would ignite serious violence in the already super-heated campaign, as thousands of the rejected voters vowed that they would show up to cast their votes. The tension was so high that ten days before the elections, an anxious Muñoz called for a meeting with the police chiefs and the heads of all the parties to agree to suspend all political rallies and other activities that could set off violent confrontations.

The veteran Coalition leader, Leopoldo Figueroa, representing the Republican Party, challenged Muñoz to "give instructions" to the 85,000 rejected voters to stay away from the precincts. Figueroa expected Muñoz to flatly reject the idea. But he answered that he was in "total agreement." As Muñoz recorded the scene: "Doctor Figueroa was shocked. He was a personal friend and he confessed to me after the elections that it was at that moment that he felt in his bones the certainty of his party's defeat."[9]

On November 7, 1944, Muñoz received the "overwhelming mandate" that he was after. The Popular Party received 64.7 percent, 383,280 votes,

---

8. Ibid., 655.
9. Muñoz Marín, *Memorias* Vol. II, 134.

168,423 more than in 1940, 174,764 more than the three opposition parties combined. It was almost a clean sweep. The party won seventeen of the nineteen Senate seats; thirty-seven of the thirty-nine House seats; seventy-two of the seventy-six municipal governments. Its candidate to represent Puerto Rico in Congress, Jesús T. Piñero, won with almost a two-to-one margin.

As much as Tugwell had admonished Muñoz for his excessive appetite for votes, he was moved by the size of the victory. Clearly, after three years of such sustained attack by politicians and the press, it was also for Tugwell a moving vindication. He believed that he had "made heroic gestures of neutrality." But "I was, in spite of myself, caught in the campaign. I was, in fact, a principal issue." In the U.S., Roosevelt was elected to a fourth term with 53.4 percent of the votes, only slightly down from his 54.4 percent in 1940. In Europe, the Allies liberated Paris and were driving relentlessly towards Berlin. Still Tugwell felt a certain sadness as American officers and men he had befriended over the past three years were now reassigned from the island. "What to us in La Fortaleza was the most noticeable change of all was now complete—the training squadrons of PBMs which had roared and glided over and around us for more than a year has melted away into the west towards the Pacific."[10]

With the resumption of civilian shipping, the island began to receive what promised to be an economic windfall. Puerto Rico was able to meet the big demand for Puerto Rican rum. In late 1943, Tugwell and Muñoz fought back a proposal from the Bell Committee to eliminate the U.S. excise tax rebate. Now Puerto Rico had the potential of undreamed-of funds to finance the reform laws that had been enacted.

Unlike in 1940, this time the Coalition could not deny Muñoz's victory. But it offered an explanation: what Muñoz called "the politics of the poor" was in fact the "politics of demagoguery." Yes, Muñoz had ended vote-buying, but he had spent four years in a more sophisticated form: buying the votes of the *jíbaros* giving away thousands of plots of land, *parcelas*, and doing countless other favors, all at the government's expense—and all this with the fervent support of Rexford Tugwell and the Roosevelt administration. No one could deny that Munoz was a spellbinder. *El Vate,* the Bohemian

---

10. Tugwell, *The Stricken Land*, 615.

many had refused to take seriously, had become a ferocious campaigner, a political fighter with a "killer instinct." For the opposition, Muñoz's overwhelming power had made him another Latin American strongman. From now until his retirement a quarter century later, the essential campaign against Muñoz was that he had so much power in his hands, that he had become a "caudillo."

A HARD QUESTION

Muñoz indeed emerged from the 1944 elections as the most powerful political leader in island history. He had surpassed his father in the sheer magnitude of popular support. Yet he insisted that what he had told the voters in his unusual November 14, 1944 "conversation-speech," his deepest purpose in public life was not to win elections: it was to lift the *jíbaro* from extreme poverty.

Through most of his life, it had seemed evident: the cause for economic and social injustice could be summed up in one word: sugar. Since coming to power however, he believed he had to prove that he was not out to kill the one industry that sustained the economy. He insisted now that sugar itself had never been the "real enemy." In a 1943 statement published in *El Mundo*, he wrote: "We have never been against sugar cane, but against the unjust and inefficient way sugar distributes the fruits of its production in Puerto Rico." He spoke of expanding agriculture into other crops, including cotton, vanilla, and fruits and vegetables. The following year, he said: "Sugar cane creates wealth. That is why we must sustain it, and if possible, increase it... from cane we can get justice for our people. From cane we got extreme injustice for our people before the beginning of the Popular Democratic Party. We fought that injustice that came from the cane. Let us create the greatest justice that we can extract from the productivity of that same cane."[11]

There was another shift in his thinking. Wealth was not the real enemy either. "The Popular Democratic Party does not want to abolish wealth," Muñoz said. "What it wants to abolish is extreme poverty. There can be no

---

11. Muñoz Marín, Draft Speech, 9.

objection to having rich people, especially if they have worked to earn their wealth, as long as that is not the result of having the majority of the population living in misery but the result of work that is constructive and socially useful."

Muñoz went on to state the economic goals of his party: that no Puerto Rican family have less than a $1,000 annual income. To reach the first step towards a minimum family income of no less than $400, discounting U.S. military spending and federal social funds, the island needed to double its current income, an increase of $150 million. Faced with this reality, Muñoz said, "from now on, our greatest effort has to be, as the improving war conditions permit, to increase production within the norms of justice." It was obvious: he and his party could not create justice distributing what did not exist. To "increase the production" of wealth was now the priority.

But how? Was it tourism? The island's spectacular scenic beauty and balmy weather were its "natural resources" aided by the fact that it offered the security and conveniences of being under the U.S. flag—no visas necessary, the same monetary system, the protections of the U.S. federal court system.

But when Muñoz and the Popular Party came to power in 1940, they brought with them a political and ideological hostility to tourism. It was associated with Governor Winship and the Coalition government: In the 1930s, they imposed a salt tax to finance tourism development. The funds were used to establish an Institute of Tourism with a promotional office at New York's Rockefeller Center. A Puerto Rico News Bureau distributed to the U.S. media photographs and material depicting a beautiful, pristine clean island populated by swimsuit models. Winship, ignoring the criticism, reported to the Legislature the "encouraging progress" being made with the funds: $221,372.02 in 1937, increasing up to $303,031.76.

But for Muñoz and his party, the salt tax became the symbol of economic exploitation. The poorest of the poor were being forced to pay for what Muñoz considered a futile attempt to whitewash, through road "beautification" projects and public relations, the ugliness of the island's extreme poverty. After he had the tax repealed in 1941, the Institute of Tourism was transferred into the Department of Agriculture, its budget reduced to $200,000.

As the euphoria of his great political victory subsided, Muñoz was faced with a sobering reality. If extreme poverty was the real enemy, with all the political battles fought and won, and all the new agencies and programs created, Muñoz and Tugwell wondered if in fact they were losing the "war." For Tugwell, the answer was distressingly clear:

> What there was to do in contrast with what we could do was maddening...we had to suffer the slums and the filth; we had to think of the thousands of diseased without care of any kind; we had to see the children neglected and unschooled... we got nowhere. The fact was that in health work, education, public works, housing, water supplies, sewerage disposal and garbage collection, street repair—all the items of state and municipal housekeeping we fell further and further behind.[12]

Puerto Rico's fundamental reality—too many people on too little land—was getting worse. At the start of the century there were one million desperately poor human beings in 3,435 square miles of land—over 70 percent of it too mountainous for agriculture. In the mid 1940s, there were two million. The island had become "one of the most densely populated areas of the world which depends chiefly upon agriculture for existence;" 645 persons per square mile, 220 persons per 100 acres of arable land.[13] Several year later, economist Harvey Perloff wrote: "Puerto Rico may have the highest rate of natural increase in the entire world. Thus, in the race between economic progress and population growth, the island finds itself in an Alice in Wonderland situation, where one had to run very fast merely to stay in the same place."[14]

As Tugwell thought about this he recalled his meeting with the President back in 1941 when he showed him the revolting photos of *El Fanguito*, and Roosevelt's full voice ordering that this slum finally be cleared up: "I want action!" Yet Tugwell knew that neither the President's order nor the years

---

12. Tugwell, *The Stricken Land*, 616.

13. Perloff, *Puerto Rico's Economic Future*, 8.

14. Ibid., 9.

of his and Muñoz's crusade had detained, much less reversed, the "rising tide of the slums." He wrote: "the war did not keep boys and girls from getting married..." throwing together "scarps of lumber, tin, leather—any material which could be scavenged in back yards or rubbish heaps. They had no latrines, no access to supplies of water, no streets, they were an invitation to the parasitic life of the subtropics; and the rats ran in hordes through the yards and into and out of the homes."

The people of Puerto Rico had indeed put an enormous amount of political power in Muñoz's hands, but to use it he had to find the answer to the hard question that had defied all of the improvement attempts since the arrival of the Americans in 1898: if not the sugar industry, if not American welfare and public-funded economic reconstruction, if not large scale tourism, then exactly what was going to lift these Puerto Rican boys and girls from the slime and rats of *El Fanguito*?

18 Industrialization

Teodoro Moscoso believed that the answer to Puerto Rico's economic problems was industrialization. The idea was not new. Going back to the first report on island conditions by Dr. Henry Carroll in 1899, through the 1930 Brookings Report, and then the Chardón Plan, "industrialization" was always mentioned. Muñoz also alluded to "industrialization" in many of his speeches and writings. The activist Governor Theodore Roosevelt, Jr. had created a Bureau of Commerce and Industry in 1928. All the efforts failed: neither Muñoz's "assignment" in New York in 1922 nor Roosevelt's Bureau, which was finally dissolved in 1942, brought a single industrial investment to the island.

The fact was that no one really believed that the island could be industrialized. As late as 1950, University of Chicago economist Dr. Harvey S. Perloff, brought to the island to prepare the first ten-year economic development plan, wrote: "Agriculture is the backbone of Puerto Rico's economy and will undoubtedly continue to be the major key to the island's welfare for a long time to come." Perloff concluded that "industrialization must be conceived...as an extension of agricultural production, and the measure of its success will be to an important extent, in terms of value added to the products raised in the farms of the island."[1]

Moscoso was determined to prove the economists and everyone else wrong. His first move was to go up to Cambridge to convince the Arthur D. Little firm, related to the Massachusetts Institute of Technology, to serve

---

1. Perloff, *Puerto Rico's Economic Future*, 334.

as his economic and technical advisor. Through the ambitious public corporation's borrowing, and later by convincing Muñoz to turn over a large chunk of the "rum tax windfall" from the U.S., Fomento, the organization that promotes the development of industries in Puerto Rico, began to build factories: a $3 million glass plant to produce bottles for the rum industry; a pulp and paper plant mostly to manufacture containers to ship the rum bottles; a clay products plant to produce home construction and sanitary ware; and a shoe and leather goods factory for the local market. Moscoso was also pushing for a big textile factory and a major tourist hotel. By 1945, he had converted the initial $500,000 into a $21 million program.

But as he barreled forward, there were mounting problems in the construction and operation of these plants. There were almost continuous labor conflicts with union leaders that had politically backed Muñoz and the Popular Party. And there were big operating loses. Only the cement plant was making profits, and it was not built by Moscoso, but by the U.S. government during the war, under the Puerto Rico Reconstruction Administration, principally to provide cement for military and infrastructure construction. The fact was that the program was creating a minute fraction, about one percent, of the new jobs needed just to keep up with the population explosion. Again Moscoso was faced with the unforgiving reality to simply catch up to the annual growth in the labor force, he would have to spend more than the entire government budget. He was back at the Alice in Wonderland treadmill.

A new approach was needed. Instead of Fomento building plants, somehow Puerto Rico had to find a way to do what it had never done: attract private capital not related to agriculture. At first, the problem was Tugwell. "The fact is," wrote Fomento historian David Ross, "that Governor Tugwell was firmly and emphatically opposed to the kind of development program which relied heavily on the offering of inducements to private capital. He expected no miracles from the government plants... He did not regard them as the only, or even the best answer to Puerto Rico's economic problem..."[2]

Muñoz, crossed another ideological bridge. He admired Moscoso's great energy and ability to "get things started." Most importantly, Moscoso was clearly right. It was not a question of whether one wanted or not to

---

2. Ross, *The Long Uphill Path*, 79.

industrialize this green island: the more Muñoz went into Puerto Rico's economic condition, the more evident it became that it was the only option. Rigid ideology, dogma, Muñoz argued, should not become another obstacle to the uphill battle against poverty:

> Puerto Rico must give its maximum effort, its maximum intelligence, its maximum study, its maximum will, the maximum good faith of all the people, its maximum facilities, to this process of industrialization. And in guiding its development, it cannot afford the luxury of theories concerning it. We cannot afford the luxury of sustaining exclusively the theory that the Government must be the sole provider of the industrial function. Nor can we permit the luxury of sustaining the theory that only private initiative will develop and maintain the industrial function... Our people, who must carry the overwhelming weight of so many difficulties, of so many problems, of so much tragedy, cannot add on to itself the weight of an inflexible theory concerning how it will overcome it. Let the private initiative have all the opportunities that seem compatible with a system of justice for all. Let the government be in charge of the entire industrial production that private enterprise cannot or will not carry out under a civilization of justice.[3]

Muñoz had come a long way from his "anti-capitalism" of the 1920s and 30s.

Tugwell's Pessimistic Mood

Finally, Tugwell said to himself, it was time to leave. Roosevelt's death on April 12, 1945 plunged Tugwell again into one of his "pessimistic moods." With his leader and friend gone, he believed that his effectiveness as Governor and his usefulness to Muñoz and Puerto Rico were greatly diminished. But his gloomy mood went deeper. His old misgivings about Muñoz came back and he wondered if all the reforms, so viciously attacked by the opponents

---

3. Muñoz Marín, *Draft Speech*, May 31, 1944, 16.

in Puerto Rico and Washington, would hold up after he left: "Why...with the war crisis over, with finances in order and with such institutions as the Planning Board, the Development Companies, the Bank and a reformed civil service, should I be pessimistic about the future? I must confess that it was because I doubted whether Puerto Ricans would be permitted to keep the gains they were making with the administrative machinery we had set up...Puerto Rico is...also completely at a loss in both political and economic sense."

Tugwell saw great difficulties in the island's adjustment to a post-war economy. It would lose the significant military spending that had generated $106.4 million in income in 1944. The great demand for Puerto Rican rum would decline as Americans began again to produce and import other spirits. The impact would be significant. From 1941 to 1945, the island had received $115 million in the run tax "rebate:" it went up another $44.8 million in 1946 before it dropped precipitously. This directly affected two of Moscoso's biggest factories, bottling and carton plants, both dependent on the rum exports.

Tugwell's pessimism extended in particular to Moscoso's program. He saw another problem regarding industrialization: the endless labor conflicts in the factories, and more important, Muñoz's politically-motivated interference. "I am even profoundly doubtful," Tugwell wrote, "whether the experiments in government enterprise will succeed: not that I doubt their complete feasibility, but for one weakness: that however is a profound one; it is the lack of discipline among the workers themselves and their leaders; and this is inextricably mixed with the perils of political interference because the leaders of the workers also are inner members of the Popular party."[4] In this, Tugwell proved prophetic.

In August, 1945, Tugwell informed President Truman that he had decided to return to the classroom at the University of Chicago. Muñoz, he was also convinced, "was obviously ready for a change." But Truman urged Tugwell to remain. "He thought," Tugwell wrote in his journal, "there might be prospect of action looking toward self-government for Puerto Rico and that I must see it through until I could hand [it] over to a newly constituted government."[5]

---

4. Ibid., 669.
5. Ibid., xviii.

19 Why? Why? Why?

The magnitude of the 1944 victory had an unintended and paradoxical effect on his party's leadership. For Muñoz, the lesson could not be clearer: the people had overwhelmingly responded to his economic and social reforms because they trusted that a vote for him and his party was not a vote for independence. The size of his victory had strengthened his conviction to keep his promise. But many party leaders had a diametrically opposed interpretation. They felt that Muñoz had the influence to "educate" the people and lead them out of their irrational and demeaning "fear of independence." No, Muñoz grimly answered, they were wrong. The moment he broke his promise, the people, specially the *jíbaro* would abandon him and their party.

It had, in fact, been difficult for Muñoz to keep the lid on the political status issue. Senator Millard Tydings never abandoned his desire that the United States would "solve the Puerto Rican problem" by persuading the island to favor independence. On April 2, 1943, he had introduced in Congress another pro-independence bill. In a telegram he taunted Muñoz, demanding to know "Why? Why? Why?" he continued to oppose his independence bills.

Once again, a Tydings bill impacted island politics. Leaders and militants of the Popular Party held a Pro-Independence Congress on August 15, 1943. Muñoz did not attend but sent a telegram congratulating them. The following day he issued a long statement reiterating the party's non-status commitment. Each party member, he said, had a "democratic right" to his own status views, as to his religious or other personal views. But he reassured the voters that only they, through a direct vote separate from the general elections, would decide how the island would emerge from its "colonial condition." Muñoz ended the emphatic message: "This commitment had been fulfilled! It is being fulfilled! And it will be fulfilled!"

A month after the election, on December 10, 1944, another Pro-Independence Congress was held under the presidency of Gilberto Concepción de Gracia, a 35-year old lawyer with a doctorate in law from George Washington University, who had been close to Nationalist Party leader Pedro Albizu Campos, but was now seen as a member of the Popular Party. For Concepción the question was no longer "why?" but "when?" On November 11, he sent Muñoz a telegram requesting an answer. Muñoz's reply was read at the Congress. He reiterated his party's commitment to address the status issue after the war, advising Concepción that his organization should carry out its work "within the spirit...of wide democracy, and of sincere fraternity with the people of the United States" and its government.

But Muñoz's conciliatory response did not reflect what was taking place within him. Two days later, he issued another statement warning the leaders and all members of his Popular Party that they might be falling into a trap: that the supposedly "educational" assembly was in fact setting itself up to become a rival political party. In blunt, tough language, Muñoz invited the dissident leaders to openly challenge him and his Popular Party. Concepción answered immediately that Muñoz was wrong: "The firm attitude of the Pro-Independence Congress on this occasion is ...a frank and absolute rejection of all intents to convert the Congress into a political party."[1]

For Concepción and his followers, the answer to the question "when?" was clearly "now." The United States and the victorious Allies had pledged themselves in the August 11, 1941 *Atlantic Charter* to end colonialism throughout the world. The Roosevelt-Churchill agreement committed the free world to "respect the right of all people to choose the form of government under which they will live and ...to see sovereign rights and self-government restored to those who have been forcibly deprived of them." In January, 1945, Senator Tydings introduced still another independence bill, his third. This time it seemed to provoke a full-scale rebellion against Muñoz: 33 of the 55 Popular Party legislators and 45 of the 75 PDP mayors cabled Tydings their support. Muñoz could no longer postpone coming to grips with the status dilemma.

---

1. Bothwell, *Puerto Rico: cien años de lucha política*, Vol. III, 426.

Muñoz responded to Tydings. He had the new Resident Commissioner, Jesús Piñero, work with the Senator to draft a totally different independence bill that provided for a long economic adjustment period: the island would continue to enjoy free trade with the U.S., receive federal grants and aids, U.S. tax exemption for Puerto Rican products, and protection for the island's sugar industry.

But the Tydings-Piñero bill, introduced on May 15, 1945, was another exercise in futility. Like the scores of other status bills introduced in the U.S. Congress, its purpose was "educational:" to argue the point that the United States "was morally obligated" to grant whatever concessions were necessary to make independence economically viable. But it was one thing to get Congress to accept a "moral" point, another to have it accept a bill with extraordinary, unprecedented benefits and concessions to Puerto Rico. Muñoz was, in fact, aware of this and asked himself how much longer would he continue to waste his time, his party's time, Puerto Rico's time?

There was, however, something new in this last bill. Muñoz had included a third option in addition to independence and statehood, "dominion status." For his *independentista* challengers it was another ideological contradiction. They revived Muñoz's many writings and speeches specifically denouncing the very idea of a "dominion" or "commonwealth" status as a disgraceful subterfuge for prolonged "colonialism." In the 1930s he had fought against the Liberal Party's "autonomy" wing. In his long discussions with Tugwell, Muñoz had brushed off his lecturing on settling on a transitory status somewhere between statehood and independence. The Pro-Independence Congress issued a long manifesto "roundly condemning" a dominion status as not only "colonial," but unconstitutional. What, the *independentista* leadership asked itself, was happening to Muñoz? The suspicion going back to 1940, when Muñoz campaigned with the slogan "status is not the issue," emerged again before their eyes.

In Washington, the Pro-Independence Congress had the enthusiastic support of the radical New York representative Vito Marcantonio. On March 26, 1945, Marcantonio introduced his own independence bill. Unlike Tydings, Marcantonio thrust the island's "freedom" into what became the post-war ideological battle between the Soviet Union and the United States. On the island, meanwhile, Concepción de Gracia's strategy was evident: to drive a wedge between Muñoz and the great majority of Popular Party leaders.

Muñoz could not govern without the legislators, the mayors, the municipal and *barrio* leaders, the militants that physically took the *jíbaros* to vote. Just as Muñoz had taken the old Liberal Party out from under its aging, conservative leadership, Concepción and his followers expected the party leadership to remain loyal to its independence "ideal," rejecting what he now denounced as Muñoz's "personal tyranny."[2]

But for Muñoz, more important than meeting and defeating Concepción's political confrontation—something he had no doubt he would easily accomplish—the real challenge was to convince his party leaders that they were simply wrong—that he himself, all his life, had been wrong, that independence was not the "solution" to the island's dreadful economic and social problems and that neither he nor his party should continue in the hopeless quest for a magic formula that simply did not exist. By the end of 1945, Muñoz set out to get these leaders that so loyally followed him in so many political battles since 1938, to now follow him, in his own words, down "the road to reality."

"THE PROBLEM"

The time had come for Muñoz to directly, explicitly, make his transformation public. He wrote four long articles published in *El Mundo*, the first on February 7, 1946. The title was simply "The Problem." In traditional island politics, no one had to ask what "the problem" was: it was Puerto Rico's political status, it was "colonialism." No, Muñoz began, "the problem" is the island's population explosion. While its only source of economic activity, sugar production, had reached its peak in 1934, in 1940 there were 270,000 more mouths to feed. What sustained these 270,000 additional people, Muñoz continued, was the influx of U.S. welfare and other forms of federal economic assistance: $8 million in 1934, $35 million by 1943. Puerto Rico had changed its life-or-death dependence from sugar to federal welfare.

But since coming to power in 1940, Muñoz said, Puerto Rico's population explosion accelerated even more. As a result of the social and economic

2. Anderson, *Party Politics in Puerto Rico*, 59.

reforms, the death rate had dropped in the past five years from 18 to 14 per thousand, while the high birth rate remained constant. When Muñoz and the Popular Party promised in 1940 to lift Puerto Rico, it meant lifting 1,870,000 men and women. When it reiterated the promise in 1944, the task was now to lift 2,100,000 million people.

"Without understanding in all its seriousness the population problem," Muñoz wrote, "one cannot in all conscience live up to one's grave responsibility in relation to the future of our people and their civilization."

But Muñoz took this grim scenario further. By the year 1960, he said, the island's population will have reached 3.1 million. "What we must do, what we are absolutely obligated to do, if we don't want to be criminally responsible for a catastrophe more tragic than a lost war, is to increase production...."

In the next article, Muñoz spelled out the awesome magnitude of the task before them, "Increased production," he said, had to be fast enough to abolish the existing, massive, chronic unemployment; faster still to absorb the explosive increase in population and the labor force; faster still to liberate Puerto Rico from "artificial economic help"—U.S. welfare and other funds: and still faster to lift Puerto Rico's standard of living to the level where there is a decline in the island's birth rate. Again using apocalyptic language, Muñoz warned: "If Puerto Rico does not achieve this by 1960—if possible before, and if not possible, not much later—Puerto Rico is lost!"

This was a remarkable public confession for Muñoz. After pounding the drums for five years, heralding the achievements of his great democratic reforms of land and income distribution, he was saying that unless Puerto Rico changed its course, it was headed towards a "catastrophe."

In the fourth article, February 10, 1946, Muñoz asked: Was Puerto Rico, after all, an "American colony?" Politically, of course, the island did not possess full self-government. But, he went on, there must be a purpose to "colonialism." How does the U.S. benefit from keeping Puerto Rico as a "colony?" Where is the self-interest? Throughout the world, he said, 700 million people in colonies sustain a much higher standard of living for the 100 million living in the European countries.

The case of Puerto Rico is peculiar. It does not fit the general design of colonialism. The United States does not possess Puerto Rico because it needs to improve its standard of living. The United States possessed Puerto Rico by mistake. A mistake in the Spanish-American War, corrected in Cuba and the Philippines, to be corrected in Puerto Rico.

The days when American companies took large profits from the island, Muñoz continued, are over. For at least the past 12 years, the inflow of American government funds had exceeded the outflow of private profits. As far as the military bases were concerned, Muñoz noted that it was obvious that the United States would continue to have in the Caribbean and in Central America bases needed for national and hemispheric security—with or without Puerto Rico: "All this means that the United States has no interest whatever to deny Puerto Rico its freedom. Therefore, to obtain freedom is relatively easy. Indeed it is not the task of liberators to convince the United States to do something that benefits it."[3] Finally Muñoz got to his point:

> We must understand that whatever political freedom is established at the expense of ineluctable economic realities will perish in the same holocaust in which the structure of an unsustainable economy will perish. And nothing will be gained but tragedy, even for those that thought of freedom as something isolated from the economic realities of our people... Let us think that dignity, that imperishable attribute of the human being, should not be devalued to the category of an excuse to not understand economics: nor, honorably, can the dignity of those few of us that can resolve our own personal problems under any circumstance, be subsidized by the suffering and the destruction of two million souls that cannot resolve it, if we do not conduct its march towards freedom and justice and civilization with the deepest sense of responsibility towards them.

---

3. Muñoz Marín, *Memorias* Vol. II, 355.

Muñoz was engaged in more than an ideological struggle within his party, or within himself. There was a brutal power struggle to control the party and he went on the warpath. He issued an ultimatum to the dissident leaders: they had to choose between the Pro-Independence Congress and the Popular Democratic Party. The *independentistas*, of course, had every right to organize themselves into a political party in opposition to the PDP. But "there is no right to attack the Popular Party with the prestige of its own name... One cannot be a *Popular* and an enemy of the Popular Party at the same time."[4]

Muñoz made a distinction between those Puerto Ricans who longed for independence "in good faith," and those who seemed to be driven by a "passion for nationalism" that "can become the driving force behind an occult and barbarous Nazi-fascism." He called on his "*independentista* friends" who aspired to have a democratic, peaceful, tolerant Puerto Rican republic, open to the cultures of all other peoples and nations, to reject the rigid, stubborn, narrow "nationalism of Franco in Spanish, of Mussolini in Italian Fascism, of Hitler in nationalist-socialist Germany."

Muñoz ended the article by stating that "Every Puerto Rican must always have very clear in his mind the deep difference. And if only a few words of mine are to survive my life, let them be these that I have just written!" But Muñoz, curiously, declared that he was "not referring under any circumstances to the Nationalist Party." Pedro Albizu Campos was still serving time in a prison hospital in New York and would not return to the island until December, 1947.

The Iceman

The journey that led Muñoz to abandon independence, which began in 1936 with the "sledgehammer" effect of the first Tydings Bill, which jolted him in his 1940 encounter with the dark *jíbaro* Nicanor Guerra on a rural road,

---

4. Ibid., 432.

now came to a climax with an unlikely technical document written by an unlikely bureaucrat. Again, it was the consequence of an action by Senator Millard Tydings. In opposing the Tydings independence bill at the May 8, 1945 public hearings, Muñoz ominously predicted that if Congress approved it "the Puerto Ricans will physically perish within five years." The Senator asked Muñoz to submit his own proposal for an economically viable independence. When Muñoz responded several days later with what became the Tydings-Piñero bill, the Senator sent it over to the U.S. Tariff Commission asking it to report on the economic consequences of the Muñoz formula for independence, and the other two status proposals included in the bill, statehood and "dominion."

In March, 1946, the Commission's chief economist, Ben Dorfman, submitted the report titled "The Economy of Puerto Rico." It was a dry, statistical, 67-page analysis that confirmed Muñoz's doomsday's scenario of Puerto Ricans dying of starvation. But it went further. Even the Tydings-Piñero bill, with all its generous economic provisions, he wrote, spelled doom for Puerto Rico. Dorfman revived the essential conclusion of the 1930 Brookings Report that had so offended Muñoz and the island's political leaders. No change in the island's current status, he declared, would of itself improve Puerto Rico's economic condition.

> Inasmuch as Puerto Rico's economic distress does not stem from political causes, a change in political environment alone would not be capable of creating the additional resources and productive capacity from which the island could reap as large economic benefits as it now receives by virtue of its present trade and fiscal relations with the United States. Moreover, such large numbers of Puerto Ricans are now living so close to a subsistence level that it is questionable whether they could afford to make the economic sacrifices necessary to obtain any non-economic benefits, real or illusory, that would accompany political independence, either as proposed in pending legislation or on any other terms likely to be attained.[5]

---

5. U.S. Tariff Commission, *Dorfman Report*, 24

Dorfman's gloom even engulfed what Muñoz and many were counting on—Teodoro Moscoso's industrialization. Noting all the enthusiasm and expectations surrounding the program, he declared that it was illusory to expect that it would make a significant dent into the mass of 170,000 unemployed workers, with a labor force growing over 12,000 a year. In any case, Dorfman went on, the entire industrialization program is based on the *status quo*—on continued free trade with the U.S.

Was there then no escape, no hope for Puerto Rico? Since the rock-bottom source of its economic misery was simply too many people on this small, land-depleted, resourceless island, the only exit, Dorfman wrote, was to reduce by half its two million population. This could not happen naturally since no one would think of increasing the death rate and in such pervasive poverty it was unreal to expect the birth rate to go down significantly. So somehow Puerto Rico had to induce one million islanders to abandon the island.

But even this outlandish idea "would merely make a solution possible." There is no guarantee, Dorfman warned, that the island's population would not again explode to two million in a short time. In any case, he added in a rare understatement, "Whether an emigration program of the above dimensions is within the realm of possibility needs further consideration."[6]

Dorfman's report was received in Puerto Rico as blasphemy. Three decades later, the island's leading historian, Dr. Arturo Morales Carrión, who in 1962 served in the Kennedy Administration as undersecretary of state for Latin American Affairs, and later as President of the University of Puerto Rico, described the report as a "dogmatic" attempt to absolve the United States of all blame for Puerto Rico's extreme poverty.

The report was essentially a 'no-exit' document. Puerto Rico would remain a stricken island, as long as its population grew. Neo-Malthusian factors were blamed for what was the implicit acknowledgment of the shortcomings of [American] tutelage. There was little the United States could do and Puerto Rico was destined to a gloomy

6. Ibid., 31.

future, according to the iron logic of Dorfman's dismal science. After nearly half a century of dependency, this was Puerto Rico's balance sheet.[7]

In fact, there was nothing in the report that Muñoz did not already know, indeed that he had not stated in his remarkable four articles in *El Mundo*. But it is one thing to know intellectually that a beloved person is terminally ill; it's another to hear the attending doctor say that it is terminal. The Dorfman report, stripped of all emotion, ideological, partisan bias, in the ironclad, irrefutable logic of its statistics and charts, was for Muñoz the death certificate of his lifelong dream of independence. Years later, Moscoso recalled seeing Muñoz emerge from the meeting with Dorfman. He had never seen Muñoz cry before, but now he saw tears in his eyes.

---

7. Morales Carrión, *Puerto Rico: A Political and Cultural History*, 268.

20 The Wake for a "Lost Ideal"

I t was time to get the Popular Party leadership to finally end the status "agony." The crucial meeting took place on July 3, 1946 on José Berríos Berdecía's farm up in the mountains near the town of Barranquitas. It was a strange gathering. Unlike the typical meetings with its festive atmosphere, perpetual noise, everyone speaking at the same time, long speeches and posturing, this one was almost entirely silent, except for Muñoz's voice in a low monotone.

He talked into the morning hours. Muñoz described the long odyssey that brought him to the conclusion that he and the Popular Party must end this "ballet of phantoms." He went over all the arguments and reasoning he had used in the *El Mundo* articles. He described a recent trip to Washington, where he closely followed the congressional hearings on independence for the Philippines, focusing on the trade relation between the U.S. and the new nation. As Dorfman had insisted, if the U.S. granted free trade to one independent nation, it would be obligated to grant it to all others with "most favored nation treaties." This seeming technicality, Muñoz insisted, was the fatal blow to Puerto Rican independence. Without free trade, the sugar industry and the surging industrial development program would collapse. "I was convinced that it was impossible, totally impossible, undoubtedly impossible, that Puerto Rico could obtain the right to chose separated independence in a plebiscite if not under economic conditions disastrous to the people's welfare, destructive of all hope of continuing to improve the lives of the people of Puerto Rico."[1]

---

1. Muñoz Marín, *Los gobernadores electos de Puerto Rico*, 290.

As Muñoz spoke, his voice lowered and he felt the silence of his leaders deepen, their spirits falling. This had become a wake for a "lost ideal." The sun was beginning to appear over the mountains when Muñoz made his plea to end the quest for independence, and instead focus on getting Congress to approve the elective governorship, as proposed by President Roosevelt and now Truman. A vote was taken: 50 voted for Muñoz, nine against.

More silence. "The anguish in their spirits," Muñoz wrote, "was evident and painful, and the absence of rhetorical oratory made it even more real and moving." Then one of the leaders spoke out. No, he said, let's not give up; let's continue to search. Convinced that it was "futile," Muñoz answered that he would do so only if the party leadership delegated in him the decision of when to finally give up. It was agreed.

While this drama took place in an open yard, sitting in a balcony in the house some forty meters away, Muñoz recorded years later, "sat a poet... She heard all night long the murmur of tired voices seeking salvation for a fallen ideal and the voice of another poet that led the gathering, heavy with the additional sorrow of talking in practical prose of an ideal of which he preferred to have talked in lyrical poetry."[2] The poet in the balcony was Muñoz' cousin, Clara Lair.

Piñero!

Who would replace Rexford Tugwell? Roosevelt had appointed two of the worst Governors, and also the best. Now, with Harry Truman in the White House, what surprise was in store for Puerto Rico? Muñoz got the Popular Party to approve a bill calling for a political status plebiscite and asking the President to name a Puerto Rican that had been elected to public office. But it was not with himself in mind. Muñoz insisted that he would never accept an appointment to the governorship, and, while no one believed him, that he was not interested in being elected to the office. The idea was to pressure the President to name Jesús Piñero, the Resident Commissioner. But Muñoz joked with Tugwell, insisting that it was to safeguard the island from another

---

2. Muñoz Marín, *Memorias* Vol. II, 176.

"Oligandul"—a nonsensical word that they had used to ridicule the awful Governors in the past.

But this time Tugwell was not amused. Muñoz was again overstepping his power and Tugwell, who at the time did not have a high opinion of Truman, believed that it would backfire. Tugwell vetoed the bill. Muñoz insisted. He had the Legislature override the veto. The Organic Act gave the President the final word, and Truman sustained Tugwell.

As far as the plebiscite was concerned, Truman explained that he had always been opposed to having the President and Congress "mislead" the people of Puerto Rico by authorizing a status vote unless it was willing to accept the result.[3] Senator Tydings backed the President, insisted that the only status Congress would commit itself to approve was independence: "Congress would not give Statehood or Dominion Status even if the people of Puerto Rico voted for it."

Muñoz did not back down. He came back again with a resolution not requiring the Governor's signature, this one explicitly pointing at Piñero as the "elected islander." All 54 *Populares* voted in favor, the three minority legislators against.

On July 25, 1946, the anniversary of the American landing in Guánica, Muñoz and friends were spending the day on a boat off Luquillo beach on the north coast. Muñoz noticed a man on the shore shouting something at him. In the distance he noticed the tall, roundish figure of his affable personal secretary, Luis Laboy. Muñoz could not distinguish the words Laboy was shouting. Was it, he asked himself, "Oligandul?" No, it wasn't. As the boat got closer to the shore, Muñoz got Laboy's word: "Piñero!" For the first time in four and a half centuries, a Puerto Rican was appointed governor.

"Neither Wind Nor Sea"

Tugwell left Puerto Rico filled with nostalgia mixed with a strong dose of the pessimism that had overtaken him since Roosevelt's death. Were Puerto Ricans, in fact, ready for self-government? He had fought hard to give Puerto

---

3. Trías Monge, *Historia Constitucional de Puerto Rico II*, 332.

Rico the right to elect its governor, but he now feared the consequences: "President Roosevelt may have been right, I thought, when he had said to me that when we withdrew and established self-government there would ensue an awkward period of—at best—bad government... after three years of thinking about this remark, I was still wondering whether he was right in concluding that there was no alternative."[4] Tugwell felt pangs of guilt. He asked himself: "were there not elements in this situation which made the abandonment of Puerto Rico to such a future particularly irresponsible?"[5]

In June, 1946, Tugwell led a team of agricultural experts to the small island off Puerto Rico's east coast, Vieques. It was mostly occupied by the U.S. Navy as part of the big Roosevelt Roads naval base complex on the eastern tip of Puerto Rico. If England had fallen to Germany, this would have been the home for the British navy. Now Tugwell had a particular interest in developing the civilian third of Vieques as part of his new Agricultural Development Program.

But something strange happened to Tugwell. The university professor of economics, the New Deal battler, the "Red Rex" that had put so much fear into the hearts of conservative Republicans in Washington and Puerto Rico, was now overtaken by emotion. As much a writer, and at times a poet, as Muñoz, he attempted to capture these deep emotions:

> I was far out on the thin tip of Vieques where its rocks, thrust into the Atlantic rollers, are continuously buried in heaving seas. The windward shores of the Caribbean islands are dry and rocky, conditions which are attractive to a certain kind of vegetation. Out there I found myself wading waist deep in orchids, flowering sage and frangipani; the combined perfumes were delicately aromatic; the burning sun was deceptively cooled by the freshets of air which flowed in from the sea...
>
> There were, for once, no people; not even the limpet-like *jíbaros* had found it possible to exist there. And none would, it was the only place I have ever found in the Puerto Rican islands where one could escape from the sight or sound of other humans. It struck me that

---

4. Tugwell, *The Stricken Land*, 686.
5. Ibid., 686.

out there I might be able to re-create a plan and policy; for all had become confused and chaotic in my mind. Perhaps I could see what lay ahead for Puerto Rico or what might lie ahead if all of us who were of good will conduct ourselves in accordance with wise provision. But neither wind nor sea, sage nor orchid, solitude nor effort, yielded anything further. Before long, as most other men have done, I got hungry and came home...[6]

Three months later, September, 1946, Tugwell finally left the island.

THE UNWORKABLE GOVERNORSHIP

President Truman's appointment of an "elected resident" constituted another breakthrough in the relationship between Puerto Rico and the United States. "Whether it was in the law or not," Muñoz wrote, "never again would it be possible to name a governor that did not respond clearly to the people of Puerto Rico."[7]

But the duality at the very heart of the governorship that previous Governors had found unworkable—administrative responsibility and authority separate from political power—now took on a different form. Jesús Piñero found himself in a situation that was even even more awkward. The tug-of-war between Muñoz and Tugwell over who really "governed" Puerto Rico was over. Piñero was handpicked by Muñoz to run for Resident Commissioner and now as Governor. Piñero was technically a federal official appointed by the President and confirmed by Congress, but in fact he was Muñoz's surrogate at La Fortaleza.

Muñoz still insisted to his friends that he had not made up his mind whether to run for Governor or not in 1948. But he acted as if he were, often giving instructions directly to the administrative department and agency heads. He ordered his chief assistant, Roberto Sánchez Vilella, to organize regular meetings of the cabinet at his Trujillo Alto home. Now that Tugwell

---

6. Ibid., 688.

7. Muñoz Marín, *Memorias* Vol. II, 183.

was gone, Muñoz drove through the Legislature important laws to promote economic development, including a law offering new industries 100 percent tax exemption. Moscoso and Fomento finally had the promotional tool they had been fighting for.

It was, Muñoz admitted, an "awkward situation" that became worse as he pushed the administrators harder and Piñero began to resist. The pressure was too much for his principal aide, Sánchez Vilella, who suddenly resigned and went to work for his brother-in-law, Moscoso, in establishing a new, costly tourism hotel, the Caribe Hilton. Several of Piñero's own attempts to make the sugar industry more competitive through greater mechanization clashed with the labor unions that were still the backbone of the Popular Party. Several other bills proposed by Piñero died in the Legislature.

The incipient conflict broke into the open when, to Muñoz's and the Popular Party's dismay, Piñero accepted an invitation to attend the inauguration of Generalísimo Rafael Trujillo as President of the Dominican Republic. Meeting at a rustic cabin up in *El Yunque*, Muñoz and his friend, Jorge Font Saldaña, set out to convince Piñero that it would be "disgraceful" for the party, and for all Puerto Rico, that he attend an event of a "murderous" dictator. Piñero clearly wanted to prove that he was his own man, but Muñoz wondered if he was yielding to pressure from the U.S. State Department. Piñero went to the inauguration. "Piñero was a good man," Muñoz wrote later, "and at the same time firm—on that occasion, I would say bull-headed—in his decisions."[8]

THE PUERTO RICO INDEPENDENCE PARTY

On July 25th, as Muñoz received the news of Piñero's appointment, the Pro-Independence Congress met in Río Piedras, under the leadership of Concepción de Gracia, and decided to meet Muñoz's challenge. A new political party would be organized. A number of *independentista* Popular Party

---

8. Ibid., 187.

leaders now considered themselves "expelled" by Muñoz. A constitutional convention was held in Bayamón on October 20. Formal inscription began in the summer of 1947. In less than four months the Puerto Rican Independence Party had enough petitions to appear on the 1948 ballot.

The party's fundamental program was the exact opposite of Muñoz's doctrine: first independence, then economic and social reform. Its leadership consisted predominantly of the island's intellectual elite: lawyers, university professors, students, writers, artists. From the beginning, the new party was torn by internal contradictions. On one hand it denounced the "colonial" structure on the island, but on the other it would participate in the "colonial elections." It admired and supported as "patriots" Pedro Albizu Campos and the Nationalist Party, but at the same time committed itself to non-violent, democratic action. The new party placed great emphasis in its internal democracy in contrast to Muñoz's "dictatorial" control.

There was also a conservative, Catholic wing in the new party that saw Americanization, and Muñoz in particular, as agents of "materialism," destructive of Puerto Rico's traditional Hispanic culture and values. Behind Muñoz's "obsession with economic reality," they believed, was a profoundly anti-religious attitude towards life. Héctor Ramos Mimoso, a young lawyer first attracted to Muñoz, now the treasurer of the Independence Party, saw his fallen idol as Cervantes's Sancho Panza: "The triumph of the belly, "*la panza*"—representing the material—over the ideal of a free fatherland."[9] Although Muñoz deliberately avoided reopening the old birth control issue, the Catholic community believed that Muñoz was, in another one of his deceptions, promoting experimentation with new birth control pills. The Independence Party program strongly condemned the "mass sterilization of Puerto Rican women."

An important defection from the Popular to the Independence Party was Dr. Francisco M. Susoni, Speaker of the House since 1945. In May 1948, he informed Muñoz that he could not turn his back on his ideal of independence, so he had decided to "retire to his home." Two months later, however, Susoni resurfaced as the new party's candidate for governor.

---

9. Ramos Mimoso, *Seis décadas de lucha*, 17.

Muñoz selected Dr. Antonio Fernós Isern to replace Piñero as Puerto Rico's resident commissioner in Congress. The 51-year-old Fernós was a veteran in government, having served as Health Commissioner in 1931, as a professor at the University of Puerto Rico School of Tropical Medicine, and at the same time active in politics, joining Muñoz in the founding of the Popular Party. In 1940 he lost to Bolívar Pagán as candidate for resident commissioner. He again headed the Health Department in 1942 after a bitter exchange between Muñoz and Tugwell over political patronage.

Fernós, with his pince-nez, resembling an Old World diplomat, had another attribute that was to prove vital to his critical missions in Congress during the next decade. Like Muñoz, not a lawyer, Fernós shared Muñoz's non-legalistic, non-doctrinaire approach to the thorny issues of the Puerto Rico-U.S. relationship. His pragmatic approach infuriated many of Muñoz's political colleagues and legal advisors. Fernós, they believed, was much too cautious. But Muñoz was determined not to waste any more time with "educational" demands from Congress that stirred island politics to a frenzy but got nowhere.

In January, 1947, Muñoz attended a luncheon in Washington organized by Interior Department Under Secretary Oscar Chapman. He informed Muñoz and new Resident Commissioner Fernós Isern that President Truman wanted to be sure that Puerto Rico's leadership was behind his proposal for the elective governorship. Muñoz reiterated the traditional Popular Party position that the elective governorship should be part of a comprehensive bill to "resolve" the entire status question. He declared, however, that he and his party would support the bill while making it clear that it was not their initiative. Chapman responded that he would get it introduced by the Chairman of the Senate Interior and Insular Affairs Committee, Senator Butler, and House Territories Subcommittee Chairman, the old hand on Puerto Rican matters, Representative Fred Crawford. Back in Puerto Rico, Muñoz applied great pressure on Fernós to get it rapidly through Congress. Muñoz knew that Chapman was right. Once Puerto Rico elected its own Governor it would be much easier to return to Congress with a status bill.

The legislation seemed to be moving quickly through Congress. In May, it was approved unanimously by the House Subcommittee on Territories and Possessions. Muñoz congratulated Fernós on the "rapid progress," adding, "I suppose that the next step, approval by the full Committee on Public Lands, will not be difficult nor will it be much delayed."[10] A week later the full committee approved it. If Fernós succeeded in getting the bill into the "calendar of unanimous consent" for June 16, 1947, it would certainly clear the House floor without debate. For this, he needed Crawford's enthusiastic support.

Muñoz could not escape the irony of now having to depend on the man that back in January 1943 he had denounced for "one of the most shameful actions in the colonial system in Puerto Rico," Crawford's resolution to have Congress repeal the entire Muñoz-Tugwell reform program. But Crawford's hostility was against Tugwell, not Muñoz, and now Fernós reported that he was an ally.

Early Monday morning, June 16, Crawford discovered that representative Sterling W. Cole wanted to make several amendments. This would open the bill to floor debate and other amendments, endangering its passage. Crawford and Fernós met with Cole. Puerto Rico could not accept one of his amendments: giving Congress control of the spending of the U.S. excise tax rebated to the insular government. In any case, Cole informed Fernós, New York representative Vito Marcantonio, an ally of the island *independentistas*, was also determined to open the bill to further amendments. Fernós rushed to Marcantonio's office and convinced him to state his objections but not to tie up the bill.

Cole insisted on delaying it. Fernós replied firmly: "I leave the bill in your hands." In fact Fernós stepped up his lobbying among representatives known to be friends and influential with Cole. It occurred to one of Cole's closest friends, Representative Dean Taylor, that the amendment could be challenged as "out of order" since it was, in fact, an amendment to the Internal Revenue Code. Fernós got a Democrat from New Mexico, Antonio Fernández, to raise the objection. Fernós then rushed to the House Parliamentarian, who would advise the presiding "Speaker" on the question of order.

Late that evening, the bill finally came to the floor. Cole submitted his amendment. Fernández raised the objection, and the "Speaker" consulted

---

10. Fernós Isern, *Estado Libre Asociado de Puerto Rico*, 73.

the Parliamentarian, who proceeded to declare the amendment "not germane." The open debate that Fernós and Crawford feared was avoided. The bill was passed unanimously.

Fernós was informed by Senator Butler that the bill would also clear the Senate "without difficulty." But on July 3, 1947, there was bad news. Republican Party leader Senator Robert Taft wanted two major changes: to restore the President's authority to name the Auditor and the creation of the post "Coordinator of Federal Agencies." This, Fernós knew immediately, would effectively kill the bill. Both proposals were unacceptable to Muñoz as patently "colonial." But Butler pointed out that it was impossible to get the bill out of the Senate over Taft's objections and the Senate was running out of time. Fernós had more bad news for Muñoz. Meeting with Taft, he learned that the Senator wanted still another major change: the President, not the elected Governor, would continue to appoint the judges to the insular Supreme Court. Governor Jesús Piñero rushed up to Washington. Should everything fail to dissuade Taft, he wrote back to Muñoz, he should accept whatever elective bill emerged from the Senate. Piñero sensed that they were facing a devastating defeat. He urged Muñoz "to take an airplane to be here in this decisive moment. I do not want to assume the responsibility by myself."[11]

On the last day of the session, a Saturday, Fernós, in the Senate room behind the floor, heard the bill's title being read. He crossed his fingers: if there was no objection, it stood approved. But then he heard Taft's voice shout, "Over!" Automatically, the bill was bypassed. Fernós found Butler, who still assured him it would pass. But when its title was reread, again Taft said, "Over."

The clock was ticking. Crawford had warned him that the House would end its session at midnight sharp. He began to feel a sickening foreboding. Taft was clearly intent on killing the bill. Fernós approached the Democrat from New Mexico, Senator Dennis Chávez. Chávez agreed to intervene. An Interior Department lawyer, present to oversee the bill, overheard Fernós and solemnly informed him that he had just killed it. Taft, he said, would never accept Fernós having "crossed party lines." Fernós had nothing to lose. He waved off the lawyer murmuring: "The die is cast."

---

11. Ibid., 76.

Chávez waited for the reading of the title of a military appropriation bill that he knew was of interest to Taft. Chávez pronounced the "fatal word." Taft swung his head in surprise and walked over to Chávez. Fernós observed them in animated conversation. Chávez then came back to report that Taft agreed to let the Puerto Rico bill come to a vote if he did the same with the military bill.

Fernós looked at the clock. It was ten, then ten thirty, and the bill was still not read. He saw Crawford walking towards him, a look of defeat on his face. He was convinced that Taft would stall until it was impossible to get the amended bill through a conference committee and into the House by midnight. In any case, Crawford added glumly, even if the bill reached the House, there would be no time to remove the Taft amendments.

But then Crawford quickly scribbled on a piece of paper a note to Taft. If he wanted to retain presidential appointments of insular Supreme Court justices, the House would approve it. When Taft returned to his seat, he read the note and nodded his head.

It was minutes before midnight when the bill was read. Taft introduced his amendment and it was immediately approved. Fernós was overcome with a crushing emotion: so much effort and it would all end in nothing. But then he looked at Crawford, and without saying a word to each other, they agreed not to give up. Crawford went running to the House to ask that the session be extended for several minutes. Fernós went running to the Senate secretariat. The amended bill was quickly prepared and given to a messenger to take to the House. Fernós grabbed the messenger by the arm, forcing him to run with him to the House. Crawford was waiting. He had convinced the House to extend its session. It was approved unanimously.

Five days later, on August 5, 1947, President Truman signed the bill, giving one pen to Interior Under Secretary Chapman, another to Governor Piñero, the third to Fernós. Muñoz, now, everyone assumed, certain to become the first elected Governor in Puerto Rican history, had decided not to attend.

21 The First Elected Governor

U niversity of Puerto Rico Chancellor Jaime Benítez had the reputation of being fearless, intrepid. Rexford Tugwell described him as "vivid, voluble, ardent for his country's good and obviously talented."[1] During Tugwell's governorship, according to one of his aides, Ángel Martín, there were only two people who would enter La Fortaleza, up the stairs pass the guards and secretaries, and right into the Governor's office: Muñoz, and the then young university professor.

Back in 1942, after the Tugwell university fiasco, Muñoz turned to Benítez, then 34, to carry out a major reform under a new University law. The Chancellor had been an ardent *independentista* in the 1930s who followed Muñoz through the ideological transformation. Although a primary goal of the university reform was to "depoliticize" the institution, Benítez was seen by the *independentista* students and the large number of *independentista* faculty as Muñoz's and the Popular Party's surrogate. Like Muñoz, Benítez was denounced as a "traitor" to their ideal. Benítez had indeed a particularly close relationship to Muñoz; although ten years younger, he saw himself as Muñoz's mentor and often as his critic. Their wives, Inés and Luz, had grown up together in Yabucoa and were still each other's best friends.

In December, 1947, Albizu Campos returned to Puerto Rico from a mainland prison hospital. The following year, in April, the students' association applied for permission to use the University Theater for a speech by Albizu. Benítez saw this as another act of deliberate "provocation" since

---

1. Tugwell, *The Stricken Land*, 93.

the students knew that partisan rallies on campus were prohibited; a rule strictly enforced during this, an election year. Back in December, four *independentista* students were expelled for violating campus regulations in activities related to Albizu's return to the island. Now, some 300 *independentista* students and faculty members held an unauthorized meeting to commemorate the tenth anniversary of the Ponce Massacre.

Benítez turned down the request. The denial, he later explained, had the "deliberate intent of clarifying that, as far as this university administration is concerned, the gentleman that orders the shooting in the streets of particular groups that differ from him, the gentleman that orders university youths to arm themselves and ignore the laws and repudiate the courts in order to use force, the gentleman that preaches that terrorist doctrine has no place on the university tribune. While I am the Chancellor of the University, it will be futile to pretend that this house will willingly welcome that propaganda."[2]

Benítez was doing something that island political leaders avoided: he was directly taking on Albizu and his followers. He believed that more than deliberately challenging his authority, the Nationalists were intent on introducing into the institution a "fascist" militancy of "hostility and intolerance." Having failed to take over the Popular Party, Benítez informed Muñoz, the *independentistas* were attempting to take over the state university.

The Nationalists accepted the challenge. Stepping up their campaign, they demonstrated throughout the campus, denouncing Benítez as "despotic...abusive...tyrannical" while announcing: "Albizu Campos will speak at the University." Flyers were distributed convoking an "assembly" on April 9th in front of the University Tower. One student that refused to take the flyer was struck in the face. Puzzled, he asked: "Why? What happened?" The answer came back: "Because you are colonial, you are submissive!"

A student strike was declared to shut down the University on April 14th. Again Benítez met with the student leaders, this time in his house. In his presence their conciliatory attitude bore no resemblance to the strident "manifesto" approved at the assembly. Expressing their fears that "all the

---

2. Benítez, *Junto a La Torre*, 158.

hostility will destroy the University," they pleaded for more communication to dispel the "misunderstanding and incomprehension." The students declared that they wanted to submit a list of grievances to discuss with him "in an atmosphere of understanding of good faith." They confessed they were personally opposed to the strike but that it was too late to call it off. They promised not to interrupt the classes nor incite other students to join the strike. Benítez answered that this was precisely what he wanted from them: honest, open dialogue. With their personal "guarantee" to him that there would be no violence, he allowed them to proceed. The next day, Benítez regretted that decision.

Early Wednesday, April 14, it seemed that the Student Council was keeping its word. Benítez, who every day walked across the campus to his office, noticed a large number of students and others in front of the University entrance. But most students were entering without any problem. He continued on to his office and began a scheduled meeting on the budget. Soon he was interrupted to be informed that the four Nationalist students expelled in December and other militants had taken over. The leaders were crying out: "To the Chancellor's office! We will throw him out the window!" One held up a piece of rope "to lynch the Chancellor!" The crowd took up the chant demanding "the recognition of Albizu as the Grand Master" that must be allowed "into the University classrooms."

It was too late for Benítez to react. Led by the Nationalists, the crowd entered the campus, poured into the University Tower, up the stairs into the Chancellor's reception room, shouting: "This is the Bastille—now we take over!" Benítez and 20 administrators and secretaries were trapped inside their offices.

The state police arrived. Benítez demanded that they do not attempt to rescue them: he would not allow "at any cost" another Ponce Massacre. Six hours later, the students sent an ultimatum: either Benítez would meet with two of their leaders, Juan Mari Bras and Jorge Luis Landing, "or we will walk over dead bodies. Whoever has to be killed will be killed, but we are entering that office." A tragedy now seemed unavoidable. The University Tower was surrounded by 70 heavily armed policemen. The Chief of Police telephoned Benítez: "This is zero hour...it is almost inevitable that there will be deaths." Dean of General Studies Mariano Villaronga agreed: "There will be at least six or seven deaths." Benítez was adamant: "The first will be mine." He gave the order to allow Mari Bras and Landing, one of the expelled Nationalist students, into his office. They came straight to the point: either Benítez resigned, or he would be responsible for "spilling the blood of the students." No, he answered: "ask the University board for my resignation!" Mari Bras and Landing then demanded that Benítez come out and give his answer directly to the students outside. "I will guarantee your life," Landing said. "My life does not interest me," Benítez snapped back. "I can see," Landing said as they walked out.

Benítez believed that by nightfall the students outside would tire and leave. He was right. With a few students remaining, surrounded by policeman, he and the others walked rapidly out of the office. The strike, however, succeeded. Classes were suspended, the University closed.

On April 16, Albizu Campos, from his residence at the Normandy Hotel in San Juan, issued another threat. The policemen that rescued Benítez "should die of shame," Albizu said. He also assailed the parents of University students "who were cowards by not going to the streets, pistol in hand, to defend their children whose lives were threatened... We have a university without students. When disciples reject their master it's because the master is a dog. The hour of the armed revolution has arrived, which is what awaits all despotism, and the good pay with the bad, because people, in their outrage, do not stop to think. The hour of the armed revolution is now. This is the hour!"[3]

Fascist Tendencies

Muñoz decided that it was time to stop Albizu. He got the Legislature convened in an emergency session that quickly approved three laws, one of them almost identical to the U.S. Smith Act, making it a crime to "advise or incite" anyone to commit a crime or to "overthrow, destroy or paralyze the government by force or violence, or to organize any meeting, assembly or group that advises or incites" anyone to do so.

---

3. Ibid., 167.

Muñoz expected considerable support. But the new laws were widely censured as a violation of "freedom of speech." Not only did the *independentistas*, as expected, condemn it, but also the conservative leaders, among them Republican Party President Celestino Iriarte and Socialist Party President Bolívar Pagán. Muñoz was furious at *El Mundo*'s headline: "Legislature Approves Bills to Punish Attacks on Government." This was, he raged, a deliberate, malicious attempt to make it seem that the laws made it a crime to criticize the government. "This headline is one of the greatest lies ever published in the country's press... knowing that these laws are only and exclusively for those that incite to force and violence." Referring to the newspaper caricature of a gagged Puerto Rican *jíbaro*, Muñoz said: "These laws are precisely to prevent anyone from gagging the people of Puerto Rico through fascist threats of force and violence."[4] The campaign of "lies," he said, will expose itself when the "reactionaries and the fascists," while insisting that "the Government does not allow them to talk," will continue to carry out their campaigns by freely attacking the Government in every public plaza in Puerto Rico and through the airwaves.

But what most troubled Muñoz was the failure of these critics to see, or accept, the ugly underside of all this violent rhetoric. Tugwell had pointed it out repeatedly, and now Benítez did at the University: there were indeed "fascist tendencies" on the island that cut across ideological and partisan lines. Tugwell had seen them in the Right, the conservative business and political class, in those who admired the Spanish *falangistas*. Muñoz and Benítez saw it come from the radical *independentistas*.

"What is fascism?" Muñoz asked in his annual speech at his father's gravesite on July 17, 1948. Quoting from India's Nehru and several English and European writers, he answered his question: "the ancient concept of the fatherland (*la patria*), formed by living and working together within a given region, of men and women in serene pursuit of their individual happiness, has been converted by the fascists into an abstract concept of the fascist fatherland that is like a pagan goddess to which one must sacrifice the lives, the rights, the freedoms of the men and women of flesh and blood..."

---

4. Bothwell, *Puerto Rico: cien años de lucha política* Vol. III, 516.

The 1948 campaign was like no other for Muñoz. The opposition, throughout his entire political life, had been "*los republicanos,*" the sugar barons, and the conservatives on the island and in Washington. Now the attacks came from the new Puerto Rico Independence Party and from Albizu and the Nationalists. In the past Muñoz had been accused of being "anti-American" and "communist." Now it was the opposite: that he had "sold his soul to the Devil," betrayed his independence "ideal" in exchange for the "glory" of living at La Fortaleza as Governor of Puerto Rico.

This was an attack meant to hurt him personally as well as politically. In the late 1930s, he had been accused of having "betrayed" Antonio Barceló in exchange for satisfying his lust for "the title of party president." Now Muñoz felt the need to respond. In his July 4, 1948 speech he did:

> Personally I would not be harmed by either immediate independence or statehood. I could be the President of the republic, or a Senator in the great Senate of the United States that exercises so much authority over the destiny of the entire world. And neither the President nor the Senator would die of hunger. You are the ones that would bear the weight of the tragedy. The glory would be mine and the hunger would be yours. I could have that glory if I had the irresponsibility of spirit that would interest me in the glories founded on the hunger of my people, or to interest me in the superficiality of glory in any form. Glory is a poor nourishment for impaired spirits. The healthy spirit hungers for justice and responsibility. Its greatest strength is honesty and patience.[5]

Muñoz ridiculed the *independentista* argument that once Puerto Rico had the power to impose tariffs to protect its local industry, the island economy would expand rapidly. The tariff wall for Puerto Rican products, he argued, now extended all the way from New York to San Francisco. It was absurd to believe that island industry would flourish making that wall many times smaller, reaching only to Mayagüez. "Puerto Rico," he declared, "has the

---

5. Bothwell, *Puerto Rico: cien años de lucha política* Vol. III, 531.

world's most favorable economic relation to the United States." It is the "political—not the economic—relation the United States maintains in Puerto Rico [that] is unjust. It is also not intelligent. It is unjust and dumb... Because it is unjust, it should be corrected, from their and our point of view. And because it is dumb, it should be corrected from their point of view."[6]

In August, 1948, the Popular Party approved a platform that for the first time included political status. It asked for a mandate to petition Congress to "resolve" the status issue. Puerto Rico, under its own constitution, would have authority over all internal matters, while "preserving the existing economic and fiscal relationship between Puerto Rico and the United States." Muñoz, still faced with the enormous task of reconciling his party leadership to the "impossibility" of independence, was not ready to close the door. The platform called on Congress to authorize a future independence versus statehood plebiscite whenever the Legislature deemed that Puerto Rico's development had reached a level where it could become one or the other without economic hardship and without special economic benefits from the United States.

At that assembly, held before a mass of *Populares* at the Sixto Escobar baseball stadium in San Juan, Muñoz was nominated to run for Governor. In four and a half centuries of history, Puerto Rico had had ninety-eight Spanish governors, eighteen American, and one Puerto Rican, Jesús Piñero. Muñoz would be the first elected by the people of Puerto Rico.

This historic moment, however, was marred by a mistake Muñoz made and came to regret for the rest of his life. In keeping with his disdain for titles, he announced that once elected governor, he would step down as president of the Popular Party. He nominated Piñero to replace him. Muñoz also meant this to be a reward to Piñero, especially after his recent difficult relationship with Muñoz. But the delegates reacted with wrath, shouting Muñoz down, forcing him to retract. Piñero was humiliated. It was a mistake that was to resurface, and come close to repeating itself, at another historic Popular Party assembly sixteen years later.

The Coalition parties virtually ceded the elections by nominating as their candidate for Governor the 66-year-old Martín Travieso. It was a symbolic gesture to reward a man who had come so close to realizing his

---

6. Ibid., 531.

life-dream. Travieso, who resigned as Supreme Court Chief Justice, a distinguished and respected figure, was the personification of "old politics"— a relic from the age of Luis Muñoz Rivera, José Celso Barbosa, Antonio Barceló, and Santiago Iglesias.

There was, however, great enthusiasm in the new Independence Party, reminding some observers of the electrifying ardor the Popular Party had back in its initial 1940 campaign. The comparisons increased when the new party held a well-attended general assembly on July 25, 1948, at the same baseball park in San Juan where back in 1940 the Muñoz party had first demonstrated its rising political power. The media reported that there were from fifteen to 20,000 people at the rally; 5,216 delegates from all the 786 barrios throughout the island. Party leader Concepción de Gracia had the candidates dramatically take an oath to implement the party's elaborate social and economic platform, just as Muñoz had done in 1940. "It was certainly an impressive event," Bolívar Pagán wrote years later.[7] Would the renegade *Populares*, many of whom had participated with Muñoz to produce the astounding PDP victory in 1940 and the massive sweep of 1944, pull off another political miracle?

There was no "miracle" on November 2, 1948. Muñoz and the Popular Party again won overwhelmingly. They received 392,033 votes, 61.2 percent, captured all the legislative districts and all but one of the 76 municipal governments. As expected the three Coalition parties together polled only 28.6 per cent, 180,513 votes. The surprise was the unexpectedly disappointing Independence Party vote. Getting only 66,141 votes, it did not elect a single legislator or mayor.

Muñoz had the electoral mandate he wanted to address the status issue. But for Muñoz, it was more than a mandate. The ideological question that had plagued his party leadership since his 1940 victory was now answered. In his resignation as Speaker of the House and from the Popular Party, Francisco Susoni insisted: "80 per cent of Puerto Ricans are *independentistas*." This was true of the Popular Party leadership in 1940 and 44. Now the Puerto Ricans had spoken for themselves. With an "Independence Party" for the first time on the ballot, led by articulate, attractive candidates, ninety percent of the people voted against it.

---

7. Pagán, *Historia de los partidos políticos puertorriqueños*, Vol. II, 269.

From the early morning hours of January 2, 1949, thousands of *jíbaros* come down from the mountains in trucks and buses, hundreds walking for hours, some bearing gifts. "The deep and abiding love between Muñoz on the one hand and the *jíbaros* on the other," Earl Parker Hanson wrote in 1955, "which began to manifest itself during the 1940 elections, has never diminished."[8] The swearing-in ceremony dramatized the identity that Muñoz had achieved with the Puerto Rican people. In his inaugural speech moments after taking the oath of office, Muñoz said: "I have just sworn faithful service to the people of Puerto Rico in the position that today I begin to occupy. Understand that it is with sincerity, and not with lack of modesty, that I will say that it was not necessary. With an oath of office or without it, forces of conscience have made of my life an oath of service to my people. With the governorship or without it, this is the obligation of all those that see ways of serving, feel the force to do so. By the vital nature, not merely the legal, of this oath, there is no reason why everyone should not share it with me..."

8. Hanson, *Transformation: The Story of Modern Puerto Rico*, 186.

22 The Take Off

When Muñoz moved his office from the Senate to La Fortaleza, he was faced with a radically different challenge—he had to become something he had never been, nor wanted to be in his life—an administrator. For the first time in the island's history, political and administrative power were united.

For a revolution to succeed, Charles Goodsell wrote in a study of Puerto Rico in this period, "it must be administered—and well. Power must not just be seized but used: revolutionary techniques of government must be converted to concrete action and the revolutionaries themselves with the practical techniques of government. If this is not done the revolution will likely become a meaningless *coup d'etat* involving a transfer of power rather than a transformation of society."[1]

Now as Governor, Muñoz found that Tugwell had left behind administrative tools, but they were disorganized. There were programs and agencies that lacked structure, hierarchy, and control. No one, in fact, could tell Muñoz exactly how many agencies existed. The University of Puerto Rico's School of Public Administration, organized in 1945, did a survey and reported that there were "around 100." He asked his young and talented Director of the Budget Bureau, Roberto de Jesús, to make his own study. Many of the public corporations were so "independent," De Jesús reported, that they often made "very important decisions" without informing the Governor or the Legislature. It was not surprising, he went on, that "the Government often appeared to follow a contradictory policy."

---

1. Goodsell, *Administration of a Revolution: Executive Reform in Puerto Rico under Governor Tugwell 1941-1946*, 1.

Muñoz knew that he had himself mostly to blame. It was under his leadership and drive that this "administrative monster" had been created. But it was also the result of Tugwell's peculiar, administrative style. While demanding that politicians not "interfere" with these agencies, he himself kept his hands off, allowing them to run their programs with virtually no supervision. When young Teodoro Moscoso was hired by Tugwell as his assistant back in 1942 and asked for a "job description," Tugwell answered that if he needed to be told what to do, he was in the wrong job. This management style had a positive effect. Goodsell points out that it was one major reason why so many of the young and inexperienced administrators that Tugwell recruited, with all their trial and error, were remarkably innovative in the early years of the Tugwell-Muñoz era.

But this was not Muñoz's style. In theory, he was told, 57 agencies reported to him: in practice very few did. And there were 11 agencies that no one could determine to whom, if anyone, they reported. This was intolerable: he was responsible, he had a mandate, the party's program to fulfill, and he wanted control.

As one of his first actions as Governor, he got the Legislature to establish a commission to come up with a government reorganization plan. He appointed a Washington attorney, James H. Rowe, Jr., who had served in the 1947 Hoover Commission to reform the Federal Government. Along with five prominent Puerto Ricans, he also appointed Louis Brownlow, described by Tugwell as "the dean of public administration that had done the most to upgrade the quality of government."

Working rapidly, the commission submitted its recommendation in five months, and by the summer of 1950, Muñoz had the new structure in place. The number of agencies was reduced to 23: none fully autonomous. Several of the public corporation's board of governors were eliminated giving the Governor a direct line of authority over them. No one had taken greater advantage of Tugwell's hands-off style than the free-wheeling Moscoso, considered by many a "loose cannon" in the administration. Muñoz reigned him in. His autonomous public corporation was made part of a newly expanded Economic Development Administration. Moscoso was now Muñoz's economic "Czar" in charge not only of industrialization, but of tourism and the critically important Ports Authority. But on the other hand Muñoz could keep him on a shorter leash now that he reported directly to him.

In its simplicity and logic, the new organization, with its centralized power structure, won the acclaim of experts and professionals as a model of efficient and action-oriented public administration. Henry Wells, a consultant to Puerto Rico's Constitutional Convention who wrote extensively on the island's modernization, wrote in 1956, "The Puerto Rican executive branch might be said to be the professional organizer's dream come true. Nowhere on the mainland have the goals of the reorganization movement been realized so completely as in the island Commonwealth."[2]

But the key to successfully "administering the revolution" was not its streamlined organization, but whether Muñoz succeeded in making the transition from the Senate to La Fortaleza. Muñoz wanted to prove that Tugwell's misgivings about him were wrong. "It caused me profound irritation," he wrote years later, "that Tugwell thought that he believed in good government and I did not: that I was committed to patronage. That offended me..."[3] According to Henry Wells, Tugwell would have been proud of his difficult disciple:

> The leadership provided by Muñoz was doubtless the most important factor. His success in keeping the administrative machine operating at a high level of efficiency and accomplishment was in part a product of the force and charm of his personality, a basic reason for his popularity among the people as a whole. But it was also a result of his superior grasp of political and administrative affairs, his imaginative approach to problems, and his willingness to make decisions after consulting [with] associates and weighing alternatives, his ability to keep track of details without getting buried in them or losing sight of long-run objectives, and, above all, his capacity to issue orders and reprimands to able subordinates without losing their respect and steadfast support. Muñoz, was in short, a strong executive in a culture that valued forceful leadership.[4]

---

2. Wells, *The Western Political Quarterly*, Vol. IX, 470-486.
3. Muñoz Marín, *Memorias* Vol. II, 116.
4. Wells, *The Modernization of Puerto Rico*, 201.

"Production For What?"

In May, 1947, Muñoz received a man who identified himself as a "spiritualist from Moca." He brought, he said, great news: he had "discovered gold" in the north-western tip of the island. He handed Muñoz a "sample." Muñoz's eyes opened and sent him immediately to Moscoso, who reported back: Sorry, the spiritualist had shown him a rock of iron sulfite. Since this mineral is abundant on the island, Moscoso continued, it is possible someone will again bring him a sample. All he had to do was hit the shiny part of the rock with a hammer, and if it shattered, it was not gold.

There was no magic formula for Muñoz's primary goal: to win "The Battle of Production." While Muñoz pushed his administration to reach the "four speeds" of development, he himself was constantly pushed by the irrepressible Moscoso. At La Fortaleza and his Trujillo Alto home, Muñoz and his aides were bombarded with letters, memos, clippings, articles from Moscoso, many with a breathless note of urgency: "It is of vital importance that Muñoz take ten minutes to read this memo—above all the last paragraph." In one letter he instructed one aide: "I include copies of two letters that I would appreciate that you get Muñoz to read. It is so essential that he learn of their content that if he does not have the time to read them, then have someone read them to him while he is having his breakfast or lunch or dinner." Moscoso commented years later "I think I scared Muñoz a bit."

Muñoz had asked Moscoso to organize his January 2, 1949 inaugural ceremony. Moscoso gladly accepted. It was clearly another indication of Muñoz's trust in him and his staff. Moscoso had another reason to celebrate. He knew that Muñoz's swearing-in would attract the national and international media. Muñoz would bring down political leaders from Washington and Latin America, and many of his American friends from his days as journalist and poet. But Moscoso used the occasion to invite over fifty top American businessmen, including David Rockefeller, president of the Chase Manhattan Bank, and Beardsley Ruml, Macy's president. Both became deeply involved in Puerto Rico and Moscoso's program.

For the American media, the story in Puerto Rico had always been the "Broken Pledge," and occasionally Nationalist violence. Now there was something new and surprising happening. *Life* magazine, in a glowing story, described Muñoz's conversion: "the once Greenwich Village Bohemian, now hobnobbing with hardheaded businessmen", convincing them that the "island is now a good place for investment and industry... Governor Muñoz said there was a good time coming and most were inclined to believe him." Moscoso took the media out to the center of the island for the inauguration of a $10 million dam. *The New York Times* reported on its front page that the dam would serve "as a major link in a power system being developed as the hub of a movement to change."

On May 2, 1949, Muñoz appeared on the cover of *Time* magazine. The four page-story ended: "Don Luis is sure that the only fundamental cure for the island's troubled is more plants, more jobs and more goods at home." This picture of Muñoz turned industrial promoter was accurate. He understood the importance of this favorable publicity in the U.S. to drive Moscoso's promotional programs.

But it was accurate only in part. From the beginning, Moscoso's program provoked ambiguous and increasingly opposing emotions in Muñoz. Of course, lifting the *jíbaro* from extreme poverty was not only the priority, but the most fundamental aspect of his "democratic revolution." But how would the program achieve this? How to make the profound transformation from an agricultural to an industrial economy, without destroying his beloved *jíbaro* civilization?

Another inner "civil war" had begun within Muñoz. In his first message to the Legislature, on February 23, 1949, he reaffirmed his solid support for the Fomento program: "We continue to give ample opportunities for new industries and we prefer that they be established and developed by private initiative as long as it fulfills the public responsibilities involved in all actions that affect the lives of many. Tax exemption for those industries... and the cooperative attitude of the government and people in general... those are the incentives."[5] But then he went on to ask a question he was to ask for the rest of his life:

Dedicated as we are to production, we must ask: Production for what? Production to serve what kind of life? Economic production for mere compulsion to produce, without an objective of life to guide

---

5. Muñoz Marín, *Los gobernadores electos de Puerto Rico*, Vol. I, 25.

it, in the modern world can only lead to gluttony of property and spiritual confusion...People do not exist for industrialization. Industrialization exists for people, and most people are workers.

The Fomento Rebellion

Over in Fomento, the young professionals working with Moscoso, many of them recruited by Tugwell, were aware of Muñoz's internal "civil war." The fact was that at every critical crossroads, as much as the poet in Muñoz seemed to agonize, in the end the pragmatic, realistic political leader in him would be on Fomento's side. Moscoso and his people also realized that there was a deep "cultural" gulf between them and the leaders and militants of the Popular Party. They were "Americanized" in education, appearance, and style, worlds away from the *jíbaro* culture. But they also recognized and appreciated that Muñoz scrupulously lived up to his promise to keep the Fomento plants free from political patronage.

With Muñoz's blessing, however, all the plants were unionized, and from the beginning there were costly labor conflicts. The union leaders vigorously protested when Moscoso recruited skilled workers from the mainland. At one of the plants, the Americans brought down for their skills and experience were themselves so frustrated and unhappy that they too went on strike.

In Moscoso's mind, these conflicts, like Muñoz's internal ambiguity, made no sense. To win the "Battle of Production" was to serve Muñoz's *jíbaro*, and to do so he had to be given the freedom to run plants as private businesses. It was obvious: the profits, after all, were not going into the pockets of greedy capitalists, but reinvested for establishing new plants and creating new jobs. None of this was at all obvious to the labor leaders. They demanded that the profits be used for higher salaries and benefits. And they reminded Moscoso and his people that they were loyal followers of Muñoz and the Popular Party and that Muñoz himself was firmly behind them.

Finally it all came to a head at the big cement plant that Moscoso had inherited from the old Puerto Rico Economic Reconstruction Administration. Each time Moscoso drove by the plant, he saw hundreds of workers at the nearby limestone quarry, nearly naked, burnt by the scorching sun, cutting the stone by hand. The purpose of Fomento was "the workers." But this was inhuman work. In his imagination, he visualized ant-like slave laborers building ancient monuments. He decided to end this by purchasing mechanical shovels he had seen in the U.S. The reaction of the union was immediate: it promptly shut down the plant. After frantic negotiations that would lead, Moscoso believed, to a settlement, he learned that the union leaders had also been negotiating separately with Muñoz, who had accepted precisely the demands Moscoso and his people had adamantly resisted.

For Moscoso and his people, if it was impossible to run these plants as a business, they preferred not to run them at all. They "resigned in mass." But one of his top lieutenants, the bright, former cement salesman that Moscoso had elevated to president of the Fomento plants, Guillermo Rodríguez, did not trust Moscoso's resolution. Too often in the past, he had seen Moscoso rage in anger and defiance, but then yield to Muñoz like a lamb. Certainly he would again. Rodríguez insisted that they all take refuge in his home and stay there for as long as necessary to make their "resignation" stick. Muñoz would not get to Moscoso. Along with the Fomento attorney, the Cornell educated Mariano Ramírez, and several others, they "went into hiding" at the Rodríguez home.

Muñoz was stunned. Suddenly his Fomento people had vanished. Finally he located them. Moscoso and his people were dead serious. Unless Muñoz and his party kept their hands off the labor situation, they simply would not return. They had no interest in wasting their time in endless conflicts with the labor leaders. Their interest was only in creating the thousands of new jobs the island desperately needed and that Muñoz himself was demanding. Of course, Muñoz answered, they were absolutely right. The Fomento rebellion ended.

Operation Bootstrap

Moscoso was even more pleased when on July 12, 1949, while testifying before a congressional committee in Washington, Muñoz declared: "We are trying to lift ourselves by our own bootstraps with the help that Congress has always given Puerto Rico. I want to say that the people there deserve all the help they can get because they are courageously helping themselves. They are not lying back and waiting for someone to lend them a hand. They are doing the utmost they can to solve their problems."[6]

The Fomento program now had a name. Muñoz told the committee: "We have abandoned what we might call 'Operation Lament' and are now in the midst of 'Operation Bootstrap'."

The "mass resignation crisis" had, for Moscoso, another positive result. He convinced Muñoz that the Government should quit the business of running industrial plants, and sell the cement, glass, paperboard and clay products plants to private investors. It was not, however, until September of 1950 that Moscoso received an offer from an unexpected source, the Ferré family in Ponce. This was a problem: among their many businesses, the Ferrés owned the only other cement plant on the island and Moscoso had declared that he would never permit a monopoly on this vital product. Now he changed his mind.

But how far could he take Muñoz? It was one thing to get the old "socialist" behind a capitalistic Fomento program, but it was another to sell these plants to the Ferré family, who were not only Puerto Rico's principal capitalists, but Muñoz's political opponents. One of the brothers, Luis, a graduate of MIT, an accomplished fencer and pianist, had emerged as the island's top statehood leader. He ran for Mayor of Ponce back in 1940, and for resident commissioner in 1948. He lost each time but his personal popularity seemed to grow. He was a charming, soft-spoken man and at the same time, a persistent, determined critic of Muñoz, often attacking him, as did the *independentistas*, of being "dictatorial."

The Ferrés offered $10.5 million for the plants. The Government would recover its original investment in the plants and the monopoly issue would be resolved by government control of the price of cement. Muñoz relented. The negotiations were quick. "It felt," Moscoso commented, "as if a giant slab of lead had been lifted from Fomento."[7] For Muñoz, it was one of the critical decisions in his life, politically and personally.

---

6. Ibid., 34.

7. Moscoso, *Oral History*, 122.

Fomento was now free to carry out the massive promotional campaign throughout the United States envisioned by Moscoso. But there was still something missing. What exactly was going to attract private investment to the island? To bring the program up to the speed Muñoz was demanding, its incentive had to be powerful enough not only to compete with the many U.S. cities and states attempting to attract industry, but to overcome the obstacles to successful operation on this small island one thousand miles from the mainland. Moscoso by now knew that the promise of profits was not enough: he had to make a "frank appeal to cupidity." As Fomento economist Hubert Barton put it in 1959, it was an appeal to the American "gold rush psychology...the possibility of making a killing."[8]

When Moscoso convinced Muñoz, once Tugwell was gone, to approve a comprehensive tax exemption law in 1947, it ignited a debate as heated and impassioned among the Muñoz administrators as the political status debate among the political leaders. But in 1948, led by the economist Sol Luis Descartes, later to become his Secretary of the Treasury, Muñoz was convinced that Moscoso's tax exemption was not only bad tax policy, bad developmental policy, but intrinsically "unfair and immoral." How could Muñoz justify heavily taxing existing Puerto Rican businesses, yet exempting newly arrived American corporations? The incentive, Descartes and the other economists he recruited argued, also rewarded those that didn't need it: obviously, the more money a company made, the more it benefited from the exemption, and, in turn, the greater the "cost" in lost revenue to the government. And it was bad developmental policy because it would deprive Puerto Rico of urgently needed tax revenue to build the infrastructure essential for growth. Finally, Muñoz was warned that the Moscoso plan was a "trap:" as much as he wanted to believe that this was a "temporary" incentive, once into it, Descartes argued, there was no way to escape.

Muñoz convened a meeting of his administrators at his home to air all of this out completely. Moscoso was surprised that there was virtual unanimity against his plan. Muñoz was quiet but it was evident that he was again torn within himself. Finally he decided against Moscoso: the

---

8. Barton, *"Puerto Rico's Industrial Development"*, 17.

1947 tax exemption law would be allowed to expire. But Moscoso was counting on Muñoz's emotional ambuiguity. Early the next morning he returned, and pleaded with Muñoz to give him an opportunity to try the new exemption plan. Puerto Rico, he argued, had nothing to lose. Again, Muñoz relented. All right, he said, go ahead, try it.[9]

On May 13, 1948, Moscoso's new tax exemption bill was approved. It was at that moment, he believed, that Operation Bootstrap was born. Puerto Rico's economic take off began. In 1949, Moscoso brought 28 new private-capital industries to the island, more than duplicating all the Fomento plants established since its founding six year earlier. Exercising his flair for promotion and public relations, he had big signs with the Fomento logo—a muscular worker pushing a huge industrial wheel—placed in front of each new factory. His agency, meanwhile, launched an ambitious industrial building construction program. Visiting potential investors were taken to plant buildings, ready to move in. In addition to 100 percent tax exemption, Fomento offered a package of multiple incentives, including low lease rates and employee training.

It was hard, painstaking work. As one Fomento economist pointed out, for every hundred companies visited by a Fomento "industrial representative," working out of the new Fomento offices throughout the U.S., ten would actually visit the island, and of these, one would establish a plant.

But the perception in Puerto Rico, and within Muñoz's Popular Party, was that Fomento had indeed created a "gold rush stampede." In the U.S., the glowing newspaper and magazine articles created the perception that the island had become one big "tax haven," raising concerns and objections in Congress and mainland organize labor. In testimony before Congress and in numerous speeches, Muñoz emphasized that he had a firm policy against attracting "runaway industries." Puerto Rico's industrialization, he insisted, would not be at the expense of other regions of the nation, such as New England, which was then beginning to lose its textile industry. Puerto Rico only aspired to a minute slice of America's industrial expansion. By law, he said, "runaway industries" were denied tax exemption.

Muñoz also made a special effort to communicate to the American labor movement that his administration rejected "sweatshops" and welcomed the

9. Maldonado, *Teodoro Moscoso and Puerto Rico's Operation Bootstrap*, 57.

unionization of the new industries. Moscoso, while accepting Muñoz's directive to push for the highest possible salaries, insisted that Puerto Rico be exempt from automatic U.S. minimum wage increases. Again, Muñoz's pragmatism was put to the test. One of the initial reform bills Muñoz had approved in 1941 was precisely to set an insular minimum wage. Now he was convinced by Moscoso that full applicability of federal minimum wages killed all hopes of attracting the labor-intensive industries desperately needed, especially in the small towns away from San Juan. Congress legislated, and American labor leaders grudgingly accepted a special "escape clause" for industries in Puerto Rico that proved they were unable to pay the minimum wage.

Muñoz's fame in the U.S. continued to grow. On May 14, 1958, he appeared again on the cover of *Time* magazine. Puerto Rico, the story declared, was about to cross a historic boundary. "Two lines will meet and cross on a graph in Puerto Rico this week and thereby touch off a great celebration. The crossed lines mean that, for the first time in history, manufacturing has edged ahead of farming as Puerto Rico's main source of income...Puerto Rico's self help program is a smashing success." That week, the report continued, "no fewer than 20 new factories are to be officially opened. Heading the list is a $2,000,000 General Electric plant to make circuit breakers..."

THE FOMENTARIAN REVOLUTION

Nothing pleased Muñoz more than an article by economist K.E. Boulding published in June 1961. After analyzing the American and Russian revolutions, he wrote, "there is a type of revolution which does not fit comfortably into any of the above categories and which may be the most important of all in the long run. I call it the 'Fomentarian Revolution' in honor of a remarkable institution in Puerto Rico which embodies it known as Fomento." The four outstanding aspects of the "Fomentarian Revolution," he said, are: "A charismatic leader who can inspire a large number of people with a vision of the future," thus creating a political consensus. Second, great emphasis on education and human resource development. Third, "the skill to strike clever bargains with foreign capitalists." And the fourth: the ability to affect a fundamental cultural transition from traditional to an "economic culture."

Muñoz was pleased to have this important economist confirm that what was taking place in Puerto Rico was indeed a "revolution," but it was the fourth point, regarding cultural impact, that rekindled the concerns he had first raised, back in 1949, in his first Message to the Legislature.

23 The Road to Reality

The transition from agriculture to industry did more than transform the economy: it changed the island's psychological landscape. On July 5, 1949, the new Governor met with President Truman to bring a message never before heard from a Puerto Rican politician. Puerto Rico, he said, was not asking but offering.

In his January 20, 1949 inaugural address, Truman announced a "bold new program" called Point Four. Outlining his principal foreign policy objectives—the Marshall Plan, the United Nations, the military buildup to deter Soviet Union aggression in Western Europe—his "fourth point" was to assist underdeveloped countries with American know-how. "The material resources," he said, "which we can afford to use for assistance to other people are limited. But our imponderable resources in technical knowledge are constantly growing and are inexhaustible... Democracy alone can supply vitalizing force to stir the people of the world into triumphant action, not only against their human oppressors, but also against their ancient enemies—hunger, misery and despair."[1]

The speech was received as surprisingly "eloquent and moving...many thought it was the finest he ever made." To Muñoz it sounded as if Truman was describing his own "democratic revolution." After centuries of listlessness and hopelessness, the Puerto Rican people had indeed been "stirred" into "triumphant action." Muñoz offered Truman the use of the Puerto Rican experience in rapid economic development within a democratic system as a

---

1. McCullough, *Truman*, 731.

showcase for the Point Four Program. And what better way to combat the anti-American challenge in Latin America, demonstrating that in this small, overpopulated, Hispanic island under the U.S. flag, democracy was indeed the "vitalizing force" in the world?

Interior Secretary Julius A. Krug, also at the meeting, followed up with a July 18 memorandum informing the President that the State Department enthusiastically welcomed Muñoz's offer. Muñoz got the insular Legislature to institutionalize the program. By the mid 1950s, Puerto Rico had received over 10,000 Point Four professionals, government officials, academics, journalists, and students. In Muñoz's eyes, this was still another change in the relationship between Puerto Rico and the United States that was not spelled out in Puerto Rico's legal status.

The time had arrived, however, to address the legal nature of the relationship. Muñoz promised all along that he would turn to the status issue after the war: now it was part of the 1948 electoral mandate. Two years earlier, Resident Commissioner Dr. Antonio Fernós Isern had mapped out a different approach to dealing with Congress. He urged Muñoz and the party to separate the "constitutional" from the "final political status" determination. Mixing the constitutional process with the question of whether the island should ultimately become a state or independent, Fernós argued, was the mistake that led to paralysis. There was no reason, Fernós believed, for Congress to object to Puerto Rico having its own constitution.

Muñoz, however, understood that getting Congress to move involved more than political strategy. Beginning with his teenage days beside his father in Congress and through his roller-coaster experiences in Washington in the 1930s, he understood that the great obstacle in the relationship between Puerto Rico and the United States, more than political or economic, was at its heart cultural. It was the wide, deep canyon of miscommunication that had swallowed his father during the tortured bartering over the Jones Act and American citizenship. Muñoz was the first Puerto Rican politician who felt that he did not have to cross that cultural canyon to communicate with the Americans. He believed that he understood American civilization. The key, Muñoz and Fernós believed, was keeping the constitutional bill as straightforward, as practical and simple as possible, and this meant keeping it as free as possible from the abstract ideological arguments loved by island politicians, as in all Latin America.

The other critical element was to approach Congress not with the old attack strategy, the traditional accusation that "we are a shameful colony," but with the positive attitude that Muñoz had brought to the meeting with Truman. The essential message would be: now that Puerto Rico had finally found the formula to climb out of centuries of poverty and injustice, let's proceed to resolve the political defect in the relationship. In the new psychological landscape, Muñoz would back his words in Congress with the fact that the Operation Bootstrap spirit had replaced Operation Lament.

The week after his successful visit with Truman, Muñoz appeared before the House Committee on Public Lands and immediately put into practice his strategy. Politically, he said, Congress already made the big improvement when it allowed the island to elect its Governor. "In my view...Congress is practically giving shape to a new kind of State. You find no dependency anywhere in the world that elects its own executive and legislative government. The step taken in Puerto Rico is tradition-breaking. It is a completely new departure which does a very high honor to the United States Congress and to the United States President."[2] But, he continued, there is "something missing which I do not anticipate will be very difficult to correct...What is missing to make Puerto Rico a new kind of State is that the people of Puerto Rico should have the right to make their own constitution."

That this was precisely the right tactic became evident to Muñoz and Fernós immediately. "Muñoz Marín," wrote Surendra Bhana in 1975, "made an overwhelming impression upon the legislators. The Public Lands Committee...broke tradition by giving the Governor a standing ovation. Secretary Krug noted in his memorandum to the President that the *Popular* leader had been received by congressmen with 'extraordinary cordiality'."[3] Never before, the Secretary added, had Puerto Rico communicated better with the United States.

2. Muñoz Marín, *Los gobernadores electos de Puerto Rico*, 100.
3. Bhana, *The United States and the Development of the Puerto Rican status Question*, 117.

Muñoz returned to the island feeling that he had indeed achieved a breakthrough in Washington. But he needed a breakthrough also in Puerto Rico. On the S.S. Suzanne with his family, Inés and daughters Viviana and Victoria, Muñoz carefully prepared a statement: the essential message would be the same as in his long *El Mundo* articles back in 1946, but this time it was short and precise. "I believe that you, with your votes, charged me to exhaust every effort to rescue you from the confusion over political status, and setting us on the road to clarity, good sense and firm orientation...I think we are now on this road."

Read at the docks in San Juan on August 1, 1949, Muñoz went on:

> Puerto Rico is not a colony... An important part of what we Puerto Ricans believe is that freedom has to be understood more through the observation of the reality than by the mere reading of political or juridical documents... If Puerto Rico is not a colony, nor a federated state, nor a separate, independent state, then, what is it? What is being created in Puerto Rico, not by theoretical plans or ivory tower jurists, but by creative dynamism... is a new kind of state. A new kind of state in association with the United States... I repeat, liberty has to be judged more through intelligent observation of its reality than by the naïve perusal of its document.

In the tranquility of his ocean voyage, Muñoz had put down in a few words his essential approach to Puerto Rico's maddening political status dilemma. Rooted in his father's pragmatic, anti-ideological attitude towards politics, and in his own long process of "de-dogmatization" beginning with his July 4, 1922 letter to Epifanio Fernández Vanga, Muñoz believed that he had finally discovered the "road to reality" that would lead his people out of the political status wilderness.

But Muñoz wanted to communicate something else. His voice deepening with indignation, he attacked the political opposition, the statehooders in the U.S. and the *independentistas* throughout Latin America, for "humiliating and reviling" the island with the "title of colony."

The people of Puerto Rico have the respect and admiration of all those in all of America who know that there is not a more vigorous democracy in any part of the American hemisphere, neither in the North nor in the South... What right do a handful of its own compatriots have to scoff at it with slander and false titles? To pretend to fight a colony that does not exist is to fight a straw man in order to avoid the responsibility of fighting against the true problems of Puerto Rico.[4]

THE TRÍAS APPROACH

But within Muñoz's own inner circle, there was a fundamentally different view. Muñoz had recruited a Harvard and Yale-trained, young lawyer, José Trías Monge, as his principal legal advisor. Trías, as well as several top leaders of the Popular Party, disagreed with the Fernós strategy and the message in Muñoz's S.S. Suzanne statement. Simply authorizing the island to adopt its own constitution, they insisted, did not create "a new kind of state" but left the island's essential "colonial" condition unchanged. Instead, they argued that it was necessary to ask Congress to totally scrap the existing Organic Act and enact a radically different status law.

Contrary to what Muñoz was saying, they believed that precisely the content of the "juridical document" was critical: that both the new law and the legislative process in Congress should leave no doubt that the United States yielded its "sovereignty" over the island. The basis of the new relationship would be a bilateral, mutually binding "compact." Congress would then explicitly acknowledge that the island was no longer a "possession" under the constitutional "territorial clause." Only after this happened, Trías and the lawyers believed, would it be correct to declare that "Puerto Rico is not a colony."

World events seemed to favor making the case of Puerto Rico in terms of "colonialism." On September 23, 1949, President Truman issued a short statement declaring that "an atomic explosion had occurred" in the Soviet

---

4. Muñoz Marín, *Los gobernadores electos de Puerto Rico*, 61.

Union. Two years earlier, Secretary of State George Marshall, returning from Moscow, "reported to Truman what Truman had already privately concluded, that diplomacy with the Soviet leadership was futile, that the Russians were determined to provoke the collapse of Europe. Now the 'enemy' was a nuclear power, producing an atomic bomb three years 'ahead of prediction'." The Cold War had begun.

With the terror of nuclear war in the background, much of the anti-U.S. offensive from the Soviet block and throughout the emerging Third World, especially in Latin America, revolved around "colonialist exploitation." Truman countered the offensive: "In all the history of the world we are the first great nation to feed and support the conquered. We are the first great nation to create independent republics from conquered territory, Cuba and the Philippines".[5]

This was seen by the lawyers and party leaders as the opening Puerto Rico needed to demand from Congress and the President fundamental legal changes that would disarm the anti-American propaganda.

"Keep it Simple"

Muñoz trusted and liked his young, soft-spoken legal advisor, who was also an expert on Spanish Literature and, to Muñoz's delight, advised him on fine wines. Two years later, after the Constitution went into effect, Muñoz appointed him the first Secretary of Justice. Their personal friendship would last throughout the rest of his life. But Muñoz was determined to follow his instincts and Fernós's advice to "keep it simple."

This was precisely the advice that Muñoz received from the experts in the Truman administration. James D. Davis, Head of the Interior Department Division on Territories, found that even Muñoz's simplified bill "is somewhat complicated...it tries to do too much with the result that is it very difficult to figure out exactly what effect it does have on existing law... We think a fairly simple bill should suffice, authorizing the people of Puerto Rico to draft a Constitution".[6]

---

5. McCullough, *Truman*, 583.
6. Trías Monge, *Historia constitucional de Puerto Rico* Vol. III, 31.

The division's legal counselor, Irving Silverman, was less diplomatic. He flatly refused to include the concept of a "bilateral compact." Now working closely with Muñoz was the veteran Washington lawyer, Abe Fortas, who had served in the Interior Department during the tumultuous Tugwell years and remained well-connected to the White House and Congress. Fortas was also an accomplished violinist, and years later would play a key role in establishing the world famous Casals Festival in Puerto Rico. As with Trías, Muñoz not only depended on his legal experience, but enjoyed his company, his knowledge and taste in the fine arts. Now Fortas emphasized the importance of retaining the compact concept in the bill. He pointed out that it was not a novel or radical concept in American history. On the contrary, it was well-known by the Founding Fathers, discussed in the Federalist Papers and in subsequent U.S. Supreme Court decisions. Indeed, the Constitution prohibits states from entering into "any Agreement or Compact with another State or with a foreign Power." Fortas agreed that the strategy must be to "keep it simple." But he strongly agreed with Trías and the other lawyers that there should be no confusion in Congress over the new relationship was precisely a "compact."

On March 7, 1950, Muñoz gave Fernós instructions to introduce the bill. On the surface, it was "kept simple." Bill HR 7674 had only 59 lines. The question of *how* to introduce the compact concept into the bill so as to make the least amount of waves was resolved. Fortas and Trías came up with the wording: "Be it enacted by the Senate and House of Representatives of the United States of America in Congress assembled, that, fully recognizing the principle of government by consent, this act is now adopted in the nature of a compact so that the people of Puerto Rico may organize a government pursuant to a constitution of their own adoption." Fernós and Muñoz, and finally Congress, approved it.

But Trías and the Muñoz lawyers were still not satisfied. Instead of totally repealing the old Jones Act of 1917, HR7674 merely amended it and gave it a new title: The Puerto Rico Federal Relations Act. Puerto Ricans would continue to be U.S. citizens, to have free access to the U.S., and would retain exemption of U.S. taxes. The amendments, they argued, made only "cosmetic" changes that did not resolve the difficult and crucial defects. One of the most important was that it did not address the matter of Puerto Rico's lack of representation in the U.S. Government. Although the island remained subject to most laws of Congress, Puerto Rico continued to be represented by only a non-voting resident commissioner. Puerto Ricans, of course, like all U.S. residents, were subject to be called for military service, but the island would not participate in presidential elections. For Trías and the others, even with congressional recognition of the "compact," the terms themselves left the relationship essentially "colonial."

Muñoz did not refute this argument. But he came back to the essential goal, to resolve the constitutional issue without upsetting the existing economic relationship between Puerto Rico and the U.S. To totally discard the old Jones Act meant having to renegotiate with Congress the highly beneficial and now vital economic conditions Puerto Rico already possessed. In theory, of course, it was conceivable that the island could negotiate even better conditions, but Muñoz was not willing to take the risk at this precise moment when the economy was beginning to take off under Operation Bootstrap.

Muñoz kept returning to the spirit of his S.S. Suzanne declaration. He was after the reality of freedom, not the freedom "of political or juridical documents." Puerto Rico's "fiscal autonomy," he believed, gave the island real self-government. An American in the states pays most of his taxes to the Federal Government: taxes imposed and spent by a Congress composed of 435 members of the House and 100 Senators. Think of it, Muñoz argued, Puerto Ricans now pay taxes imposed and spent by a Legislature and Governor all elected by themselves. If the power to tax is the power to govern, the new status was juridically untidy, but in the real world "fiscal autonomy" gave Puerto Ricans real power over their government and themselves.

But Muñoz, as much as he wanted, could not ignore the insistence by Trías and other legal experts that a juridically flawed political status was being created. As he was to do throughout this process, Muñoz attempted to meet the objections half way. Seeking voting representation in Congress was, of course, out of the question since it would inevitably mean assuming the federal tax burden. Then, why not statehood? This, of course, was not what Trías and the other "autonomists" in the Muñoz group wanted.

But this, in turn, revived the Fernós warning that Puerto Rico should not make complex, unorthodox demands that would threaten the entire initiative. Muñoz asked Trías to come up with a more moderate mechanism that gave the island some participation in the applicability of Federal laws without affecting its "fiscal autonomy." Finally, Muñoz agreed to add Section 6 to the bill: "The President of the United States, when requested by legislative enactment of the government of Puerto Rico, may exempt Puerto Rico from the application of any Federal law, not specifically made applicable to Puerto Rico by Congress, which he deems inapplicable by reason of local conditions." Muñoz had reason to believe that Congress would not object. This, after all, was almost identical to what Congress had approved in the 1947 Elective Governor Act.

On March 6, 1950, Muñoz met with the President and the new Interior Secretary, Oscar L. Chapman, and both reacted positively. The skeptical legal counsel, Irving Silverman, was now on board. Picking up on Muñoz's Cold War argument, Silverman lobbied key senators that it would have the "greatest propaganda value in Latin America."

On the eve of congressional hearings, the entourage of aides, lawyers, and administrators that accompanied Muñoz to Washington had never seen him so tense. Senate hearings were held the same day the bill was introduced, March 13, 1950. "Muñoz always had great difficulty writing speeches and statements," Trías commented decades later. "He suffered acutely from writer's block. He would be unable, at times, to write a single word until the night before, then spend the entire night writing frantically, making changes until the very last moment." But this was more than "writer's block." Although everything seemed to be going well in Washington, Muñoz seemed strangely insecure about the congressional reaction to his bill.

Budget Director Roberto de Jesús recalled: "All day Sunday—his Senate Interior and Insular Affairs Committee hearing was on Monday—we wondered if Muñoz would pull back, not introduce the bill, not testify. We had lunch that afternoon with a prominent Washington figure who casually asked what Muñoz intended to say. Muñoz tightened up and refused to talk about it." After lunch, De Jesús continued, they spent an hour driving around Washington, seeing the sights they all had seen scores of times. Muñoz took them to the Georgetown University buildings where he had lived and studied for a few months. Then he announced that he "wanted to go to the movies." De Jesús sat next to him: "I can tell you that he never watched the movie. From the corner of my eye, I could see him rehearsing his testimony, his hands moving up and down as he emphasized his points."

Muñoz followed his strategy and began on a positive note. "Puerto Rico is one of the best working democracies in the world...The main result of our proposal is that the law will catch up with the fact..."[7] He again grounded the proposal on economics. Using a dramatic analogy first employed by University of Puerto Rico Chancellor Jaime Benítez: to understand the island's economic reality, one must imagine the United States without any natural resources, with very little arable land, yet with the entire world's population living within its borders.

At one point, while Muñoz was describing the role of tax exemption in attracting industry, assuring the committee members that his intention was to phase it out as soon as possible, committee chairman Senator Joseph C. O'Mahoney interrupted him to emphasize that Puerto Rico had never been taxed by the U.S. Government: "Governor... I would like to have it clearly on the record that the relationship between the Federal Government of the United States and Puerto Rico, since the island came under the jurisdiction of this government, has not been one of colonial exploitation of the people. Is it not a fact that it has always been one of seeking to create more opportunities for the people to support themselves?" Muñoz answered:

I would say that not only has the attitude of the Federal Government been helpful, but that by all modern definitions of what constitutes colonialism, it has not been a colonialist policy in Puerto Rico. The most clear and significant fact in this is that one of the characteristics of colonialism is to prevent colonies from establishing and developing industry...that is so far from being true in Puerto Rico that we are now developing industrialization not only without any opposition from the Federal Government, but actually with much sympathy, understanding and aid from the Government of the United States.[8]

Muñoz then turned to the Cold War argument. Allowing Puerto Rico to have its own Constitution "will free both the Puerto Ricans and the people of the rest of the States of the malicious accusation of colonialism so constantly

---

7. Muñoz Marín, *Los gobernadores electos de Puerto Rico*, 95.
8. Ibid., 100.

wielded against them by the Communists groups in Latin America. It will put us politically and morally on an equal level to the great democratic practices and the great effort to continue solving the difficult economic problems of Puerto Rico."[9]

Once more the members of the committee "were so thoroughly impressed" by Muñoz that they gave him a standing ovation.[10] Even Trías, who felt that Muñoz was being overly conservative, was impressed: "With his voice deep and clear, his elegance and ease of expression, his perfect command of English, his agility in debate and authority of his presence, Muñoz Marín clearly has impressed the Committee. One could sense in the majority of its members a favorable disposition towards the bill."[11] Trías also noted that Muñoz demonstrated "exquisite care" in sidestepping the legal pitfalls. The implications and the constitutionality of the "bilateral compact" were not raised once.

The issue, however, came up quickly in the House hearing the following day. One representative asked pointblank if the island would remain "a possession or Territory of the United States." Harping on semantics, Muñoz answered, "certainly not as a possession. Sir, I do not believe that some Americans can be a possession of other Americans." North Dakota Representative William Lemke shot back: "As a Territory of the United States?" Committee chairman J. Hurdin Peterson broke in: "Occupying a peculiar status under the Constitution of the United States, and by an Act of Congress it being neither a State nor a possession." Muñoz added: "It is a community of American citizens that should have whatever name is proper to govern themselves fully in their local function of government under the Federal Constitution."

The Muñoz lawyers hoped that this exchange would finally clarify on the record that the island would no longer be a "possession," a "territory," or in the language of island politics, a "colony." They were also pleased by how Fernós answered a direct question by committee chairman O'Mahoney at the May 17 hearing. "Should Puerto Rico," Fernós said, "adopt its own constitution, it would certainly constitute a compact between the United States...and the people of Puerto Rico."

---

9. Ibid., 123.

10. Bhana, *The United States and the Development of the Puerto Rican status Question*, 123.

11. Trías Monge, *Historia constitucional de Puerto Rico* Vol. III, 45.

Back in Puerto Rico, however, nothing said in the congressional hearings diminished the pro-statehood and *independentista* opposition to the bill. Independence Party President Concepción de Gracia decided not to testify, expressing his condemnation of the process in a telegram. The insular Republican leaders asked for changes in the bill's wording to imply that the new status was a transition to eventual statehood. Industrialist Luis A. Ferré assured President Truman in a letter that if an honest plebiscite is ever held, "an overwhelming majority will choose statehood."

Several members of Congress, opponents of statehood for Hawaii and Alaska, wanted to make certain that the Puerto Rico bill did not inadvertently open the doors to these two territories. Muñoz and Fernós were asked to clarify whether under the new arrangement, Puerto Rico would become an "incorporated territory" and thus on track to eventual statehood. No, they answered emphatically: there was absolutely no intent, no mandate for this from the people of Puerto Rico.

When news of this exchange reached Puerto Rico, the opposition rejoiced, insisting that Muñoz and Fernós had finally confessed that the new law did not "change" the island's status: that it remained "colonial." Muñoz found himself again in a debate over semantics. What did the word "change" mean? Even though the bill did not "incorporate" Puerto Rico, it did indeed change Puerto Rico's legal relationship to the U.S. The Muñoz lawyers, meanwhile, warned him that it was more than a silly game of semantics: that several troubling statements were getting into the congressional record. One, by the Interior Department Division on Territories and Insular Possessions, categorically declared that the bill "will not change Puerto Rico's political, social and economic relationship to the United States." Fernós was not worried: the bill, after all, was now sailing smoothly. Yet Trías and the lawyers wondered if it was sailing too smoothly and whether these contrary statements would eventually come to haunt them and the new status.

Suddenly the bill encountered an unexpected tempest that momentarily shook Muñoz and Fernós. The Senate committee, in approving the bill, eliminated Section 6, the clause to partially overcome the flaw of the applicability of federal laws. "Muñoz was indignant," Trías wrote, "and was on the verge of withdrawing his support of the bill." Abe Fortas, however, strongly urged Muñoz to go ahead. On June 9, the Senate approved the amended status bill without debate.

Fortas disagreed with the other legal advisors who felt that without Section 6 the bill was unacceptable. He wrote to Muñoz: "I am personally enthusiastic about the bill passed in the Senate because it retains the basic theory of consent—in fact, it may even incorporate the principles of consent more clearly than in the bill as introduced because of the requirement of positive approval of the Congress and the detailed requirement of a referendum of the people of Puerto Rico to accept the Act. The bill also represents the principle that the people of Puerto Rico shall draft their own constitution and that it further retains the language which to my mind is of paramount importance, that the Act is in the nature of a compact."[12]

Three days after the House approved the bill, on July 2, 1950, President Truman signed what was now Law 600.

In Puerto Rico, the reaction of the opposition, that in fact nothing had "changed," was expressed in an editorial in the leading independent newspaper, *El Mundo*: "The Constitutional bill is an additional concession to that already made in the elective government, but it cannot be presented to the eyes of the world as something comparable to the Day of Independence of the United States..."[13]

This was precisely what Law 600 represented for Muñoz, Fernós, and the Popular Party. In just sixteen weeks, they had achieved what the previous generation had not in a half century. A new form of political relationship, "a new kind of state," to be named Commonwealth status, in Spanish, *Estado Libre Asociado*, Free Associated State, had been created with Congress and the President of the United States.

---

12. Ibid., 53.
13. Ibid., 57.

Muñoz did not underestimate, much less discard, the misgivings and warnings of his legal advisors that there were serious juridical defects in this new status. Nor that the congressional record was not clear enough, lending itself to hostile interpretations of "congressional intent". But what was critical for Muñoz was the breakthrough in getting Congress to approve any status bill. The "keep it simple" strategy had worked. Fernós had again demonstrated his skill in skirting the pitfalls and land mines that had defeated so many other Puerto Rican initiatives. There will be time, Muñoz assured the skeptics among his advisors and in his party, to address and correct the defects. This was only the beginning.

24 The Nationalist Revolt

"**H**e comes to kill," Jaime Benítez commented to Muñoz after listening to a Pedro Albizu Campos radio speech soon after he returned to the island in December, 1947.[1] Muñoz pointed out to the University Chancellor that Albizu seemed to be in a time warp. Albizu spoke as if he had returned to a Puerto Rico, frozen in the 1930s, not to the existing Puerto Rico, still beset with enormous problems, but now bursting with enthusiasm and hope.

Albizu's new goal was to "kill" the Muñoz constitutional process. When Muñoz raised his right hand to take the oath of office as Governor and swore allegiance to the American constitution, Albizu declared, he committed an act of "high treason" against the Puerto Rican nation. In his speeches Albizu reaped scorn on Muñoz as "degenerate...an idiot...fat...a poor devil...a puppet...the High Priest of slavery." He ridiculed Muñoz for having turned La Fortaleza into a "hotel" to serve the "satanic *yanquis*," getting down on his knees, walking on all fours, so that they could ride piggyback around the mansion.

On March 21, 1949, the anniversary of the Ponce Massacre, Albizu accused Muñoz and his Health Secretary of plotting to "exterminate the people" through forced sterilization and "castration of all Puerto Ricans." But when the Secretary approached him with his knife, Albizu cried amid cheers and laughter from his followers, "Muñoz Marín tells him 'No, no, not me! Don't cut it off!' " There were also threats: "Mr. Truman must remember, and his representatives in Puerto Rico, Muñoz Marín and Dr. Pons, that it

---

1. Muñoz Marín, *Memorias* Vol. II, 192.

may well be that the doors of power will fall over them as they did over the Germans in Nuremberg, for in their day they will be hung in this very plaza."[2]

Independence and statehood leaders would, of course, campaign against Muñoz's new status bill. But Albizu's attacks, always extreme, now seemed surreal to Muñoz. Did Albizu really believe, as he said in his speeches, that President Truman and Secretary of State George Marshall were shaping American policies and actions in the United Nations and other international forums in response to his attacks? Did he believe that Muñoz and the "*yanquis*" had brought down thousands of "blond and blue-eyed" agents to spy on his every move? Did he really believe that Muñoz and Health Secretary Pons were "injecting a poisonous virus" into the blood stream of Puerto Rican children under the guise of a program to inoculate all school students?

Benítez, having survived the frightening confrontation with the Nationalist students at the University, said that it was Albizu who was "injecting the poisonous virus" of hate into his followers. One of Muñoz's closest friends, writer and university professor Antonio Colorado, himself a former Albizu follower, described him as a "mentally deranged mystic," driven by "an elemental hatred of life and of history... For him, whoever does not respond with a gunshot, or with a stone, or with a fist, with physical brutality against any offense, real or imagined, is a coward and deserves to die. Should this doctrine survive and take root, force will replace reason."[3]

But Muñoz was faced with the same question that American governors had dodged. In openly calling for the violent overthrow of the government, Albizu was in violation of the insular 1948 sedition law. But the uproar over that law impressed on Muñoz not to repeat the error of Governor Winship, converting Albizu and the Nationalists into martyrs. Yet, there was reason to believe that Albizu and the Nationalists would indeed attempt to "terrorize" the Puerto Ricans into not participating in the constitutional process. Albizu's threats became more explicit: "That puppet that is called Muñoz Marín" and all the "*yanquis*" that surround him were "going to die here." The status bill, he declared, represents the disappearance of the Puerto Rican nationality: all Puerto Ricans would become "yanquis". The hour had arrived to "get the

---

2. Acosta, *La palabra como delito*, 55.

3. Bothwell, *Puerto Rico: cien años de lucha política* Vol. III, 560.

enemy out of here by any means." Albizu directed his words at Muñoz: "You are going to lose your neck, nothing will save you, not even the atomic bomb." In another speech, he challenged his followers: "The cup has overflowed. It depends on you! Are you willing or not?... This is the hour for immortality, for the greatness of Puerto Rico."[4]

The Law 600 status referendum was set for June 4, 1951. On October 27, 1950, four days before the inscription of new voters, the police stopped a car in San Juan that had run a red light. One of the passengers was Albizu, returning from a meeting in Fajardo. Although the police found several weapons in the car, they made no arrests and let them go. Coincidentally, just a few yards away, Muñoz was having dinner at a restaurant with his Commissioner of Education, Mariano Villaronga, who was leaving the next day on an official trip to Paris.

Two days later there was a massive breakout of inmates from the state prison in Río Piedras. The insular police was mobilized throughout the island to round up the fugitives, many of them dangerous. In the early morning hours of the following day, October 30, forty Nationalists, led by the well-known social worker, Blanca Canales, attacked the police station in Jayuya, a small town in the coffee-producing central mountain region. The station was set on fire, one policeman burned alive. The Nationalists took over the town. At the same time, bands of Nationalists attacked the police stations in the towns of Ponce, Peñuelas, Naranjito, and Arecibo, where another policeman was killed.

Muñoz received news of the uprising at his home on the outskirts of San Juan. His daughters, Viviana and Victoria, had already left for school. He had them brought to La Fortaleza as he and Inés sped back to Old San Juan. At 11:30 a.m. Muñoz was at his office meeting with Attorney General Vicente Géigel Polanco when they heard the repeated cracking sound of machine gunfire outside at the entrance to La Fortaleza. Bullets smashed through the wooden blinds. Muñoz and Géigel dropped to the floor and crawled out of the office. Outside, on her knees, his secretary was praying. The La Fortaleza police returned the fire. One policeman, up on the roof, ran out of bullets. Budget Director Roberto de Jesús stuck his head out the window of his office and threw him his loaded gun. Viviana and Victoria, who had

---

4. Ibid., 170.

attempted to look out the residential third floor window at the commotion outside, were now cringing behind a large bureau, crying.[5] Moments later, five of the six Nationalists that had gotten out of a car in front of La Fortaleza were dead. The sixth, under the car, wounded and bleeding, continued to fire for another half hour and was finally taken. Two of the La Fortaleza guards were badly wounded.

Having seen the bodies of the Nationalists lifeless in pools of blood, and afraid for the lives of his wife and children, Muñoz was overcome by two emotions. Once again, Albizu's "madness" had produced an unspeakable tragedy. What struck Muñoz was its absurdity. The very idea of a "revolt" was senseless. This mindless violence, far from stopping the constitutional process, would further terrorize the people of Puerto Rico against independence. But what, Muñoz asked himself, if they had succeeded in killing him? Had not the killing of Police Chief Riggs in 1936 led to his bitter fight with Ernest Gruening and eventually led to the collapse of the New Deal in Puerto Rico?

The emotions quickly gave way to anger and Muñoz moved quickly. The Puerto Rico National Guard was mobilized—all 296 officers and 4,017 men. A company was dispatched to retake the town of Jayuya. There were mass arrests of Nationalists and independence sympathizers: some 800 persons were arrested. The next day, October 31, the "revolt" was crushed. There were 28 deaths: 16 Nationalists, 7 policemen, one National Guardsman, and four civilians. Among the 43 injured, there were 9 Nationalists, 23 policeman, 6 National Guardsman, and 11 civilians.

Years later, Muñoz's own Civil Rights Commission severely criticized the mass arrests. Muñoz agreed that there had been "violations of law," including not having declared martial law before activating the National Guard.[6] He also agreed that there were indeed unjustified arrests of *independentistas* not engaged in the revolt. But he declared that when he learned of them, he immediately ordered their release.

---

5. Muñoz Marín, *Memorias* Vol. II, 238.
6. Ibid., 239.

November 1, 1950, two days later, was a hot day in Washington. The temperature was up to 85 degrees. President Truman, after having lunch with his family, went up to the third floor bedroom for a nap. They were living in Blair House, across the street from the White House, which was in repair. Truman opened the window in his room. Downstairs, the door was also open, only the screen door was closed. It was so calm and quiet inside that, as one usher later confessed, "it was a struggle to stay awake." Outside, the White House police were also fighting boredom, killing time, one of them joking about getting new eye glasses to better follow "the girls walking by." Three White House policemen were posted, two of them inside wooden guard booths. In the hallway, there was one Secret Service agent. A fourth policeman, just relieved, was making his way back into the house.

No one noticed two neatly-dressed men approaching from opposite directions. They were so "subdued and unobtrusive" that the day before, when they checked into a hotel near Union Station, they had been "mistaken for divinity students" by the hotel clerk.[7] Suddenly both men pulled out guns and fired at the policemen. Upstairs, Truman leaped from the bed and looked out the window. He heard frantic shouts "Get back! Get back!" and retreated. In seconds it was over: one of the men was dead. White House policeman Private Leslie Coffelt was fatally wounded. Two other policemen, critically wounded, survived.

Truman's immediate reaction was that these were two "crackpots or crazy men." When informed that they were Puerto Rican Nationalists from New York City, in anger he commented that they were "stupid as can be." The Washington newspapers had published that he was scheduled to visit Arlington Cemetery that afternoon. Twenty minutes later and they would have caught him leaving Blair House. Everyone was aware of Truman's daily walks with notoriously lax security. Albizu Campos, in fact, had made mocking references to the walks: "...they have Truman making exercise every day, the poor old man, walking fast. Look, Truman, when you get drunk we are going to give you a beating; leave the bottle, Truman! Don't

---

7. McCullough, *Truman*, 813.

eat so much, do your exercise at five in the morning, Truman, up and down with Truman. The poor old man walking, walking, walking...”[8]

Two letters from Albizu were found on the body of 25-year-old Griselo Torresola, naming him the head of the mainland Nationalist movement. The other Nationalist was 36-year-old Oscar Collazo, later convicted and sentenced to death.

On November 2, Muñoz ordered Albizu's arrest at his home in Old San Juan, on the corner of Sol and Cruz Streets. He ordered that Albizu be taken alive, however long it took to get him out of the house. After a long wait, the police fired several gas bombs at the building. Albizu lifted a broomstick with a towel from his window and emerged without resistance.

As "stupid" as the attempted assassination of Truman had been, of course the reaction of American public opinion would be outrage. Muñoz immediately telephoned the President and that night transmitted a coast-to-coast radio message to the American people, assuring them that only several hundred Nationalists and "communists" were involved in the uprising. The vast majority of Puerto Ricans, he said, treasure their democracy and their American citizenship.

But the real test took place on November 4th, the first day of the new voting inscription. The night before, in his traditional election eve radio message, Muñoz vented his anger:

> I want to say...that the greatest indignation that I have felt these days was not for the attempt against my life and that of my wife and little girls at La Fortaleza. The greatest indignation that has shaken my soul in all this episode has been to observe the following: how the passions of young men who could have been of good service to their people, have been pushed to violence and suicide; and how, after they were killed, the author of all this...profanes the sacrifice provoked by himself, lifting a used towel at the end of a broom stick as a flag of surrender after the first tear gas bomb.[9]

---

8. Acosta, *La palabra como delito*, 113.
9. Muñoz Marín, *Memorias* Vol. II, 248.

The policemen and National Guardsmen, he continued, sacrificed their lives to safeguard the right of the people of Puerto Rico to their democracy; their right to register during the next two days and then participate in the status referendum. Now it was up to each Puerto Rican to "do his part" to vindicate those that gave their lives. The appeal and the emotion worked. On the 5th and 6th of November, 157,393 new voters registered, by far the largest new-voter inscription in island history.

As Muñoz knew would happen, the Nationalist revolt strengthened him. It cleared the road to drive forward the status initiative, creating a consensus unique in Puerto Rican political history. The shock of the attempt on his life further undermined the conservative, pro-statehood campaign that there was an *independentista* secret agenda behind the status initiative. In the United States, his powerful and effective radio message and his strong reaction crushing the revolt generated even more support for him in Congress.

Meanwhile, Concepción de Gracia and the Independence Party leadership found themselves in the familiar dilemma of how to react to Nationalist violence. Their only hope to challenge Muñoz in the 1952 elections was to distance themselves from Albizu and the Nationalists. But as *independentistas* it was emotionally impossible. The day after the Truman assassination attempt, Concepción and other party leaders met in Aguadilla and their predicament became evident. On one hand the party reaffirmed its commitment to "work peacefully" and democratically for its independence ideal. But then it severely attacked Muñoz for having provoked the violence and expressed "its most profound respect...for the compatriots that have offered and are offering their lives for the independence of Puerto Rico."[10]

For Muñoz, history repeated itself, except that the roles were reversed. Back in 1936, Ernest Gruening and the conservative coalition lambasted him for not denouncing the Riggs killing and thus "condoning murder." Now it was Muñoz who passionately attacked the *independentistas* for "condoning" the bloody attempt to destroy Puerto Rican democracy.

---

10. Pagán, *Historia de los partidos políticos puertorriqueños* Vol. II, 297.

There was another casualty from the Nationalist revolt. For Muñoz, it was a particularly painful experience. Under the 1947 elective governorship law, the attorney general was first in line to replace the Governor. Muñoz gave the job to one of his closest and most trusted political allies, a cofounder of the party who had served as Senate majority leader, Vicente Géigel Polanco. Géigel was the prototype of the men, like Trías and Fortas, Muñoz liked to have around him: a writer, university professor, founder of the Puerto Rican Academy of History, President of the *Ateneo*, journalist, and a successful lawyer who defended the working class. Géigel was also the prototype of the ardent *independentista* in the Popular Party who in 1940 had rebelled against Muñoz, but then accepted his leadership and ideological transformation in order to carry out the much-needed social and economic reforms.

After the October 28, 1950 prison riots and breakout—a total 108 inmates escaped, two prison guards were killed—Géigel came under fire for mismanagement of the prison system. He was accused of "pampering" the prisoners and demoralizing the guards, all contributing to the disorder that spread to other prisons throughout the island.

But the accusations went beyond incompetence. It seemed obvious to many that it could not be a coincidence: that there was a connection between the prison riots that diverted the entire insular police force, deployed to round up the fugitives, and the Nationalist uprising. If Muñoz had been killed, Géigel, who was with Muñoz in his office when the Nationalists attacked La Fortaleza, would have become Governor.

Was Géigel part of a conspiracy? The island newspapers published sensational reports that supposedly confirmed he had indeed been approached by the Nationalists. *El Mundo* reported that Albizu Campos himself had sent an emissary urging Géigel to "cover himself with glory" by proclaiming the "*La República de Puerto Rico*" from La Fortaleza after Muñoz's assassination.[11]

Muñoz refused to believe the rumors and did not replace Géigel, who refuted the stories in articles strongly supporting Muñoz and the creation of the Commonwealth status. By early 1951, however, Puerto Rico already

---

11. Anderson, *Party Politics in Puerto Rico*, 163.

into the constitutional process, Muñoz had evidence that his intimate friend may have indeed been involved in a conspiracy.

Géigel had named a picturesque personality who called himself "Conrad Kaye" to run the prison system. When Muñoz inquired about the appointment, Géigel responded that they had met the previous year and had become "good friends." Kaye had an extraordinary background: from labor organizer in New York, to fighting against Generalísimo Franco in the Spanish Civil War, serving in Europe in the American Army in World War II, then to Mexico, and finally to the island after marrying a Puerto Rican. This was precisely the battler of leftist causes that Muñoz had often welcomed to the island. But after meeting him for the first time at La Fortaleza, Muñoz suggested to Géigel that "he should be investigated" to see if the story of his life was true.

Muñoz was informed by the FBI that "Conrad Kaye" was not his real name and had indeed misrepresented the story of his life. In fact, he was born in Russia and had been an active communist at least until 1943. When Géigel was unable to refute this, Muñoz ordered that "Kaye" be removed. Before Géigel acted, the prison breakout took place.

On February 1, 1951, finally convinced by the evidence that "Kaye" was indeed responsible for the riot, Muñoz asked for Géigel's resignation. Anticipating Muñoz's action, Géigel counterattacked, blaming Muñoz and his administration for the conditions in the prison system and thus making him responsible for the breakout. Géigel left Puerto Rico, went to New York to work for the Spanish language daily newspaper, *El Diario*, and while still calling himself a member of the Popular Party, he attacked Muñoz as a "dictator" and the constitutional process as a gigantic "fraud."

The Telegram From Cuba

The day after the Nationalist uprising, Muñoz got a telegram from the President of Cuba, Carlos Prío Socarrás, asking him to "intercede" with the American authorities "to liberate Albizu Campos." Muñoz's first reaction was to ignore it: what right did the head of an "undemocratic and corrupt" government have to request anything from him? But as he thought about it, he decided to answer. Albizu's wife, Laura Meneses, was in Cuba at the time, as well as other Nationalist leaders, and had certainly influenced the Cuban president.

Muñoz wrote to Prío Socarrás that he had made two fundamental mistakes. It was not necessary for him to "intercede" with the American authorities since he had the power, given by the free votes of the Puerto Rican people, to deal with Albizu under Puerto Rican law. The second mistake, Muñoz went on, was to consider the Albizu revolt a battle for freedom. This was not a battle between Puerto Ricans and the American government. On the contrary, it represents "fascist purposes of tyranny by a minute group of armed fanatics that want to impose, with grotesque and tragic futility, their own interpretation of freedom on two million Puerto Ricans."[12]

There was no need for anyone to fear for Albizu's life or rights. "Although 48 hours ago Albizu Campos ordered that I and my family be assassinated, every one that knows me knows that he will have the full protection of the laws of this government that safeguard even the worst and most irresponsible citizens."

The Albizu revolt had still another effect. Muñoz's position and that of the Popular Party had been that the autonomy status being negotiated with Congress was a "transitory" solution to give Puerto Rico the time to develop its economy to the point where it could realistically choose between statehood and independence. However, after the events of October 30 and November 1, Muñoz changed. He wrote in the early 1970s: "I arrived at the conclusion that I, personally, could not continue to sustain that fictitious attitude: that I owed it to Puerto Rico to express my conviction." The new status, he now said, was Puerto Rico's "final" status solution.

---

12. Muñoz Marín, *Memorias* Vol. II, 241.

25 The Compact

M uñoz knew that most Puerto Ricans, and certainly the *jíbaros* had practically no interest in the ideological political status conflict and much less in the juridical issues which lawyers and political leaders considered vital. Puerto Ricans wanted economic security. This meant security that the island would not be cut loose from the United States, now guaranteed with Muñoz in power. There was no question that he and his enormous political machine would produce another huge victory in the Law 600 referendum.

But this was not another election. Muñoz did not want another manifestation of his popularity and that of his party's. Now that he was insisting that Commonwealth was the island's "permanent, final" status, it was evident that it must outlast him and his party. It was crucial to somehow get Puerto Ricans to understand what they were voting for. Everyone knew, or thought they knew, what statehood and independence were. But what exactly was this new status, "The Free Associated State?" Everyone understood what a "colony" was, but what was this thing called a "compact?"

Muñoz faced the most difficult communication challenge of his political life. It was one thing to have "taught" the *jíbaro* not to sell his vote or to get his followers excited about voting "against the *republicanos*." But how to communicate complicated concepts such as "fiscal autonomy?" How to translate this dry, boring phrase into emotionally charged concepts of freedom, real self-government? How to keep the voters awake explaining the "compact"?

On July 17, 1950, in his annual speech at his father's grave site in Barranquitas, he declared: "I have tried to make this entire matter of Puerto Rico's political situation, instead of a dispute over juridical words, a dynamic of developing reality." Muñoz announced that from now on he would refer to Law 600 as "the Compact and Constitution Law between the Congress of the United States and the People of Puerto Rico."

Muñoz, however, could not keep the Law 600 campaign from becoming precisely a "dispute over juridical words." The opposing parties, after all, were led by prominent lawyers who had spent their lives arguing the juridical aspects of the status conflict. The veteran Miguel Ángel García Méndez, the Coalition leader of the 1930s who had served as Speaker of the House, now again at the helm of the Republican Statehood Party, considered himself a constitutional expert. The Independence Party was still led by the equally prominent lawyer Gilberto Concepción de Gracia. Both insisted that Muñoz was indeed committing a monumental "fraud" on the people. Who, when, and where, they asked, determined that there could be a "new kind of state" within the American constitutional system? Anyone who knows anything about the American system knows that there are two, only two ways to be part of the U.S.—either a federated statehood or a territory. Contrary to Muñoz's "deception," they insisted that Law 600 merely allowed Puerto Rico to adapt its constitution and did not, in any way, change the island's "colonial" status.

To make their point, the opposition lambasted the very concept of a "compact." Only a "sovereign" Puerto Rico could have a mutually binding "compact" with the United States. Where, García Méndez and Concepción demanded of Muñoz, did Congress even hint that it intended to give up its "sovereign" power over Puerto Rico?

Muñoz and Fernós responded that whether the "compact," whether Commonwealth status itself, was "constitutional" or not, would not be decided in this campaign debate, but eventually in the U.S. courts. This, after all, was the history of the island's status since the very beginning with the 1900 Foraker Act. Congress and then the U.S. Supreme Court had struggled to find a way to "fit" this small, extremely poor, Hispanic, overpopulated island into the American system. Unlike Cuba and the Philippines, the island clearly did not want independence. To make it an "incorporated territory," like Hawaii and Alaska, meant eventual statehood and full federal taxation. The Court, in effect, created a new status for Puerto Rico: "unincorporated territory." If the American political system was flexible enough to find a unique solution back in the early century, Muñoz and his people argued, why not again?

García Méndez and Concepción also attempted to nail Muñoz on what they insisted was a flagrant contradiction. Muñoz had been declaring all along in Puerto Rico and before Congress that Commonwealth status "closed no doors": that the island remained free to chose another status whenever it wanted. How then, they asked, does Muñoz reconcile this with his latest assertions that Commonwealth is "permanent and final?"

The answer, Muñoz declared, was evident: legally, of course, nothing prevented Puerto Rico in the future from seeking a change in its status. What he was saying was that Puerto Rico's reality, as far as he could see into the future, made both alternatives to Commonwealth "impossible." In theory the "doors were open," but in the real world they were closed.

Muñoz, it was clear, was being drawn into the abstract debate he detested:

> It was painful having to deal with this: for me, independence, as well as statehood, would be, yes, "final," but in the sense of the "Final Judgment," that is, they would end everything else. It is curious and tragic, this compulsion of a number of Puerto Ricans to deny themselves of the options of freedom—the creativity to work out with their own spirit, their own experience, their own circumstance, their own freedom—in stubborn sacrifice to the God that is worshipped under the names of 'final' or "permanent."[1]

Why, he asked himself, wasn't it evident to everyone in Puerto Rico that while this island was trapped in the statehood-versus-independence "dilemma," there had been no political, economic, social progress? How could the statehooders and *independentistas* avoid admitting that in the eight years since he put aside the ideological status conflict issue, Puerto Rico had experienced its greatest economic and social growth ever and the most progress in self-government since the turn of the century? "I want," Muñoz declared early in the campaign, "to liberate the minority of that dilemma

---

1. Muñoz Marín, *Memorias* Vol. II, 257.

that unnecessarily tortures many and makes their lives less useful than they should be before the true and great problem of integral freedom in Puerto Rico, economic, social, and political."[2]

Undeterred by the furious juridical attack, on June 4, 1951, the day of the referendum, Muñoz made one last attempt to define the "compact." "The compact between the United States and Puerto Rico establishes the following: (a) full self-government in Puerto Rico, (b) voluntary association as the basis of the federal relations to exist between Puerto Rico and the United States and (c) the principle that those federal relations can only be implemented by [mutual agreement]."[3]

He then stated the exact meaning, as he and his party saw it, of the Law 600 vote:

> The relation from now on between the United States and Puerto Rico will derive from a compact freely entered into by both peoples. The people of the United States thus fulfill the highest moral obligations with the people of Puerto Rico, initially in virtue of the Treaty of Paris and subsequently in virtue of the Charter of the United Nations.

Law 600 received the overwhelming popular support he wanted: 76.5 percent voted in favor. Two months later, the delegates to the Constitutional Assembly were elected. Seventy members of the Popular Party, the maximum permitted by law, were elected, including Muñoz and Fernós Isern, who was chosen its president. There were fifteen Statehood Republicans and seven more pro-statehood Socialist Party delegates. The Independence Party boycotted the convention.

Muñoz believed that he had succeeded in communicating with the voters. If the opponents were right in asserting that there were individual members of Congress that had not understood what they were doing in approving Law 600, Muñoz would now insist that the people of Puerto Rico clearly understood. Politicians and lawyers could continue to debate the "congressional intent." For Muñoz, no one could question the "Puerto Rican

---

2. Muñoz Marín, *Memorias* Vol. II, 267.

3. Muñoz Marín, *Los gobernadores electos de Puerto Rico*, 272.

intent" in massively approving "The Compact and Constitution Law between the Congress of the United States and the People of Puerto Rico." For Muñoz, the sheer power of the huge electoral victories in June and August was the real world answer to the juridical questions.

THE CONSTITUTIONAL CONVENTION

Republican Party leaders Luis A. Ferré and his brother-in-law García Méndez, faced with certain defeat, had both urged their followers not to participate in the June referendum. But now they decided to do so in the Constitutional Assembly that met between September 17, 1951 and February 6, 1952. They explained once more that they were not against the adoption of the constitution. Their goal was to ensure that Muñoz and the Popular Party wrote nothing into it that "closed the door" to eventual statehood. Indeed, they believed that the adoption of the constitution, because it made the island look more like a state, became, in itself, a "step" in that direction.

The active participation of the opposition Republican leadership, as well as the Socialist Party delegation, was critically important to Muñoz. It was vital to prove to American public opinion, as well as everyone in Congress, that he and his party did not have a "dictatorial" stranglehold on the constitutional process. But a price had to be paid. The legal debate that Muñoz scorned was now brought full-fledged into the assembly. Another delegate, Republican Party President Celestino Iriarte, joined García Méndez and Ferré, bringing together a team of lawyers that produced an extensive legal brief that concluded that Muñoz's "compact" thesis was unconstitutional.

Muñoz himself wrote the preamble: "The Commonwealth of Puerto Rico is hereby constituted. Its political power emanates from the people and shall be exercised in accordance with their will, within the terms of the compact agreed upon between the people of Puerto Rico and the United States of America." *Not explicit enough,* some of his own party leaders complained. In his four-volume "Constitutional History of Puerto Rico" written three decades later, Trías Monge recorded his disappointment: failure to make the "compact" concept definitive was "the most critical decision of the Popular Party leadership in the Constitutional Assembly."[4]

An "Inoffensive Document"

Muñoz was in fact wrestling with the same dilemma that he had with Law 600: how far could he risk taking Congress without losing the entire battle? The Constitution, after all, had to be approved by Congress as well as the Puerto Rican people. Another one of his key legal advisors, Insular Attorney General and convention delegate Víctor Gutiérrez Franqui, argued that it should not be a "slavish copy of any American document." Another person who believed that Muñoz was being excessively conservative was Dr. Pedro Muñoz Amato, Dean of the University of Puerto Rico School of Public Administration, who now headed a team of Puerto Rican and American legal and constitutional consultants. He argued that while Congress and the President had to ratify the Constitution, this was not a "law of Congress" where every dot and comma had to meet their approval. The Constitution, he said, had only to comply with the directives of Law 600: to establish a republican form of government, include a bill of rights, and conform to the applicable provisions of the U.S. Constitution. This gave Puerto Rico space, Muñoz's advisors insisted, to produce a modern, advanced, and innovative document.

Muñoz was being pulled in opposite directions. No one had to sell him on a progressive document that went beyond the American Constitution. He wanted a Constitution with a bill of rights, not only protecting individual, private rights against government abuse, but also guaranteeing "social and economic rights." Fernós, the Constitutional Assembly President, aware that over one third of the delegates were lawyers, warned Muñoz against producing a beautifully idealistic Latin American-type document with very little opportunity of success in Washington. It was, after all, his responsibility to get it through Congress before 1952, President Truman's last year in office. If Puerto Rico failed in this congressional session, would a conservative

---

4. Ibid., 66.

Republican president, as now seemed likely, support it as much as Truman? Muñoz's chief legal aide, Trías Monge, once more, was disappointed: "Due to the conservatism of Congress, it was resolved to make it (the Constitution) the most inoffensive possible."[5]

One good example of what concerned Fernós was the irrefutably important issue of "sovereignty." But as he had argued with Law 600, it was not necessary, nor wise, to provoke a juridical debate over what had always been a contentious issue in American political history. Even after the American Civil War, there were constitutional lawyers and politicians that still argued if the states had "sovereignty" or not. Puerto Rico's "sovereignty," Fernós insisted, would be implicitly recognized in the amendment clause. Once ratified by Congress, it would become Puerto Rico's exclusive power to amend its own Constitution.

The Bill of Rights, as Muñoz desired, went far beyond the federal constitution. Freedom of the press was strengthened, prohibiting the government from expropriating printing presses and other publishing equipment; workers were given the right to unionize, to bargain collectively, and to strike, including employees in the government's public corporations, but not in the regular agencies. Other workers' rights included equal pay for equal work, extra pay for extra hours, an eight-hour day and a "reasonable minimum wage." Capital punishment and wire-tapping were prohibited. Discrimination "on account of race, color, sex, birth or religious ideas" was prohibited. Illegitimate children born after the enactment of the Constitution were given the same rights as legitimate children, including inheritance.

There were several innovations in the structure of the government. The principle of separation of powers was strengthened. Legislative autonomy was reinforced by making it a continuous body during its four-year term, with the power to determine the length of its sessions. Muñoz himself introduced a constitutional guarantee that, regardless of election returns, no less than one third of all House and Senate seats would belong to the minority parties. Since nearly all Puerto Ricans voted straight party tickets, the party that won a mayority of votes got nearly total control of the Legislature. The assembly strengthened also the independence of the judicial branch. It created a unified judiciary administered by the Supreme Court

---

5. Trías Monge, *Historia constitucional de Puerto Rico*, Vol. III, 69.

Chief Justice, a system that was to receive recognition as one of the most progressive under the U.S. flag.

Pushing Muñoz to make the document as liberal and "creative" as possible was Harvard University professor of government, Carl Friedrich, brought down as a consultant. Friedrich, however, believed that the delegates went too far in giving too much power to the Governor. The state government performed many of the services that, on the mainland, were local responsibilities, including public education, utilities, police protection, and fire fighting. "The government of Puerto Rico," he wrote in 1958, "is probably the most unqualifiedly monolithic and centralized administration under the American flag."[6]

The Constitution was indeed Muñoz's document: every idea, every line, was personally approved by him. But was the convention also, consciously or not, making a constitution "for Muñoz?" The question of "what will happen after Muñoz?" finally came up in what became the most hotly debated issue: the Governor succession clause. Inevitably the issue became a personality conflict. When the outspoken, flamboyant Jaime Benítez energetically campaigned for an elected "vice governor," it was seen by other Popular Party delegates that he was attempting to position himself as Muñoz's successor. Other leaders, determined to stop Benítez, came out passionately against his proposal.

More than with any other clause, Trías Monge recorded years later, Muñoz seemed totally unsure of himself, constantly changing his views, at one time or another favoring and opposing the elected vice-governor idea, then the appointed lieutenant government option. Finally, Muñoz decided that it would be the insular Secretary of State, who would have to possess the same qualifications as the Governor and whose confirmation required approval of both House and Senate. The idea that sometime in the future there would be an "after Muñoz" had crept and momentarily disrupted the consciousness of the Popular party, and of Muñoz himself.

---

6. Friedrich, *Middle Road to Freedom*, 42.

26 The Battle to Create Commonwealth Status

On April 9, 1952, Resident Commissioner Antonio Fernós Isern, as President of the Constitutional Convention, accompanied by Interior Secretary Oscar Chapman, handed President Truman the Constitution of the Commonwealth of Puerto Rico. Muñoz's letter to President Truman read: "The significance of this process, both for Puerto Rico and for the democratic leadership of the United States, is great and heartening... The present process is based on bilateral action through free agreement... the principle that the relationship is from now on one of consent through free agreement, wipes out all traces of colonialism."[1]

The assembly had already approved the Constitution: 88 votes in favor, three against, one absent. Puerto Rican voters, already suffering from "electoral fatigue," responding again to Muñoz's appeal to go once more to the polls—the fourth time in three years—overwhelmingly approved the Constitution: 373,594 votes in favor, 82,877 against, 7,357 protest votes. The percentage of registered voters participating went down to 59 from just over 65 per cent in the Law 600 referendum. But the 80 percent voting in favor was up from the 76.5 percent favoring Law 600.

As expected, President Truman enthusiastically endorsed and sent the document to Congress. "The people of the United States," he declared, "and the people of Puerto Rico are entering into a new relationship that will serve as inspiration to all who love freedom and hate tyranny..."[2]

---

1. Trías Monge, *Historia constitucional de Puerto Rico* Vol. III, 271.
2. Ibid., 273.

Both Muñoz and the President's letters underlined that this was indeed a "new relationship." That same day Fernós introduced in Congress a ratification resolution that specified that Law 600 had been "adopted by Congress as a compact with the people of Puerto Rico." Fernós seemed to be once more off and running. On April 25, the House Interior and Insular Affairs Committee approved the resolution after hearing only Fernós's short statement. There was, however, one ominous note. Several committee members, while voting in favor, expressed doubts about Section 20 of the Bill of Rights, inspired by the United Nations Declaration of Human Rights that, under the leadership of Eleanor Roosevelt, the United States Government had endorsed in 1948.

Drafted and defended mostly by Jaime Benítez, Section 20 declared that "the Commonwealth also recognizes the existence" of a list of economic and social rights: "to receive free elementary and secondary education...to obtain work...to a standard of living adequate for the health and well-being of himself and of his family, and especially to food, clothing, housing and medical care and necessary social services...to social protection in the event of unemployment, sickness, old age or disability...the right of motherhood and childhood to special care and assistance."

Senate members, meanwhile, were flooded with messages from Independence Party President Concepción de Gracia and other party leaders alleging that Muñoz was guilty of numerous electoral irregularities in the constitutional voting: that he had denied 100,000 new voters, presumably *independentistas*, the right to vote and had grossly distorted the process by making false claims as to the new status. The protest had an effect. At the Senate hearing on April 29, 1952, Republican Senator Guy Cordon, from Oregon, questioned Muñoz on the allegations. Muñoz calmly denied them.

But then a letter from Senator Olin Johnston, a Democrat from South Carolina, was read before the committee. Johnston revived the old accusation that Muñoz was "anti-American," that years earlier, speaking at a Liberal Party meeting, he had demanded that the American flag be brought down. "I have repeatedly asked about this incident from the Senate floor but have received no reply from Mr. Muñoz Marín." It was evident to Muñoz and Fernós that the pro-statehood opponents were also active in the campaign against him.

But Muñoz's attention was caught by something else in Johnston's letter: "there is nothing in this constitution which would prevent its being amended in Puerto Rico without the consent of the Congress of the United States." The Senator set his sight at the heart of the Constitution. Fernós, after all, insisted that it was precisely this clause that established the transfer of "sovereignty" to Puerto Rico. If Congress retained the right to approve or reject any amendment to the constitution, Muñoz's entire edifice of a "new status," of eliminating all "vestiges of colonialism," of a "bilateral compact," would come crashing down.

LONG'S REVENGE

Senator Johnston was a friend of the contractor that had built Puerto Rico's first low-cost private housing in San Juan. After Muñoz became Governor in 1949, the contractor, Leonard Long, informed Muñoz that former Governor Jesús Piñero had committed the government to grant him tax exemption and other Planning Board considerations. Piñero denied it. When Muñoz rejected the request, Long turned to his friend from his home state. Johnston had never hidden his hostility toward Muñoz. Now it was clear that he was out to kill the constitution.

Muñoz and Fernós were shaken. Suddenly the ratification resolution was in crisis. Muñoz established "battle headquarters" at the Mayflower Hotel in Washington, mobilized a campaign to drum up support from major mainland and island newspapers, and from friendly labor and business leaders. Editorials appeared in *The New York Times*, *The Washington Post*, and *The New York Herald Tribune*. Influential columnists, such as Drew Pearson, joined the battle. It was a good story: a disgruntled American businessman, bent on revenge, was sabotaging the constitutional process of over two million American citizens. The campaign received strong support from the White House and Interior Secretary Chapman. Abe Fortas went to work. Muñoz also turned to his friends in Latin America, the so-called "democratic left," to apply "international pressure."

As Trías Monge recalled it, Muñoz and his people actively debated two alternatives: to create a showdown, forcing Congress to either approve the constitution as it was or withdraw it; or to delay the process to allow the Muñoz campaign to take effect on American public opinion and members of Congress. But to delay the process, they concluded, could effectively kill it. To keep it going required "giving the tiger a big chunk of meat." One thing was certain: that "chunk of meat" could not be the amendment clause that Johnston was demanding. It would likely have to be the social and economic rights of Section 20 of the bill of rights.

It was. On May 27, Fernós received word that the Senate Interior and Insular Affairs Committee had approved the ratification bill, eliminating Section 20. The Senators expressed fears that these unrealistic and "socialistic" provisions would be seen as constitutional mandates beyond Puerto Rico's economic capacity, and that in the end they would be paid for by American taxpayers. Muñoz considered this absurd. The constitution merely "recognized the existence" of these rights: they were clearly not "mandates" but the goals of the people of Puerto Rico. But it was not worth risking the entire constitution. In any case, once the Constitution was adopted, the Legislature of Puerto Rico was free to approve into law each item in the Section 20 "wish list." Muñoz instructed Fernós to turn over the "chunk of meat."

Back in Puerto Rico, the Senate action added fuel to the *independentista* and statehood campaigns that Congress retained total power over Puerto Rico. In this legal battlefield the process of eliminating Section 20 became crucial. Muñoz and Fernós insisted that it be done through mutual consent with Puerto Rico. Congress would make its ratification of the constitution contingent on Puerto Rico accepting its elimination. Of course, if Puerto Rico refused to do so, there was no constitution. Muñoz and Fernós knew that the assembly would follow his and Fernós's decision to accept the loss of Section 20.

The Poison Pill

But the constitution crisis deepened. In the House, the Republican representative from Michigan, George Meader, introduced an amendment flatly stating that Puerto Rico remained a "territory:" "...nothing herein contained shall be construed as an irrevocable delegation, transfer or release of the power of the Congress granted by article IV, section 33, of the Constitution of the United States." This time Fernós welcomed a full debate on the Meader amendment.

Meader came well-prepared although he was not a member of the Interior and Insular Affairs Committee. He read from a Library of Congress opinion that he had requested: "While the adoption of this constitution with the approval of Congress may create a moral obligation not to override the compact made with the people of Puerto Rico pursuant to Public Law 600, Eighty-first Congress, it would not diminish the constitutional power of Congress to deal with this Territory as it deems best."

No, Fernós insisted. The U.S. was bound not only by a "moral obligation" to honor the "compact," but by law. After intensive and at times heated debate, the Meader amendment was taken to a vote and defeated. Finally, what the legal advisors had been clamoring for was achieved. This seemed to be the defining moment: the issue over the "legislative intent" in Law 600 was resolved, and the legitimacy of the "new relationship" was established.

But time was running out. The ratification resolution was not scheduled to reach the Senate until June 23, 1952. Fernós was up against two deadlines. First, he had only seven days to get the resolution approved. The other deadline was emotional. The 25th of July was the anniversary of the landing of American troops in Guánica, for Muñoz and his party the appropriate date to inaugurate the new Constitution and Commonwealth status.

It was agreed that if the resolution was not approved by four in the afternoon, there would be only a half hour to introduce motions and amendments, and an additional half hour for debate. After short statements by committee chairman O'Mahoney and New York Senator Herbert Lehman, Fernós's heart sank when Senator Olin Johnston took the floor armed with numerous amendments, all unacceptable. He *is*, after all, Fernós said to himself, going to kill the Constitution.

"We have received," Johnston said, "nothing from Puerto Rico in return for all we have given them, all the millions of dollars that we have spent in Puerto Rico. We have asked for nothing in return in the form of taxes or anything else. I think we have been very good with the people of Puerto Rico. In relation to the Constitution of Puerto Rico I can say that we can give them a constitution or not give it to them: I want the Puerto Ricans to know this."

Then he introduced an amendment to limit the Governor of Puerto Rico to one term. To Fernós's shock, Senator Dennis Chávez, in the past a knowledgeable friend of Puerto Rico, rose to back the amendment. Muñoz, Chávez said, would certainly agree with the amendment: it was an error on the part of the Puerto Rico constitutional assembly not to include the term limit—an "error of the heart." Fernós had no idea what Chavez was talking about. But the clock was ticking. Lehman and O'Mahoney came to the rescue, pointing out that as far as they knew, Congress had never before attempted to rewrite a state constitution. Taken to a vote, the term-limit amendment was defeated.

O'Mahoney's Gamble

Now Johnston came with his already announced intention to require congressional approval to amend the constitution. As other Senators rose to support it, Fernós could see the "poison pill" taking effect. The ratification was dying before his eyes. Then O'Mahoney himself took the floor to agree to the Johnston amendment and it was quickly approved. Fernós's heart stopped. But O'Mahoney came rushing to tell him that this was a desperate gamble to save the ratification. Among the large number of amendments Johnston intended to introduce was one identical to the Meader amendment that the House had rejected. O'Mahoney had gotten Johnston to agree that if his "poison pill" was approved, he would not introduce any more amendments. Either Johnston was stopped, O'Mahoney coldly told Fernós, or it was all over. Let the bill go to the House with the "poison pill," O'Mahoney said, and then remove it there. It was a terrible gamble, but there was no alternative.

When news of the Senate approval of the Johnston amendment reached Muñoz in La Fortaleza, Trías Monge recorded years later, "what happened there...reached the proportions of a nuclear explosion."[3]

What had gone wrong? As Muñoz, Fernós, Fortas, Trías, and the Truman administration officials attempted to understand how the ratification got derailed, it became evident that there was more at stake than constitutional issues or the personal revenge of a disgruntled "continental." The campaign of the Puerto Rican opponents, mostly the incessant allegation by the *independentista* leadership that Muñoz had dictatorially steamrolled the constitutional process, had taken effect in Congress. It was a paradox of the American political system: the partisan opponents that could not defeat Muñoz in Puerto Rico, were now attempting to defeat him in Congress. Political leaders that denounced "American colonialism" were now desperately seeking to get the American Congress to kill a Constitution written and approved by the people of Puerto Rico. And it seemed to be working.

The anti-Muñoz campaign had surfaced during the public hearings. Johnston questioned why the "Federal Coordinator" established in the 1947 elective governorship act had never been named. The implication was clear: that Muñoz and his party wanted to dispense the millions in federal funds without U.S. oversight. It was these funds, according to the critics, that oiled the Muñoz machine to grind out one great electoral victory after another.

The Truman administration stepped in to defend Muñoz. The "Federal Coordinator" was never named, Interior Secretary Oscar Chapman replied, because on two occasions Congress itself had failed to appropriate funds for the post. No one, the Truman people pressed on, had done more for Puerto Rican democracy than Muñoz, who in 1940 eliminated the practice of vote-buying, in 1950 sold the Fomento factories to one of his principal political opponents, and who now, in the proposed constitution, guaranteed the opposition parties no less than one third representation in the Legislature.

Joining the pro-Muñoz campaign were two members of the House that had personally observed the island referendums: Representatives Frank

---

3. Trías Monge, *Historia constitucional de Puerto Rico* Vol. III, 307.

Bow of Ohio and Chester McMullen of Florida. They were particularly adamant in refuting the charges of Independence Party President Concepción de Gracia of pervasive fraud in the voting. The Michigan Republican Fred Crawford came to Muñoz's defense: "...I think it will be found that the administration of the present Governor of Puerto Rico is just about as constructive and helpful and cooperative as between and with everybody concerned, as any appointee, military or civilian, who has been sent from the United States to Puerto Rico."[4]

El Mundo, the pro-statehood newspaper that often drove Muñoz up the wall with its relentless criticism, published stories pointing the finger at the contractor Leonard Long as responsible for getting his friend, Senator Olin Johnston, to upend the constitutional process. In Washington, Representative Bow added to the pressure by calling for an investigation into Long's role in the Johnston amendment.

Muñoz got many of the constitutional convention members, including several from the opposition parties, to cosign a telegram to the members of the House-Senate conference committee: "...we sincerely believe that amendments now under consideration in conference destroy the high moral significance of the Constitution by implying that American citizens of Puerto Rico cannot be trusted as American citizens of the States, and thus need extra limitations on their political liberty." While Commonwealth status is not statehood, the Muñoz cable went on, it is not "an inferior" status of "second class citizens... Meagerness cannot possibly do anybody any good."[5]

The Republican Statehood Party leadership, seeing the possibility of Muñoz and the Popular Party suffering a devastating defeat, accused its president, Celestino Iriarte, of being too supportive of Commonwealth status. Led by García Méndez and Ferré, Iriarte was removed. At a stormy assembly on June 22, the day before the Senate action, García Méndez replaced him as president and Ferré became vice president. As with the Independence Party in relation to Nationalist violence, the new statehood leadership was torn between conflicting attitudes and strategies. García Méndez and Ferré, as well as Iriarte, had all voted for the constitution as convention delegates. Now they joined the assault to kill it. Finally, García issued a statement

---

4. Bhana, *The United States and the Development of the Puerto Rican status Question*, 152.

5. Muñoz Marín, *Memorias* Vol. II, 307.

saying that the party neither favored nor opposed the Johnston amendment since it was unnecessary and irrelevant. With or without it, he insisted, Puerto Rico continued as a "colony" where Congress retained total power over the island, including the right to amend the island Constitution.

MUÑOZ RAISES THE FLAG

The O'Mahoney gamble worked in the House. Fernós lined up solid opposition to the amendment. Once back in the Senate, however, it was unclear if O'Mahoney would succeed. *El Mundo*'s respected Washington correspondent, William Dorvillier, reported that the possibilities of withdrawing the amendment seemed remote.[6] But by June 27, Muñoz and Fernós began to see light. Several Senators that had strongly backed Johnston appeared to be wavering. O'Mahoney began to iron out with Muñoz and Fernós an alternative: that any amendment to the constitution must be consistent with the congressional ratification act, Law 600, the Puerto Rico Federal Relations Act, and those parts of the U.S. Constitution applicable to the island. This was, in fact, already the case. Muñoz and Fernós were yielding nothing and the "bilateral compact" concept remained intact.

The breakthrough came when Leonard Long, affected by the stories in *El Mundo* and the threatened Bow investigation, asked his friend Johnston to withdraw his opposition to the constitution. Johnston announced that he was accepting the House version. The conference committee approved the Fernós-O'Mahoney compromise. On July 1, hours before recessing, the House and Senate approved what was now Public Law 447 ratifying the Constitution of the Commonwealth of Puerto Rico. Two days later, President Truman signed it.

Less than 24 hours after the President's historic signature, Muñoz gave the July 4th speech in Puerto Rico, always a major event on the island. He was clearly still shaken by the terrifying near-miss that brought his four-year constitutional process to the brink of disaster. And he was still fuming at the "atrocity against the people of Puerto Rico," that one disgruntled

---

6. Trías Monge, *Historia constitucional de Puerto Rico* Vol. III, 308.

American businessman and his friend in the Senate came so close to destroying the process.

"If the people of Puerto Rico were not armed to the teeth in one of the most honorable histories of democracy in action," Muñoz roared, "there would have been no hope of winning. But rectitude and democratic honesty in this battle proved invincible. And how perfect and poetic was justice. All who acted wrong were defeated. All who acted right won!"[7]

But Muñoz's strongest invective was directed against the *independentistas* that had conducted the furious campaign aimed at the right wing of the Republican and Democratic parties. In an attack reminiscent of his emotional denunciation of the Nationalist uprising, he said:

> The Congress received letters, telegrams, and memorandums demanding and arguing that it should not respect the will of the Puerto Rican people as expressed in the ballot box on three occasions. And those who did this call themselves defenders of freedom and enemies of colonialism. "In the name of freedom," they vociferated and they whispered, "tell Puerto Rico that the vote of its good and simple people is worthless." "In the name of freedom," they murmured to Congress, "tell the Puerto Ricans that their clean exercise of democracy means nothing before the Congress of the greatest democracy in the world!" "In the name of freedom" they insisted in divesting the Puerto Ricans of their deep faith in the means of the vote and of peace...
>
> These people, now it is clear, carry in their hand a cardboard doll marked with the name of freedom, but what's inside is the most ragged colonialist spirit. While here a man, for the most sordid business motives, sought to detain, in the most nakedly colonial way, the will of the people, the others, those with the cardboard box with the name of freedom, said to those in Congress that could defeat Puerto Rico: "Master, punish the voters of Puerto Rico!" They said: "Master, slap the face of the democratic will of the people of Puerto Rico!" Whoever despises the dignity of the votes of a people,

---

7. Muñoz Marín, *Los gobernadores electos de Puerto Rico*, 450.

despises the people and despises their freedom. Whoever despises a people, offends the name of freedom. Those are, people of Puerto Rico, the only colonialists that you still have among you.[8]

On July 25, 1952, before 35,000 people gathered in front of the Capitol building, the pristine, blue water of the Atlantic ocean behind them, Muñoz proclaimed the Constitution and Commonwealth status. He announced that at his request, President Truman commuted to life imprisonment the death sentence of the Nationalist Oscar Collazo, who had attempted to assassinate him at Blair House on November 1, 1950. This action was in deference to the island's constitution that prohibited the death sentence, symbolizing the new relation between Puerto Rico and the United States.

"It was a striking feature of the ceremonies attendant of the Constitution on July 25th that so large a share of the attention was focused upon the rising of the Puerto Rican flag,"[9] one of the dignitaries present, Rubert Emerson, former head of the Interior Department's Territories and Insular Possession Division, wrote in 1953. Now as the National Guard Band played *La Borinqueña*, after a two-year battle and a desperate race against the clock in Congress, it seemed as if Muñoz went into slow motion as he very slowly raised the Puerto Rican flag to the same level as the American flag.

---

8. Ibid., 451.

9. Hanson and Well, *Puerto Rico: A Study in Democratic Development*, 10.

27 An Odd Situation

N o one was more intrigued by the creation of a "new state," Commonwealth status, than Carl Friedrich. Born in Leipzig, Germany, the 50-year-old Harvard professor was the author of numerous books on government and philosophy, had played a big role in the adoption of West Germany's constitution, and served as a consultant to Puerto Rico's constitutional assembly. Tiny Puerto Rico, he wrote, had become the scene of a major "act of political creation." He stated, "The new status of Puerto Rico as a free and associated state or commonwealth is a new dimension of federal government. Nothing like it was envisioned by the fathers of the American Constitution."[1] So unique was Muñoz' status, that "it goes beyond known form of federalism...existing categories do not suffice for comprehending what has happened."

As Rexford Tugwell was a decade earlier, Friedrich was also intrigued by the figure of Muñoz:

> His personality is complex. He is friendly, and yet aloof, highly intelligent and yet resistant to notions which do not fit in with his experience and thought, sincere in basic outlook and yet calculating and shrewdly expedient in his everyday dealings. He loves wine and song, and is admired far beyond Puerto Rico in the Spanish-speaking world as a poet of genuine merit. The vigor of his imagination, the true gift of the poet, is held in check by a cautious, even

---

1. Friedrich, *Middle Road to Freedom*, 18.

suspicious streak of sharp-eyed circumspection. While profoundly confident of man's capacity to contribute to his own well-being, he is no builder of utopias, no happy warrior who would expose himself to unnecessary risks. His humor is strong and ever-ready, but it is a somewhat sardonic one, familiar with Cervantes as a Spanish heritage. With such a personality it is not surprising that Muñoz Marín should have become the remarkable inspirational leader that he is today.[2]

Even more than Muñoz's legal advisors and political leaders, Friedrich believed that Muñoz should have been more willing to take "risks" in dealing with Congress, especially in resolving the "defect" in the applicability of federal law to Puerto Rico without voting representation. In 1959 he wrote: "this framework is so unsatisfactory, in my opinion, a review and revisions are overdue." Optimistic in his perception of the flexibility of the American constitutional system, he saw no reason why it could not be greatly expanded to include Puerto Rican participation not only in the applicability of the laws of Congress, but in U.S. foreign affairs, international relations, and even defense policy.[3]

A MORAL OBLIGATION

Another "defect" in the new status, Friedrich wrote, was that it did not "envision a contribution by Puerto Rico to the federal treasury."[4] In fact, this was an issue that Muñoz felt strongly about. When Muñoz first talked about industrialization, the "Battle of Production," he emphasized that one of its principal purposes was to reduce Puerto Rico's dependence on "artificial aid." It was below Puerto Rico's self-respect, its dignity, while not paying federal taxes, to continue to receive the ever-growing flow of federal funds. But when he brought it up at the constitutional assembly, the statehood

2. Ibid., 15.
3. Ibid., 33.
4. Friedrich, *Middle Road to Freedom*, 33.

delegates jumped from their seats to proclaim that Muñoz was talking about eventual statehood. No, he answered sharply: statehood would mean extracting federal taxes "from the poverty and the misery" of the Puerto Rican people. Instead he envisioned a system that would be tied to the island's development, to its ability to pay, without undermining the island's vital "fiscal autonomy." If current economic trends continued, Muñoz declared, by the 1960s the island should have reached the same level as the rest of the United States and then should begin to make payments to cover the costs of federal services on the island.

Muñoz's proposal created confusion within his party. His legal experts and most Popular leaders were more interested in extending the island's autonomy. The idea—that Muñoz was to bring up repeatedly throughout his life—struck them as it did the statehooders: it would take the island into greater integration into the U.S. and eventually towards statehood. Others saw it as "unreal" since there was no time in the foreseeable future when the island could afford to send millions to the U.S. Treasury. Muñoz answered that this was not an ideological nor an economic issue, but a matter "of the dignity and respect" of Puerto Ricans to their new union with the United States.

An Odd Situation

An odd situation had developed. Those who had brought about this "act of political creation—beginning with Muñoz himself, his political leaders and legal team consultants as Friedrich, now seemed to be harping on its "defects." Muñoz reminded everyone that back on December 26, 1951 he had declared to the constitutional convention: "I have said many times that this is a vital formula, full of life, full of the power of growth: that this is a dynamic form full of energy, full of movement towards the future..." While the statehooders and *independentistas* exploited each mention of a "defect" in the new status, Muñoz insisted that the "potential for growth" was not a weakness, but the strength of Commonwealth.

In any case, the hope of making Commonwealth "grow," of course, depended on continuing to gain the support of the Puerto Rican voters. On

November 4, 1952, Muñoz achieved his biggest victory yet, getting 65 percent of the vote. The big surprise was the emergence of the Independence Party as the principal opposition with 19 percent. The Republican Statehood Party dropped to 13 percent. Nationalist Party leader Albizu Campos, convicted on August 29, 1951 of inciting the violent overthrow of the island government, was back in prison, serving a sentence of up to 44 years.

The 1952 election also marked the disappearance of the old Socialist Party. It failed to retain its legal standing with only 3 percent of the vote. It was for Muñoz a nostalgic and sad event. This was the party that first attracted him to political action, campaigning in the cane fields, defending bloodied cane workers fighting for humane wages. The Socialist Party, like everything else in Puerto Rico, had changed. It had become conservative and trapped in absurd alliances. Muñoz himself wanted to believe that in his innermost core and motivation, he himself had not changed, that he was still, in his heart, the same "socialist" that joined Santiago Iglesias for the 1920 campaign. The demise of the Socialist Party meant something else: it underscored the reality that political parties tend to live and die with their leaders, making Muñoz think again about the future of his own party, and his own creation, Commonwealth status.

At The United Nations

Three days before President Truman left office, on January 17, 1953, Muñoz sent him a letter asking that the United States Government officially notify the United Nations that Puerto Rico was no longer a "colony." The UN required member nations to report on the steps taken to "decolonize" its non-self governing "dependent territories." The United States reported on Alaska, Hawaii, the Panama Canal Zone, Guam, American Samoa, the Virgin Islands, and Puerto Rico.

The removal of Puerto Rico from the list constituted international recognition of its new political status. Yet, whether to proceed provoked a debate within Muñoz's inner circle. Several party leaders argued that a UN "stamp of approval" undermined their resolve to return to Congress to remove the "defects" in Commonwealth status.[5]

---

5. Trías Monge, *Historia constitucional de Puerto Rico* Vol. IV, 9.

Muñoz decided to go ahead. The U.S. was met by surprising difficulties and opposition. Puerto Rico's political relation to the United States became a pawn in the Cold War power struggle taking place in the United Nations. The Soviet Union block worked aggressively to have the UN reject the American petition. Meanwhile, the resurgent Puerto Rico Independence Party mounted an intense campaign among Latin American nations, historically in favor of Puerto Rico "joining the community of free nations."

Fernós was named to the American U.N. delegation. It became one more uphill battle that came down to the wire. On the day of the vote, November 23, 1953, U.S. Ambassador to the U.N., Henry Cabot Lodge, read a message from President Eisenhower to the General Assembly declaring that "if at any time, the Legislative Assembly of Puerto Rico adopted a resolution in favor of more complete or even absolute independence," he would "immediately thereafter recommend to Congress that such independence be granted."

Something was gained during the seemingly endless U.N. debates: members of the American delegation repeatedly and forcefully sustained that the U.S. Government had indeed entered into a "compact which cannot be amended or abrogated unilaterally."[6] On August 20, 1953, following a presentation by Fernós, U.S. delegate Mason Sears declared:

> A most interesting feature of the new constitution is that it was entered into *in the nature of a compact* between the American and the Puerto Rican people. A compact, as you know, is far stronger than a treaty. A treaty usually can be denounced by either side, whereas a compact cannot be denounced by either party unless it has the permission of the other.[7]

Finally, eleven months after Muñoz's original letter, the General Assembly voted to remove Puerto Rico from the list of colonies. It was anything but a consensus vote: of the U.N.'s sixty member nations, 26 voted in favor, 16 against, mostly Soviet block members plus several Latin American and African nations, and 18 abstained.

---

6. Ibid., 20.
7. Ibid., 28.

But now it was evident that Muñoz himself was suffering from "status fatigue." Returning triumphantly to San Juan, Fernós, Trías Monge, and other members of the Puerto Rican team were anxious to narrate to Muñoz the intensity and drama of the battle at the United Nations. But they could not locate him. He was not at La Fortaleza, nor at his Trujillo Alto home. Finally they caught up to him in a tiny island off the east coast, Palominos. Muñoz greeted his visitors with his usual warmth and at first seemed to listen intently: his face "somber." But soon it became obvious that he was, Trías Monge wrote years later, "singularly disinterested...in this theme. Soon the conversation turned elsewhere."[8]

The Cold War, however, kept the issue alive in the UN. After the Fidel Castro revolution in January, 1959, the Cuban delegation, backed by the Soviet block, took the initiative to revive the Puerto Rican question at the Decolonization Committee. Castro, who greatly admired Albizu Campos, had a strong personal interest in promoting Puerto Rican independence. But the U.S. frustrated the Cuban initiative.

HEADY TIMES

The 1950s, when Muñoz and other leaders were not brooding about the political status, were exhilarating times for Puerto Rico. Muñoz was especially pleased by one convert: his old mentor and tormentor, Rexford Tugwell. Nothing had vexed Muñoz, Moscoso, and other protégés, like Tugwell's 1946 memoirs of his years as Governor, expressing a fundamental pessimism about his own accomplishment and the survival of the revolution itself. The book, one of his admirers, Earl Parker Hanson wrote, "was one of Tugwell's greatest mistakes...under the title *The Stricken Land*...it should have been called *The Stricken Tugwell*."[9] By 1953, however, Tugwell had reached a conclusion to the enigma that had bedeviled him, whether Muñoz would turn out to be another "political boss" or a "statesman." Now, describing Muñoz's achievement, he wrote: "it is not too much to say that a

---

8. Ibid., 56.
9. Hanson, Transformation: The Story of Modern Puerto Rico, 197.

transformation is in process which for a long time will be one of the wonders of human history."[10]

In his first visit with President Eisenhower in 1953, as he had with Truman seven years earlier, Muñoz offered even greater Puerto Rican participation in promoting American democracy and development throughout the Caribbean and Latin America. The island's new State Department, created under the 1952 Constitution, was given the responsibility and means to expand the Point Four technical and cultural exchange programs. Muñoz appointed Insular Assistant Secretary of State, Dr. Arturo Morales Carrión, to run the programs. By 1959, among the nearly 10,000 visitors, there were 6,500 technical trainees from 118 countries, and 1,400 politicians, journalists, and other "opinion makers" from 79 countries. Numerous international conventions were organized on the island to discuss issues ranging from public health to economic development to social and political theories. "The results," Morales Carrión wrote in 1983, "were hailed in the United States and in much of Latin America. The program turned Puerto Rico into a hemispheric meeting ground and added to the Puerto Rican sense of pride and accomplishment."[11] Now at the height of the Cold War, Tugwell's *Stricken Land* was heralded as the American "Showcase of Democracy" in the Caribbean, the democratic alternative to the dictatorship in the Soviet "showcase," Fidel Castro's Cuba.

THE MIGRATION

Muñoz had his own "flattering statistics" which he used often. Life expectancy, which had been 46 years in 1940, was up to 64 years in 1955. The mortality rate, down to 7.5 percent per thousand population, was lower than all but two mainland states. In just a decade and a half, 18 years had been added to the life of the Puerto Rican. This, as in the past, made the population treadmill move faster. Puerto Rico experienced a classic "revolution of rising expectations." Hundreds of thousands abandoned the

---

10. Hanson and Wells, *Puerto Rico: A Study in Democratic Development,* 145.
11. Morales Carrión, *Puerto Rico: A Political and Cultural History,* 292.

rural zones and small towns, their hopes aroused by the Muñoz rhetoric and the physical reality of the clusters of Fomento plants in the urban areas. Thousands settled in San Juan and other cities, again swelling the slums. Thousands of others were drawn to the mainland pulled by the labor shortage caused by the Korean War. The massive migration of young Puerto Ricans, mostly to New York City, had begun. The net outflow reached 75,000 in 1953: by the end of the decade, a half million islanders had left the island.

While providing the island with a crucial escape valve from the population pressure, the enormous migration became another emotional political and ideological issue. Opponents accused Muñoz of carrying out a policy of "pushing" young Puerto Ricans off the island, most of them to live in city slums, many to live off U.S. welfare. In New York, Representative Vito Marcantonio, a fierce critic of Muñoz who had described Puerto Rico as a "saturnalia of corruption" during the status debate in Congress, was himself accused of "importing" these voters to feed his New York political machine.

Another primary target of the criticism was Teodoro Moscoso, who periodically made controversial statements supporting birth control and other means of population control. Singled out as the mastermind behind "the migration policy," Moscoso had indeed convinced Muñoz to have the insular government provide services and orientation to the migrants on the mainland—from urging them to take warm clothing in winter to teaching rudimentary English, to supervising the mainland contracts for migrant farm workers.

But there was in fact no "conspiracy" by Marcantonio or Moscoso to ship Puerto Ricans to the mainland. Muñoz's policy reflected his own views and emotions. In the past he scorned the idea of attempting to solve the island's economic and population crisis through migration. Now he accepted it as inevitable. The policy was to neither promote nor discourage it. It was identical to his policy on government-sponsored birth control programs. After airfare from San Juan to New York plummeted to $45, it became a moot issue. As American citizens, there was no way for Muñoz or Moscoso or anyone to stop or control the Puerto Rican exodus.

The Nationalists Strike Again

On March 1, 1954, Fernós's aide at the U.S. Capitol, Orville Watkins, informed him that something "suspicious" had happened that morning. Several Puerto Ricans appeared at the office and asked when he, Fernós, was expected to arrive. Orville gave evasive answers that clearly displeased the Puerto Ricans, who turned and left. As Fernós left for lunch, his aide warned him to be careful.

Shortly after 1:00 p.m., four Nationalists from New York City, led by Lolita Lebrón, a 34-year old garment woker that had migrated to New York in 1940, entered the visitors' gallery of the House of Representatives, pulled out handguns and fired at the Representatives on the House floor. Five were wounded. Michigan representative Alvin Bentley survived after several days in grave danger. The Nationalists had positioned themselves directly above Fernós's empty seat. He had not returned from lunch.

The following day, Fernós took the floor to speak, but when he pronounced "Mr. Speaker..." the entire House broke out in applause, all on their feet. Deeply moved, Fernós expressed the indignation of the people of Puerto Rico. The House gave him another standing ovation after his brief words. Muñoz flew up to Washington. Speaker of the House Joe Martin suspended the House session, invited Muñoz to enter the floor and stand in front of the presidency. One by one the House members filed by Muñoz and Fernós, shaking their hand. That afternoon, Muñoz and Fernós met with President Eisenhower at the White House. From there they visited each of the wounded congressmen, except for Bentley, whose life was still in danger. Several months later, during the New York City trial of the Nationalists, one state witness declared that Fernós was indeed on the Nationalist hit list.

The timing of the shooting of Congress at first puzzled Muñoz and the federal authorities. There seemed to be nothing going on in Puerto Rico or in Congress to provoke it. Then it was learned that it was timed to coincide with an Inter-American Conference being held in Caracas, Venezuela. Once again, this struck Muñoz as surreal. In his speeches during the 1940s,

Albizu gave great importance to these conventions in Latin America, events that were, in fact, mostly ignored in the U.S. and in Puerto Rico.

A year earlier, in September, 1953, Muñoz had pardoned Albizu, in jail for the Nationalist 1950 uprising. Doctors reported that the Nationalist leader suffered from paranoia. He wrapped himself in wet towels, convinced that the United States was sending atomic "death rays" to torture and kill him. Muñoz now revoked Albizu's pardon. Progressively ill, by 1956 he was confined at the island's Presbyterian Hospital. On November 15, 1964, as one of his last acts before stepping down from the governorship, Muñoz again pardoned him. Five months later, April 21, 1965, Albizu died.

THE STATEHOOD RESURGENCE

Nationalist violence had once again backfired. In the 1956 elections, the Independence Party suffered an unexpected decline in votes, down to 86,838 from 126,228 in 1952. Meanwhile, the Statehood Republican Party, appeared to be terminally ill in 1952, more than doubled its votes from 85,591 in 1952, to 172,838. Nationalist violence was certainly one factor that helped the Republican candidate for Governor, 52-year-old Ponce industrialist, Luis Ferré. He had been running for office since 1940, served in the Legislature in the 1952-56 term, and was now emerging as an effective vote-getter, mostly in the new urban middle class. Known as a modern "progressive Republican" similar to New York's Nelson Rockefeller, he worked closely with his brother-in-law, veteran politician Miguel Angel García Méndez, who as Statehood Republican President and senator looked after the party machine.

But for Muñoz there were deeper reasons for the resurrection of the statehood movement: the revival of an attitude that he hoped had died with the old politics: the will, or the lack of resistance, to cultural "assimilation." As he had warned back in his first message as Governor in 1949, Puerto Rico was in danger of allowing itself to be Americanized, not by decree from Washington nor misguided educational policies, but by his own "democratic revolution"—the enormous thrust of the island's industrialization, the great migration from the rural to the urban centers, and the increasing flow of Puerto Ricans between the island and the American mainland.

It was all too obvious that the "Battle of Production" was still far from won. And he was determined to launch a new battle in Congress to make the Commonwealth "grow" and hopefully become more acceptable to the statehood and *independentista* voters. But there was a more fundamental battle he was now convinced would be lost if not waged urgently: the battle to save Puerto Rican culture from sinking in inexorable assimilation.

PART IV

Serenity
1953-1980

"Can a culture be efficient in production and at the same time wise and modest in consumption? Can it be feverish in output and serene in intake? I say that we are getting to a time in which it must be."

Muñoz Marín
1955

28 Serenity

In one of his frequent escapes to Puerto Rico's lush, beautiful rural areas, a sign painted in front of a small, wooden building caught Muñoz's eyes: *Agapito's Bar*. Nothing symbolized *jíbaro* culture like the thousands of small grocery stores, *bodegas* and bars that dotted the entire island. "When a young man gets married," wrote Stuart Chase in 1951, "a frequent practice is to borrow a hundred dollars from his prospective father-in-law and open a retail store. Everywhere one goes one sees these tiny, inefficient, unsanitary shops, sliding into bankruptcy."[1]

Most of these *bodegas*, economist Harvey Perloff pointed out, "were no larger than oversized packing crates, stretched along the highways and mushroomed in towns and villages, often several to a block. The total inventory is frequently no more extensive than a well-stocked pantry in a middle-class home. The prices of retail products, which are uniformly high, reflect the inefficiency of distribution..."

But as inefficient as they were, these tiny *bodegas* and bars played a vital role in the culture, tying over the *jíbaros* and their families over the dead periods in coffee picking and sugar harvesting with seemingly endless credit. The bars, of course, served as the *batey*, the meeting places to drink rum, play dominoes, perhaps see a cockfight, and always to talk politics.

Muñoz knew that the vast number of them were in danger of extinction, victims of the modernization of Puerto Rico. Back in 1941, he eliminated the odious salt tax and other sales taxes that principally hurt the poor. But the *jíbaro* consumers were still paying a heavier "tax" with the exorbitant

---

1. Chase, *Operation Bootstrap in Puerto Rico*, 28.

prices for a pound of rice or codfish due to the inefficiency of the *bodega* system.

Soon after becoming Governor, Muñoz asked Moscoso to deal with the problem. Moscoso quickly mobilized a team of experts, bringing down from Harvard University economist John Kenneth Galbraith, who had run President Roosevelt's wartime price regulation program. Galbraith made clear that the modernization of the food retail industry through larger stores and supermarkets, then beginning to appear in the U.S., meant the economic dislocation of thousands of poor Puerto Ricans including the newly-married couples that depended on the meager *bodega* income.

But what moved Muñoz when he saw the sign in this particular little bar was another price that Puerto Rico was paying for its modernization. At the December 29, 1953 convention of the Puerto Rico Teachers Association, he said:

> In a town in the interior of the island I saw a sign that said "Agapito's Bar." Why did you do it, Agapito? If by that street of that little town not even once a year is there a client whose vernacular is English. Is it that it makes you feel better saying it in a language that is not yours? And if you reject your language, are you not to a certain point also rejecting yourself? And if that attitude spreads to thousands and thousands of people, unconsciously as in the case of Agapito, from where will they get the spiritual vigor to continue contributing a respectable culture to itself and to the United States and to America and to the Western world?[2]

Why use English words, Muñoz asked, when there are perfectly good Spanish words, and in some cases, "good Puerto Rican words?" Why use the word "drink" if there is the good Spanish word *trago* or *copa*, and the better Puerto Rican words *palo, matracazo, juanetazo*? Why is it, Muñoz continued, that in the public and private schools, teachers are still called "Mister" and "Miss?" Isn't that evidence of an "absurd colonialist" mentality?

Muñoz was aware that he had entered a danger zone. Americanization, cultural assimilation, and English itself were acutely sensitive issues in

---

2. Muñoz Marín, pamphlet, Luis Muñoz Marín Foundation.

the ideological status conflict: the *independentistas* and Nationalists denouncing the "extermination" of Puerto Rico's cultural identity, the statehooders extolling the necessity of English and Americanization as synonymous with progress and prosperity.

Muñoz attempted to avoid this battlefield. English, he said, is "a great language that every Puerto Rican should learn and learn it well..." It was not the Americans, he continued, who were to blame, but the Puerto Ricans themselves, the existence of a "psychic blandness...a weakness in our culture" that is producing, not a bilingual people, but a people "semi-lingual in two languages."

Reiterating his belief in Puerto Rico's "permanent union" to the United States, he said that loyalty to American citizenship cannot mean "the inert cultural assimilation of the language, the way of life, the spirit, of what is to become of the Puerto Rican as a Puerto Rican..." Instead, it imposed on Puerto Ricans the obligation to choose what is positive and reject what is negative in American culture: learn and practice fundamental American democratic principles and attitudes, but seriously question "whether economic activity is an end in itself": reject "habits of consumption that can lead even a very rich country to feel poor or insufficiently rich..."

Puerto Rico, he said, has arrived at a crossroads: the "precise historical moment has arrived when if we do not take deliberate command of the cultural process...the Puerto Rican personality can be damaged in an inexorable hybrid without feet or head."

"A NEW FANGLED POVERTY"

To "take command of the cultural process" required putting a harness on the enormously powerful forces of economic development, industrialization, and urbanization that he himself had unleashed on this island.

"Production for what?" he had asked back in 1949 in his first message to the Legislature. Now, speaking to the Harvard graduating class on June 16, 1955, he proposed an answer. In one of the most important speeches of his life, he proposed a political and social philosophy called Operation Serenity:

In Puerto Rico we are trying in our modest setting to bring to a harmonious success, for the good of our souls and bodies and for the observation of our fellow citizens and of such parts of the world as may care to look, Operation Bootstrap—the right to life, Operation Commonwealth—the right to liberty; and Operation Serenity—the pursuit of happiness with some hope of really catching up to her...

Operation Serenity is undoubtedly the most difficult... We might say that it aims to give some kind of effective command to the human spirit over the economic process. It attempts to make the human spirit an effective ruler, albeit a constitutional one limited by the strong parliament of economic forces. It aims at making high objectives for man's earthly life real, familiar and simple in the daily life of the community...

Serenity may perhaps be defined as the habit of seeing your world whole, instead of just economically; as the living society of man and forces and facts in which you as an individual conduct your life. To see it whole you must see it simply. And to see it with intelligent simplicity you must see it deeply. A society in which Operation Serenity had been successful would use its economic power increasingly for the extension of freedom, of knowledge, and of the understanding imagination rather than for a rapid multiplication of goods, in hot pursuit of a still more vertiginous multiplication of wants...

Priority obviously goes to fighting old-fashioned poverty... There is room also, it seems to me, for an awareness of a newfangled poverty, that of the feverish desires outstripping the feverish production and of the feverish production inventing new desires that must go for many unfulfilled.[3]

The Gandhi Statuette

Putting a harness on Operation Bootstrap meant putting a harness on that intrepid "human dynamo" that drove it forward, Teodoro Moscoso.

---

3. Ibid.

In meetings with Moscoso, Muñoz had a habit of pushing forward a statuette that was on top of his desk, of one of the men he most admired, Mahatma Gandhi. Finally one afternoon, Moscoso felt his blood boiling in anger and frustration. He resented the perception that Operation Bootstrap was a bulldozer indiscriminately leveling everything in its path, the good and bad, and in the process destroying Puerto Rican culture and values. "Don Luis, please don't push Gandhi at me," he said, pushing the statue back at Muñoz.

If there was one person in Puerto Rico, Moscoso believed, that did not have to be lectured on the vital importance of culture it was precisely Moscoso. It was he, after all, who had begun the restoration of Old San Juan, even before Muñoz had created the Institute of Puerto Rican Culture, bringing specialists that had worked for the Rockefeller family in restoring the colonial town of Williamsburg.

There was, Moscoso believed, at best, a naiveté, perhaps even self-delusion in Muñoz's evangelical sermonizing over the "good life" of temperance. Yes, in many ways, Muñoz's lifestyle exemplified the *jíbaro* culture. Muñoz certainly had very little interest in material possessions. In his rustic two-bedroom home outside San Juan, there were certainly no traces of the "conspicuous consumption" Muñoz decried. As he had been all his life, Muñoz remained poor. Before the 1956 elections, his net "wealth" was itemized at $562, his home still heavily mortgaged with 16 years to go.[4]

But Moscoso, as much as anyone in Puerto Rico, knew that in his love of life, of the pleasures of life, no one was more removed from the austerity of his idol Gandhi. In the thatched-roof open *bohío* where he loved to spend his evenings, sitting with friends in a small circle of wicker rocking chairs, Muñoz would carefully select and savor a bottle of vintage wine given to him by friends, including Moscoso. Muñoz, like Moscoso, loved to travel. He was untiringly curious about the history of the places he visited, pestering his hosts with endless questions. When his friends traveled, they scrupulously jotted down the names and addresses of good restaurants to report back to him. But, unlike Moscoso, Muñoz was not an adventurer. He avoided exotic experiences, seeking always the comfort, security, and familiarity of Western culture. When a friend who had just returned from Japan asked if he ever

---

4. *Time*, 30.

intended to "explore the mysteries of the Orient," Muñoz shook his head and said: "I'm a European."

A Fearful Engine

As long as the Operation Bootstrap engine ran (and it was now running as never before), Moscoso said to himself, Muñoz could philosophize and indulge the poet in him. Bootstrap, in fact, now seemed unstoppable, having driven the island's economy forward through the two recessions in the U.S. in the 1950s. Puerto Rico's net income was expanding at a rate of 7 1/2 percent, over twice the rate of the U.S. Projections for the 1960-61 fiscal year were even higher: an 8 1/2 percent growth. Fomento had established 111 new factories in just one year, and more were on the way. Capital investment in new plants and machinery was up to $292 million, a 21 percent jump in one year. There were already 45,000 Puerto Ricans working in the Bootstrap factories, 9,000 more than the year before. Total industrial salaries were up by nearly 30 percent. For the first time, Fomento was promoting heavy, capital-intensive industries: Union Carbide, Grace and other chemical and petroleum industries were building giant plants along the island's south coast. Moscoso's risky venture into tourism hotels was also beginning to pay off as jet travel brought the island closer to the mainland. Private luxury hotels had gone up on both sides of San Juan, the San Juan Intercontinental Hotel to the east, and Laurence Rockefeller's Dorado Beach Hotel, with a Robert Trent Jones gulf course, to the west.

No one believed that Muñoz would suggest slowing down the Bootstrap engine. On the contrary, it was evident that it still had a long way to go: while the labor force had grown in the past decade from 624,000 to 786,000, and unemployment had declined from 18 to 13 percent, the cold reality was that at that same rate, it would take 100 years to "abolish unemployment." Even with all the new public housing, Muñoz knew that still 43 percent of all Puerto Rican families, 94,000, lived in slums. Puerto Rico annually spent one third of its total budget on education, a statistic Muñoz used often. Yet still less than half of all public school children completed high school. In 1940, 94 percent of all families had an annual income of less than $2,000.

The improvement had been dramatic: Bootstrap had nearly cut this in half. But by mid-1950, still 55 percent of the families were below the poverty line.

In fact, while Muñoz pushed Gandhi at Moscoso, he was also pushing him to get the great industrial Fomento wheel to turn faster. Again on the cover of *Time* magazine on May 14, 1958, Muñoz specified the targets: by 1960, 91 percent of the families should be above the $2,000 level: by 1975, Puerto Rico should have reached the 1957 U.S. per capita income. This required that there should be no less than 2,500 factories by 1975, five times the number in the late 1950s. When a reporter asked: "Where do you want to go from here?" Moscoso could not have been more pleased with Muñoz's answer. "Man, we are not here yet!"[5] On the *Time* cover Muñoz was described as "The Bard of Bootstrap."

All this, Moscoso and the Fomento people realized, was the manifestation of the old internal ambiguity, the "civil war" within Muñoz. Yes, he did indeed act like the "Bard of Bootstrap," but inside he was also Hamlet-like, second-guessing himself and his policies. Muñoz continued fundamentally uneasy with the tax-exemption program, and at times publicly reiterated that it could not be the "long term solution." In 1958 he suggested that casino gambling licenses, which drove hotel construction and the entire tourism industry, be phased out. That also came to nothing. Aware of the danger of sending mixed signals, he asked in the 1955 Harvard speech:

> Can a culture be efficient in production and at the same time wise and modest in consumption? Can it be feverish in output and se-rene in intake? I say that we are getting to the time in which it must be—and if it must, it probably can... Economists could tell us that a higher and higher rate of multiple consumption is necessary to a high rate of production, and therefore of employment and of income, and that what I am talking about would bring economies tumbling down on our heads. It need not be so, because of the evi-dent possibility of re-gearing high productivity to higher ends. If it were so then it would most certainly be time to ponder what to do about a situation in which Serenity could bring about catastrophe.

---

5. Ibid., 30.

One economist in the audience at Harvard who agreed wholeheartedly was John Kenneth Galbraith. Three years later, in the preface to his book, *The Affluent Society*, he wrote: "Governor Luis Muñoz Marín first persuaded me to question the wisdom of our preoccupation with more and more consumer goods as a goal."[6]

THE CASALS FESTIVAL

In December of 1955, Muñoz and Puerto Rico had a stroke of good luck that gave a boost to Operation Serenity. The 79-year-old Spanish cellist, conductor, and composer, Pablo Casals, decided to make Puerto Rico his home. Having nearly lost his life during the Spanish Civil War, Casals became in exile an international symbol of opposition to the *Falangista* regime, refusing to perform in any nation that recognized the Generalísimo Francisco Franco government.

Casals's mother was a Puerto Rican, born in the western end of the island, Mayagüez, taken to Spain at the age of eighteen, never to return. His first visit to the island, and to her birthplace, in 1955, was an event that attracted worldwide interest, made even more newsworthy by the fact that his constant companion was an attractive, talented nineteen-year-old Puerto Rican student, Marta Montáñez. Casals's decision to live in Puerto Rico was in part in homage to his mother, but also because he had fallen in love with the young Montáñez.

At dinner at La Fortaleza, Muñoz urged Casals to organize a festival in Puerto Rico similar to his renowned Prades Festival in the small French town near the Spanish border. There was the problem that the United States recognized the Spanish regime, but Muñoz convinced Casals that because of Puerto Rico's "unique" political status he would not violate his anti-Franco oath. Casals agreed.

In Washington, the power-broker and amateur violinist, Abe Fortas, promoted the new festival, delighted to help. Fortas biographer Laura Karman wrote: "When the seam on Casals's cello broke at the last rehearsal

---

6. Gailbraith, *The Affluent Society*, x.

before the 1958 festival opened, the Maestro entrusted the instrument to Fortas, who flew it to New York where an expert could repair it."[7]

But before the inaugural concert two years earlier, 1956, there was a greater crisis. In rehearsals, Casals slumped off his stool. He suffered a heart attack. In spite of this, the festival was held on schedule. The musicians from around the world that had come to pay tribute to Casals performed behind an empty stool and before an international audience of admirers. Casals slowly recovered and the following year, on August 3, 1957, he and Marta were married.

The Casals Festival projected to the world precisely the portrait of Puerto Rico that Muñoz wanted. David Ogilvy, founder of the advertising agency Ogilvy & Mather, had been recruited by Moscoso as the creative force behind Fomento's hard-nose promotional advertising. Now Ogilvy dedicated the big-budget full-page color ads in the major U.S. magazines to picture a beautiful island where not only fabulous profits were being made, but a "cultural renaissance" was taking place.

CAMELOT

The culmination of this renaissance came years later, on Monday, November 13, 1961, when President Kennedy and his wife Jacqueline invited 153 guests to a White House banquet in honor of Muñoz, followed by a Casals concert. Fortas engineered the event. "The arrangements were so complex that Fortas swore to his friend Isaac Stern he would not get involved in such an activity again even if Jesus Christ were available for a Jew's harp concert."[8] The event was a big success. Among the guests were American composers and conductors, Aaron Copland, Leonard Bernstein, Leopold Stokowski, and Eugene Ormandy. There were labor and business figures such as David Dubinsky, Henry Ford, and Paul Mellon; journalists and publishers Walter Lippman, Edward R. Murrow, and Randoph Hearst. Introducing Casals, Kennedy commented that the cellist had performed for the Spanish Queen María Cristina in 1892, and for Britain's Queen Victoria in 1892. Alice

---

6. Gailbraith, *The Affluent Society*, x.

Longworth, President Theodore Roosevelt's daughter, also present, had heard Casals perform in the White House in 1904. "In no part of Europe," Italian composer Gian-Carlo Menotti declared, "can an event like this be seen. The British royalty invites movie stars. Our president invites artists." For Kennedy, the Camelot legacy was born. For Muñoz, this was the triumph of his Operation Serenity.

The Institute of Culture

In 1955 the Institute of Puerto Rican Culture was organized. Muñoz turned it over to a 34-year-old graduate of the University of Chicago and Harvard, anthropologist Ricardo Alegría. Although low-key and soft-spoken in contrast to Moscoso's driving personality, Alegría proved as energetic and enterprising in promoting cultural events as Moscoso was in promoting new industry. Taking over Moscoso's Old San Juan restoration, Alegría brought about a dramatic improvement that, like the Casals Festival, received worldwide recognition. This was another opportunity for Ogilvy to promote Puerto Rico's "cultural renaissance." One of his advertisements for Moscoso read: "Can this really be the Puerto Rico everyone is talking about? Is this the island American industry is now expanding to, at the rate of three new plants a week? Is this truly the scene of a twentieth-century renaissance? Ask any proud Puerto Rican. He will surely answer—yes."[9]

Alegría and the Institute soon found themselves in the crossfire of the island's political and ideological battles. The Institute's mission seemed innocuous enough: to "preserve, enrich and promote the cultural values of the people of Puerto Rico." But this provoked the strong opposition of pro-statehood leaders who often accused Muñoz of deliberately "de-emphasizing" the teaching of English in the public schools. They saw the Institute, Alegría, and Muñoz's "community education program" as engaged in a conspiracy to promote "cultural nationalism" and disparage the influence of American culture.

---

8. Ibid., 177.

9. Maldonado, *Teodoro Moscoso and Puerto Rico's Operation Bootstrap*, 118.

In fact, many of the island's top painters, graphic artists, and moviemakers hired by the Education Department to carry out the community education program were fervent *independentistas*. Several of them produced works that denigrated Muñoz's promotion of tourism, and, in their view, "Americanization." The program, however, was one of Muñoz and his wife Inés's favorites.

Another important initiative in Serenity was taking place at the University of Puerto Rico. Muñoz's close collaborator and friend, Jaime Benítez, brought to the island world famous figures, academics and intellectuals, including the Spanish Nobel Prize laureate, Juan Ramón Jiménez. "The rapid growth of the University of Puerto Rico," Carl Friedrich wrote in 1959, "may be cited as one clear indication of the vitality of this growing local culture. Nowhere else has so much been accomplished in so little time with such limited resources. The brilliant leadership of the chancellor, a man of great breadth of cultural understanding, and a trained social scientist as well, has made of the university a genuine meeting place of the Spanish-speaking and the English-speaking world."[10] By 1960, UPR had become one of the biggest land-grant universities in the U.S., and had the distinction of being considered the best institution of higher learning in all Latin America.

WHAT KIND OF CIVILIZATION

By the end of the 1950s, Moscoso and others began to wonder if the idea of retiring had crept into Muñoz's mind and emotions. When they heard Muñoz's January 19, 1960 message to the Legislature, they asked themselves if this was his last. It sounded like Muñoz summing up his career. Muñoz began:

> We are at the beginning of a new decade. We should, of course, continue and accelerate the integral development of Puerto Rico in all its aspects. There is something, however, that merits our principal attention, our most devoted dedication, in these new times.

---

10. Friedrich, *Middle Road to Freedom*, 11.

We dedicated the decade that began in the year 1940 to the battle to abolish poverty. And to do so, we put aside the political status issue. In the beginning of the 1950s we put special energy in the creation of a new political status, vitally adapted to the economic necessities of Puerto Rico. In the decade we now begin I propose that we put special attention to the kind of civilization, the type of culture, how deep and good a quality of life the people of Puerto Rico want to create on the basis of the growing economic prosperity.

Economic development is not an end in itself, but the basis for a good civilization. Political status is not an end in itself, but a means to economic realization and the development of a good civilization.[11]

In several weeks, Muñoz would celebrate his 62nd birthday. Muñoz did think about making this his last legislative message. Moscoso had heard correctly. It had the aspect of a blueprint of development and priorities for the future. But there were too many things that remained undone. The timing was not right. Muñoz put aside the idea of retiring as he prepared himself for another political campaign.

---

11. Muñoz Marín, *Mensajes al pueblo puertorriqueño*, 226.

29 The Statehood Challenge

The statehood movement had always had an emotional argument against Commonwealth status—the "blood tax."

During the constitutional process, Muñoz and Fernós had been aided in Congress and American public opinion by Puerto Rico's participation in the Korean War. Soon after the North Korean invasion of South Korea on June 27, 1950, Puerto Rico's 65th Infantry Regiment was activated. On September 23, it was in combat in Pusan, Korea. The Puerto Rican troops, disparaged by General MacArthur during the Second World War, now received recognition for their courage. The regiment suffered numerous casualties in rescuing the First Marine Division, besieged and surrounded by the Chinese. One out of every 42 American killed in action, a total of 743 Puerto Ricans, gave their lives.[1] In relation to population per state, Puerto Rican casualties were twice as high as for the rest of the nation. At the July 25, 1952 Commonwealth inauguration ceremony, there was an "overwhelming" wave of Puerto Rican pride when the soldiers of the much-decorated 65th marched by in the parade.[2]

But the heroism of Puerto Rican soldiers, both statehooders and *independentistas* insisted, only highlighted the fact that under the new status Puerto Ricans called to war and sacrifice were still not able to vote for the American Commander-in-Chief. While Muñoz extolled tax-exemption for industry, Puerto Ricans were paying a "blood tax."

---

1. Morales Carrión, *Puerto Rico: A Political and Cultural History*, 286.
2. Hanson, *Transformation: The Story of Modern Puerto Rico*, 16.

Now statehooders had another strong argument. The admission of Alaska into the Union on January 3, 1959, followed by Hawaii on August 21, 1959 sparked a renewed militancy: it removed what had been two obstacles of statehood. These were the first non-contiguous territories admitted into the Union, and Hawaii had a different cultural heritage.

For Muñoz, who had always seen statehood as "unreal," this was further proof. Hawaii and Alaska revealed precisely why Puerto Rico could not follow. Both had been "incorporated territories" for a half century. They had all the obligations of American citizenship, including paying all federal taxes, but no self-government, no elective governor, and no votes in Congress or presidential elections. So statehood for both was a political achievement without an economic price. Alaska required a period of economic adjustment as federal programs were taken over by the local government. But both new states had natural wealth and economic potential. Hawaii already had a prosperous economy, with a high per capita income based mostly on agriculture and defense spending, and now jet travel placed it on the verge of great tourism development. And there was no cultural price to pay. Both were Americanized. Alaska was the last American frontier. In Hawaii, the early 19th century New England missionaries had begun the process of cultural assimilation that engulfed the later waves of Asian and European immigrants.

But the status issue, as Muñoz saw it, had never been rational. He had always seen the statehood movement more as a "cultural defect" among a number of Puerto Ricans: a distrust of the ability of Puerto Ricans to govern themselves: a mentality that "everything American" is superior. In 1955, he concluded his message to the Legislature with an emotional appeal: "I believe in the moral greatness of association, but not because I believe in the moral inferiority of the Puerto Rican. I believe in association for high reasons of dignity, not because of insulting fears of the capacity of the people of Puerto Rico to create and grow and respect itself in its freedom... I do not want to be at the head of those that follow me because they fear themselves, because they do not believe in the moral integrity of our people."[3]

But if the statehood phenomenon was a demeaning "cultural defect," a malignant manifestation of the "Agapito's Bar" syndrome, there was no

---

3. Muñoz Marín, *Mensajes al pueblo puertorriqueño*, 120.

question that it was growing, Muñoz's speeches on Serenity and his emotional appeals were not slowing down this phenomenon. The solution, Muñoz was increasingly convinced, was to tackle the "defects" in Commonwealth status. Muñoz agreed with his party leaders who insisted that Commonwealth will either "grow" or die. Back in his February 24, 1954 legislative message, he said "It is growth [in Commonwealth status] that will guarantee its permanence".[4]

The time to return to Congress had arrived. There was, however, no consensus in the Popular Party on just how to make the Commonwealth "grow." This powerful political machine, one of the most efficient and effective anywhere under the U.S. flag and in the hemisphere, was in fact, as had been his father's political parties, built over a deep ideological fault. In its early days, its survival depended on Muñoz's ability to bridge the remarkable phenomenon that "ninety percent of our leaders favor independence, while ninety percent of our voters are opposed." After the *independentista* revolt of 1948, the fault line separated a "left wing" that wanted "maximum autonomy," and a "right wing" that favored greater participation and integration into the American economic and political system. The autonomous wing consisted predominantly of political, legislative, and academic leaders that agreed that Puerto Rico was drifting towards total "assimilation," pushed inexorably by Moscoso's industrialization. It was delighted and encouraged by Muñoz' Serenity pronouncements. Semantics was important. It disliked Muñoz referring to Commonwealth as a form of "union", much less "permanent union" with the United States, preferring the word "association." Commonwealth status, after all, was called, in Spanish, the "Free Associated State."

For the "right wing," most of it in the administration, the core of Puerto Rico's status was American citizenship and "fiscal autonomy." Whatever the legal interpretation, Puerto Ricans were part of the United States in an arrangement that, contrary to all the talk about "defects," was working very well.

Days after his 1954 legislative message, Muñoz received an unusual, and in some ways, remarkable letter from Jaime Benítez. The university chancellor felt that the Commonwealth status was as much his to protect

---

4. Muñoz Marín, *Los gobernadores electos de Puerto Rico*, 111.

and defend, as it was Muñoz's. He had played a role in the Constitutional Assembly second only to Muñoz. In the letter, he expressed disappointment that Muñoz had made such major pronouncements on the future of the status without, as he had done in the past, discussing it with him. Benítez was famous for his often blunt style, but in this letter there was a tone of rebuke, of censure.

Muñoz, Benítez believed, was damaging the status he, they, had created. Why, he wanted to know, the rush to change a status that they had so recently created? The very idea that the Commonwealth had to grow in order to survive was wrong, even self-defeating: "I think that your reiterated insistence that the stability of Commonwealth status is conditioned to its growth creates confusion...What some people doubt, myself among them, is that announcing sudden changes, at this difficult time in world politics, promotes confidence in Commonwealth status, and even its growth...I find it unjustifiably risky to play a type of roulette where one risks losing a great deal more than what one wins if one hits the right number."[5]

Muñoz, the pragmatic, realistic political leader, Benítez was convinced, was making a big mistake. Clearly influenced by the "autonomous wing," the more he tampered with Commonwealth to make it "grow," the more he played into the hands of the opponents by instilling more insecurity and confusion in the people. In a few words, Benítez pleaded, it is working well. Leave it alone!

THE WAR AGAINST BENÍTEZ

Benítez was by now the scourge of the Popular Party left wing. He had always been seen, like Tugwell, as intellectually overbearing, arrogant, egocentric. Now he was accused of not only accepting what the lawyers and some party leaders insisted was still a "colonial status," but of being principally responsible for the "Agapito's Bar" syndrome. The University of Puerto Rico, instead of serving as the incubator of Puerto Rican cultural nationality, had become a wellspring of American materialistic values. His

---

5. Bothwell, *Puerto Rico: cien años de lucha política*, Vol. IV, 190.

concept of the "House of Studies," a university run by a strong central administration, while guaranteeing total academic freedom in the classroom, was seen as the "Americanization" of the institution.

After the 1948 Nationalist Party attempt to take over the institution, Benítez found himself in an ongoing "cold war" with a good part of the faculty and student groups, led by *independentistas*, demanding a "university reform" along the lines of the Latin American universities where early in the century much of the institutional power was transferred from the administration to the faculty and students.

A good part of the war within the Popular Party against Benítez, and the party's right wing, was spearheaded by an emerging "new generation" that Muñoz was actively recruiting into the party and administration. Many were well educated, some with degrees from Ivy League universities. Several of the more prominent "new generation leaders," such as Severo Colberg and José Arsenio Torres, had been protégés of Benítez at the University and were now among his harshest critics.

In 1956, the war broke out into the open: Ernesto Ramos Antonini, Speaker of the House and Popular Party Vice President, informed the media that Muñoz "has withdrawn his confidence in Benítez." Soon after that, a vote was taken at the University's governing board to fire him: members close to Muñoz voted for expulsion. Benítez survived by one vote, but his friendship with Muñoz was broken.

THE CRASH AGAINST THE REEF

In 1959, Muñoz made the decision to send to Congress a totally new Commonwealth status law. On March 23, Fernós introduced what was to become the Fernós-Murray Bill. It explicitly declared that Puerto Rico was no longer a "U.S. territory," that Commonwealth status was based on a now totally rewritten "bilateral compact." Puerto Rico would begin to pay for federal expenses on the island, major federal responsibilities and programs would be transferred from the federal to the insular government, and the island would have direct participation in such federal areas as negotiating U.S. commercial treaties, setting special tariffs on certain Puerto Ricans imports. The bill also included two changes that Fernós had first introduced in the 1953 "cosmetics bill" and that Muñoz had pulled back: one would have insular Supreme Court decisions go straight up to the U.S. Supreme Court on appeal; the other, of economic importance, would allow Puerto Rico to set its own public debt limit.

If back in 1950, the strategy was to "keep it simple," Muñoz and Fernós were now aware of the magnitude and complexity of this bill. This was the kind of "total autonomy" bill that Muñoz's legal advisors, constitutionalist Carl Friedrich, and the party's left wing believed Muñoz and Fernós should have fought for in Congress in the first place. The first major obstacle was to overcome the inevitable reaction of the members of Congress. Echoing the admonition of Benítez back in 1954: if it isn't broke, why fix it? Had not Congress "resolved" the status issue just a few years ago? There could not have been a more positive account of how well the Commonwealth was working economically, politically, culturally, than the *Time* magazine cover story on Muñoz a year earlier.

But Fernós saw still another obstacle: the perception in Congress that however "generous" it was in bestowing "privileges" to the island, the Puerto Ricans kept coming back complaining and asking for more. In 1958, Fernós warned Muñoz:

> The generalized but erroneous concept that Puerto Rico has enormous economic privileges makes it practically impossible to perfect the terms of the political association without resuscitating these alleged privileges. Any attempt to clarify and widen political autonomy, without clarifying the economic relationship, will crash against that reef.[6]

The "crash" came quickly and unexpectedly. It resulted from Muñoz's impatience. Fernós had carefully planned to get the bill through relatively safe waters in the House where he trusted he would receive the same support as he had in the past. At Muñoz's urging, however, he had Senator James E. Murray, chairman of the Interior and Insular Affairs Committee,

---

6. Fernós Isern, *Estado Libre Asociado de Puerto Rico*, 411.

introduce the bill in the Senate on May 25th. Several days later, Fernós was surprised to learn that following Muñoz's visit with Senate leader Lyndon Johnson, it was agreed to hold early Senate hearings. Johnson acted so quickly that when Fernós received the June 9 date for the hearings, he had to get Muñoz, on his way to New York, to turn around and return to Washington. Muñoz and Fernós were unprepared. On such a complex bill, it was vital to have visited the key Senate committee members to familiarize them and their staff members. It was also vital to adequately prepare and brief the executive departments that would report on the bill. Fernós felt it in his bones that he and Muñoz were taking a huge risk in these rushed hearings.

After a short statement, Fernós turned to introduce Muñoz. Senator Henry "Scoop" Jackson broke in to say that he had "one or two philosophical questions." In the novel, unique Commonwealth arrangement, the Democratic Senator said, Congress had thrust itself into constitutional "uncharted waters" and it was now essential to address this central issue that was extremely troubling to him. "Is it your judgment that in fact your present status, Commonwealth, is based on a compact that cannot be changed except with the consent of the people of Puerto Rico?" The tough, 47-year-old former prosecuting attorney from the state of Washington, in the words of Trías Monge, went "straight to the jugular."[7] Muñoz answered yes. Incredulously, Jackson asked just where in the American constitution did he find the authority for the "compact?" Muñoz went back to his emotional argument: since statehood and independence were both effectively untenable for generations to come, "I find it impossible to believe the United States can not find a way to abolish what would be in essence a colonial relationship."

Muñoz had used the words that rattled members of Congress— "colonial relationship"—and Jackson reacted, interrupting him: "No. Let's put this in perspective." And Muñoz shot back: "I think we found the road in 1952." But Jackson persisted:

Governor, let me tell you something. If I had the constitutional power to give Puerto Rico the power of local self-government that

---

7. Trías Monge, *Historia constitucional de Puerto Rico*, Vol. IV 151.

resides in the state, I would not waver to do so. Here we are talking about being asked, in effect, that we declare that we cannot pass federal laws (for Puerto Rico) that are applicable in the other states, even when the states are not in favor.[8]

This was indeed the "jugular." The Fernós-Murray bill, effectuely gave the Commonwealth powers constitutionally denied to the states. Jackson was not a conservative tied to island reactionaries. He had always been supportive of Muñoz. Before ending, however, there was more bad news for Muñoz. It was evident that Jackson was determined to prevent Muñoz and Fernós from railroading the bill through Congress. These deep constitutional questions, he insisted, required careful studies that "will take time." He announced his intention to bring the greatest number of Puerto Ricans into the debate. Extensive public hearings, he said, would be held on the island. "We cannot, naturally, receive the testimony from each one of the two and a quarter million American citizens in Puerto Rico. But we will give a complete and just audience in which all the differences of opinion will be expressed."

Muñoz and Fernós, of course, could not oppose making the process as open and democratic as possible. But, for Muñoz, this was the opening for the opposition parties, led by prolific and articulate lawyers who did indeed consider themselves "constitutional experts" to capture and dominate the process, turning it into another exercise in abstract ideology.

The Fernós-Murray bill was in trouble. The Jackson interrogation had exposed the gulf that existed between the two irreconcilable visions of the Puerto Rican relationship to the United States. Muñoz's position was that what Congress had created in 1952 was incomplete, unacceptable, and required major surgery. According to the Friedrich thesis, the American system was flexible, "creative" enough to permit a new kind of status with "total autonomy." Jackson's position was the opposite: Congress had given the island a unique status of political and economic privileges and now it was demanding even more privileges that were not possible. Any hope that the Fernós-Murray bill would sail through Congress like the status bills in 1947 and 1951 was now dead. It had "crashed against the reefs."

---

8. Fernós Isern, *Estado Libre Asociado de Puerto Rico*, 464.

Muñoz needed all the support he could get from the Republican Eisenhower administration. Muñoz, of course, had always been identified as a liberal Democrat since his relationship with President and Eleanor Roosevelt. There was, in fact, a strong affinity between the Popular Democratic Party and the national Democratic Party. The local Democratic Committee was invariably controlled by members of the PDP, principally San Juan Mayor Felisa Rincón de Gautier, who was active in mainland Democratic campaigns. But Muñoz had deliberately refused to affiliate himself or his party to the Democrats, in part because of deference to his concept of political autonomy but also for practical reasons. He wanted the freedom to deal with both Republicans as well as Democrats in Congress and the White House outside party lines.

Now, in this crisis, he felt he could count on the good relationship he had developed with Vice President Richard Nixon. Muñoz had dramatically demonstrated his "neutrality" in national politics when he organized a warm welcome in Puerto Rico for Nixon in May, 1958. The non-scheduled visit followed Nixon's disastrous trip to Latin America, with anti-American demonstrators in Venezuela rocking and nearly overturning his limousine. "It was a close brush with death," Nixon wrote in 1990.[9] Muñoz had thousands of Puerto Ricans line the streets of Old San Juan shouting "Arriba Nixon!" The highly publicized visit highlighted the island as the "showcase" of American democracy. Back in Washington, convinced that the U.S. needed a new Latin American policy, Nixon became an enthusiastic booster of Muñoz and his "democratic revolution."

On June 17, Muñoz met with Eisenhower. "It has come to my attention," Muñoz said, "that within the Executive Department there are persons who do not fully understand the position of Puerto Rico, and who do not fully realize its importance. I believe it to be of great importance for the United States in its relationship with Latin American countries and the rest of the world that the United States should not be seen to be abandoning its position regarding the existence of a compact between it and the people of Puerto Rico..."[10] Eisenhower was receptive and promised that he would personally

---

9. Nixon, *In the Arena*, 181.

10. Trías Monge, *Historia constitucional de Puerto Rico*, Vol. IV, 153.

examine the drafts of his administration's reports to Congress on the Fernós-Murray bill.

A "MONUMENTAL HOAX"

It was also vital to address Jackson's attack on the constitutionality of the new status. Muñoz had his lawyers prepare an extensive legal brief that cited a growing number of favorable federal court decisions, several by the Supreme Court. While not dealing directly with the status question, the courts used language and arguments sustaining that the island was indeed no longer a "territory," but fully self-governing. Particularly favorable was a 1957 decision by First Circuit Court Chief Justice McGruder, who flatly rejected the argument "that the Constitution of the Commonwealth is just another Organic Act of the Congress. We find no reason to impute to the Congress the perpetuation of such a monumental hoax."[11]

But Fernós wanted an even more direct and convincing answer to Jackson's objections. Four days after the Senate hearing, on June 13th, he traveled down to the University of Princeton to meet with the man considered a "maximum authority" on constitutional law, Dr. Edward Corwin, editor of the Congress publication of the annotated edition of the Constitution. When Fernós entered the professor's home, he found him with a bad throat infection that made it impossible for him to speak. He proceeded to explain the purpose of his visit, Corwin writing his responses on pieces of paper. Finally, Corwin agreed to study the matter. On June 20, Corwin sent his opinion: the "compact" was constitutional. Since Puerto Rico was an "unincorporated territory," thus not "an internal matter for the United States," Congress could "enter into a valid compact with the people of Puerto Rico."[12]

---

11. Documents on the Constitutional Relationship of Puerto Rico and The United States, 326.

12. Fernós Isern, *Estado Libre Asociado de Puerto Rico*, 471.

In Puerto Rico, meanwhile, the Fernós-Murray bill set off a collective frenzy not unlike the reaction to the 1936 Tydings bill. While Hawaiian and Alaska statehood seemed to make statehood for Puerto Rico imminent, the Fernós bill was interpreted by a growing number of Puerto Ricans as indeed a move towards independence. Federal employees on the island, fearful that they would lose their jobs, mobilized to campaign in San Juan and Washington. In his interrogation, Jackson made reference to the many alarming letters he was receiving from these employees.

Just as there was a "new generation" of Popular Party leaders with strong autonomist and Serenity views, the bill motivated a new generation of young professionals, including some of the disgruntled federal employees, to get into the new statehood crusade. They described themselves as nonpartisan and decried that the insular Republican leaders attempted to monopolize the "statehood ideal." A vigorous group, Citizens for State 51, sprang up to organize letter-writing campaigns and boisterous pro-American manifestations that impressed the members of Congress during hearings on the island, while back in Washington, contrary to Eisenhower's assurances, the administrative agencies were tearing the original bill apart with amendments and legal qualms.

THE BISHOP FROM PONCE

It was an ominous sign. The Catholic Church Bishop of Ponce, James McManus, jumped into the status battle, sending the Jackson and House committees a letter denouncing the bill as precisely a move towards independence and calling on the members of Congress to further "clarify" that Puerto Rico indeed remained a U.S. "territory."

Muñoz and the *Populares* were not surprised. The charismatic and outspoken Bishop had never hidden his disdain for Muñoz and his sympathy for statehood. They strongly suspected that McManus was in tandem with one of Ponce's leading residents, Luis A. Ferré, a practicing Catholic and now the leader of the statehood movement. McManus's major project was the establishment of a Catholic University in Ponce, built on land donated by the Ferré family. As Jackson promised, the Senate and House committees held seven days of hearings throughout the island. In Ponce, New York representative Leo W. O'Brien, who had managed the Alaskan and Hawaiian statehood bills through the House, was quoted in local newspapers predicting eventual statehood for the island. Fernós was convinced that O'Brien, a "fervent Catholic" had fallen under the spell of McManus. The energetic Bishop, Fernós reported, had become "very close to the members of Congress during the hearings."[13] Responding to a letter from Fernós, O'Brien backtracked. He clarified that he didn't think the island would be asking for statehood "now or in the near future," but reiterated his belief that most of Puerto Rico would favor it "as a final solution."[14]

CONFUSION

Muñoz's biggest problem, however, was confusion. Trías Monge recorded years later: "There existed in Congress a great desire to help Puerto Rico, but a marked ignorance of its spiritual torture before the marked deficiencies of its status. We could not count on a single representative or senator with whom we could discuss, frankly and to the point, the political problem of the moment."[15]

Members of Congress, far from understanding the "spiritual torture" of Popular Party leaders, suspected that behind the bill was simply partisan politics. Even the strong Muñoz admirer and Commonwealth supporter, the Democrat from Colorado, Interior and Insular Affairs Chairman Wayne Aspinall, reacted to the incessant accusation from Puerto Rico. He asked Muñoz during one of the hearings: "You would deny, then, that these proposals have any purpose whatsoever which would perpetuate yourself, your associates, or the Popular Democratic Party in influence or power?" Muñoz attempted a satirical response: "I am afraid that we have to work a little bit hard to get ourselves out of the confidence of the people of Puerto Rico."

---

13. Ibid., 493.

14. Ibid., 493.

15. Trías Monge, *Historia constitucional de Puerto Rico*, Vol. VI, 161.

But, in fact, Muñoz seemed to be wavering. On September 13, he gathered the leadership of his Popular Party in the cool mountain town of Cidra from which he had begun to organize the party in 1938. It was another endless "soul-searching" encounter. Muñoz declared that he had "sincerely and honestly believed" that the creation of the Commonwealth status would bring "tranquility and serenity" to the people. Yet he had to admit that the effect of the Fernós bill was the opposite. It was evident that Puerto Rico had "regressed" to the terrible status ideological wars of the past. The opposition parties and "other opposition forces" were principally to blame, he said, but that was beside the point: "Now we have to admit that the tranquility that should exist, does not exist, and Puerto Rico has a profound need that it exist."

Muñoz announced major changes in his status initiative. He had long ignored the demands of the Republican Statehood Party leaders for a plebiscite, insisting that it was a "sterile and dangerous" waste of time as long as statehood was economically impossible. A new bill, however, would include a clause to trigger a plebiscite when the island reached the per capita income of the poorest state. Puerto Rico then would be free to discard the Commonwealth and turn towards statehood without economic hardship. Independence, Muñoz declared, would not be included because his "thinking revolved around the fundamental concept of permanent union based on irremovable common citizenship."[16]

Again Muñoz insisted on a formula for Puerto Rico to contribute to the national treasury when the insular economy allowed it. This had never made any sense to most of the party leaders since it would clearly make even more difficult future efforts to increase the island's autonomy. It was obvious to leaders that the hysteria over the Fernós-Murray bill had shaken Muñoz.

Muñoz did something that further baffled both wings of his party, including Fernós himself. On April 6, 1960, while in Washington, he decided on the spur of the moment to testify at a House hearing on a constitutional amendment to allow residents of the District of Columbia to vote for the

---

16. Bothwell, *Puerto Rico: cien años de lucha política*, Vol. IV 241.

president. Muñoz came out strongly for Puerto Ricans, as well as all other American citizens regardless of where they lived, having the presidential vote.

The last thing the Popular Party leadership needed was another internal ideological bloodletting over an idea that had virtually no probability of becoming reality. Muñoz, in any case, declared that he was not formally petitioning to have Puerto Rico included into the constitutional amendment, but merely expressing a personal view "of principle."

Fernós wondered why Muñoz did it. He doubted that Puerto Rico could retain federal tax exemption if it participated in national elections. And would the presidential vote, he wondered, have the effect of incorporating the island into the U.S., thus undermining the status that they had been working so hard to "perfect?"

THE DEATH OF FERNÓS-MURRAY

By spring of 1960, it was hopeless. One of Muñoz's public relations specialists in Washington, Scott W. Runkle, wrote that the sense in Washington was that Muñoz and his party were simply moving too fast and applying too much pressure to make fundamental changes in the status that was still short of eight years old. The island, meanwhile, was now rushing towards the 1960 elections. Muñoz gave up. On May 3, Fernós formally withdrew the bill.

Muñoz and Fernós tried to minimize the political backlash. Committee chairman Aspinall and sub-committee chairman O'Brien tried to help by insisting that it was not "dead" but that simply time had run out to consider such an extremely complex bill. O'Brien held another public hearing to receive the testimony of former judge Paul D. Shriver, who had been commissioned to study the constitutional implications of the bill. O'Brien specifically declared that the primary reason for the hearing was "to demonstrate that we have not killed the bill but merely delayed action on it." He expressed absolute confidence that a bill "changing in some aspects" Commonwealth status would be approved by the next Congress. But the truth was that the bill was dead.

Muñoz, as always, attempted to anticipate the effect of the national elections on Puerto Rican issues. It seemed likely that Vice President Nixon would be elected. On the other hand, Muñoz did not know what to make of the young Senator from Massachusetts. Senator John F. Kennedy had written him several letters suggesting that Puerto Rico was indeed seducing "run-away-industries" from his state, offering a "tax-haven" and "cheap labor."

As always, Muñoz was edgy before an election. No one remotely believed that Ferré would defeat him. But he was concerned by the boost that Alaskan and Hawaiian statehood had given the Republicans. And as he had confessed in Cidra, the Fernós-Murray bill had certainly provoked insecurity among many Puerto Ricans. It was a major electoral challenge to match the 63 percent of the vote he obtained in 1956. And there was the natural wear and tear of a political party already twenty years in power. Muñoz had instituted a new appraisal of property value that had the effect of increasing property tax precisely in the urban areas that were becoming Republican Statehood strongholds. The Popular Party, "the party of the poor," was now seeing thousands of *jíbaros* entering the growing middle class.

As he had learned during his old Marxist days, profound economic changes inevitably change the political landscape. Island politics had shifted again. The challenge was no longer from the Left, from the *independentistas*. He was back to battling the Right, the statehooders.

But there was another change in his political hegemony: a change in the psychological landscape. The Fernós-Murray bill was not only his first failure in Congress since 1943, but his first important political defeat since 1940. His image of invincibility had cracked. Now he turned his attention to meet and roll back the statehood thrust, a movement still led by the same old Republican "capitalists" but that were now getting a lot of new blood and had a different dynamic. The 1960 campaign, however, took a bizarre turn that Muñoz and the confident statehood leaders could not imagine.

30 The "Sin Against God"

José Luis Feliú Pesquera, a 41-year-old lawyer, was one of the Popular Party legislators that switched to the Independence Party in 1948. First elected to the House of Representatives in 1944, Feliú returned as an *independentista* in 1952 and again in 1956. The following year, soon after the opening of the new legislative session, he introduced a bill to release all public school children an hour a week for voluntarily religious training in their church. The bill, one of hundreds introduced by minority legislators, was ignored.

Feliú was a somewhat offbeat politician: always with a colorful bow tie, his eyes hidden behind thick glasses, he spoke very fast in short, choppy sentences, and always seemed to be off in a rush. Now and then he took the floor to give a long, emotional speech, but he seemed strangely aloof, detached from the partisan warfare. He was definitely not part of the legislative political club and was rarely mentioned in the island media.

Early in 1960, however, several reporters began to take note. Every afternoon, after the House ended its work, Feliú spoke to an empty House floor defending his Bill 84. There was now an occasional story, not on the religious instruction bill, but on Feliú's lonely, seemingly hopeless crusade. The bill, on the surface, appeared to raise constitutional questions of separation of Church and State. In terms of educational policy, it appeared to make no sense. Half of all public school students were still in "double matriculation," receiving only three hours of instruction a day. Although there had been steady progress in reducing this percentage, new schools were simply not built fast enough to absorb the school population growth.

Muñoz and the PDP leadership saw no reason to cut off another hour of instruction when families already had so much time to send their children to receive religious education.

As Feliú continued his crusade, the bill began to gather support from other legislators, including from the Popular Party, and favorable newspaper editorial comment. Late one afternoon, Feliú somehow got his bill to the floor where it was quickly approved. But the PDP leadership immediately flip-flopped, recalled the bill and tabled it.

Now Feliú's daily House speech attracted more attention. He began to rally support from Church organizations that saw this as a gratuitous slap in the face of the island's large Catholic population. Soon there were demonstrations in front of the Capitol building. Feliú now displayed a surprising ability to whip up enthusiasm with electrifying speeches.

On May 7, 1960, the Bill 84 controversy escalated. *El Mundo* published a long statement by the Catholic Bishop of San Juan, James P. Davis, strongly criticizing Muñoz: "In this matter of religious instruction, Mr. Muñoz Marín cares very little how the Catholic *Populares* think who, after all, are the ones who made him Governor of Puerto Rico." Referring to Muñoz's opposition to the bill, the Bishop said: "A blow with the whip hurts, but it awakens us."[1]

Two weeks later, on May 22, the Catholic Church organized a massive demonstration in front of the Capitol building. The event had a strong effect on public opinion. Standing before a giant white cross and life-size photograph of Pope John XXIII, Bishop Davis cried out the words that the "frenzied crowd" demanded: "You are free to organize yourself into a political party!" The great mass broke out in chants: "*Viva el Papa!* For God! For God!"

On June 4, the Catholic newspaper, *El Piloto*, published another statement by Bishop Davis:

A Catholic has the grave duty not to give his vote to any anti-Catholic candidate: nor to any candidate that is not willing to defend the national right of parents to education: nor to any candidate who is not willing to repudiate publicly and legislatively the neo-Malthusian and sterilization laws... If for the very grave duty of conscience,

---

1. Bothwell, *Puerto Rico: cien años de lucha política* Vol. VI, 281.

it becomes indispensable that Catholics organize a political party, the Bishops declare that Catholic citizens have total freedom to organize themselves.

Muñoz was puzzled by what was taking place. There seemed to be no relation between the unwillingness to approve a relatively unimportant bill and the reaction of the Catholic Bishops and the thousands of laymen who were now on the warpath. How did his opposition to Bill 84 become such an oppressive "anti-Catholic" act? What had gotten into Bishop Davis, an affable person who had seemed to avoid controversy and with whom Muñoz always had a good relationship? Did he really believe that Muñoz was "whipping" him and island Catholics?

There was, of course, the open hostility of Brooklyn-born Bishop James McManus in Ponce, who had been on the island since 1929. Muñoz recalled that at the inauguration of Moscoso's 500th Fomento factory, a plant employing 2,000 Puerto Ricans, McManus, out of the blue, surprised everyone by turning to him to criticize his refusal to repeal the existing birth control laws. After the ceremony, knowing of the Bishop's feelings, Muñoz was still disturbed and confused, asking Moscoso: "Why did he do that?"

In March, 1960, openly critical of the Fernós-Murray Bill, McManus again publicly attacked Muñoz. He sent a letter published in *The New York Times*: "The present condition in Puerto Rico is that Governor Muñoz Marín is, by his own will, imposing upon the people of the island and on the Congress of the United States, an independence which was never granted and a 'voluntary association' which is absurd unless independence has been granted."[2] To Muñoz and his people, this again sounded like the Bishop was echoing precisely the Ferré-García Méndez "fear campaign."

In his reply published in *The New York Times*, Muñoz pointed out that McManus had quoted him as saying "We are happy to say that Puerto Rico is a free, self-governing Commonwealth, joined to the United States by its own choice." Not true, Muñoz said: it was President Eisenhower that said it in his recent visit to the island. This made the Bishop even sharper in his rebuttal to Muñoz: "The Puerto Rican people should choose statehood as their permanent status if they desire a safe and prosperous future... I am a clergyman because I am not, like the Governor, an opportunist..."

2. Alonso, *Muñoz Marín vs. the Bishops*, 43.

Clearly a remarkable phenomenon was taking place in Puerto Rico. The Catholic Bishops and the Church were actively organizing, not a party of Catholics as in Europe and Latin America, but a "Catholic Party:" a virtual Church party. This could not be explained solely on the Ponce Bishop's personal hostility nor on his suspected links to island statehood leaders. Many Catholic party activists were, in fact, *independentistas* that equated Muñoz's "betrayal" of independence and his passion for Operation Bootstrap to his materialistic, "*pancista*" mentality, his willingness to sacrifice spiritual ideals to satisfy the demands of the "stomach."

THE GROVAS MEETING

The Chancellor of the Diocese of San Juan, Msgr. Rafael Grovas, an island-born *independentista*, convened all parish priests to a meeting on May 30, 1960, a week after the Catholic mass rally. Each one was asked to bring a well-known and reliable Catholic layman. To his surprise, several priests spoke out strongly against the "Catholic Party." One Spanish priest recalled the anti-clericalism during the Spanish Civil War. Another who had served in 14 countries declared that nowhere were priests as respected as in Puerto Rico.

Informed of this meeting, and that it had ended "in chaos," Muñoz assumed that the new party initiative was "dead."[3] But he and many of those attending the meeting were surprised to find that immediately afterwards an island-wide drive began to inscribe the new "Christian Action Party." Inside Churches and throughout the island inscription forms were distributed and filled out. In many towns, priests joined laymen in actively promoting the party.

On June 30 there was another major escalation. Bishops Davis and McManus issued the first of a series of pastoral letters, read at all masses. "As guides and religious pastors to more than two million Catholics in Puerto Rico, we urge and exhort all the people to give their help and support to the new Christian Action Party."

---

3. Ibid., 52.

Muñoz still could not figure out what was taking place. Into his reelection campaign, as he stared out the window of the campaign bus, he shook his head and muttered: "It's as if some time-machine had flung us back to the Middle Ages. Incredible... incredible." In forty years of public service it seemed that everything had been thrown at him—from allegations of being a drug user to the Nationalists' bullets. Now he was facing a campaign where the Bishops denounced him as "anti-religious, anti-Catholic, anti-God."

KENNEDY GETS THE NEWS

It was "incredible" also for John F. Kennedy, a Catholic, who told his campaign manager Ted Sorensen: "If enough voters realize that Puerto Rico is American soil, this election is lost."[4] Kennedy had achieved a critical victory in the predominately Protestant state of West Virginia. This not only knocked Hubert Humphrey out of the race, but, Kennedy hoped, would begin to defuse the "religion issue." He followed this with a major speech in Houston before Protestant clergy where he declared: "I believe in an America with separation of Church and State—where no Catholic prelate would tell the President (should he be a Catholic) how to act, and no Protestant minister would tell his parishioners for whom to vote—where no church or church school is granted any public funds or political preference...where there is no Catholic vote, no anti-Catholic vote, no bloc voting of any kind..." Kennedy's people were delighted by the reaction. "It was the best speech of the campaign," Ted Sorensen wrote, and one of the most important of his life.

But then the stunning news broke that the Catholic Bishops in Puerto Rico were indeed "ordering" all island Catholics how to vote. "Their action," Sorensen reported, "aroused a bigger storm in our election than in Puerto Rico... American protestant leaders saw in the Puerto Rican pastoral letter a confirmation of their worst fears. On that basis, said Denver's Methodist Bishop, 'I shall not mark my ballot for a Roman Catholic candidate for the Presidency.'" The Puerto Rican story, Serensen continued, "was featured in

---

4. Sorensen, *Kennedy*, 209.

publications ranging from hate sheets to denominational newspapers, often under the headline, "They said it couldn't happen in America."

It was happening in Puerto Rico. The political status issue was buried in a campaign that became an ordeal for Muñoz and hundreds of thousands of his followers. At Church masses throughout the island, priests told the parishioners: "A vote for the Christian Action Party is a vote for Christ."

Muñoz racked his brains: *What have I done to provoke this?* Yes, he was not, and never had been, a practicing Catholic, although his wife, Inés, was, as was her family. But he considered everything he had attempted to do in Puerto Rico "profoundly Christian." Was there anything more authentically Christian than his life-long crusade and his success against economic exploitation and social injustice? What were all his speeches and philosophizing these past five years on Operation Serenity about if not an emotional rejection of a "materialistic" lifestyle, an exaltation of "spiritual and moral" values? What was all his sermonizing on the need to direct economic development towards a "good civilization" if not a plea for a profoundly Christian society? Had he not given Puerto Rico an uncompromisingly honest government administration, as honest as anywhere in the world? Wasn't this in keeping with Christian morality?

Even the attack that he was an "advocate" of Church-banned artificial birth control was not totally accurate. The law legalizing birth control had been approved in 1936 by the old Coalition before he came to power. Yes, he resisted Catholic pressure to repeal it. But his government policy towards birth control was neutral, as it was towards migration to the mainland. Indeed, Moscoso and others in his administration were frustrated by Muñoz's refusal to implement activist "family planning" programs.

Even the old attacks on his lifestyle, Muñoz insisted, were outdated. Everyone in Puerto Rico knew that since coming to power in 1940, and since his family and marriage to Inés Mendoza, he had given up his womanizing, his heavy drinking, even his smoking. Muñoz believed in the existence of God and confessed to intimates that he prayed. Once, talking to friends, he wondered out loud if his prayers had to be "translated thousands of times before it reached God."

Muñoz was now under the most ferocious attack against a political leader in Puerto Rican history. Yet how could he, himself a fierce political campaigner, counterattack without falling into the trap of sounding as if he were indeed "anti-Catholic, anti-God?" Just as important, he had to combat the new party and the Catholic hierarchy, using all the power of his political machine and personality, without deepening the wounds that the conflict was inflicting on thousands of Catholics that followed him. It was a thin but a vital line.

He came upon the strategy. He would combat the "Catholic Party" without attacking the Catholic Church in Puerto Rico, or even the Bishops. He would campaign, not against the Bishops, but against their "error." "We Puerto Ricans," he said in a rally in Coamo, "shall fight to defend the traditional religion of the majority of the Puerto Rican people against the grave errors of the Bishops who are transitory, while our religion is permanent."[5] At another meeting in late August, he said, "My advice to all Puerto Ricans is to respect the priests." Then, after a long pause, his voice deepening, he added: "My advice to the priests is to respect the free political ideas of their parishioners."

In the Popular Party's massive convention in August, organized to be a show of force, Muñoz deliberately omitted all mention of the Church conflict in his long and passionate address. He told reporters afterwards, "To bring up the topic of religious intervention in politics before 100,000 people is as improper in August as in May, just as dangerous to the peace in the heart of the Puerto Rican family. That is why I did not do it."

But at the convention, Muñoz and the Popular Party unwittingly made the conflict even worse. Muñoz believed that the party platform approved at the convention appeased the Catholics. It stated the importance of religion in "the aspiration of the Puerto Rican people for a good civilization." It detailed all the actions taken by the government to benefit the different religions, including helping to establish the Catholic University, setting rural land aside for chapels, extending school lunch programs to religious schools that

---

5. Alonso, *Muñoz Marín vs. the Bishops*, 97.

served poor children. But then it added: "We are concerned that part of our public opinion wishes to impose dogmas of personal conduct on another part of our public opinion by means of laws which prohibit and sanction... The political philosophy of the Popular Party implies that only those acts that the general consensus of Puerto Rican public opinion considers immoral, such as murder, robbery, perjury, etc., may be prohibited with sanctions..."

Muñoz and his party, confused from the beginning by the "Catholic Party," were now jolted by the reaction to the platform. Bishops Davis and McManus, now joined by the Puerto Rican Titular Bishop of Lares, Luis Aponte Martínez, issued another pastoral letter on October 23, two weeks before the elections. Quoting extensively from the Popular Party platform, they declared that it constituted "morality by consensus." It was now beyond doubt that Muñoz and his party were determined to "exclude God from government... This philosophy ends the Ten Commandments of God... to be substituted by the popular and human criteria."

Read at all masses, the letter made explicit what had been implied since the party was first organized. The Bishops "prohibited Catholics" from voting for the Popular Party. The following Sunday, still another and longer pastoral letter was read at the masses. A vote for Muñoz and the Popular Party, the Bishops declared, was "an offense to God." Now just days before the election, all Catholics were reminded that to disobey their Bishop "is to commit a sin."

THE VATICAN MISSION

Teodoro Moscoso was in Madrid, on his way to Edinburgh, Scotland to give a speech on economic development. His hotel room phone rang. It was Muñoz from San Juan. Did he know about the latest pastoral letters? Yes, Moscoso answered, he had read about them just moments earlier in the European edition of *The Herald Tribune*. "Cancel your trip to Scotland," Muñoz said. "I want you to go to Rome and see the Pope personally and tell him what is happening in Puerto Rico." Was Muñoz panicking? Certainly he was aware that the Vatican, from the beginning, had refused to get involved in the conflict. When it did issue a statement, on October 27, it declared: "The Holy See has no knowledge of the document prepared by the Bishops of Puerto Rico, which is not surprising, because the prelates are free to give to the faithful in religious and moral matters such instructions as in their pastoral consciences they consider useful and necessary."[6]

In the United States, however, Church leaders were clearly disturbed. Muñoz had sent prominent members of his administration who were active in the Catholic Church, such as Roberto de Jesus and Rafael Picó, to urge American Cardinals to publicly express their opposition to Davis and McManus. Back in July, at a meeting in New York attended by De Jesús, Francis Cardinal Spellman personally attempted to dissuade Davis and McManus from proceeding with the new party. But the Cardinal found it "impossible to deter McManus."[7] Questioned by reporters whether Catholics voting for Muñoz would be "excommunicated," Spellman answered that while he agreed that it would be a sin of disobedience, it was "without penalty."

In Senator Kennedy's home state, Boston's Cardinal Cushing came closest to explicitly attacking the Puerto Rico Bishops. On October 29th, he declared that it was "in total disagreement with the North American tradition if the Catholic authorities in [Puerto Rico] would attempt to dictate the political vocation of its citizens. This has never been a part of our history and I pray to God that it never will."

While the Vatican refused to intervene, the Apostolic Delegate to the United States, Archbishop Egidio Vagnozzi, declared that he "was confident that the Catholic hierarchy in the United States would never assume a political attitude similar to that of the Bishops in Puerto Rico."[8] Cushing, in turn, declared that he was "pleased to add his voice to that of Archbishop Vagnozzi."

In Puerto Rico, meanwhile, behind the scenes, Muñoz attempted to get the Bishops removed from Puerto Rico. On September 14, 1960, he appealed directly to the Pope. The departure of the Bishops, he wrote, was "the only remedy which at this point could avoid graver consequences that I fear could develop. His Eminence may be assured that as far as I am concerned,

---

6. Ibid., 125.

7. Ibid., 58.

8. Ibid., 124.

as Governor and political leader, I shall always exercise the maximum of my influence so that religion would not suffer by this situation, but I am afraid that it might not be possible unless measures are applied to the situation."

The Vatican did not reply until a month later, on October 20th. Cardinal Domenico Tardini, the Secretary of State, wrote: "Please accept my sincere thanks for having transmitted the information to me. The Holy See follows with great interest the religious situation in Puerto Rico." He added that "the contents" of his letter "have been given due consideration." The Bishops themselves reacted in the last pastoral letter: "to change the Bishops would resolve nothing... the principles would have to be changed and these are immutable, as are immutable the truths of God..."

Moscoso knew that his trip to Rome would evoke the same response. But receiving the force of Muñoz's rage through the telephone, he knew better not to argue with him. At the Vatican, Cardinal Tardini did not receive him. He was taken, instead, to Msgr. Agostino Casaroli, who insisted he knew very little, not only about the Church situation on the island, but about Puerto Rico itself. Moscoso, however, could see on top of Casaroli's desk a high stack of press clippings, documents, and communications from the Bishops of Puerto Rico. In his report back to Muñoz, Moscoso conceded: "The mission you asked me to fulfill was a failure."[9]

The Eerie Silence

Muñoz's campaign became more difficult. As he did in 1940, he appealed to Puerto Rico's "manhood." Having freed themselves from the "economic interests," Muñoz asked if now the Puerto Ricans were going to permit the Bishops to again "enslave" them by dictating how to vote.

The campaign ended on a surreal note. The Church crisis had so overwhelmed the campaign that instead of pleading for continued support for his economic and social programs, or for Commonwealth status, Muñoz's traditional election eve radio address sounded like a confession:

---

9. Ibid., 100.

On this solemn occasion, I swear to you by the God I believe in with all the force of my soul that there is nothing in the Popular Party, nor in its program, nor in its attitude, nor in its history that is not profoundly Christian, that is not based on the deep respect of all creatures of God on earth, on the deepest respect for man's justice, his human person and his freedom.

Finally, on November 8th, an eerie silence descended on all of Puerto Rico. The sun-drenched streets were empty: for once, not a radio or loudspeaker was heard. Voters were inside the precincts, seated in school rooms, many squeezed into small children's seats, waiting for the doors to close and the voting to start at 2 p.m. It was, in many ways, like a religious ritual where everyone displays respect, even reverence for the voting process. Political antagonists, waiting for their names to be called to cast their votes, quietly, pleasantly talked to each other. It's all over. Everyone can return to being human, civil, and respectful again. Now it's a matter of depositing the ballot, going back home, putting on the radio, and in the early evening begin to hear the earliest return, usually from some small, rural precinct in the center of the island.

The returns that evening gave Muñoz another big victory: 58 percent, 431,406 Puerto Ricans, voted for him and his party, the vast majority of them Catholics ignoring the Bishops' order and admonition that they were committing a "sin." Even more striking, the Christian Action Party got only 52,096 votes, five percent. Muñoz had won the most emotionally-wrenching political battle of his life.

Catching Up

Lost in the ordeal was Muñoz's original goal for this campaign: to stop the pro-statehood momentum. He had hoped, at least, that the Statehood Republican Party's "neutrality" in this storm would hurt them at the polls. Both Ferré and García Méndez stated that while they supported the doctrine of separation of Church and State, Muñoz was to blame for the crisis for having established a "totalitarian" government. Privately, Muñoz seethed with anger at what he saw as a "petty" partisan reaction in the face of such a threat to island democracy.

The Statehood Party, however, registered another big increase in votes: from 172,838 in 1956, to 252,364. It would have been bigger, García Méndez was convinced, if not for the Church battle. Many of the CAP votes, he believed, would have gone to his party, while many "pro-American" Protestants were induced to switch to the Popular Party. "The Bishops," García commented to his brother-in-law and party candidate for governor, Ferré, "gave Muñoz the issue that he lacked in order to combat the formidable issue of statehood..."[10] In any case, the 1960 elections placed the statehood party as Muñoz's major opposition force. It was still far behind, but it was catching up. Since 1952, the Popular Party had increased its votes by only 26,474: the Statehood Republican Party by 166,776.

One year later, President Kennedy revealed to Teodoro Moscoso, whom he had named Ambassador to Venezuela and then Coordinator of the Alliance for Progress, how close the Puerto Rican Bishops' "incredible action" came to costing him the elections. Kennedy asked Moscoso to sit in at a meeting with special assistant Larry O'Brien, who had done a survey among Democratic Party chairmen throughout the nation. One of the questions was the effect of the Puerto Rico issue. The estimate was that it cost Kennedy "over one million votes." Kennedy's margin over Richard Nixon in the popular vote was 119,460 votes.

For Muñoz, it was a personal political achievement that paralleled his 1940 victory. Somehow, he had walked the thin line: he crushed the "Catholic Party" without provoking the anti-clericalism that he feared, and, remarkably, without any damage to the Church itself. After the elections, however, Muñoz did not forgive. The Popular Party-controlled Legislature launched a full-scale investigation into the "miraculous" registration of the Christian Action Party. No one had understood how in just months its organizers had filed over 70,000 inscription forms, a laborious task that required the certification of each one by a judge.

Massive forging of the petitions was uncovered. A district judge in Bayamón who had certified most of them pleaded guilty before the insular Supreme Court and was removed from the judiciary. Two party candidates that had been awarded seats in the House and Senate under the constitutional

---

10. Bothwell, *Puerto Rico: cien años de lucha política* Vol. IV, 325.

guaranteed minority clause were expelled, among them the energetic representative that had started it all with his religion education bill, José Feliú Pesquera.

On July 2, 1962, Muñoz finally traveled to Rome and was received by Pope John XXIII. It had been agreed beforehand that he would not bring up the battle with the Bishops. The Vatican, of course, knew of Muñoz's insistence in having Davis, now Archbishop of San Juan, and especially McManus, taken out of the island. Muñoz had asked Rafael Picó, the former head of the Planning Board and now president of the Government Development Bank, to intervene. President Kennedy had named Picó as his emissary to the Dominican Republic after the fall of the Trujillo dictatorship. There he met and worked with the Papal Nuncio with jurisdiction over Puerto Rico, the Archbishop Emanuelle Clarizo. While anxious to end the conflict, the Archbishop assured Muñoz and Picó that his demand to remove the Bishops was simply unacceptable. Following the Muñoz visit with the Pope, Picó met privately with the same Church official that had declined to meet with Moscoso two years earlier. Picó brought up Muñoz's demand. "Monseigneur Tardini," Picó wrote, "expressed great surprise and even indignation at such a request."

But in fact, the Vatican was responding to Muñoz's request. The Papal Nuncio Clarizo and Picó arranged a meeting between Archbishop Davis and Muñoz. Picó and Roberto De Jesús had never seen Davis as the person that provoked the conflict, but as one who allowed himself to be swept by the passion and anti-Muñoz militancy of McManus and Rafael Grovas. This meeting, however, did not go well. Both Muñoz and Davis had still not recovered from the battle.

But one afternoon, working at his La Fortaleza office, Muñoz instructed his personal assistant, Luis Laboy, to call "Bishop" and ask him to come over as soon as possible. Muñoz was referring to Fred Bishop, the head of the FBI office in San Juan. But Laboy heard "the Bishop." Davis was surprised by the sudden request to go to La Fortaleza. On the way, he wondered if there was another crisis. When Laboy ushered him into Muñoz's office, Muñoz first was shocked, then broke out in laughter. He explained the error—"No, Laboy sent for the wrong Bishop!"—profusely excusing himself. Then Davis laughed. "Wouldn't you join me for a glass of sherry?" Muñoz asked. Davis agreed. The ice was broken.

By 1964, Muñoz got his wish. Both Bishops had left Puerto Rico: Davis returned to New Mexico and McManus to Brooklyn. The third Bishop that signed the last two pastoral letters but had always remained at the margin of the conflict, the Puerto Rican Luis Aponte Martínez, was elevated to Cardinal. The Church-State crisis of Puerto Rico was over.

31 John F. Kennedy

The Kennedy presidency, historian Arturo Morales Carrión wrote, became "the high water mark in the Muñoz era in Puerto Rican history."[1] It was a period that "saw the closest relationship ever established between a Puerto Rican political leader and a U.S. president. Kennedy had a genuine liking for the people of Puerto Rico and great admiration for Muñoz and his achievements."

Kennedy first met Muñoz in 1958, when he decided to give his first campaign speech on Latin America in Puerto Rico. "For U.S. officials entrusted with reshaping policy after the warning-laden Nixon trip," *Time* magazine reported, "the Puerto Rican advance is a textbook of imaginative lessons."[2] Kennedy, seeking a dramatically distinct Latin American policy for his upcoming campaign, became familiar with these "imaginative lessons." His principal advisor on Latin America was the veteran New Dealer with vast experience in the region, Adolf Berle, who was also an advisor and friend of Muñoz.

Berle agreed with Muñoz that revolutionary change was inevitable in Latin America and the United States found itself "on the wrong side"—the reactionary, totalitarian side—that was doomed to lose. This, in fact, was also the view of Republican candidate Nixon after his near-fatal experience in Venezuela. The Nixon visit had dramatically alerted the Americans that the Cold War competition was now raging throughout a Latin America

1. Morales Carrión, *Puerto Rico: A Political and Cultural History*, 298.
2. *Time*, 38.

sinking in poverty and social injustice. The difficult question for the U.S. was not which side to be on, but who to trust and support in this "revolutionary ferment." Muñoz argued strongly that it should be the "democratic left" then emerging in such countries as Venezuela, Costa Rica and Colombia.

There was indeed an element of risk in distinguishing the democratic from the totalitarian left. Muñoz urged American policy makers to trust popularly-elected leaders such as Venezuela's Romulo Betancourt, who had begun his career as a communist but evolved into a democratic reformer. Betancourt spent several years in exile in Puerto Rico, carefully observing Muñoz's social and economic transformation. Muñoz assured the Kennedy people that the rhetoric of these leaders was always deeply nationalistic and may sound hostile to Americans. But he could attest that Betancourt, like José Figueres in Costa Rica, were essentially committed to American democratic principles. These were also, Muñoz pointed out, tough warriors who had survived many battles: only they were dedicated and hard enough to "compete with the totalitarians."[3]

Berle, in turn, assured Kennedy that he could trust Muñoz. The Senator did, declaring in the 1958 speech in Puerto Rico that it was a mistake to believe "all Latin American agitation is Communist-inspired—that every anti-American voice is the voice of Moscow." Kennedy went on to express his conviction that "most citizens of Latin America share our dedication to an anti-Communist crusade to save what we call free enterprise."

Several weeks later, Fidel Castro made his triumphant entry into Havana. Prodded by Nixon's push for a new approach to Latin American dictators, the Eisenhower administration had turned against Cuban strongman Fulgencio Batista. Muñoz and the Puerto Ricans enthusiastically believed the "lessons" of Puerto Rico were applicable to Cuba and looked forward to Castro becoming part of the "democratic left." Muñoz quickly offered the new Cuban leader Puerto Rico's assistance, sending a team of high-level administrators to Havana. Cuban Minister of the Treasury, Dr. Rufo López-Fresquet enthusiastically responded leading a mission of 12 important businessmen to San Juan.[4] Castro, however, rebuffed Muñoz

---

3. Schlesinger, *A Thousand Days: John F. Kennedy in the White House*, 765.

4. López-Fresquet, *My Fourteen Months with Castro*, 102.

and his offer. By early 1961, López-Fresquet was in exile and Castro was actively supporting and training subversive groups in Puerto Rico.

As Cuba moved deeper into the Soviet orbit, the new Kennedy administration turned more to Puerto Rico. Another of President Kennedy's advisors on Latin America, historian Arthur Schlesinger, Jr., was an admirer of Muñoz. The President's Latin American Task Force, he wrote, "worked closely with Luis Muñoz Marín, the remarkable governor of Puerto Rico. Together they developed a network of unofficial relationships with the *partidos populares* of Latin America. Kennedy, whose friendship with Muñoz began with the Puerto Rico trip of 1958, fell heir to these ideas and relationships."[5]

The new President named Muñoz's associates to key administrative positions. He appointed Arturo Morales Carrión as Deputy Assistant Secretary of State for Latin American Affairs, and Teodoro Moscoso to run the Alliance for Progress. According to Schlesinger, "The Puerto Rican experience indeed was an important source of ideas for the Alliance."[6]

With such a friendly, admiring President in the White House, Muñoz decided to attempt a new status initiative. If democratic Puerto Rico was the alternative to a communist Cuba, this was the time to return to Congress to finally remove the flaws in "America's showcase of democracy." This time Muñoz would not make the mistake of rushing unprepared to the U.S. Senate. Now he would make sure he had the understanding and support of Kennedy and his administration beforehand. In addition to the old Washington establishment liberals, Adolf Berle and Abe Fortas, Schlesinger returned from a tour of Latin America even more solidly behind Muñoz's "democratic left." There was also support from the young lawyer Richard Goodwin, who during the campaign was Kennedy's speechwriter and stayed on at the White House as an influential advisor on Latin America. A free spirit, Goodwin was distrusted and disliked by many in the State Department, as being a loose cannon. But that was just the type of person, Muñoz believed, who would deal creatively with the island's status. Muñoz was further encouraged by the appointment of Steward Udall as Secretary of the Interior. Udall had been a member of the House Territories and Insular Affairs Committee and a good friend of fellow committee member, Resident Commisioner Fernós.

---

5. Ibid., 192.
6. Ibid., 765.

Kennedy came through. On July 25, 1961, the ninth anniversary of the Commonwealth of Puerto Rico, he issued instructions to "all departments, agencies, and officials of the executive branch of government to faithfully and carefully observe and respect" the "singular position of Commonwealth status." The executive order specifically mentioned that the island's status was "in the nature of a compact." All fundamental matters regarding the status would now be referred directly to the Office of the President.

Kennedy named a commission of high-level administrators to meet with Muñoz and his advisors. Berle, Goodwin, Schlesinger, and the newly-appointed special assistant to serve as liaison on Puerto Rican matters, Lee White, were joined by William Bundy from the Defense Department, Nicolas B. Katzenbach from Justice, and Abraham Chaynes, legal advisor to the State Department. With Muñoz were Fernós, legal consultant Trías Monge, and Muñoz's chief of staff, Heriberto Alonso. Insular Secretary of State Roberto Sánchez Vilella, whom Muñoz was quietly grooming to eventually replace him as Governor, joined the committee later on.

Muñoz and his people had never before felt so uninhibited in proposing and discussing ideas to achieve "maximum autonomy." So as not to restrict the free flow of ideas, the committee's existence was undisclosed. This would hopefully insure that the ideas were not leaked and used by the statehood and independence opposition to sabotage their efforts. And indeed Muñoz and his people began brainstorming with a radical idea: as an "intellectual exercise," instead of asking how much power the U.S. was willing to yield to Puerto Rico, why not start with the assumption that all power resided on the island? And the question became: how much power should Puerto Rico yield as absolutely essential to its "association" with the United States? The Kennedy members of the committee, aware of the President's strong desire to please Muñoz and Puerto Rico, at first went along. As the brainstorming continued, the Puerto Ricans came up with one "creative idea" after another, such as instituting a joint United States-Puerto Rico Supreme Court. But gradually the Kennedy people became uneasy as they began to suspect that this "intellectual exercise" seemed to be drifting further away from American constitutional doctrine and political reality.

There was nothing wrong with the principle as Muñoz often expressed it. There were four essential pillars to Commonwealth status: common citizenship, currency, defense, and market. All other matters not vital to these "pillars" should be under Puerto Rican control. The problem was how to sort out what was and wasn't "vital." Before long, the Kennedy people found that unraveling the Puerto Rico-U.S. relationship that had evolved since 1900 was a nightmarish task. The Muñoz lawyers believed that Puerto Rico, never having been incorporated legally, was not "part of the United States." But in reality Puerto Rico was linked to the U.S. by hundreds of arteries in which authority flowed between the Federal Government and the island, from aviation, to national parks, to communications, to immigration, to off-coast and inland waterways, postal service, banking laws, the FBI and other federal law enforcement agencies. Even the U.S. Supreme Court, which considered the early-century "insular cases" among its most difficult, had never sorted out what parts of the U.S. Constitution applied to Puerto Rico and what parts did not.

The Kennedy people began to feel dazed by the complexity of the minute surgery required to follow Muñoz's "intellectual exercise." The devil was indeed in the details. Muñoz, in turn, sensed their bewilderment and misgivings when Goodwin, the most supportive and adventuresome in the committee, at one point interrupted to ask: Why not statehood? Muñoz was silent for a moment. This was returning to square one. Economically impossible, Muñoz answered. Goodwin asked why. Chaynes came in: let's suppose Puerto Rico could resolve all its economic issues, would you still be against statehood? The people could then return to statehood, Muñoz answered, but he would still be personally opposed.[7]

By late October, 1962, the misgivings in the Kennedy team had sharpened into "serious doubts." Justice Department official Harold F. Reis, regarded as the expert on Puerto Rican status matters, expressed to Trías Monge that the proposals raised "substantial problems from the point of view of the United States."[8] Reis questioned the fundamental premise of the entire exercise: that Puerto Rico, a body of two and a half million American citizens, could fit within the American system with "maximum autonomy." The new thrust to "perfect Commonwealth" was slipping away.

---

7. Trías Monge, *Historia constitucional de Puerto Rico* Vol. IV, 182.
8. Ibid., 196.

Muñoz, however, still relied on Kennedy's personal support. On December 15, 1961, a month after the glittering "Camelot" White House dinner in honor of Muñoz and the Pablo Casals concert, a radiant Kennedy and his wife Jacqueline emerged from Air Force One under the afternoon sun in San Juan. On the way to Venezuela and Colombia, Kennedy stayed overnight at La Fortaleza. Over 700,000 Puerto Ricans lined the avenues and streets from the airport into Old San Juan to gape at the beautiful young couple. After dinner, Muñoz and Kennedy talked about the Catholic Bishops and the havoc they created in the presidential campaign, then about the Alliance for Progress and Cuba. The program to put the Americans on the side of political and economic development, after the April 17, 1961 Bay of Pigs disaster, was taking on a predominantly Cold War mission. This gave Muñoz another opportunity to reiterate the need to come up with new legislation to remove the "defects" in Commonwealth status in 1962. He informed Kennedy that Commonwealth would reach its tenth anniversary, a good time to complete the unfinished business of Puerto Rico's relation to the U.S. Kennedy agreed. Seven months later, at the massive anniversary celebration on July 25, 1962, Muñoz read a letter from Kennedy enthusiastically acknowledging that the time had come to achieve the "maximum development" of commonwealth status and promising to work with Muñoz to achieve it.

WORKING FOR KENNEDY

Back on the island for the Christmas season, Teodoro Moscoso spent hours talking to Muñoz about Washington and Congress under the Kennedy presidency. Moscoso shared his experiences and disappointments running the Alliance for Progress. As they talked well into the night, Muñoz began to detect something he had never before seen in Moscoso. The always irrepressible "human dynamo" that Muñoz had so much depended on, and at times feared, now seemed disheartened.

Kennedy, Moscoso explained, had two programs that he considered "his own:" The Peace Corps, assigned to his brother in law, Sargeant Shriver, and the Alliance for Progress. It was, of course, a great honor for him and all of Puerto Rico that Kennedy had entrusted him with the enormous challenge of running a $20 billion dollar program with the monumental goal of lifting the economies of all of Central and South America. But there was a gap between Kennedy's intentions, his rhetoric, his sincere promises, and his actions. Moscoso's first jolt, after being called to Washington from Venezuela, was that in spite of the inspiring speeches and of hearing Kennedy tell him that there was no bigger challenge in American history, the Alliance for Progress was buried deep inside the State Department bureaucracy. Moscoso vehemently protested. During his trip down to Puerto Rico, Venezuela, and Colombia, Kennedy assured him that he would remove the Alliance from the State Department, giving it its own identity as with the Peace Corps. But months later, as Moscoso was about to physically move the agency out of the Department building, he was informed that Kennedy had changed his mind. Moscoso's warning to Muñoz was sobering. "Don't automatically translate his charm and friendship, his soaring rhetoric, into concrete action. Kennedy can win your heart, but he can also break it."

A few days later, on January 4, 1963, Muñoz recalled Moscoso's warning when he was informed that the Kennedy joint committee had abandoned the original Muñoz plan to go to Congress with a bill to create a totally new, fully autonomous Commonwealth status. The administration now proposed that Congress be asked only to name still another study commission that would take in all three status alternatives. For Muñoz, this was indeed to go back to square one.

SAYLOR'S MANHANDLING OF MUÑOZ

But it was only the beginning. At the May, 1963 public hearings, Pennsylvania Republican John P. Saylor subjected Muñoz to a "rude, arrogant, at times insulting" interrogation.[9] In a hostile tone, he asked Muñoz if he would appoint himself to the proposed status study commission. When Muñoz answered that he would appoint "the people that I thought would be most useful," Saylor shot back: "You didn't answer my question!"

---

9. Ibid., 205.

Muñoz tensed up: "I did." "No, sir, I asked you whether or not you would appoint yourself to the Commission." Muñoz's fists gripped the end of the table: "Let us wait until the bill is passed." Saylor then said: "This is a typical situation that I have found. The Governor of Puerto Rico, when he finally gets up right against a proposition, he doesn't commit himself. I want an answer to the question."

Since the battles with Tugwell, Muñoz was a veteran in dealing with congressional hostility and it was evident that Saylor, known to be close to island statehood leaders, was well briefed. But this was different in the directness and acrimony of his attack. Saylor then tore into the bill. He said that it denied Puerto Ricans "freedom of choice," which was in violation of the status resolution approved by all the parties in the insular legislature. Saylor then asked Muñoz whether Puerto Rican children "pledged allegiance to the American flag." Muñoz answered that Puerto Rican children do so as often as American children on the mainland: "The loyalty of the people of Puerto Rico, the same as the loyalty of the people of the States, is not judged by how many times they make an external manifestation of loyalty." Saylor interrupted in obvious disgust: "I am one of those, Governor, that believes that as you train... a child so shall he live. I find nothing wrong in seeing to it that daily we pledge allegiance to the flag of the United States of America."

"I find nothing wrong with it either," Muñoz said, to which Saylor replied, "I don't know..." He went on, asking Muñoz if when he mentions "good citizens," whether he is referring to Puerto Ricans as "American citizens." Muñoz responded: "I said so in at least five or six other places in my statement, Congressman. If your objection is to the number of repetitions..." Saylor got to the heart of his attack: "all of this commonwealth that you keep talking about" was something that Muñoz had "built up... in Puerto Rico" and was never "the intention of Congress then, and I hope not now."

Saylor finally got under Muñoz's skin. The Puerto Ricans in the hearing room wondered if he would explode. After moments of silence, Muñoz said that if the Representative was right, "then Puerto Rico is still a colony of the United States. If it is still a colony of the United States it should stop being a colony as soon as possible for the honor of the United States and for the sense of self-respect of the people of Puerto Rico."

Saylor's manhandling of Muñoz was sensationally reported back in Puerto Rico. Muñoz supporters asked why Committee Chairman O'Brien had permitted the affront. Even more puzzling was Resident Commissioner Fernós's silence: why didn't he interrupt Saylor? Fernós downplayed the confrontation, pointing out to the reporters that Saylor was famous for his abrasive and insulting style of questioning, especially high-ranking Kennedy cabinet members. The island media revealed that his questions had indeed been prepared by a Republican Statehood Party "communications consultant." Later in 1964, Republican Statehood Party gubernatorial candidate, Luis A. Ferré, a contributor to the Saylor reelection committee, traveled to Pennsylvania to campaign for him.

WHAT IS COMMONWEALTH?

As bad and "insulting" as the Saylor confrontation was, Muñoz and his people were not surprised. But they were more than surprised by the Kennedy people. They were puzzled that representing the Kennedy administration at the House hearings was a low-level official, the interim deputy director of the Budget Bureau, Harold Seidman. After expressing the administration's endorsement "in principle" of the bill, Seidman declared that it was too restrictive, that its study of the status question should be as wide-ranging as possible: "Accordingly, we believe the Commission should be directed simply to develop proposals for a new compact or for such other arrangements as it may find to be feasible and appropriate." Then Seidman dropped a bombshell. He criticized the concept of "permanent union" under the Commonwealth formula, emphasizing that he was not expressing his personal views but that of the administration. Muñoz and his team were flabbergasted. This had been precisely Saylor's argument. The Kennedy administration had placed itself squarely on the side of the enemies of Commonwealth status. What had happened? Had Kennedy, for reasons that no one could imagine, doublecrossed Muñoz? Representative O'Brien, Fernós recorded years later, "could not hide his disgust" and commented privately that he was going to drop the bill altogether.[10]

---

10. Fernós Isern, *Estado Libre Asociado de Puerto Rico*, 565.

Accepting that the Seidman testimony "created perplexity, anxiety and confusion," Fernós tried to calm Muñoz down by insisting that this was another, by no means the first, bureaucratic glitch in the Kennedy administration. Muñoz did not want explanations. He wanted the White House itself to "clarify" the President's position. After a long night of telephone calls by Muñoz, Fernós and others, the following day, May 20, the White House issued a "clarification." The press statement declared that the President "strongly endorses" the Muñoz bill and "reiterates his commitment" to continue working with Muñoz, as expressed in the exchange of letters of July 25th. As to the "permanence of a perfected Commonwealth status," the White House continued, the administration also was in total accord with Muñoz's testimony: Commonwealth was as "permanent" as determined by the "mutual consent" of Puerto Rico and the United States. The statement closed expressing the administration's desire for "prompt and favorable" consideration of the bill.

But Fernós was wrong. This was not another breakdown in communication in the administration. The fact was that no degree of good will towards Muñoz and Commonwealth status in the White House could overcome the essential reality that, as Trías Monge confessed later, Puerto Rico's position was simply "unintelligible," not only to most members of Congress and to the American people, but to the Kennedy people themselves.

Representative O'Brien admitted as much in the House debate for the watered-down bill on October 23, 1963. The veteran sub-committee chairman posed the question that many members of Congress were asking themselves: Why this study? Why not leave things alone in Puerto Rico. "The answer is this: No one in Congress or out of it knows exactly what is the Commonwealth of Puerto Rico." His committee, he declared, simply could not deal with such a "monumental task" as unraveling the Puerto Rico status issue. It could not respond to the demand for a "perfected" Commonwealth or for statehood. So this bill "calls for nothing more than a high-level study; that prejudges nothing: that commits Congress to nothing."[11]

Fernós recorded in his memoirs that after the May, 1963 hearings, "I continued alone in charge of the bill until its final approval." In Puerto Rico, the statehood leadership celebrated that they had, for the second time, stopped

---

11. Ibid., 583.

Muñoz cold. What had begun two years earlier as a Kennedy-Muñoz juggernaut to "perfect" Commonwealth status had become another "study" that "commits Congress to nothing." Disappointed, Muñoz shot back at the opposition: "If this bill finally becomes a law, it is to be hoped that the Commission's work will liberate forever the people of Puerto Rico from the superficiality and the lack of intellectual integrity to which certain leaders have taken this so important matter."[12]

Moscoso's assessment proved right again. Here was another gap between rhetoric and action. While his administration deeply disappointed Muñoz in its handling of his status initiative, Kennedy himself continued to express his admiration for the Puerto Rican leader. In 1963, he awarded Muñoz the Presidential Medal of Freedom, the nation's highest tribute to a civilian: "Poet, politician, public servant, and patriot. He has taken his people to new heights of dignity and purpose, transforming a stricken land into a vital society."

Kennedy never got the opportunity to give the medal to Muñoz. Three weeks later he was killed in Dallas.

Through Abe Fortas, intimate friend and advisor to the new President, Lyndon Johnson, Muñoz continued to have access to the presidency. The Puerto Rico-U.S. Status Commission held its first meeting at the White House on June 9, 1964, President Johnson and Muñoz present. Its chairman was James H. Rowe, who was familiar with Puerto Rico having been part of the government reorganization commission created by Muñoz in 1949. There were twelve others, six Americans, four from Congress, including O'Brien and later Senator Jackson, and six Puerto Ricans, including the top leaders of the statehood and independence parties.

Fernós, whom Muñoz had often praised as the best resident commissioner since the days of his father Muñoz Rivera, saw his reputation diminish. The unexpected failure of the Fernós-Murray bill led to rumors that he had lost his touch in Congress. The Popular Party's left wing considered him much too diplomatic, too willing to compromise and accept less than what Puerto Ricans demanded. Fernós was hurt by the criticism. He had, in fact, gained the two most important improvements in Commonwealth that

---

12. Ibid., 574.

were included in the ill-fated bill: one allowing Puerto Rico to set its own government debt limit, another to allow insular Supreme Court decisions to be appealed directly in the national Supreme Court just as with the states. Shortly after the inauguration of the new Status Commission, on July 16, 1964, Fernós announced his retirement after eighteen years in Congress. Teodoro Moscoso and Arturo Morales Carrión had already left the Johnson administration and returned to Puerto Rico.

The question all Puerto Rico asked as it entered into the 1964 election campaign was whether Muñoz would also retire. He had been so overwhelming a presence and a force in every aspect of Puerto Rican life in the past four decades, that it was difficult to believe that he would.

32 The End of the Muñoz Era

M uñoz didn't like to hear older Puerto Ricans, *jíbaros* that followed him since 1940, shout: "Papa...Papa...Papa..." In his many battles—against the reactionaries at home and in Congress, against the vitriolic *independentista* campaign that he was a "traitor" to Puerto Rican freedom, against Nationalist violence, against the bizarre attack of the Catholic Bishops—the *jíbaros* had stood by his side, supporting him, giving him the will to continue fighting back. Throughout, he wanted to believe that at heart, it was not "Papa" but the people themselves that had won all those battles. Now it was no longer possible to avoid the question he had avoided: what would happen to the party, the movement, the revolution, without his leadership?

The inevitable generational transition in the Popular Party leadership had begun. His young protégé, Santiago Polanco Abreu replaced Speaker of the House Ernesto Ramos Antonini after his sudden death in early 1963. Fernós Isern was retiring from Congress, although he later accepted to serve in the insular Senate. But there was resistance from "the Old Guard." The colorful and powerful Mayor of San Juan, Felisa Rincón, was determined to stay for at least another term. University of Puerto Rico Chancellor Jaime Benítez and Muñoz had resumed their old friendship, but Benítez continued to fight those determined to drive him out of the institution. Many of the Senators and Representatives, most of them leaders of local political machines that had been with Muñoz from the beginning, saw no reason to step down.

Muñoz made up his mind to keep his decision secret until the very last moment. His immediate family, his wife Inés, his son Luis, daughters Muna,

Viviana, and Victoria, hoped that he would retire. But it would be exclusively his decision, for in essence, it had to do not with party or family, but with the "pact" he had made with the *jíbaros* back in 1940. It was clear to him that precisely to honor that pact, in the best interest of the *jíbaro*, and all Puerto Ricans, he should step down. The question was how to convince them and his party leaders.

Among the young men and women he recruited to get involved in the party and government was a 27-year-old lawyer from Ponce, Rafael Hernández Colón, son of a pro-statehood judge Muñoz had named to the Supreme Court, and of an *independentista* mother who had run for mayor of Ponce in 1948. Muñoz was impressed by a university thesis Hernández had written on Commonwealth status. He was also impressed by other young professionals that had identified themselves with his party but were also persistent critics. The two dissident university professors, Severo Colberg and José Arsenio Torres were now politically active. Colberg zeroed in on Operation Bootstrap as destructive of Puerto Rican values and cultural identity, while Torres strongly attacked the lack of openness and democratic participation in the Popular Party.

On the status issue, the "new generation" was part of the wing favoring "maximum autonomy," a constitutional amendment to reinforce Puerto Rico's civil rights, a radical University of Puerto Rico reform, and many other political reforms. In frequent meetings, *tertulias*, under the thatched-roof, open *bohío* in Trujillo Alto, Muñoz relished that these young people, at times including his youngest daughter, Victoria, were a far cry from the unconditional, adoring *Populares* that shouted "Papa!" at him. He admired their willingness to openly and directly discuss the need for "less dependence on Muñoz's leadership". This was precisely what Muñoz wanted to hear from his party.

Some party veterans well acquainted with Muñoz's restlessness, his compulsion to second-guess himself, now wondered if he was going too far. He and these young people talked about "renovation" and "greater democracy," but to the veterans the "new generation" sounded curiously "anti-Popular," even "anti-Muñoz."

THE LAST MESSAGE

Muñoz's February 11, 1964 State of the Commonwealth message seemed unmistakably to be his last. The economy of Puerto Rico had never grown faster. The 10 percent increase in production made Puerto Rico's development one of the world's fastest. Operation Bootstrap had never been more vigorous. Fomento had established 152 new manufacturing plants in the previous year. The goal to decentralize the location of new industry was succeeding: ten years earlier, less than half of the towns, only 33, had factories. Now all but two had a Fomento plant. Dramatizing his reconciliation with the Catholic Church, he quoted "the great Pope John XXIII" encyclical "Mater et Magistrate" in proposing what Muñoz called "The Purpose of Puerto Rico."

> "The vitality of a people is the vitality of its collective purpose. A vital people will have a vital purpose. A weak people will have a weak purpose—or no purpose at all. In this case it would not be a people: it would be a conglomeration of appetites and ambitions of individuals and groups. Puerto Rico does not want to be that. Puerto Rico should not want to be that. And with the help of God, [Puerto Rico] will not be that. The Puerto Rican Purpose cannot be mere economic progress, because if Puerto Rico is to be the Puerto Rico that we want and respect, it should not only hunger for consumption, but thirst for justice, art, science, understanding, and good human conviviality."[1]

Muñoz made numerous proposals to decentralize the state government, particularly the powerful Planning Board. Although he reiterated the need to continue "importing capital investment," he called for a much greater effort to "balance" the economic development with a greater share of native investment. He proposed a big expansion in the number of cooperatives and a new and stronger anti-monopolies law. Muñoz not only leaned back to his "socialist" roots, but it was evident how much the "new generation" leaders influenced his thinking.

---

1. Muñoz Marín, *Los gobernadores electos de Puerto Rico*, 337.

Muñoz endorsed important changes in the electoral law, prohibiting campaign solicitation among government employees and an innovative plan for public financing of political campaigns to reduce the influence of "special interests." Particularly pleasing to the new leaders was his declaration that the time had arrived for a "university reform law" that would decentralize and "democratize" the institution. Muñoz ended his sixteenth and final message:

> I have not spoken of political status. If we dedicate ourselves to the great goals of the Purpose of Puerto Rico, our effort itself will demonstrate, each day with greater clarity, what is the political status that should become part of that Purpose of Puerto Rico. Everyone knows what is my conviction as to the political status. But each Puerto Rican will judge for himself. It is for each Puerto Rican to judge.[2]

MUSICAL CHAIRS

To think seriously of retiring, it was essential to "institutionalize" the Popular Party. Muñoz had given little importance to creating a permanent foundation to the party. It was run from small offices in a rented building and had little administrative structure. In 1960, he took what he hoped would be the first step: he resigned as party president and was replaced by a seven-member "presidential commission." It was a highly unusual and complicated arrangement. Following Muñoz's instructions, his trusted Secretary of State and Vice Governor, Roberto Sánchez Vilella, had come up with a new organization that would facilitate its "renovation" by keeping the top party leadership in continuous rotation. The party assembly elected a nineteen-member "presidential panel" from which seven members would serve three-month terms in a "presidential commission." Each of the seven would then serve as acting "presidential delegate" for a one-month period.

2. Muñoz Marín, *Mensajes al pueblo puertorriqueño*, 349.

When Muñoz approved the plan, the veteran party leaders were incredulous. Sánchez Vilella, the quiet, analytical, Ohio State University educated engineer, who for years had functioned as his political as well as administrative troubleshooter, understood the inner workings of the Popular Party better than Muñoz himself. He had a prodigious memory and could remember the name and personality of a *barrio* PDP leader in a remote rural area. But the PDP leaders were flabbergasted that Muñoz had approved Sánchez's mechanism with the theoretical precision of a Swiss watch, but unworkable, even absurd, in the real world of party politics. How could anyone imagine that the strong leadership and personality of Muñoz could be substituted by a perpetually revolving committee in a continuous game of musical chairs? Muñoz's initial attempt at "institutionalization" got off to a bad start.

Sánchez Vilella, however, had the solid support of new generation leaders that by mid-1964 had informally organized themselves and were meeting regularly, occasionally issuing public statements promoting the idea of Muñoz's retirement. What made Sánchez an unlikely candidate to replace Muñoz as governor, in the eyes of the party veterans, was precisely what made him attractive to the young people. On the one hand, no one had been closer or more loyal to Muñoz, but on the other he was the antithesis of the "political boss," the all-absorbing leader. No one was better prepared to "depersonalize" the Popular Party. He was as scrupulously honest as Muñoz, with a dispassionate, rational mind that appealed strongly to the university professors among the new leaders.

Sánchez had never identified himself ideologically. No one knew where he stood on most political or even administrative issues. His role had been to take apart the ideas and programs put forward by Muñoz and others to see if they would work. It was known that he had often clashed with his irrepressible brother-in-law, Teodoro Moscoso, whom he considered excessively impulsive and at times dangerously risk-prone. It was this role as critic that in part led the new generation to believe that Sánchez would naturally become part of the party's autonomous wing.

As the party's August 14, 1964 nominations assembly in Mayagüez approached, Muñoz's words and actions were increasingly ambiguous. He seemed to be zigzagging so much that, as one commentator put it, he was "making the island dizzy with confusion." Nothing was more puzzling than what Muñoz did one week before the assembly. Another of the party's 1960 "reforms," designed to facilitate the injection of "new blood," was "the exemption"—*la dispensa*. No party candidate could run for a third consecutive term in the same office unless he got an "exemption" from the rank and file. It was, like the "presidential commission" scheme, a cumbersome process. Some 3,000 party members would decide in an island-wide referendum which candidates were allowed to run for a third term.

Muñoz, of course, needed the *dispensa* to run for a fifth term. So when the press noticed that his name was not among the list of candidates in the referendum, they rushed to La Fortaleza convinced that he had finally revealed his intention not to run. But the reporters were met by a press secretary who was obviously as confused as everyone else. No, he said, Muñoz had not made his decision. But, the reporters shouted back, he cannot run without the *dispensa*. "All speculation is at your own risk," the aide said as he turned and fled.

Two days before the Mayagüez assembly, the news from La Fortaleza was even more baffling. There would be another *dispensa* referendum, this one exclusively for Muñoz. Muñoz sent a letter to all 3,000 party leaders emotionally urging them to deny him the exemption, to say "yes" to his retirement. By now no one could fathom what Muñoz was thinking. If he had decided not to run, he had merely to do nothing. If he had decided to run, why send the letter pleading with the party leaders to deny him permission?

Several days earlier he quipped to a friend that he intended to "campaign in favor and against" his serving a fifth term. He meant it. In the original draft of his letter, he gave his arguments for and against his retirement. But at the last moment he crossed out all the arguments against retirement, leaving only those in favor. He wrote:

> The people of Puerto Rico need to prove to themselves that they can follow a great path of justice and progress without depending on one man alone. The Popular Democratic Party needs to prove to itself and to all Puerto Ricans that it is strong because of the mission of redemption it has accomplished and because of its capacity to continue to fulfill that mission and not because of the candidacy of one man. The Popular Democratic Party needs to place in itself the

trust it has placed on me. No greater service than this can anyone perform for the party and for Puerto Rico.

Muñoz was attempting to communicate an idea that seemed to contradict itself: to vote against him was a vote for him. To allow him to run again meant that he had failed, that his political leadership had overwhelmed and suppressed Puerto Rico's self-confidence. Muñoz placed the thousands of Puerto Ricans that worshipped him in an impossible dilemma. His odd behavior sent chills through the new generation, now wondering if Muñoz had changed his mind. He was clearly agonizing over this. Was he panicking over the consequences? Or was he stumbling in a desperate, last minute attempt to prepare the convention delegates for the traumatic announcement of his retirement?

But if this was his intent, he had outmaneuvered himself and it backfired. When the referendum tally came in, to no one's surprise, of the 3,000 party members, 2,734 approved his *dispensa*. For the party veterans the ordeal was over. Muñoz had asked the party to decide for him and it did. As the day for the convention arrived, it seemed that he had locked himself into another four years in La Fortaleza.

On Saturday, August 15th, Muñoz called for Sánchez Vilella and his La Fortaleza Chief of Staff, Heriberto Alonso. They were to go immediately to Mayagüez and begin to canvass one-by-one all the delegates. Sánchez would make no definitive announcement but would ask each one a question: what would be his or her reaction if Muñoz announced his retirement, and nominated him, Sánchez Vilella, to replace him? Sánchez and Alonso located themselves in a room underneath the Mayagüez baseball stadium where a massive assembly would be held the next day, and began calling in each party delegate. Muñoz, meanwhile, arrived in Mayagüez Saturday afternoon and locked himself with his wife and immediate family in a Mayagüez Hilton suite. As word circulated of the Sánchez-Alonso meetings, party leaders began to appear at the door of Muñoz's room. All were stopped. Muñoz had given strict orders: No one was allowed in.

The meetings at the stadium continued until four in the morning. Sánchez, emotionally and physically exhausted, returned to his room. There was a knock on his door. It was one of Muñoz's security guards: "Don Luis wants to see you." He was waiting the hotel's pool. "Well?" Muñoz asked. "It's all right," Sánchez said. "You can make the announcement."

Muñoz knew that it all depended on his voice. The Mayagüez Baseball Stadium was a sea of red and white, the party colors. The stands and the grounds packed solidly with the party militants under the blazing sun. As he approached the microphone, he was about to announce his retirement. But before he could speak, a chant began among the delegates: "Four more! Four more! Four more!" This was not what he wanted or expected to hear.

This was in fact what the trusted Sánchez had assured him would not happen. He looked around at the party leaders behind him up at the platform, at his wife Inés, then he raised his arm, gesturing with his hand: "All right, all right. Let me begin." The chant continued. Inés, her attractive face framed by a wide, large, white hat, made her way through the party leaders to stand beside her husband. She smiled to display her pleasure at this enormous outburst of emotion for her husband. But she knew that her husband was in trouble. Her body now against his, as if to physically buttress him to ensure that he would not weaken, would not retreat, no matter what happened.

Unable to begin his speech, Muñoz' face became increasingly grim. The chant "Four more! Four more!" now sounded like a command, and Muñoz had never accepted commands. Not from his father, *El León*, not from his family, from friends, allies, political supporters, from business or media magnates, not from American presidents or governors or members of Congress, and not from the worshipping mass now before him.

Muñoz leaned forward again towards the microphone. With the power of his voice he had to take command. The leaders behind him were now waving their arms frantically to break the cadence of the chant. Lifting both arms over his head, Muñoz raised his voice over the chant.

"I am not leaving...I am returning to the hills, the valleys, to the soul of the people...I *must* return...." Inés began to clap her hands wildly, trying to get the mass of *Populares* to join in approval. "I must return..." Muñoz repeated. "Good! Good! Good!" she cried. But the delegates answered: "No! No! No! No!" waving their hands and heads from side to side. No, they would not let him go.

Muñoz raised his voice in anger. Attacking the opposition Republican Statehood Party always worked to control the *Populares*. They are the "merchants of fear," he shouted, raising his arms, shaking his head in that familiar display of disgust and indignation the *Populares* loved to see in their leader. "They want to achieve power by putting fear into your hearts!" It was now his most profound patriotic duty, Muñoz thundered, not to become an accomplice "by destroying your confidence in yourselves." It didn't work: the chant got stronger. "No! No! No!" and Muñoz angrier. "I have been your teacher, but now I want to return to the classroom—I want to return to you, the people, you are the classroom! I want to return and I *will* return... beyond all doubt I *will* return to you, to the classroom... Puerto Rican! I trust you! I am not your strength! Your strength is within yourself!"

Muñoz turned and walked away from the microphone. He had failed. It seemed hopeless. Behind him he could hear the frenzied chanting, pleading of the *Populares* grow. The convention was out of control.

Roberto Sánchez Vilella was seated off to the extreme left of the platform: leaning forward, his head bent down, staring at the floor, fidgeting nervously with his pipe and a cleaning tool. The 51-year old engineer had devoted his life to serving Muñoz. He was drained after the tension of the long months while Muñoz wrestled internally with his decision to retire or stay, and the ordeal of the meetings with the party leaders the previous night and morning hours. This was to be the biggest moment of his life. But he now sat there unseen, ignored, horrified at the spectacle before him—everything seemed to be coming apart. Muñoz's personal physician, Dr. Francisco Berio, seated next to Sánchez, placed a tranquilizer tablet in his hand.

Muñoz returned to the microphone. But Inés suddenly took the microphone and shouted: "You must respect Luis Muñoz Marín!" *She* was taking command. Again she repeated the admonition. The tough former school teacher had radically changed Muñoz's habits and lifestyle. Now she was determined to rescue him from the looming disaster. Her reprimand momentarily stunned the delegates. Her fists above her head, her lips tried to form other words, but instead she repeated, her fists coming down with each word: "*You must respect Luis Muñoz Marín!*"

Muñoz took the microphone, and mustering the last ounce of strength in his large, bear-like body, said: "Nothing will force me to change my mind." His eyes pitch black with rage, his finger pointing directly at the delegates, he cried: "Do not force me to turn my back on my duty! Do not oppose my serving you as I must...do not shout at me not to serve you as I must... you cannot force me to betray my conscience." Over the deafening chant of "No! No! No!" Muñoz nominated Roberto Sánchez Vilella for Governor.

Muñoz's dark, burly Administrator of Parks and Recreation, Julio Enrique Monagas, lifted Sánchez from his chair, his thick arms around his chest, and pushed Sánchez to the front of the platform. Muñoz and Sánchez embraced. Sánchez took the microphone and began to accept the nomination, but his words were drowned by the chant: "No! No! No!" At that instant, the Mayor of San Juan, Felisa Rincón de Gautier, standing behind Sánchez, gave a sign to her large San Juan delegation. No one was more personally hurt by Muñoz's decision to "retire," but no one in the party was more loyal. The colorful, charismatic 66-year-old San Juan leader had prepared her delegation for this crisis.

Instantly her militants began to yell at the top of their lungs: "*Ése es! Ése es! Ése es!*" A play on the letter "S" for Sánchez: "He's the one! He's the one! He's the one!" Several of Muñoz's closest political cronies and administrative aides, including writer Jorge Font Saldaña and the lawyer Hiram Torres Rigual, packed together directly in front of the platform, took up the chant, waving their arms at the delegates as conductors before a huge orchestra and chorus singing "Ése es! Ése es! Ése es!"

For a moment the convention hung suspended between the two delirious, competing chants: "No! No! No!...Ése es! Ése es! Ése es!" Everything Muñoz had planned for—for himself, his party, for Puerto Rico now hung in suspension as each chorus attempted to overpower the other. Slowly Felisa Rincón's delegation prevailed. The chant "Ése es" began to spread throughout the stadium. Sánchez spoke again, accepted the nomination, asked for everyone's support, his words unheard. He was now entirely surrounded by party leaders, all shouting "Ése es! Ése es!" drowning out the "No! No! No!"

Muñoz was no longer in sight: he had disappeared behind Sánchez and the party leaders.

The next day, late in the afternoon, I went to his home outside San Juan. He was dressed in loose terry-cloth shorts, tied around his waist with a rope, several sizes too big, making his thighs look spindly. The matching terry-cloth shirt was unbuttoned, exposing his wide, round, smooth chest. He had a drink in his hands. As a newspaper reporter, I had seen Muñoz play a cat and mouse game with the press, at times leading it to think that he had decided not to run again, and then leading it in the opposite direction.

Now his eyes seemed to say jokingly: "Well, now you finally have the story you've been after for four years. It was a close call. But it's done. It's over."

He turned and walked down the path around the small, rustic concrete home he and Inés lived in when not in the palatial *La Fortaleza*. We walked into the thatched-roof, open *bohío*, where he loved to spend his evenings, talking, drinking wine.

He expressed his absolute certainly that he had done the right thing, that Sánchez Vilella was a great administrator that would do a better job running the government. No one was more understanding, more loyal to the "democratic revolution" that had achieved so much but had so much more to accomplish. Sánchez, he went on, would be his own man and would carry out the vital renovation of the party to a "new generation" of leaders and administrators.

Yes, he still had five months as Governor, and a campaign to get Sánchez elected with a big victory margin against the perennial pro-statehood opponent, Luis A. Ferré, running for a third time. "Retirement," he said, is not the right word: call it "giving up authority." As he had cried out at the delegates, he looked forward to returning to the Puerto Rican countryside— back to what had been the happiest time of his life a quarter century ago— back to the *jíbaro's batey*.

"The Muñoz era has ended," he proclaimed again with a twinkle of delight in his eyes, and I knew what he meant and what he believed. Since his earliest years, Muñoz had felt imprisoned, first by the demand that he live up to his father's legacy, then by the enormous responsibility and power of transforming Puerto Rico. He had created a movement that had liberated his people from primitive economic exploitation and primitive partisan politics. And now, finally, he believed that he had liberated himself.

Now, he had to put everything back into place. One of the leaders that came to visit him was the Speaker of the House, Santiago Polanco Abreu, who was unhappy about being nominated to replace Fernós Isern as resident commissioner in Congress. This was one of the problems, the many problems, Muñoz knew he had to deal with in the transition. Polanco was believed to aspire, in the future, to the governorship. He was seen as having a special relationship to Muñoz, the godfather of his children. From a poor, rural family in the small coastal town of Isabela, Polanco had worked himself through college and a law degree, and up the party hierarchy. He still saw himself in his heart a *jíbaro*. Not fluent in English, he would feel alienated, lost in Congress and in Washington. And politically, although it was an honor to serve in Congress, he resented that Sánchez Vilella had taken him out of the way, sending him to the "Washington exile." Muñoz firmly assured him that this was not the case, and asked for his word that he would hold nothing back in campaigning for Sánchez.

The biggest challenge, of course, was to get the new generation leaders to jell into the party structure. He had seen to it that the vocal and prolific university professors, Colberg and Torres, were both on the party ticket for the Legislature. He brought the studious, seemingly well-organized Ponce lawyer, Hernández Colón, to work in the campaign. Most of all, he had to get his party leadership to accept that he had made the right decision, and have it campaign as hard as ever for Sánchez.

Muñoz had reluctantly decided to run for the Senate to prove to the party that he was not "leaving." He would dedicate himself to making the studies and preparing the legislation to implement the ambitious Purpose of Puerto Rico. There was also the big challenge of continuing his effort to "perfect" Commonwealth status. It was already decided that he would replace Sánchez in the new Puerto Rico-U.S. Status Commission. But he had to convince everyone, beginning with the new generation leaders, that Sánchez would not be a figurehead: that he would not attempt to run the government or the party from his Senate seat.

The Republican Statehood Party leaders believed the attempt to "depersonalize" the Popular Party was doomed to fail: that a political party not driven primarily by status ideology could not survive the exit of its founder and leader. Theirs was held together by the statehood "ideal" since it was founded by José Celso Barbosa at the beginning of the century. The island newspapers, back in 1940, were right in putting the words "Popular Party" within quotes. It had never been a true party but a conglomerate of people motivated only by the adoration of their leader. This, the Republicans believed, was the beginning of the end of what had always been "the Muñoz party."

Of course, the statehood leaders still had reason to fear the Popular political machine, driven as much by the rewards of government power, from plots of land to public housing to a job, as by Muñoz's charisma. But certainly the machine would start to break down as the educated but politically naive new generation leaders began to push out the Old Guard. And there remained the biggest question mark. The lackluster Sánchez had never before run for office. If he stumbled as a candidate, the attractive gubernatorial candidate, Luis A. Ferré, would register still another big gain in voters, and perhaps even shock Puerto Rico on election day.

There was no shock on November 3, 1964, but there was a surprise. The Popular Party won even bigger than in the previous election: it went from 58 to 59.3 percent of the vote. Roberto Sánchez Vilella impressed everyone with the magnitude of his victory. The Republican Statehood Party's dream of shattering, or at least seriously crippling the invincibility of the Popular Party, was smashed as it registered less than half the gain in votes it had achieved in the 1960 elections. The impressive, and for Muñoz deeply troubling, surge in the statehood movement had been stopped. But above all, Muñoz believed that his party had learned the lesson, had learned to "trust itself". For the first time in his life he felt he was "free at last!"

33 The Three Civil Wars

In the remaining fifteen years of his life, Muñoz was unable to write his memoirs. By his own account, he wrote "several thousand pages," at least four drafts. He wrote in his small office in Trujillo Alto, in a small apartment in Rome in the early 1970s, much of it by hand, some of it dictated to secretaries, at times to a recording machine. He wrote in notebooks, sheets of paper, scraps of paper. At one point he invited close friends to engage in a dialogue with him over the highlights of his political career, the conversations recorded, transcribed, and then almost entirely rewritten by him. On March 17, 1973 he started to write a "Diary." It lasted one year.

One major obstacle was that the November 1964 elections had not, after all, given him the freedom that he longed for. By mid-term, the Sánchez Vilella administration and the Popular Party were in crisis. Nothing, in fact, seemed to go as he had planned after his retirement. Launched with great enthusiasm after the big victory, the Sánchez governorship had become a nightmare for Muñoz. The transition he believed he had achieved broke down. The generational warfare he had worked so hard to avoid tore the party apart. The old guard Muñoz "loyalists," believing it was being unceremoniously pushed aside by Sánchez and his "new generation" administrators, rebelled. Sánchez's personal life, meanwhile, generated sensational news. He went through a highly publicized separation and divorce and immediately married a young, beautiful assistant, Jeannette Ramos, the daughter of the late Speaker of the House, Ernesto Ramos Antonini.

At first, Muñoz, spending long periods of time in Europe, strongly backed Sánchez. But in 1967, he found himself forced to return to take command again of the Popular Party. A political status plebiscite was to be held on the island for the first time, the result of the two-and-a-half year study by the Puerto Rico-U.S. Status Commission. As the voting day approached, it was evident that his party had been critically weakened. After an intense and difficult campaign, Commonwealth status won with 60 per cent of the vote. The following day Muñoz triumphantly announced: "The status issue has ended." The island, he said, must dedicate itself to implementing the "mandate" to get Congress to proceed with the "perfection of Commonwealth status."

But Muñoz was, in fact, disappointed. This was not the overwhelming "mandate" that he wanted. Now, with the defection of Sánchez, the Popular Party lost control of the governorship. Who was going to implement the plebiscite "mandate?" For the Republican leadership, the 39 percent that voted for statehood meant that it had regained the momentum lost in the past elections. This was five points more than the 1964 Republican Statehood Party vote. Just as important was the change in the statehood leadership. Luis A. Ferré replaced his brother-in-law, Miguel A. García Méndez, who had decided not to participate in the plebiscite, as the sole party leader. Discarding the name "Republican," long associated in Puerto Rico with reactionary politics, Ferré organized his own statehood movement, calling it the New Progressive Party.

By 1968, the Muñoz party was irreconcilably divided. Sánchez first announced he would not seek reelection, then changed his mind and ran under his own People's Party, quickly organized by the defecting new generation leaders. Muñoz threw his support behind a Senate veteran, Luis Negrón López, a large, soft-spoken small-town lawyer from Sabana Grande. Under his candidacy, the Popular Party campaign emerged as a nostalgic attempt to return to a *jíbaro* past.

Sánchez and the dissidents were especially hard on Muñoz. Their slogan, "Let the people decide," implied that Muñoz had indeed become a "dictator." At several campaign stops, for the first time, Muñoz' campaign bus was stoned.

On November 5, 1968, what most Puerto Ricans never thought they would live to see, happened: the Popular Party lost. Sánchez and his People's Party siphoned off 87,832 votes. Ferré, who had been running for office since 1940, was elected in this his fourth run for the governorship.

In Rome

In August, 1970, Muñoz resigned his seat in the Senate and went to Italy. One of his daughters, Viviana, lived near Rome. Muñoz rented for himself and Inés a small apartment on Via Cassia, north of the city. The apartment had a narrow balcony that wrapped around the corner of the building. Muñoz, taking a break from writing his memoirs, would walk back and forth in the balcony. Puerto Rican visitors were incredulous when they saw the smallness of the apartment for this man, who had seemed, to friends and foes alike, larger than life. But Muñoz also spent much time in his daughter's larger home, where guests were met at the entrance by a huge poster of the revolutionary Ernesto "Che" Guevara. There were frequent trips with the family to Paris, Madrid, Crete, the hometown of the husband of his other daughter, Victoria, and to the Swiss Alps, where he went to see his granddaughters skiing.

Months went by without reading a newspaper from Puerto Rico. This was one of the happiest periods of his life. Rome, in those days, seemed victimized by one labor protest or work stoppage after another, interrupting water, electricity, and transportation. Muñoz insisted to visiting friends that this did not bother him in the least. His "socialist enthusiasm" revived, he spent long hours trying to follow these protests in the leftist Italian newspapers.

Muñoz was delighted to serve as guide to his visiting friends. He recited the history behind Roman ruins and monuments. One of the privileges that he retained as ex-governor was keeping his security guard, Julio Quirós, who became an expert in getting him and his guests, usually in a rented van, around the city and often to one of Muñoz's carefully selected cafés or restaurants. Visitors also noticed that as much as he relished the freedom of "not being Muñoz Marín," the charisma Thomas Hoving described was still there. His presence and demeanor, his cane and beret, always worn with a slight tilt, made waiters and others treat him with the deference of someone they could sense was "important."

In late 1972, Muñoz's two-year honeymoon with Rome and Europe come to an end. The young lawyer from Ponce who had written the impressive thesis on Commonwealth status, Rafael Hernández Colón, to everyone's surprise, had moved in to fill the leadership vacuum after the devastating

1968 defeat. In 1969 he was elected Senate President and now, at 36, barely the age allowed under the constitution, was running for governor. No one believed that the young man, unusually introspective for a politician and who struck some in the party and media as aloof and arrogant, had the slightest opportunity against the well-liked Governor Ferré.

The old feeling of being trapped returned. Muñoz told himself that the last thing in the world he wanted was to return to another political campaign in Puerto Rico. He insisted to friends that he would return only if he was convinced that he was "needed." Was there any hope of defeating Ferré? Through the years, Muñoz had seen the affable Ferré as a unique opponent. He had been a relentless adversary in the United States, in Congress as in Puerto Rico, attacking Muñoz's "dictatorial rule." In the heat of the Catholic Bishops' attack, while not openly siding with the Bishops, he blamed Muñoz for the crisis. And he was certainly persistent in his quest for his "statehood ideal." But in their personal relationship Ferré demonstrated genuine friendship and respect.

As the 1972 elections approached, Muñoz knew that he had been fooling himself. For all his personal charm, and his image as "Puerto Rico's leading industrialist," Muñoz saw Ferré as a weak Governor. No one questioned Ferré's personal integrity, but there were frequent reports of irregularities in the administration. The line that Tugwell had drawn and doggedly defended, between partisan politics and public administration, and that Muñoz insisted that he had scrupulously honored, had eroded. And there was also Muñoz's renewed "socialist enthusiasm." He was troubled by the fact that Ferré and his family were the island's most powerful capitalists, owners of key industries, many other businesses, real estate holdings, and now, a major daily newspaper, *El Nuevo Día*. This posed for the island, Muñoz was convinced, "dangerous conflicts of interests."

At the same time, Muñoz also had a peculiar relation to his party's young candidate, Hernández Colón. After serving as Secretary of Justice in the Sánchez Vilella administration, Hernández broke with Sánchez. Never a slavish *Muñocista*, he treated Muñoz as his mentor. Yet Muñoz never felt totally comfortable with the young man, finding his intellectual aloofness disconcerting. But he admired his sharp, analytical mind, his ability to focus and organize, and now his surprising emergence as an effective political leader.

Muñoz waited as late as possible in the campaign to return. But at the last moment, in Madrid, the bags already taken to the airport, Inés urgently called the Spanish friend who had made the travel arrangements, José Antonio Sáenz de Ormijana, to cancel the trip. Their daughter Viviana was suddenly ill and they could not leave. Saenz located the doctor that had once treated Inés and whom she trusted. The doctor called: he had just examined Viviana and assured them that it was nothing serious and urged them to go ahead and return to Puerto Rico.

On October 6, 1972, Muñoz arrived secretly. He had instructed only one friend, the businessman and former representative, Jorge Bird, to meet him and Inés at the airport. From there he was rushed to the home of another friend, lawyer Omar Cancio, deep in the mountains of Cidra.

Muñoz had lost none of his old flair for dramatics. There was a reason for his minutely planned, stealth return to the island. That Sunday, before one of the largest multitudes ever assembled in Puerto Rico, over 100,000 *Populares* at the huge parking area outside the Plaza Las Américas shopping mall, most of the men and women decked out in the party colors, red and white, Muñoz slowly emerged up onto the platform. When the people recognized his figure, there was a deafening roar of elation. It was the great emotional counterpoint to the traumatic assembly in Mayagüez eight years earlier. Muñoz had returned. Again, as it was then, the roar of the ecstatic *Populares* would not allow him to speak. This time his full, powerful, masculine voice had the old electrifying effect as he slowly pronounced one word: "*Compatriotas...*" Again there was a roar of euphoria. Deep within the human mass, Teodoro Moscoso and his wife, Gloria, cried silently.

A month later, on November 7, 1972, Muñoz saw his Popular Party return to power. It was an impressive victory for Hernández Colón, defeating Ferré and the New Progressive Party by 95,000 votes, regaining control of the Legislature, and 73 of the 78 municipal governments. For many in Puerto Rico this was a return to "normality." Sánchez Vilella retired from politics, spending the rest of his life teaching at the University of Puerto Rico. He died in 1998 at the age of 85.

Muñoz's attitude towards to the new Governor remained ambiguous. Hernández had always felt strongly about the need to proceed with the "perfection" of Commonwealth status. He named Muñoz to another commission appointed by President Nixon and himself that drafted and sent to Congress a "New Puerto Rico-U.S. Compact Bill." This pleased Muñoz but he was still not satisfied. He felt just as strongly that Hernández should do more than he had done to achieve Serenity's humanistic goals. The "socialist enthusiasm" that had reawakened in him when he was in Rome was now very much alive. He wanted urban sprawl "stopped in its tracts" replaced by meticulously planned "new cities." He wanted the construction of new highways paralyzed wherever possible and to place much more emphasis on environmental protection. But after the trauma and tragedy of the Sánchez Vilella experience, Muñoz was particularly sensitive to saying or doing anything that would be interpreted as pressuring the young Governor.

Here he was, at this late stage in his life, out of office and out of power, still with the old sense of being imprisoned. On May 27, 1974, he wrote in his diary: "I am the Puerto Rican that has less freedom in Puerto Rico, in the profound sense."[1]

THE OIL SHOCK

Muñoz renewed fears about the social consequences of rapid economic development, however, become academic. Suddenly, Puerto Rico was in crisis. The robust growth that Puerto Rico had sustained now for two decades, and many, including Muñoz, seemed to take for granted, came to an abrupt halt. The island's total dependence on imported oil sent the economy reeling following the outbreak of the new Yom Kippur War on October 6, 1973, and the oil embargo. The giant petrochemical industry, the pride of Operation Bootstrap, but that Muñoz now saw with grave misapprehension due to its environmental impact, collapsed. The entire economy took a nosedive, from a 7.3 percent expansion in fiscal year 1973 to a minus two percent "negative growth" in 1975. Unemployment rocketed up to Great Depression levels, 21.9 percent by late 1975: 57,000 Puerto Ricans lost their jobs, 23,000 of

---

1. Muñoz Marín, *Diario: 1972-74*, 73.

them as a result of closed Fomento plants. Hernández Colón and his administration were locked in a desperate battle to prevent the collapse of the entire economy.

Muñoz would not live to see his party win another election. The economic crisis sent Hernández Colón and the Popular Party to defeat in 1976. The election of the 44-year-old Mayor of San Juan, Carlos Romero Barceló, as Governor of Puerto Rico, represented more than another change in administration. Romero had been a leader in the Republican Statehood Party's new generation and then President of Citizens for State 51. His style was fundamentally different from that of the "old school" Ferré. The Yale graduate and lawyer was uncompromisingly opposed to Commonwealth status.

For Romero, a burly man of exceptional energy, the key was to demolish the very concept of Operation Bootstrap. He published his political doctrine in a booklet titled: "Statehood is for the Poor." He argued that Puerto Rico was the victim of a "conspiracy" between "rich industrialists...that line their pockets" through tax exemption and low salaries, and the Popular Party that created the "Commonwealth myth" in order to fill the party coffers with the political contributions of the industrialists. Romero emphasized that the founder of his party, Ferré, was "an exception."

There was another factor driving the new Governor. It now seemed that Muñoz's political life had made a full circle. His climb to political dominance had begun almost exactly forty years earlier in the bitter conflict and emotional breakup with Antonio Barceló and the Liberal Party. The old leader, the "heir to the Luis Muñoz Rivera legacy," died soon after, it was often said, his heart broken by Muñoz's cruel "betrayal." Now, in 1976, the new Governor was the grandson of Antonio Barceló.

THE THREE CIVIL WARS

In 1982, Doña Inés found more evidence of Muñoz's struggle to write his memoirs. Looking through his papers two years after his death in 1980, deep in one of the drawers of his big desk, in the Trujillo Alto office, she found a number of sheets of paper clipped together. Muñoz had written on top: "Brief history of a long life and a deeply-felt vision for a future of good."

By 1974, after ten years of trying, Muñoz had given up. In one passage, he tries to understand why so many attempts had failed:

> They don't satisfy me although without a doubt they have some value that some miner of history and literature may dig up and refine. Why? Perhaps because of not having access to some data, or a reluctance to bury myself in the shuffling of papers or scurrilous articles, or an impatience to get to the point of converting an experience of the past into a projection of the future—which is what should be of most interest. Or, possibly, that I am right in suspecting that even in the most dramatic political life, in attempting to narrate it one discovers a certain boredom, a certain vulgarity (that is not the word—it may denote a snobbishness that is not intended) that appears alien to the purest and most sincere purposes to which that life may have been dedicated.[2]

Throughout his life, in several of his major speeches and in countless *tertulias* with friends, Muñoz referred to the "civil wars" within him. Now, in these sheets of paper, he tried once more to explain them. There were, he wrote, three "civil wars," rooted in his need to serve the "two Puerto Ricos that exist," and that clashed against one another: the clash between *"la patria"* and *"el pueblo."* Serving *la patria* was serving the "homeland" in its collective existence as a people with their own history, their own cultural identity. Serving *el pueblo* was serving "the people" in their existence as individuals, as families, as social classes. While the collective Puerto Rico demanded nationhood, the "flesh-and-blood" Puerto Rican demanded economic and social justice. It was out of the need to find some solution to this "civil war" that he came up with a new political status: "From the clash of independence with social justice is that Commonwealth status emerged."

The second "civil war" was between justice and development: the profound responsibility to wage war against Puerto Rico's desperate economic needs; the clash between "socialism that is moral but inefficient and capitalism that is immoral and efficient."

---

2. Muñoz Marín, *Memorias* Vol. II, viii.

And the third "civil war" was having for too long lived the life and served the interests of the "bourgeoisie," while within himself yearning for a life of "poetry, art, Bohemia" in "solidarity with the worker, the poor, the down-trodden."

The final years of his life were difficult and painful. In January, 1976, Muñoz suffered a stroke that impaired his speech. After months of intensive rehabilitation, he recovered enough to speak slowly, with a slight but perceptible slur. In that year's election campaign, he managed to give several radio talks in support of Hernández Colón and the Popular Party. For thousands of Puerto Ricans the impaired voice was a sad manifestation of the reality that Muñoz's days were indeed coming to an end. Muñoz gradually lost much of his eyesight, needing a thick magnifying glass to read. He struggled to continue working until the end, more and more imprisoned by his failing body. "Luis Muñoz Marín," Jaime Benítez wrote, "lived in the last years of his life the torments of a chained Prometheus."

Muñoz died on April 30, 1980.

Epilogue

Muñoz's close friends, former President of Venezuela Rómulo Betancourt and former Costa Rican President, José Figueres, were among the hundreds of thousands that filed pass the casket at the Puerto Rico Capitol Building overlooking the Atlantic Ocean. "I want to tell you," said Betancourt, "that the Puerto Rican that feels the most anguish does not feel greater grief that I." Recalling Muñoz's life-long battles against dictatorships, and his hospitality and support for the democratic exiles that made Puerto Rico their home in the 1950s, Figueres and Betancourt credited Muñoz as being a decisive force in the resurgence of Latin American democracy. "A Latin American," Figueres said, "has died as few in Latin American history."

His perennial political opponent, Luis A. Ferré, his voice broken with emotion, lamented: "To his arguments mine were opposed. To his reasons mine were opposed. And now I find the dialogue severed. He occupied an exceptional place in the frame of my political thinking. Now that frame is not the same."

"Such was the power and grandness of the extraordinary personality of Luis Muñoz Marín," *The San Juan Star* editorialized, "that people from all stations of life claim his as their own."

Jaime Benítez, closer to Muñoz than anyone else through the decades, who venerated and dissented and at time fought with him, said: "Time has run out on Luis Muñoz Marín—without days or hours to pursue his flight as poet and patriot..."

But of all the expressions of grief, the eulogies and accolades, none would have pleased Muñoz more than the words of the University of Puerto Rico professor, Gordon Lewis. A Marxist who strongly favored independence for Puerto Rico, Lewis had arrived on the island from England in 1950 and stayed. His major 1963 book, "Puerto Rico: Freedom and Power in the Caribbean," and subsequent works were sharply critical of Muñoz's "colonialist" and "capitalist" policies.[1]

So Lewis was surprised in 1963 when he received a telephone call from Muñoz saying he had read his book and wanted to invite him to discuss it with members of his administration and others. Although Lewis had always thought that he was seen by Muñoz's people as a "dangerous European subversive communist," he accepted.

Now, attempting to capture the essence of his life—what Muñoz to his death felt he was unable to do—Lewis wrote:

> There comes a time in the life of all peoples when the death of a great leader unleashes, like some awe-inspiring volcanic eruption, all of the deep and powerful emotions that constitute a sense of national being. No one, I think, who stood in the long, patient lines of Puerto Ricans of all classes and political beliefs at the Capitolio, or watched that long, tragic caravan of Don Luis' last trip to Barranquitas, reminding one of Lincoln's long last journey from Washington to Springfield, Illinois in 1865, can but have felt that he was in the presence of a truly historic event...
>
> There is no doubt that he deserved this tremendous outpouring of love and devotion. As Churchill personified England, as Franklin Roosevelt personified America, he personified Puerto Rico. He was the complete patriot...in his own person, he was the Puerto Rican incarnate...
>
> As a master craftsman in the great art of politics, he had class, as the English say... He never kowtowed to the American masters, for he knew that he was better than most of them...

---

1. Lewis, *Notes on the Puerto Rican Revolution*, 9.

Above all else, like a very great charismatic leader, he forged a bond of love and affection between himself and his people that no alien force could corrupt or outside element pollute. The bond ran deeply into the roots of the Puerto Rican collective psyche: and Muñoz used it, but he did not exploit it for narrow or selfish purposes. There was no hate in his heart. There was always love and compassion. When I ponder on the passage of time and tide in his life, and now his mourned death, I am reminded, as an Englishman, of Gladstone's graphic phrase on that great event of 1845 when John Henry Newman made his famous conversion from Canterbury to Rome, deserting the Church of England for the Church of Rome. It was as if, wrote Gladstone, some great cathedral bell had suddenly ceased tolling. For those of us who were privileged to know Muñoz, we shall hear that bell tolling to the end of our lives.[2]

2. *The San Juan Star,* May 11, 1980

MUÑOZ AT BARRANQUITAS

Every year Muñoz celebrated the birth of his father, Luis Muñoz Rivera, at his birthplace, the mountain town of Barranquitas. Here he is with Speaker of the House, Ernesto Ramos Antonini, also the vicepresident of the Popular Democratic Party.

MUÑOZ LOVED TO WALK

Always a brisk walker, he is enjoying himself with Secretary of Public Works, Francisco Lizardi, to his right, and Representative Santiago Polanco Abreu too his left.

MUÑOZ AND FERNÓS ISERN

Muñoz had success in getting the U.S. Congress to approve a new constitution and a new political status, Commonwealth. Resident Commissioner in Congress, Dr. Antonio Fernós Isern, (left) played a key role. With MuÒoz is Secretary of State, Roberto Sánchez Vilella.

INÉS THE TEACHER

Muñoz's wife, Inés Mendoza, who insisted that she was born with the vocation to teach, seen here with a public school student.

MUÑOZ THE ADMINISTRATOR

After becoming Puerto Rico's first elected governor in 1948, Muñoz had to make the transition from Senate President to government administrator. He relied on young Puerto Rican talent. From left: Rafael Picó, President of the Planning Board, Roberto Sánchez Vilella, Secretary of State, and Teodoro Moscoso, Administrator of Economic Development.

THE FAMILY

Muñoz had four children, two from his first marriage to the poet Muna Lee. Here he stands in front of La Fortaleza in 1956 with Inés and their two daughters, Viviana (left) and Victoria.

CAPTURING MUÑOZ

This 1965 photo, by San Juan photographer Gunter Hett, captured the Muñoz I knew for many years.

MUÑOZ IN DEEP THOUGHT IN GREECE

After his retirement, Muñoz spent two happy years in Europe. Here he is in deep thought in Greece in 1971.

OPERATION SERENITY

In Operation Serenity, Muñoz urged Puerto Rico to set sight beyond economic development towards what he called "good civilization" – simplicity and conviviality. For Muñoz, this included a good glass of wine at a Madrid café, in 1972.

DOÑA INÉS

When Muñoz met and fell in love with the beautiful school teacher, Inés Mendoza, in 1938, his life changed. A heavy drinker and smoker, Muñoz had begun the marathon task of organizing a new political party. Inés imposed discipline and moderation on Muñoz for the rest of his life.

THE PUERTO RICAN FLAG

One of the most emotional moments in Muñoz's life was the raising of the Puerto Rican flag on July 25, 1952, to inaugurate Commonwealth status in union with the U.S. A decade later, about to retire after four terms as Governor, he is exuberant under the flag.

AN EARFUL

By 1957, Muñoz had great political power in Puerto Rico and prestige in the U.S. But this young girl was anything but intimidated.

THE MEMOIRS

A prolific writer all his life, Muñoz was unable to write his memoirs. He produced numerous versions; several of them during his prolonged stay in Rome in the 1970's. Here he is at his home in Trujillo Alto, searching for the exact right word.

THE FREEDOM MEDAL

President John F. Kennedy awarded Muñoz the Presidential Medal of Freedom in 1963, three weeks before he was killed in Dallas. Muñoz received the award the following year from President Lyndon B. Johnson.

THE PRINCIPAL OPPONENT

The charismatic pro-statehood industrialist, Luis A. Ferré, was Muñoz's principal political opponent. Ferré finally was elected Governor of Puerto Rico in 1968; Muñoz had retired four years earlier.

PABLO CASALS AND JOSÉ FERRER

Operation Serenity took a giant leap forward in 1956 when Muñoz convinced the great Spanish cellist Pablo Casals to organize and direct the annual Casals Festival in San Juan. On July 17, 1959 wearing a tuxedo that he abhorred, he shares a moment with Casals and Academy Award winner José Ferrer.

THE BASEBALL FAN

Into his sixties, Muñoz invited friends to a baseball field where he would try to make bat contact with soft pitches. Here he is in 1949, intensely talking to Jackie Robinson, with the Puerto Rican outfielder, Luis Olmo Rodríguez at right.

THE COMMUNICATOR

Muñoz loved to talk and his favorite medium was radio. He had a strong, masculine voice that projected self-confidence, resolve, but that at the same time was friendly and intimate.

THE JÍBARO

Muñoz came to power in 1940 by talking and *listening* to the jíbaros. Here he is in 1946, after being reelected overwhelmingly as President of the Puerto Rico Senate.

Bibliography

Acosta, Ivonne. *La palabra como delito*. San Juan, P.R.: Editorial Cultural, 1993.

Aitken, Jr. Thomas. *Poet in the Fortress*. New York: The New American Library, 1964.

Alonso, María Mercedes. *Muñoz Marín vs. the Bishops*. San Juan, P.R.: Publicaciones Puertorriqueñas, 1988.

Anderson, Robert W. *Party Politics in Puerto Rico*. Stanford, CA: Stanford University Press, 1965.

Barton, Hugh C. "Puerto Rico's Industrial Development." Paper presented at a seminar of the Harvard University Center for International Affairs, Cambridge: October 29, 1959.

Bayrón Toro, Fernando. *Elecciones y partidos políticos de Puerto Rico*. Mayagüez, P.R.: Editorial Isla, 1989.

Beisner, Robert L. *Twelve Against Empire*. Chicago: University of Chicago Press, 1968.

Benítez, Jaime. *Junto a La Torre*. San Juan, P.R.: University of Puerto Rico Press, 1962.

Benítez Rexach, Jesús. *Vida y obra de Luis Muñoz Marín*. San Juan, P.R.: Editorial Edil, 1989.

Berle, Adolf A. *Latin America: Diplomacy and Reality*. New York: Harper and Row, 1962.

Bhana, Surendra. *The United States and the Development of the Puerto Rican Status Question*. Wichita: University of Kansas Press, 1975.

Bird Piñero, Enrique. *Don Luis Muñoz Marín: el poder de la excelencia.* San Juan, P.R.: Luis Muñoz Marín Foundation, 1991.

Black, Ruby. *Eleanor Roosevelt: A Biography.* New York: Duell, Sloan and Pearcew, 1940.

Bothwell González, Reece B. *Puerto Rico: cien años de lucha política* . 4 vols. Río Piedras, P.R.: Editorial Universitaria, 1979.

Carroll, Henry K. *Report on the Island of Porto Rico.* 1899. Reprint, New York: Arno Press, 1975.

Chardón, Carlos, et. al. *Report of the Puerto Rico Policy Commisssion* (Chardón Report). San Juan, P.R.: 1934.

Chase, Stuart. *Operation Bootstrap in Puerto Rico.* National Planning Association Planning Pamphlet No. 75. Washington, D.C.: September 1951.

Clark, Víctor S. et. al. *Porto Rico and Its Problems.* Washington, D.C.: Brookings Institution, 1930.

De Jesús, Roberto. "El gobierno de Puerto Rico en 1949." In Marshall Dimock and Sociedad Americana de Administración Pública, 1951.

De Jesús Toro, Rafael. *Historia económica de Puerto Rico.* Cincinnati: South Western Publishing Co., 1982.

Dietz, James L. *The Economic History of Puerto Rico.* Princeton: Princeton University Press, 1980.

Diffie, Bailey W. & Justine, Diffie. *Porto Rico: A Broken Pledge.* Whitfield, NY: Vanguard Press, 1931.

Fernós Isern, Antonio. *Filosofía y doctrina del estadolibrismo puertorriqueño.* San Juan, P.R.: Inter American University of Puerto Rico, 1996.

_____. *Estado Libre Asociado de Puerto Rico.* Río Piedras, P.R.: Editorial Universitaria, 1974.

Ferrao, Luis Ángel. *Pedro Albizu Campos y el nacionalismo puertorriqueño.* San Juan, P.R.: Editorial Cultural, 1990.

Freidel, Frank. *The Splendid Little War.* New York: Dell, 1962.

Figueroa v. People of Puerto Rico, 232 F.2d 615, 620 (1st. Cir. 1957).

Friedrich, Carl J. *Middle Road to Freedom*, New York: Rinehart & Company, 1959.

Gailbraith, John Kenneth. *The Affluent Society*, Boston: Houghton Mifflin Company, 1958.

Goodsell, Charles T. *Administration of a Revolution: Executive Reform in Puerto Rico under Governor Tugwell 1941-1946.* Cambridge: Harvard University Press, 1965.

Goodwin, Richard N. *Remembering America: A Voice of the Sixties.* Boston: Little Brown, 1971.

Gruening, Ernest. *Many Battles: An Autobiography.* New York: Liveright Press, 1973.

Hanson, Earl Parker. *Transformation: The Story of Modern Puerto Rico.* New York: Simon and Schuster, 1955.

Hanson, Millard and Henry Wells, eds. *Annals of the American Academy of Political and Social Science,* 285 (January 1953): 1-8.

Hernández Colón, Rafael. *Retos y luchas.* San Juan, P.R.: 1991.

Ickes, Harold L. *The secret diary of Harold L. Ickes.* New York: Simon and Schuster, 1954.

Johnson, Paul. *Modern Times.* New York: Harper Collins Publishers, 1992.

Karman, Laura. *Abe Fortas: A Biography.* New Haven: Yale University Press, 1990.

Karnow, Stanley. *In Our Image: America's Empire in the Philippines.* New York: Random House, 1989.

Kirk, H. L. *Pablo Casals.* New York: Holt, Rinehart and Winston, 1974.

Lewis, Gordon K. *Freedom and Power in the Caribbean.* New York: Monthly Review Press, 1963.

_____. *Notes on the Puerto Rican Revolution.* New York: Monthly Review Press, 1974.

Life, March 8, 1943.

MacGregor Burns, James. *Roosevelt: the Soldier of Freedom.* New York: Hartcourt Braze Javanovich, Inc., 1970.

Mahan, Alfred Thayer. *Interest of America in Sea Power: Present and Future.* London: Sampson, Low, Marston and Co., 1987.

Maldonado, A. W. *Teodoro Moscoso and Puerto Rico's Operation Bootstrap.* Gainsville: University Press of Florida, 1997.

Maldonado Denis, Manuel. *Puerto Rico: mito y realidad.* San Juan, P.R.: Ediciones Península, 1969.

Mathews, Thomas G. *Puerto Rican Politics and the New Deal.* Gainesville, FL: University of Florida Press, 1960.

McCullough, David. *Truman*. New York: Simon & Schuster, 1992.

Morales Carrión, Arturo. *Puerto Rico: A Political and Cultural History*. New York: W.W. Norton and Co., 1983.

Moscoso, Teodoro. "Industrial Development in Puerto Rico." Annals of the American Academy of Political and Social Science (January, 1953).

_____. *Oral History*. San Juan, P.R.: Fundación Luis Muñoz Marín, May 9, 1984.

Moscoso, Teodoro and Hubert Barton. "Puerto Rico and the Economics of Development". In Pamela Falk, ed., *The Political Status of Puerto Rico*. Lexington, Mass.: Lexington Books, 1986.

Moynihan, Daniel P. *A Dangerous Place*. Boston: Little, Brown & Co.,1978.

Muñoz Marín, Luis. *Diario: 1972-74*. San Juan: Fundación Muñoz Marín, 1999.

_____. "Development through Democracy". In Millard Hanson and Henry Wells, Annals of the American Academy of Political and Social Science, 1-8.

_____. In *Los gobernadores electos de Puerto Rico*. Vol. I. San Juan: Corporación de Servicios Bibliotecarios, 1973.

_____. *La Historia del Partido Popular Democrático*. San Juan, P.R.: Editorial Batey, 1984.

_____. *Letter to Antonio Fernós Isern*. January 22, 1948. Luis Muñoz Marín Archives, Trujillo Alto, P.R.

_____. *Letter to Getulio Vargas*. January 28, 1952. Personal papers of Rafael Fernández García's estate, to be donated to the Puerto Rican Collection of the Universidad del Sagrado Corazón, Santurce, P.R.

_____. *Memorias: Autobiografía pública 1898-1940*. Vol. I. San Juan, P.R.: Universidad Interamericana de Puerto Rico, 1982.

_____. *Memorias*. Vol. II. San Juan, P.R.: Universidad Interamericana de Puerto Rico, 1992.

_____. *Mensajes al pueblo puertorriqueño*. San Juan, P.R.: Universidad Interamericana de Puerto Rico, 1980.

_____. *Speech at ILGWU Convention*, Atlantic City. N.J.: May 18, 1958. Pamphlet.

_____. Unedited Draft *"Memorias"*, San Juan, P.R.: Luis Muñoz Marín Foundation, 1974.

_____. Draft Speech, San Juan, P.R.: Luis Muñoz Marín Foundation, May 31, 1944.

Musicant, Iván. *Empire by Default*. New York: Henry Holt & Co., 1998.

Negrón Sanjurjo, Quintín. *Los primeros treinta años de Luis Muñoz Rivera*. San Juan, P.R.: Luis Muñoz Marín Foundation, 1993.

Nixon, Richard M. *In the Arena*. New York: Simon and Schuster, 1990.

Ogilvy, David. *Confessions of an Adversiting Man*. New York: Atheneum, 1963.

Okuda, Kenji. "The Industrial Development Program in Puerto Rico. 1942-1953". Ph.D. diss., Harvard University, 1954.

O'Toole, G.J.A. *The Spanish War: An American Epic, 1898*. New York: W.W. Norton & Co., 1984.

Pagán, Bolívar. *Historia de los partidos políticos puertorriqueños*, 2 Vols. San Juan, P.R.: 1972.

Perloff, Harvey S. *Puerto Rico's Economic Future*, Chicago: The University of Chicago Press, 1950.

_____. *The Alliance for Progress*. Baltimore: Johns Hopkins Press, 1969.

Pike, Frederick D. *FDR's Good Neighbor Policy*. Austin, TX: University of Texas Press, 1995.

Ramírez Lavandero, Marcos and José A. Ortíz Daliot, *Documents on the Consitutional Relationship of Puerto Rico and the United States*, Washington, D.C.: Puerto Rico Federal Affairs Administration, 1988.

Ramos Antonini, Antonio. *Discursos*. San Juan: Cámara de Representates, 1984.

Rivera, Jose A. *El pensamiento político de Luis Muñoz Marín*. San Juan,P.R.: Luis Muñoz Marín Foundation, 1996.

Romero Barceló, Carlos. *La estadidad es para los pobres*. First edition. Publisher unknown, 1973.

Roosevelt, Theodore. *Colonial Policies of the United States*. New York: Doubleday and Co., 1937.

Rosario Natal, Carmelo. *Luis Muñoz Marín: Juicio sobre su significado histórico*. San Juan, P.R.: Luis Muñoz Marín Foundation, 1990.

_____. *Luis Muñoz Marín, servidor público y humanista*. San Juan, P.R.: Luis Muñoz Marín Foundation, 1998.

_____. *La juventud de Luis Muñoz Marín*. San Juan, P.R.: Editorial Edil, Inc. 1989.

_____. *Luis Muñoz Marín y la independencia de Puerto Rico*. San Juan, P.R.: Producciones Históricas, 1994.

Ross, David F. *The Long Uphill Path*. San Juan, P.R.: Talleres Gráficos Interamericanos, 1966.

Safire, William. *The New Language of Politics*. New York: Random House, 1968.

Schlesinger, Arthur M. *The Crisis of the Old Order*. Boston: Houghton Mifflin Co., 1957.

_____. *The Coming of the New Deal*. Boston: Houghton Mifflin Co., 1959.

_____. *The Politics of Upheaval*. Cambridge, Mass.: Riverside Press, 1960.

_____. *A Thousand Days: John F. Kennedy in the White House*. Cambridge, Mass.: Houghton Mifflin Co., 1965.

Sorensen, Theodore C. *Kennedy*. New York: Harper and Row, 1965.

Szulc, Tad. *Fidel: A Critical Portrait*. New York: Avon Books, 1986.

The American Mercury, "The Sad Case of Puerto Rico", Feb. 1929.

The Nation, "The American Colony", April 8, 1925.

The Nation, "What Next for Puerto Rico", Nov. 20, 1929.

The San Juan Star, Sunday Magazine, May 11, 1980.

Time, June 23, 1958.

Tobin, James. *The Tobin Report*. San Juan, P.R.: University of Puerto Rico Press, 1976.

Torruella, Juan R. *The Supreme Court and Puerto Rico: The Doctrine of Separate and Unequal*. Río Piedras, P.R.: Editorial de la Universidad de Puerto Rico, 1988.

Trías Monge, José. *Historia constitucional de Puerto Rico*. Río Piedras, P.R.: Editorial Universitaria, 1981.

_____. *Puerto Rico: The Trials of the Oldest Colony in the World*. New Haven: Yale University Press, 1997.

Tuchman, Barbara W. *The Guns of August*. New York: Bantam Books, 1989.

Tugwell, Rexford G. *The Stricken Land*. Garden City, N.J.: Doubleday and Co., 1947.

_____. *The Art of Politics*. New York: Doubleday & Company, 1958.

U.S. Tariff Commission. *The Economy of Puerto Rico: With Special Reference to the Economic Implications of Independence and other Proposals to Change its Political Status* (Dorfman Report). Washington, D.C.: March 1946.

Wagenheim, Kal. *Puerto Rico: A Profile*. New York: Praeger Publishers, 1970.

Watkins, T.H. *Righteous Pilgrim: The Life and Times of Harold L. Ickes*. New York: Henry Holt and Co., 1990.

Wells, Henry. *"Administrative Reorganization in Puerto Rico."* Western Political Quarterly, Vol. IX (1956).

The Modernization of Puerto Rico. Cambridge, Mass.: Harvard University Press, 1969.

World's Week. "TR-PR", July 1931.

Zimmermann, Erich W. *Staff Report to the Interdepartamental Committee on Puerto Rico*. Washington, D.C.: September 1940.

Index